D0660774

MACHINERY
OF DEATH

**THE REALITY OF AMERICA'S
DEATH PENALTY REGIME**

**EDITED BY DAVID R. DOW
AND MARK DOW**

WITH A FOREWORD BY CHRISTOPHER HITCHENS

ROUTLEDGE
NEW YORK LONDON

Published in 2002 by
Routledge
29 West 35th Street
New York, NY 10001

Published in Great Britain by
Routledge
11 New Fetter Lane
London EC4P 4EE

10 9 8 7 6 5 4 3 2 1

Library of Congress Cataloging-in-Publication Data

Machinery of death : the reality of America's death penalty regime / edited by
David R. Dow and Mark Dow ; with a foreword by Christopher Hitchens.
      p. cm.
    Includes bibliographical references and index.
    ISBN 0-415-93266-1 — ISBN 0-415-93267-X (pbk.)
    1. Capital punishment — United States. I. Dow, David, 1959– II. Dow, Mark.

  MV8699.U5 M29 2002
  364.66'0973 — dc21   2001048409

CONTENTS

FOREWORD

SLOUCHING TOWARD
ABOLITION

CHRISTOPHER HITCHENS

Abolitionist is a term with a noble pedigree, even though its exact lineage cannot be determined. We cannot really know at what point it was determined to cleanse America of slavery. Was it the murder of Elijah Lovejoy? The publication of *Uncle Tom's Cabin*? The attack on Harper's Ferry? Abraham Lincoln's Second Inaugural? A whole train of alternately disgraceful and heroic events has to be reviewed. I would personally select, as the moments that sounded the end of man's legal property in man, the *Dred Scott* decision by the Supreme Court and the passage of the Fugitive Slave Act. For it was only in the moments of its greatest apparent triumphs that the cause of slaveholding revealed itself in all its inhumanity, irrationality, and exorbitance.

I believe that we now live in the preabolitionist phase of capital punishment in the United States. And, by a somewhat extended analogy, I believe that the great triumphs of the death-penalty faction were precisely the moments that prefigured that penalty's coming eclipse. I mean by these "triumphs" the passage by President Bill Clinton of the Anti-Terrorism and Effective Death Penalty Act [hereafter AEDPA] and the consequent federal execution of the death sentence passed upon Timothy McVeigh.

Clinton's AEDPA vastly increased the number of capital crimes, and greatly shrank the opportunities open to those charged with such offenses. While the judicial killing of McVeigh, widely advertised as a potential moment of catharsis and clarification, became instead an occasion of monumental state and police bungling, resulting in a spectacle that was obscene both as climax and—perhaps more importantly—as anticlimax. It turned out, both in the "macro" sense and also in the specific and "micro" sense, that the machinery of human sacrifice was suffering from an irreparable series of malfunctions, and falling victim to rapidly diminishing returns.

One might profitably pause for a moment and recollect the argument as it stood at the beginning of the 1990s. The only real question seemed to be, Could the Democratic Party become as plausible a spokesman for human sacrifice as the Republican Party? Governor Clinton's execution of the lobotomized Rickey Ray Rector during the New Hampshire primary elections of 1992 seemed to close this apparent gap, and voters continually reported to pollsters and others with much the same lack of concern about such episodes as liberal intellectuals had registered in the case of the Rector atrocity. To be an abolitionist at that period was, in the terms of our beloved consensus, to be a quixotic or freakish curiosity, the equivalent of a village atheist in the Bible Belt.

The difference made by the ensuing decade is a truly remarkable one. Today, it is the proponents of human sacrifice who are on the defensive. One might mention the following factors in almost any order:

1.   Republican governor George Ryan of Illinois, a strong and consistent advocate of the death penalty, felt compelled to announce a moratorium on executions after discovering that his state's death row contained more innocent than guilty occupants. Illinois had at that moment come within a day or two of murdering an innocent and mentally defective man.

2.   Republican George W. Bush, then governor of Texas, had been secure enough in what he imagined to be popular esteem as to make jokes about the execution of a woman named Karla Faye Tucker, and about the execution of a Canadian whose sentence had not been disclosed to the Canadian consulate. His state was found to be putting down the mentally retarded, and to be failing to furnish defendants in capital cases with even the decent minimum of a court-appointed defense. His evident lack of concern about this, and his puerile celebrations of his own "toughness," had the effect of disturbing more people than it enthused or reassured. (Al Gore's solidarity with Bush on the subject, evidenced in the presidential debates, probably did little to dispel the gathering sense of revulsion.)

3.   The findings of the Sentencing Project, with its expertise in the new field of DNA evidence, materialized the already widespread and justified suspicion that innocent people have been framed, or railroaded, or made the victims of incompetent and slovenly procedures.

4.   Partly transmitted from America's darker past, and partly confirmed by recent disclosures and examples, the ineffaceable stain of racial discrimination was associated with the death penalty and remained, in the public mind, a specific misgiving about it.

Whenever a luckless person was saved from death row at the last moment (as recently happened because of the chance efforts of a class in a journalism school in Illinois), he invariably turned out to be a member of the so-called underclass, a class somewhat conspicuously color coded.

To these recent developments, several of them directly related to the "fast tracking" of capital cases and the abbreviation of the appeals procedure—ghastly features of the Bill Clinton/Dick Morris AEDPA initiative—we can add three tendencies that have had a longer-term and slower but germinal effect. The first of these is the moral influence of Pope John Paul II. I say this with due reluctance, as a committed atheist and critic of the Church, but the reign of the present pope has seen the principled near-condemnation of capital punishment. Rome has not yet seen fit to anathematize the practice, but has made abundantly clear that it can be justified only in the most extraordinary cases. (There is a latent relationship here with the debate on a "consistent life ethic" that arose from the abortion controversy, but this is not the place to discuss it.) I remember interviewing Mario Cuomo a short while after his electoral defeat as governor of New York. He complained wryly that the papal encyclicals on the death penalty were read from the pulpit—but on the Sunday *after* the election rather than the Sunday before it. This is no longer the case; every serious and believing Catholic is quite aware of Church teaching on the subject, and the pope himself has made several very public intercessions for clemency in a number of "high-profile" American cases.

In parallel with this development, the condemnation of the United States by international bodies and independent human-rights organizations has gathered pace and momentum. From a number of instances I'll select the United Nations resolution, sponsored by the nations of the European Union, that called for a ban—while the larger subject was being debated—on the execution of the insane, the pregnant, and the underage. The United States was among the contemptible handful of despotisms and theocracies that voted against this motion. The number of Americans who travel overseas, and who are exposed to the astonishment and disgust felt by civilized countries, is not small. In June of 2001 President George W. Bush himself was exposed to a little of it on his first official visit to Western Europe. On the eve of his departure, a clutch of senior retired American diplomats, including the prominent conservative Thomas Pickering, wrote him an open letter saying that they had become convinced that the practice lowered the worldwide reputation of the United States.

The third development is the emergence of a significant group of victims—relatives and survivors of those who have been murdered—who oppose the execution of the perpetrators. The trial of Timothy McVeigh helped give prominence to this hitherto-ignored constituency. The tableau outside the prison on execution days used to be a predictable one: a group of opponents of the death penalty holding candles, and a crowd of celebrants with signs and slogans of sadistic relish. To this has now been added a third and morally decisive actor: the mourner and victim who insists that human sacrifice is not the answer. (This of course does nothing to diminish the ardor of those whose idea of a good time is to daub Fry Him on a piece of dirty cardboard.)

Taken together, these long- and short-term evolutions occasionally produce what is crudely called "critical mass." Depending on the immediate circumstances and on the way that the issue is framed or phrased, an actual or potential majority can be found for either (a) a moratorium on the death penalty or (b) its replacement by a sentence of life without parole. Again, I remind you how unthinkable this would have been even a decade ago.

Ostensibly, there was no such public feeling when it came to the execution of Timothy McVeigh. (Incidentally, I here use the term *execution* for the sake of familiarity and convenience. It is the sentence, not the prisoner, that is executed, and it is interesting to note how our newspapers also describe certain kinds of cold-blooded murder as having been conducted "execution style.") McVeigh was even described as "a posterchild for capital punishment." Remorseless, butcherlike, proud of his evident guilt, and sane at least to outward appearances, he could not avail himself of the usual doubts or reservations. How boldly and frequently it was asserted that his death would bring "closure."

Has there even been such a sordid, paltry disappointment? The grotesque spectacle of the closed-circuit broadcast opportunity (itself declined by very many of Attorney General John Ashcroft's invitees) was overshadowed by the breath-stopping incompetence of the FBI, which claimed to have mislaid no less than 40,000 pages of documents that had been promised to McVeigh's defense. The resultant "stay" only protracted the time in which the state could torture McVeigh, and he torture his victims, with further uncertainty. The end when it came was banal and empty: who can forget the stammering, secondhand phrases with which the witnesses to this state occasion confessed their confusion? Some of them were only half-ashamed to say that they had hoped for something more cathartically agonizing; an *auto da fe* in which McVeigh would at least writhe a little. Much street opinion was of the same tone. Alas, the U.S. Constitution forbids the rack and the wheel, and this in itself makes an absurdity of the supposed stress on the priority of victims' "feelings." Given full rein, some (though by no means all) would have demanded a whole-hog lynching, that ceremony of burning and dismemberment that persisted well into the twentieth century and of which our current "procedures" are a shame-faced hypocritical descendant. (The tawdry trade in souvenir T-shirts in Terre Haute was likewise a wretched simulacrum of the brisk selling of amputated "souvenirs," and bits of rope and firewood, that used to feature so prominently in the states of the Old Confederacy.)

Though you may still be shot, gassed, hanged, or electrocuted in these United States (this depending, like the rest of the process, on your zip code) the preferred method is now "lethal injection." Itself a repugant parody of a medical event, this supposedly humane solution has managed to negate itself. It neither provides "closure" nor catharsis—I once witnessed one in Missouri and saw the frowns of pointlessness on the faces of all present—and it can go horribly wrong. But because of that very contingency (a blown-out catheter; a hard-to-find vein; a sudden spray of blood or chemicals) it is never shown in its entirety to the witnesses. The patient has been "prepped" before the curtain is drawn, and thus even the traditional dignities of a last address are vanishing. Woe to those who try and civilize the process of human sacrifice.

Having employed this last term several times now, I declare openly what I hope is already obvious. There is no chance of reforming this system, and there is no limited avenue of attack upon it. Some of the essays in this excellent collection (I might instance Clive Stafford-Smith's article on the *Green Mile* moment, if to do so were not invidious) are humane and well-reasoned efforts to show that certain methods of execution are so barbarous as to be illegal, or that certain defendants have been denied their rights as citizens. This is well and good, and cannot be said enough. The original verdict on "the machinery of death" was pronounced by a Supreme Court justice who had had more than enough experience of its caprice. And attorneys must do the best for their clients with the legal recourses that are available.

But one should not become trapped or tricked into demanding that the death penalty be made more humane, or more "equal opportunity." The whole tendency of all investigation, into its origin and nature, makes it plain that a candid and unambiguous abolitionist position is the only justifiable one. Take any route you like into death row; there is no emerging from such a place with any demand save that it be demolished.

Let me take the two extreme, limiting cases. Many people become abolitionists because they fear the ultimate horror of executing the innocent. And many cling to the opposing view because murderers have killed again, either in prison or upon their release. However, these two atrocities are not in fact morally equivalent. Even in a system that retained the death penalty, some murderers would draw life sentences and some would even get parole. It follows—unless we assume a 100 percent execution of all convicted homicidal types, and further assume that they are put to death as soon as they are convicted—that no society can ensure against the awfulness of another murder being committed by a convicted murderer. We do not, in other words, have the power to "abolish" that contingency. But we *do* have the power to ensure that no innocent person is executed, and we must at all times remember that such an outrage is a double outrage, because it means *ex hypothesi* that a guilty murderer has gone free and can slay again. To have such an option and to choose not to exercise it is morally delinquent. The only society that can say it has made this choice rightly is a society that has adopted abolition.

Another potent argument is, I believe, underused and underestimated. The state, in the history and evolution of civilization, is regarded by all but a few extreme theorists as a necessary evil. The struggle for civil society is a struggle to keep state power within bounds. In the days of absolutism, the ruler was defined precisely as the one who had the power of life and death over his subjects. Democracy itself is involved in the rejection of exactly that definition. Ever since Cesare Beccaria published the first critique of capital punishment, the Enlightenment and abolitionism have been partners. (Consult the dates on which European countries abolished the death penalty, and in some cases in the 1930s restored it, and you will see that this calculus works every time.)

In the United States, many of those who endorse capital punishment are also convinced that "big government" is barely competent to collect the taxes or deliver the mail. Not every aspect of this suspicion is laughable; it possesses the elements of an honorable libertarian tradition. Indeed, when the French Socialist government abolished the guillotine in 1982, their justice minister Robert Badinter told the National Assembly that it was above all a question of ending this "totalitarian" conception of the relation between the state and the citizen. Well, if you want to see "big government" at its worst, take the tour at Terre Haute and see, as I have seen, the black-leather cruciform "gurney" bed, combined with the manifest, culpable incompetence of the FBI. When the authorities killed Timothy McVeigh they destroyed, among other things, an important piece of evidence in an argument that will never be over.

I am not myself a pacifist, a Buddhist, or a vegetarian, and I can easily conceive of circumstances in which it would be immoral *not* to take the life of another. However, to kill a prisoner is something from which even the harshest practitioners of violence have traditionally refrained. There are good reasons for this, not all of them merely utilitarian. It is ignoble, to begin with. The prisoner may change his mind, or even his heart. He may supply useful information, or form the basis of a valuable scientific or clinical inquiry. If he is guilty, he may provide—in time—important evidence. If he eventually proves to have been innocent, then as already noted there will be laughter in hell at the ease with which the guilty have gone free. You hear it said by last-ditch defenders of human sacrifice that there is no certified case in the United States of the execution of an innocent person. This is palpable and vicious nonsense, both in theory and in practice. In the first place, the proposition is self-justifying in that a principal witness has in all cases been physically destroyed. In the second place, very many such miscarriages have been uncovered in societies with far fewer executions than the United States and it seems unlikely that, even given the special dispensation of providence, only one nation should be immune from such error. The number of innocents recently salvaged from death row by last-minute DNA disclosures is sobering enough, though not as sobering as the number of jurisdictions that still refuse to allow such evidence to be heard. In the third place, this would require defining all past lynchings as extrajudicial when in fact many took place with official approval and collusion. Finally, we have Hugo Adam Bedau and Michael Radelet's indispensable documentation of twenty-three cases of prisoners put to death by the state and later found innocent (another 116 convicted and sentenced to death were found innocent before the state could execute their death warrants).[1] And I am morally certain, as are most of those concerned, that the man to whom I bade farewell at Parchman Prison Farm, Mississippi, in 1987, Edward Earl Johnson, was killed by cyanide gas at the public expense for a murder committed by someone else.

I have kept repeating the term *human sacrifice* for one more reason. In primitive antiquity, it was thought apt that one person's death could or would expiate the sins of the collective. On this calculation, which was sometimes made explicit, guilt or innocence did not matter. The example was all. I have actually heard modern proponents of "deterrence" make the identical point. Even today, in tribal or theocratic societies—though in relatively few of them—an offender can be taken straight from the sentencing to the stoning. No doubt this fulfills some elementary requirements. But in a developed and complex society, with rules of evidence and appeal, the death sentence becomes a mockery of itself. It mutates into a protracted, depressing, degrading torture. (Incidentally, all the arguments for capital punishment can be employed as arguments for torture without changing a phrase.) And, even after this death row foulness is over and the rope, gas chamber, or immolating chair have done their work, all the above objections still apply with full force. This is why so many of those charged with running the "machinery" have revolted against it, and this is why for so many of us it is already clear that our descendants will view this debate with the same fascinated curiosity that we bring to the arguments for slavery, or the galleys, or the Inquisition. Abolitionism is one of the firmest steps we can take in voluntarily leaving our debased prehistory behind us, placing the instruments of the "machinery" in a museum of the superstitious past.

—Christopher Hitchens
Palo Alto, California
July 2001

NOTE

1. See Hugo Adam Bedau and Michael L. Radelet, *Miscarriages of Justice in Potentially Capital Cases,* 40 Stanford L. Rev. 21 (1987).

INTRODUCTION

DAVID R. DOW

One entirely unexpected consequence of George W. Bush's successful quest for the White House was that a national debate over the death penalty erupted. Unfortunately, the debate that Bush provoked is the wrong debate, focusing on the wrong issues, for the wrong reasons.

Death penalty opponents thought that the debate was going to begin when Karla Faye Tucker was executed in 1998. As Texas was preparing to execute a woman for the first time since Reconstruction, the international news media descended on the state. From the sky, Huntsville looked to be tiled with satellite trucks. People who ordinarily support capital punishment were given pause. Pat Robertson, for example, publicly opposed Tucker's execution. Many people began to suspect that a death penalty debate was getting ready to start. Some were critical of the fact that it took an attractive, articulate, white Christian woman to get the conversation jump-started, but so what: at least we were going to have a conversation.

The beauty of the Tucker case was that she was not innocent; she committed a gruesome murder and never denied it. (She killed Jerry Dean with a pickax, stabbing him numerous times.) Consequently, the death penalty debate, had it actually occurred in the wake of the Tucker execution, would have been a debate about the death penalty itself: about whether it is necessary, useful, or moral. But there was no debate to speak of at all. Tucker was put to death, the reporters went home, and the conversation ended. Except for a little hiccup, caused by a report that then Governor Bush had mocked Tucker's final plea for her life, the story, like all death penalty stories, died.

Then came a decision by George Ryan,[1] the Republican governor of Illinois, to suspend the use of the death penalty in his state. He suddenly realized what anybody who thinks about the question for more than a nanosecond already knows: that innocent people get sent to death row, and innocent people get executed. This is simply a fact, a stubborn and ugly fact that will not go away. Innocent people go to prison because the criminal justice system is made of people, and people make mistakes. No matter how good the lawyers, no matter how ample their resources, no matter how assiduous the appellate courts, there will still be mistakes. Perhaps not as many as occur in the current system, with all its ineptitude and corruption, but still some. If you are going to support capital punishment, then you had just better go ahead and bite the bullet and get used to the idea of, every now and then, executing someone who did not do the crime.

For whatever reason, Governor Ryan apparently decided that an occasional mistake is one thing, but a batting average of under .500 is quite another. Illinois has executed twelve people since the death penalty resumed in 1976; it has released thirteen from death row after concluding that they were innocent. So Ryan, an erstwhile supporter of capital punishment, said enough is enough.

At the time of Ryan's decision, George W. Bush was cruising toward the Republican presidential nomination. On NBC's *Meet the Press* he was asked about the Illinois death penalty moratorium, and he responded that there was no need for such a halt in Texas because he was 100 percent sure that everyone who was executed in Texas during his tenure as governor was guilty. It is hard to overstate the sheer idiocy of that remark. Hardly anybody who has been executed in Texas has been convicted on the basis of DNA evidence, and in the absence of such evidence, how anyone can be 100 percent certain about anything is a mystery.

The absurdity of Bush's remark, however, precisely because it was so absurd proved pivotal in framing the national death penalty debate. With Bush running for president, the national media became obsessed with proving Bush wrong, with identifying at least one innocent person who has been executed in Texas since 1995.

Along came Shaka Sankofa, nee Gary Graham, hurtling into the path of Governor Bush's stroll to the nomination. The scene in Huntsville was like the scene at the time of the Tucker execution—only bigger, if that is possible. All the major television networks had Graham stories every day for a week. Geraldo Rivera and Larry King and the cable news outlets as well were there, not to mention the weekly newsmagazines. Major newspapers, including the *Chicago Tribune* and the *New York Times*, had major, multiday stories about Graham, about indigent defense, about the Texas Board of Pardons and Parole, and about the governor's power to commute a death sentence. On the day of the execution, I happened to be at lunch with a group of death penalty lawyers from across the country. All of us were on our cell phones the entire time, talking to different reporters. We didn't exchange a word with one another for the entire meal. In Houston, the three local newscasts were on the air covering the execution from 5:00 P.M. until 10:00 P.M, with only a thirty-minute break for national news at 5:30, which led off, of course, with news of the impending execution. Each of the 10:00 P.M. newscasts then led with the Graham story. It was all Gary, all the time.

Graham, who was executed in June 2000, is certainly not the first arguably innocent person to be executed in Texas. Odell Barnes, who was executed in 2001, had a compelling innocence claim, and David Spence, who was executed in 1997, quite likely did not commit the murder for which he was executed. But Barnes was an unappealing character, who may not have been a murderer but was a serial rapist, and Spence was put to death long before Bush was running for president. Graham was the right case at the right time.[2]

During George W. Bush's run for the White House, every death penalty lawyer I know received a call from a major media organization asking for the name of an innocent person who had been executed in the past six years. I do not know how they answered, but this is what I said: Since 1977, when the modern death penalty era resumed with the execution of Gary Gilmore by firing squad in Utah, there have been thirteen people released from death row for every one hundred killed. Overall, around eighty people have been released. Does this mean that there were eighty innocent men on death row? Not exactly. They might have been innocent, but nobody knows.

Which brings us to the critical fact that the single-minded focus on innocence has almost entirely obscured: Of the eighty or so men who have been released from death row, five or six, or maybe seven at the most, have been released on the basis of DNA evidence. All the rest have been released not because there is irrefutable DNA evidence of innocence (although after the O. J. Simpson trial it is hard to say exactly what is meant by the term "irrefutable DNA evidence") but because the evidence of guilt has been undermined. Our confidence in the verdict of guilt has been undermined because the evidence that supported the conviction has been vitiated because we discover that the police coerced a confession or fabricated evidence; or because we discover that the prosecutors withheld exculpatory evidence or failed to disclose that they had promised leniency to another defendant in exchange for testimony; or because the defendant's lawyer was incompetent.

In recent years in President George W. Bush's home state of Texas alone, Henry Lee Lucas was moved off of death row and at least six other men (Randall Dale Adams, Clarence Brandley, Ricardo Aldape Guerra, Muneer Deeb, Vernon McManus, and John Skelton) have been released from death row and have walked out of prison altogether. These men were released because of police or prosecutorial misconduct, or because of incompetent defense lawyers. We say that they are innocent, and I have no reason to believe that any one of them has ever had anything to do with a homicide. Nevertheless, although not a single one can be shown to have committed the murder for which he was sent to death row, there is not a speck of DNA evidence in any of the cases to prove that he did not. Proving innocence is proving a negative: it is philosophically and practically impossible.

We can rarely if ever state with metaphysical certainty that a particular person did not commit a crime. Recognizing this truth, the world of law uses the word *innocent* as a term of art; it means that the state cannot prove beyond a reasonable doubt that someone is guilty. What it means to say that someone is innocent, therefore, is *not* that we are certain that the person did not commit a crime; it means that there is not reliable evidence of guilt. Thus, when governor Bush said that none of the more than 135 death row inmates who were executed during his tenure as governor were innocent, he said something that, as a metaphysical matter, is almost certainly wrong. At the same time, the fact that it is almost certainly wrong does not mean that it can be *proven* wrong. And most importantly, as a legal matter, Bush's assertion, irrespective of whether it was right or wrong, is irrelevant.

In all of this there is a lesson, and that is that it is a mistake to focus single-mindedly on the question of innocence. It is a mistake for two reasons. The first is that the concept of innocence is the wrong concept; the second is that the fact that there are innocent people on death row is a symptom of a broader problem. This volume identifies examples of men who have been executed and who were probably innocent, but it also examines the broader problem, which has numerous dimensions.

At the time that a capital trial occurs, the word *innocent* means "not guilty"; it means, in other words, that the state has not proved beyond a reasonable doubt that the defendant committed the murder that the state is accusing him of having committed. But when the concept arises years later, it does not necessarily mean the same thing. George W. Bush can insist that Gary Graham was "guilty" because there is no DNA evidence that proves that Graham did not commit murder. But when Graham was tried, that conception of guilt would have been entirely untenable. It was not Graham's job to establish conclusively that he did not commit the crime; rather, it was the state's job to prove that he *did* commit murder.

Most of the time the state succeeds at trial. In Houston, Dallas, and San Antonio, around 99 percent of all capital murder defendants over the past decade have been convicted. In Virginia, Alabama, Mississippi, and Louisiana, the prosecution's success rate in obtaining convictions ranges from better than 75 percent to better than 90 percent. The number is not quite as high in other states with death row populations comparable to that of Texas, like Florida and California, but even in those states the prosecution succeeds well over half the time. What these data mean is that for the typical capital murder defendant, the truly critical phase of the trial is the punishment phase. (A death penalty trial is actually two trials. At the first, both the state and defense put on evidence, and the jury determines whether the defendant is guilty; at the second, both the state and defense present additional evidence, and the jury decides whether to sentence the defendant to death.) When people like Governor Ryan and President Bush use the word *innocent*, however, they are thinking only about the guilt-innocence phase of the trial, not the punishment phase. They ignore the fact that someone can be found guilty of a crime, and then—in the punishment phase—be found "innocent" of the death penalty.[3] What it means to say that someone is innocent of the crime is that there is insufficient reliable evidence of guilt; how does this concept translate in the context of punishment? Twenty percent of the men who were executed under Governor Bush had lawyers who called no more than one witness at the punishment phase. In Gary Graham's case, could a better lawyer have persuaded the jury to sentence the then seventeen-year-old defendant to a life sentence rather than death? Nobody knows the answer to that question, but the real problem is that the language and terms of the current death penalty debate have no capacity even to consider it.

Of the nearly four thousand people on death row in America, conservative estimates are that 1 percent—forty people—did not do what they were sent there for. Ninety-nine percent is a pretty good batting average, until you realize the price that the 1 percent has to pay. Moreover, even of the 99 percent who probably did what the state accused them of doing, probably half of them had serious constitutional violations at their trial. We know this because between the reinstatement of the death penalty in 1976 and the mid- to late 1980s, federal courts set aside the conviction or the sentence in death penalty cases around half the time. Further, although most of the men on death row may well have done what the state said they did, many of them would have been spared the death penalty—would instead have been sentenced to life in prison—if they had had better lawyers, or if their lawyers had had more resources.

All these inmates are missing from the current debate because their cases cannot be discussed in the language of "innocence." But what about a defendant who did commit the murder but has redeeming qualities that would warrant a life sentence rather than death? What about a mentally retarded defendant whose lawyer puts on no evidence of retardation or who somehow overlooks the importance of importuning the jury not to sentence a retarded man to death? What about a youthful defendant, a boy of fifteen or sixteen at the time of the crime, whose lawyer neglects to emphasize youth at the punishment phase? Or what about a defendant who, high on drugs, commits a murder but who also has a reputation in the community for being productive and for being a loving father, husband, and son? What about a lawyer who fails to call as witnesses the defendant's loved ones? What about a defendant who confesses because he is coerced by police? What about a defendant who is sentenced to death because the jury erroneously believes that a life sentence means he will be out on the street in twenty years or less? How does the concept of innocence pertain to any of these defendants?

It is bad enough that the present death penalty debate, by focusing on the concept of "innocence" is fixated on the wrong concept; what is worse is that the present debate obscures the fact that innocence is better understood as a symptom of the problem, rather than as the problem itself. The reason that people who did not commit the act are found guilty, and the reason that people who ought to be sentenced to life in prison are instead sentenced to death, is that the system is not working. From the police to the prosecutors to the defense lawyers to the judges who are supposed to be overseeing the entire operation, the system is broken.

Former Supreme Court Justice Harry Blackmun, appointed to the Court by President Richard Nixon, was, from the 1970s through the 1980s, a steady vote for the state in death penalty appeals. In the 1976 cases that reinstated the death penalty, he voted with Justice William Rehnquist in every case. Eventually Justice Blackmun saw the system for what it is: a colossal mess that defies repair. At last in the case of death row inmate Bruce Callins, Justice Blackmun threw up his hands. He wrote:

> From this day forward, I no longer shall tinker with the machinery of death. For more than 20 years I have endeavored—indeed, I have struggled—along with a majority of this Court, to develop procedural and substantive rules that would lend more than the mere appearance of fairness to the death penalty endeavor. Rather than continue to coddle the Court's delusion that the desired level of fairness has been achieved and the need for regulation eviscerated, I feel morally and intellectually obligated simply to concede that the death penalty experiment has failed. It is virtually self-evident to me now that no combination of procedural rules or substantive regulations ever can save the death penalty from its inherent constitutional deficiencies. The basic question—does the system accurately and consistently determine which defendants "deserve" to die?—cannot be answered in the affirmative. It is not simply that this Court has allowed vague aggravating circumstances to be employed, relevant mitigating evidence to be disregarded, and vital judi-

cial review to be blocked. The problem is that the inevitability of factual, legal, and moral error gives us a system that we know must wrongly kill some defendants, a system that fails to deliver the fair, consistent, and reliable sentences of death required by the Constitution.

This volume brings together lawyers, prison officials, social workers, journalists, and relatives of murder victims who have one thing in common: intimate knowledge of the machinery with which Justice Blackmun tinkered for so many years. For a generation, Justice Blackmun participated in the effort to repair the system incrementally. He tried to eradicate racism, yet as Stephen Bright and Mark Dow demonstrate in the following pages, racism continues to infest the death penalty apparatus in America. Justice Blackmun tried to give the states enough leeway so as to spare people who did not deserve to die, without giving the states so much leeway as to make the dispensation of the death penalty entirely random, but as Andrew Hammel and Phyllis Crocker show, that aspiration too was thwarted. Justice Blackmun supported superprocedural safeguards, to ward off the execution of someone innocent, but as Bob Burtman, Shawn Armbrust, and Richard Burr and Mandy Welch point out, even that goal has proven elusive.

Justice Blackmun, even from his early days as an upholder of the death penalty, realized that death is different, that the carrying out of this sentence should never be routine. Yet, as Mark Dow's interview with Donald Cabana, and Stacy Abramson and David Isay prove, the implementation of this punishment has become routine—routine, at any rate, to those who must put prisoners to death. To the lawyers who represent the condemned and to the social workers who counsel them, the death penalty is never routine, as the chapters by Cecile Guin, Sarah Ottinger, and Clive Stafford-Smith attest. But to the rest of America, the issue is easy not to think about.

Justice Blackmun, both as a death penalty upholder and in time as a death penalty reverser, never confused law with politics. While, as Ken Silverstein discusses, some judges charged with overseeing death penalty cases act lawlessly because acting lawlessly is consonant with their political impulses, Justice Blackmun never did. He distinguished, as great jurists must, between the legal dimension of an issue and its political face. He never equated respect for the rule of law with antipathy toward the family members of murder victims. At both the beginning of his career and at the end, he would have had no difficulty discussing death penalty issues with either proponents of capital punishment or with the small number of men and women in America, represented in these pages by Bud Welch and Renny Cushing, who have had family members murdered yet feel no urge to take another life in turn.

Ironically, the contemporary debate over the death penalty is one that Justice Blackmun's own change of heart did little to provoke, for this change of heart was not a story of great national import and came at a time when national sentiment concerning the death penalty was rather static. It is a debate, nevertheless, about the very system that Justice Blackmun helped construct, and then abandoned. The following pages identify at least some of the reasons Blackmun decided that he for one could no longer tinker. That decision represented opposition to the death penalty itself, for the machinery of death cannot run without human hands to turn the dials.

NOTES

1. The context of Governor Ryan's decision is provided in Shawn Armbrust's essay in this volume.
2. Gary Graham's case is discussed in this volume by Mandy Welch and Richard Burr; the case of Odell Barnes is discussed in this volume by Bob Burtman.
3. This difficult issue is addressed in this volume by Sarah Ottinger.

PART I

THE REALITY
OF THE REGIME

HOW THE DEATH PENALTY
REALLY WORKS

DAVID R. DOW

ore people are executed in the United States every year than are executed in either Saudi Arabia or Afghanistan, countries that have a reputation for using the death penalty liberally. The company America keeps is not flattering. Only China and the Republic of Congo (and possibly Iraq, where the number of executions is difficult to verify), execute more people annually than does the United States. Until very recently, the execution machine in America did not trouble very many people; to be sure, a steady minority has endeavored for around a generation to abolish the death penalty, to bring the United States in line with all other Western democracies, but the majority of Americans have remained somewhere between indifferent and in favor of capital punishment.

One reason for the indifference is that, for all the executions, the death penalty system in America is largely invisible. People notice high-profile executions—like those of Timothy McVeigh, Ted Bundy, or Karla Faye Tucker, the first woman put to death in Texas since Reconstruction—but the routine execution of state prisoners goes almost entirely unnoticed, even in the very state where the execution occurs. Executions in America are banal. In many states, they occur in the middle of the night or at dawn, which makes protests inconvenient; in Texas, which is the nation's pacesetter for executions, the death penalty is so common that the state's leading newspapers do not even send reporters to cover many of the executions.

Where there is invisibility there is often ignorance. People assume that life on death row is pleasant, or that murderers are able to engage in numerous and lengthy appeals. But these assumptions are by and large false. There is a common misperception, for example, that death row inmates have unlimited access to cable television and modern exercise equipment. The facts are rather different. In Texas, inmates spend twenty-three hours a day in a sixty-square-foot cell that has four solid walls and a slit of a window. None can have a television. About one-fourth are allowed radios. The men exercise by themselves in a chain-link cage. There is no air conditioning, despite summer temperatures that routinely approach one-hundred degrees. Conditions are similar in Oklahoma, except that the entire death row facility is underground, so there is no natural light. In Oklahoma, a death sentence means never seeing sunshine again. That might help to explain why about one in every three Oklahoma death row inmates decides not to pursue any appeals, preferring a quick death to years in a subterranean tomb.

Supreme Court Justice Thurgood Marshall, who unequivocally opposed the death penalty, used to say that if Americans knew how the system really worked, they would turn against it in an instant. Justice Marshall's conclusion is open to doubt: whether knowledge will cause a change of heart is difficult to predict. But his premise—that an informed opinion is superior to an uninformed one—seems entirely uncontroversial.

In particular, three pieces of knowledge seem to be both important and lacking: how the death penalty system really works; who gets sentenced to death; and how the courts treat appeals by death row inmates.

HOW THE SYSTEM WORKS

In 1972, in the case of *Furman v. Georgia,*[1] the Supreme Court struck down all then-existing death penalty laws. It did so for one principal reason: the dispensation of death sentences was arbitrary. In Justice Potter Stewart's famous metaphor, whether an individual received the death penalty was as inexplicable as whether a pedestrian in a thunderstorm would be struck by lightning.[2] Of the thousands of criminals who committed crimes each year for which they might have been sentenced to death, only a handful actually received the death penalty. In the United States, there are around eighteen thousand homicides each year, yet in a busy year fifty or sixty people will be executed. In *Furman,* the Court could make no sense of why the vast majority of killers escaped the ultimate punishment while a handful were struck by lightning, and so the Court declared the death penalty statutes unconstitutional.

Immediately many states went about the business of rewriting their death penalty statutes in order to purge them of arbitrariness. In 1976, the issue arrived at the Supreme Court once again, and in the case of *Gregg v. Georgia,*[3] the Court upheld the death penalty. States had done two things in the intervening years that caused the Court to reverse itself. First, they had narrowed the universe of so-called death-eligible crimes. Whereas in 1972 many crimes—including murder, rape, robbery, and kidnapping—could subject a defendant to the death penalty, most statutes were rewritten to provide that only a defendant who committed homicide could be sentenced to death. (Several statutes also included rape as a death-eligible offense, but in *Coker v. Georgia*,[4] the Court declared those statutes unconstitutional, holding that the states could impose the death penalty only on someone who committed homicide.)

Second, the states created bifurcated trials. Death penalty trials would begin to proceed in two distinct phases. At the first stage, the jury would determine whether the defendant did what the state accused him of doing; this is known as the guilt-innocence phase. At the second stage, the jury, assuming it found the defendant guilty, would decide on punishment. In some states, the jury has fairly wide latitude during the punishment phase. In most states, for example, juries can assess the death penalty if they find the murder to be especially wanton, vile, or heinous. In other states, the jury's discretion is more limited. Efforts to cabin the jury too severely have been declared unconstitutional; for example, when North Carolina and Louisiana wanted to *require* juries to sentence murderers to death if they found them guilty of first-degree murder, the U.S. Supreme Court intervened and struck the statutes down.[5] But some limits on jury discretion are permitted. In Texas, for example, if the jury answers very specific questions in a certain way the defendant is automatically sentenced to death. (One of the questions asks the jury whether the defendant will probably commit future acts of violence; the other asks whether there is sufficient mitigating evidence to warrant sparing the defendant's life. In other words, once the future dangerousness question is answered affirmatively, the presumption is in favor or execution unless the jury finds sufficient mitigating evidence to justify a lesser sentence.)

The basic idea that underlies this bifurcated structure is captured by a phrase from the Court's opinion in *Gregg* itself: "death is different."[6] Because nothing compares in finality to death, the procedures that must be adhered to when death is a potential punishment are designed to achieve reliability. Reliability in this context has two meanings: first, and more obviously, that no one is convicted for a crime he did not commit. (Throughout I will use the masculine pronoun to describe death row inmates as well as capital defendants because the vast majority of such people are men.) The second face of reliability is more elusive; it means that no one should be sentenced to death who is not morally deserving of the sentence. To help achieve this end, the Supreme Court has held, in a series of decisions, that the defendant in a capital case must be permitted to place any evidence before the jury that he believes will help persuade the jury to return a sentence of less than death. This evidence is known generically as *mitigating evidence*.

For example, a defendant can try to persuade the jury that, although he may have committed a horrible crime, he still has some qualities that warrant sparing his life. This type of evidence is known as *positive mitigating evidence*; the idea behind it is to show the jury that the person who committed an animalistic act is nonetheless a human being, with human qualities, and ought therefore to be spared.

A second type of mitigating evidence consists of evidence that seeks to diminish the defendant's moral culpability: to show that although he did an unforgivable thing, there are reasons that can be pointed to that play a decisive factor in making the defendant who he is. Many death row inmates, for example, are mentally infirm; most were abused as children; many have alcohol or substance abuse problems; many were abandoned by one or both parents. None of these factors excuses the conduct, of course, and it is also true that most alcoholics, most victims of child abuse, and most children raised by single parents do not commit murder. Nevertheless, the idea behind this *negative mitigating evidence* is that the jury must be able to assess the defendant's moral culpability, and one or more of these factors may persuade the jury to conclude that although the defendant is responsible for having committed a terrible act, his moral culpability is such that he ought to be sentenced to life in prison rather than death.

When someone commits a crime for which he can be sentenced to death, the first thing that must happen in order for death penalty law to be relevant is that the prosecutors decide to charge the defendant with capital murder and seek the death penalty.[7] The next step is the trial. Figure 1.1 shows the steps of death penalty litigation beginning with the trial.

Any criminal defendant has a constitutional right to be represented by competent counsel. This right applies to the trial, as well as the appeal through the state court system. This first appeal, represented in figure 1.1 by steps 1 and 2, is known as the direct appeal. In some states, the appeal in a death penalty case skips step 1, the appeal to the intermediate court of appeals, and goes immediately to the state's highest court; in other states, the appeal proceeds initially to the intermediate court of appeals.

Well over 90 percent of death penalty cases are affirmed by the state courts of appeals. In significant death penalty jurisdictions like Texas and Virginia, the figure exceeds 98 percent. Once the highest state court has ruled on the case, the death row inmate can request that the U.S. Supreme Court hear his case. This is represented by step 3 in figure 1.1. Technically, the inmate files a petition for a writ of certiorari; the Supreme Court, however, is not required to hear the merits of the case,

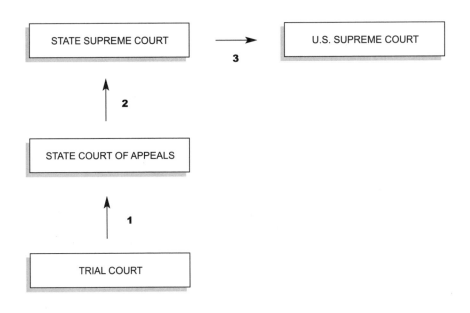

FIG. 1.1　TRIAL AND DIRECT APPEAL

and in fact, very few death penalty cases are considered by the Supreme Court during the direct appeal phase. Over four thousand parties ask the Court to hear their appeals each year, and the Court hears fewer than two hundred cases, so the odds are obviously long.

Once the Supreme Court declines to hear the inmate's appeal at step 3, the case is said to be final. *Final* is a term of art that carries a number of consequences. One of them is that the death row inmate no longer has a constitutional right to be represented by counsel.

It is important to notice that up until this stage of the proceedings, no federal court has examined the constitutionality of the state court proceedings. As a practical matter, the inmate at this point of the process has had one appeal—the appeal to the state court. Although the inmate may also have attempted additional appeals, these efforts are precisely that: *attempted* appeals; for once the inmate's initial appeal is completed, the inmate must receive permission from the superior court before the superior court will actually examine the merits of the case. And the reason it is important to emphasize that the judges who have thus far reviewed the conviction have been state court judges is that unlike their federal counterparts, who have life tenure and fixed salaries and are therefore (at least in principle) immune from transient political pressures, state court judges in nearly every state are politicians. They must run for office, or must run in so-called retention elections. Judges who are answerable to the electorate must perforce be mindful of the electorate's views concerning death row appeals. A judge who rules for a death row inmate risks her own political future. In one case from Texas, for example, a judge ruled, in a case involving the murder of a police officer, that the police had coerced the confession and that it therefore could not be used. Without the confession (and the illicit evidence to which it led), there was insufficient evidence to hold the defendant— meaning that the cop killer went free. The police and prosecutors, outraged at the judge's decision to suppress the confession, recruited a lawyer in the district attorney's office to run against the judge, and the judge was defeated handily in the next election.[8]

Habeas corpus law implicitly recognizes that there is a unique and valuable vantage point that can be brought by a federal judge, so death row inmates do have another opportunity to try to have their cases reviewed by a federal court. Both the U.S. Constitution and federal statutes allow for federal courts to issue a writ of habeas corpus. Such a writ is issued when a court determines that a prisoner, in this case a death row inmate, has either been convicted or sentenced unlawfully. These habeas corpus appeals are also known as postconviction or collateral appeals.

In theory, habeas corpus appeals are based on what are known as nonrecord claims. That is, the habeas lawyers look outside the trial record as the basis for their appeals. For example, the most common claim on habeas corpus is a claim that the defendant's trial or appellate counsel was ineffective. In part, of course, this claim is based on the record, in that the instances of the lawyer's asserted ineffectiveness will be gleaned by scouring the record to see what the lawyer did and did not do. But many aspects of an ineffectiveness claim are not apparent from the record itself. In a death penalty case, where the most important phase of the trial is the punishment phase, the trial lawyer may have put on virtually no mitigating evidence because he failed to conduct an investigation. Consequently, the habeas lawyer will conduct the investigation that the trial lawyer did not conduct and then attempt to prove that had the habeas lawyer conducted the investigation and introduced the evidence gathered during that investigation, the result would probably have been different. (For reasons discussed below, this burden of proof is nearly impossible to satisfy, further diluting the sense in which the habeas process is a bona fide appeal.)

Federal habeas corpus law is extremely complex. Yet there is no constitutional right to have an attorney when pursuing habeas relief.[9] A number of states do by statute provide lawyers for death row inmates who are pursuing their habeas appeals; moreover, under federal law, states that provide lawyers may be able to take advantage of an expedited

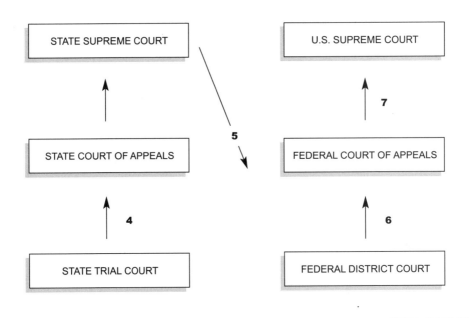

FIG. 1.2 HABEAS CORPUS

review schedule in federal court, but the essential point is that inmates do not have a constitutional right to counsel at this state of the proceedings.

The Supreme Court has held that a federal court cannot consider any issue in a habeas corpus appeal that was not first presented to the state courts to consider. This is known as the exhaustion requirement. Accordingly, the first step for inmates pursuing their habeas appeals is to return to state court to give the state court an opportunity to consider every issue that the inmate hopes for the federal court to consider. This step is represented in figure 1.2 as step 4. Obviously, the state courts that are asked at step 4 to consider the legality of the inmate's conviction or sentence are the same courts, and ordinarily the very same judges, who have already decided against the inmate at steps 2 and 3 of the process; not surprisingly, therefore, inmates lose during the state court aspect of habeas review almost all the time.

Now the inmate has, at last, an opportunity to have a federal court consider the merits of his appeal. This opportunity is represented in figure 1.2 as step 5; the inmate asks the federal district court to review the constitutionality of the state court proceedings. In a sense, *this* is the inmate's second appeal. As a practical matter, however, it is very difficult for the inmate to prevail, for three reasons. The first is that by virtue of federal law, the federal district court is required to presume that the factual conclusions reached by the state court are correct; the second is that many issues that the inmate is entitled to have the state court consider—such as whether evidence was unlawfully seized—cannot be considered by the federal court. The issues that cannot be considered by a federal court as part of the habeas corpus appeal—that are said to be not cognizable on collateral review—are not limited to esoteric legal claims. In the case of *Herrera v. Collins*, which involved an appeal from a death row inmate in Texas, Supreme Court Chief Justice William Rehnquist insinuated that even a claim of actual innocence might not be enough to warrant judicial relief during habeas corpus proceedings.[10] Similarly, in the Virginia case of *Coleman v. Thompson*, the Supreme Court, stressing the importance of finality, did not address defendant Roger Coleman's basic claim that he was actually innocent.[11]

Third, and finally, it is not only the courts that have made appellate success elusive; it is also the U.S. Congress. Responding to political pressure, and as part of Bill Clinton's effort to project a tough-on-crime demeanor, Congress and President Clinton rewrote the federal habeas statute in such a way that precludes the federal court from even considering many issues, and that further restricts the ability of the federal court to grant relief with respect to those issues that it can consider.

Thus, although there is a sense in which this trip to federal district court does represent a second appeal, the burden is on the inmate to persuade the federal court that it can even consider the merits of the issue, much less grant relief. Moreover, once the federal district court has decided against the inmate (and for reasons discussed at greater length below the courts almost always rule against the inmate), the inmate has no further right of appeal. In order to appeal the district court's ruling to the federal court of appeals, either the district court or the court of appeals must grant the inmate permission. (This permission is known as a certificate of appealability, or COA). Oftentimes, therefore, step 6 in figure 1.2 consists of the inmate's attempt to have the court of appeals grant a COA; here again, there is a sense in which step 6 represents an appeal, yet it is simply not an appeal in the ordinary sense of the word because the court of appeals is often not reaching the merits of the decision but is instead deciding whether it may reach them.

Finally, the inmate may again ask the Supreme Court, in step 7, to hear the case. Once again the inmate files a petition for writ of certiorari, and once again, although there is a sense in which this step can be denominated as an appeal, it is yet another attempt to ask a court to consider the merits of the case.

After step 7 is complete, the case is, for all intents and purposes, over. There has been one appeal through the state court system, and one appeal through the federal court system. It is likely that only a single federal court, the federal district court, has considered the merits of the case. It is possible, but by no means certain, that a federal court of appeals has also examined the case. If the inmate wishes to pursue any further appeals—if, for example, he discovers new evidence that might establish his innocence, or if a witness recants, or if evidence of police or prosecutorial misconduct emerges—he must receive permission from the court to pursue the issue. Any pleading that the inmate files, though known generically as an "appeal," is actually a request that the court consider the merits of the issue. For reasons relating to the arcana of federal habeas corpus law, these requests are almost always denied. The inmate can ask repeatedly for a federal court to consider the issue, and many inmates, especially those with compelling new evidence, do ask repeatedly. But these requests are not, in any meaningful sense, additional appeals. They are requests for an appeal, and they are almost always denied.

After his trial and direct appeal are over, an inmate might ask a federal court five times or five hundred times to consider the merits of his case. These requests are referred to as "appeals" in the popular media, and thus has developed the popular perception that the appellate process in death penalty cases is unduly lengthy. That perception is based on a myth, and is also erroneous. There is in America an elaborate appellate machinery, and although this machinery can be exploited by large corporate defendants (like tobacco companies), hostility from the courts and Congress has rendered it unusable by death row inmates. To be sure, many of these inmates ask repeatedly for some court to pass on the merits of their case, but the answer is almost always no.

WHO GETS SENTENCED TO DEATH

Since 1988 I have assisted in the representation of more than two dozen death row inmates, but when I started working on these cases it was not because I was against the death penalty. In fact, I was not even all that interested in the death penalty. I was teaching federal jurisdiction, a somewhat arcane law school course that deals with the power of the federal courts to hear certain cases; it is something of a cross between technical procedural rules and constitutional law. Habeas corpus law is part of the federal jurisdiction course. Over the past decade, many of the most important decisions in habeas corpus law have been death penalty appeals. So I thought that I would understand habeas corpus law in a deeper way if I knew substantive death penalty law.

While I was teaching myself death penalty law, Texas and other southern states were beginning to get their death penalty apparatuses in working order. And as the states were beginning to execute people,

Congress funded resource centers to recruit volunteer lawyers to represent death row inmates and to train them and give them assistance. These recruited lawyers were not death penalty specialists (in the late 1980s there were only a handful of death penalty appellate specialists— not nearly enough to represent the nation's death row population), and so they relied on the lawyers at the resource centers to teach them, on an accelerated basis, how to handle a death penalty case. I knew many of the lawyers at these resource centers and, because I was learning death penalty law, I thought I should take a trip to death row. I finally did, with a resource center lawyer, in the fall of 1988. We visited with half a dozen or more inmates that were at that time unrepresented.

On the drive home, the lawyer asked me if I wanted to represent one of the inmates, and I said no. I told the lawyer that I was somewhere between agnostic and moderately in favor of the death penalty and couldn't really see myself representing a murderer. The lawyer said that my view about the death penalty was irrelevant; only poor people get executed, the lawyer said. Well, the solution to that, I replied, is to execute more rich people.

The resource center lawyer asked if we might postpone the philosophical discussion for another time because the immediate problem was that one of the people I had just met had an execution date scheduled for exactly two weeks hence and his lawyer had quit—by writing the inmate a letter to that effect—two days earlier. I think most lawyers would find it hard to say no under such circumstances. Whatever my feelings about the death penalty, I certainly did not think the state should execute people who had no lawyers, so I agreed to handle the case.

A disproportionate number of capital murder defendants are black, and disproportionate number of capital murder defendants are people who are accused of killing a white victim. And close to 100 percent of capital murder defendants are indigent. At some level, everyone in America already knows this. If you were accused of capital murder, would you rather be black or white? If you were accused of capital murder, would you rather be rich or poor? The answers are obvious, of course. Rich people generally have advantages that poor people do not, and that is especially true in the criminal justice system. Likewise, black Americans face forms of racism that whites do not, including poorer medical care, higher disapproval rates on mortgage applications, and so on; and one instance of racism is reflected in the criminal justice system. The population of death row in America is close to 100 percent poor.

You Get What You Pay For
In the United States, there have been more than three hundred people executed since the death penalty was reinstated in 1976. Almost all have

been poor. Rich people often do not even get convicted to begin with; when they do, they never get sentenced to death. The Menendez brothers in California, for example, killed their parents with shotgun blasts; they used their money to hire first-rate lawyers, and they did not get sentenced to death. O.J. Simpson, of course, did not get convicted, but even before he was acquitted, the prosecutor's office made the decision not even to seek the death penalty against him. In almost any jurisdiction, a poor black male accused of slitting the throats of a white woman and white man would undoubtedly face the death penalty. Katherine Ann Power, as a young, white, upper-middle-class college student, participated in a bank robbery during which a policeman was shot and killed; I represented someone convicted of a similar offense, who was executed in 1995. My client was black, male, and poor. Power, in contrast, escaped to the west coast, got married, had children, and, years later, returned to Boston, where she was sentenced to fifteen years.

There is a simple reason that money matters. The reason is that the single most important factor that determines whether a defendant will be sentenced to death is the quality of the defendant's lawyer. In jurisdictions without public defender systems, indigent defendants get lawyers who cannot afford—and who are at times simply unqualified—to put on effective and vigorous defenses. In many jurisdictions in the so-called southern death belt, caps on fees that will be paid to lawyers representing capital defendants are astonishingly low. Counties in Georgia and Mississippi until recently set caps of $1000 in death penalty cases.

In contrast, where defendants have the resources to hire their own lawyers, or where there is a public defender system for capital defendants, the defendants fare much better. In South Carolina, Susan Smith, who murdered her children by strapping them into a car and then driving it into a lake, was spared the death penalty because she was represented by David Bruck, one of the nation's preeminent death penalty lawyers.

In 1997 Texas executed an inmate named David Spence. Spence was convicted of murdering three teenagers in a notorious case known as the Lake Waco murders. The state's theory was that Spence had been hired by a man named Muneer Deeb to murder a young woman who had spurned Deeb's advances. Spence, according to the State, then murdered the wrong people, in a case of mistaken identity. There is compelling evidence that Spence did not in fact commit the murders for which he was executed, but that is not the point of this story. This story is about Deeb, who was also convicted and sentenced to death. In what can only be described as a stunning development, Deeb, representing himself on his direct appeal, persuaded the appellate court to grant him a new trial. Upon hearing the news, one of the first things Deeb said was that whereas he had relied on his court-appointed trial the first time around, at the new trial he would get the "best lawyers money can buy." He borrowed heavily from his overseas family and hired Mike DeGuerin, one of the nation's preeminent criminal defense lawyers. The state did in fact choose to try Deeb again; he was acquitted. So Spence was executed for committing a murder at the request of Deeb, even though Deeb's jury found that Deeb had requested no such thing.

Every person on death row in America lacks the resources to hire a dream team. Those who are charged with capital murder in jurisdictions that lack a public defender system are represented by lawyers who have been disciplined by the bar association at a rate five times greater than the norm. Even those defendants who have had competent lawyers are doomed by a system that pays those lawyers inadequate wages and gives them insufficient funds to hire experts or conduct thorough investigations. Here are just a few examples:

A woman named Pam Perillo was sentenced to death in Texas. Her case is somewhat unusual in that she prevailed on her habeas corpus appeal in the federal court. The reason she prevailed is that she was represented at her trial by a lawyer who was also having a close personal relationship with one of the state's primary witnesses. Moreover, this lawyer appointed to represent Perillo had previously represented a different defendant in connection with the same crime, and his strategy in that prior defense had been to blame all wrongdoing on Perillo.[12]

Another capital murder defendant was represented by a lawyer who was having an affair with the defendant's wife. In the midst of the trial, the defendant was served with divorce papers, and following the conviction of the defendant, the lawyer proceeded to marry the death row inmate's former wife.[13] A defendant who is facing a death sentence is probably better off being represented by a lawyer who does not have designs on that defendant's wife.

A capital murder defendant is also best served by having a lawyer who has not traded representation for book rights to the client's story, but the lawyer who represented Betty Lou Beets, the second woman executed in Texas since Reconstruction, did exactly that.[14]

In one notorious case, a single lawyer represented codefendants even though the excuse of one of the defendants was that the other one had pulled the trigger and fired the fatal shots. In another case, a defendant was convicted and sentenced to death and then prevailed in his appeals and was therefore the beneficiary of a new trial. At his new trial, he was represented by the man who had served as the foreman of the jury at the previous trial—in other words, he was represented by someone who had already deemed him guilty and sentenced him to death.[15]

Charles Bass, who was executed in 1986, turned himself in to authorities after consulting with a lawyer who, unbeknownst to Bass, had entered into a contract with a filmmaker who was producing a film based on the life of Bass's murder victim; the attorney received $5000 from the film company in advance and a promise of additional cash if

Bass in fact surrendered. When Bass argued on appeal that he had not only received ineffective assistance but had in fact been betrayed by his lawyer, the court of appeals ruled against him, reasoning that the lawyer who betrayed Bass did not ultimately represent him at trial.[16]

Sometimes the incompetence of lawyers who represent indigent defendants can be attributed to a conflict of interest, but at other times, it is attributable to nothing other than the sheer ineptitude of the lawyer. Thus, for example, one defendant was represented by counsel who, during his closing argument, said: "You are an extremely intelligent jury. You've got this man's life in your hands. You can take it or not. That's all I've got to say." The lawyer then sat down. He was finished with his closing.[17]

Harvey Duffy was represented by a lawyer who had never tried a capital case; the lawyer spent less than a day picking the jury—even though jury selection is perhaps the most critical phase of a capital murder trial and when done properly takes weeks if not months.[18]

A handful of defendants have been represented by lawyers who did not raise even a single objection throughout the course of the trial.[19] One unfortunate defendant was represented by a lawyer who showed up drunk at the trial,[20] and another defendant, a Latino, had his lawyer refer to him during the trial as a wetback.[21]

Lawyers representing capital defendants do not perform any better on appeal. One appellate lawyer filed a brief that was one page long.[22] Another lawyer continually failed to meet deadlines for filing the appellate pleadings and was therefore jailed for contempt. The lawyer ultimately filed a brief that was eight pages long, which he wrote from a jail cell.[23] A lawyer in Alabama filed a brief for a man named Larry Heath that was one page long. The lawyer cited a single case—one that went against his position. The brief had more typographical errors than it had citations to authority. And yet, when Heath was finally fortunate enough to obtain competent counsel, all the issues he might have raised on appeal were deemed to have been defaulted upon by the previous lawyer—meaning that the court refused to review the merits of Heath's arguments after concluding that because they should have been raised by his earlier lawyer, his subsequent lawyer was precluded from raising them.[24]

Even when the lawyers are good—and there are many very fine lawyers appointed to represent indigent capital defendants—they are often prevented from mounting a fully effective defense. Two obstacles stand in their way, one concrete and one somewhat more abstract. The concrete obstacle is that they are paid insufficient wages. For example, the two lawyers who represented accused cop killer Carl Wayne Buntion were awarded $30,000 less than they had requested. The lawyer who represented Federico Martinez-Macias was paid at the princely rate of $11.84 per hour.[25] Once defense lawyers know that their bills will be scrutinized with hyperzealousness by trial judges who are loath to authorize the spending of taxpayer dollars for the representation of an accused murderer, they will stop doing anything that they think they might not get reimbursed for. Genuinely competent counsel do whatever must be done to represent their clients; lawyers who are worried about whether they will get paid do less.

Second, and somewhat more abstractly, in many states (including Texas) trial lawyers are appointed not by a central appointing authority, but instead by the trial judge who will preside over the case. This means, obviously, that the lawyer is serving two masters: the defendant, but also the judge. If the lawyer offends or alienates the judge, the lawyer will not be receiving any future appointments. The same dilemma confronts appellate lawyers, who are appointed by judges who sit on the court of appeals. Even lawyers of the firmest moral fiber cannot help but feel the impact of this conflict. Harris County, Texas, where Houston is located, sends more men to death row than does any other state except Virginia. In Harris County, there are twenty-two criminal district court judges with jurisdiction over capital cases; of these, sixteen have received campaign contributions from lawyers who have been appointed to represent capital defendants between 1998 and 2000.[26] This cozy relationship may be pleasant for the prosecutors, judges, and defense counsel, but it does not best serve the interests of the capital defendant.

Perhaps the most important quality a lawyer who represents capital murder defendants must possess is the willingness to be loathed. Lawyers who represent terrorists or mass murderers, or even simple murderers, must be willing to be reviled by the family members of the murder victims, by demagogic politicians, by the popular media, even by the presiding judges themselves. A lawyer who must count on having his or her bill paid by a judge who is accountable to the electorate will almost never be willing to incur such enmity. The rare lawyer who has such character will probably be appointed to represent only one fortunate defendant; the next time, the judge will find someone who is more compliant.

How Race Matters
Other than wealth, the most salient factor in the death penalty system in America is race. Over seventeen thousand executions have occurred in the United States. Of that number, a total of thirty-five have involved a white murderer and a black victim. In Texas, the death penalty capital of the Western world, there has never been a white man executed whose victim was black. In 1998, three white men chained James Byrd, a black man, to the back of their pickup and dragged him for miles, killing him. Two of the three were sentenced to death. Until they arrived at death row in 1999, in fact, there had never even been a white murderer on Texas' death row whose victim was black.

These data are hardly unique to Texas. In Georgia, for example, blacks represent 60 percent of all homicide victims, yet 80 percent of those executed are executed for killing a white. In Kentucky, over one thousand blacks have been murdered since 1977, but of the twenty-eight people on death row, not a single one is there for killing another black person.

These data have been known for many years. Over a decade ago, a group of researchers, led by David Baldus, examined more than two thousand homicides in Georgia and, as part of the examination, analyzed more than two hundred different variables: race of victim, race of offender, economic status of victim and offender, details of the crime, and so on. They determined that although black murderers were significantly more likely than white murderers to be sentenced to death, the truly dramatic variable was the race of the victim: murderers of whites were between four and five times as likely to be sentenced to death as murderers of blacks. This essential finding has been validated in every state where the study has been conducted.[27] Nationwide, whites make up slightly less than half the total number of murder victims, but more than 80 percent of those executed are executed for killing a white person.[28]

Not all scholars agree that the race of the accused plays a significant role in determining which defendants are sentenced to death; nevertheless, it is fair to say that a broad consensus acknowledges the impact of the race of the victim.[29] Not even the Supreme Court has denied this fact. Nevertheless, in 1987, in the case of *McCleskey v. Kemp*,[30] the Court denied relief to McCleskey, a black man sent to death row for murdering a white victim, on the grounds that McCleskey's statistical showing did not demonstrate that racism had operated *in his particular case*. The dissenting justices complained that the burden the majority placed on McCleskey could never be met; all any death row inmate can show are statistics. At some point, those statistics must be permitted to speak for themselves.

As Lon Fuller's hypothetical Justice Keen once put it, there is such a thing as overexplaining the obvious.[31] The obvious fact is that America has not solved its race problem, and one domain where this problem is highlighted is the realm of criminal justice. Race is an issue in the capital punishment arena because it is an issue in America. Any truthful portrait of death row, to be truthful, must illuminate this inescapable fact, and any supporter of capital punishment must come to grips with it.

These are thus the three unhappy truths that describe the population of the nation's death row: First, a small percentage of the inmates did not do what they were convicted of doing; innocent people get executed. Second, all of the inmates are indigent, and there is a strong likelihood that they would not have been sentenced to death had they been able to afford elite defense counsel. Third, race plays a role in who gets sentenced to death. Social scientists and partisans can debate precisely how pronounced these truths are, but only the ingenuous or the disingenuous can deny them altogether. What this means is that supporting capital punishment requires a willingness to tolerate these truths. The honest defender of the death penalty must, to be honest, be willing to say that the value of the punishment justifies the maintenance of these inequities.

THE COURTS AND CONGRESS

In one of my first cases, I was putting the finishing touches on a motion for a stay of execution when I received over the fax machine an order from the court denying the motion. In another case, the court of appeals claimed to have reviewed the entire record before denying the motion even though the record never entered the chambers of the judge who wrote the order.

Every death penalty lawyer has many such stories, because these stories are not unique. They reflect a notable phenomenon. A generation ago, lawyers who represented death row inmates were admired by the courts even as they were often scorned by the public. They were viewed, by the courts and by a small segment of the population at large, as preserving the integrity of the system. These lawyers were willing to stand by the accused and the infamous in spite of minimal remuneration and frequent obloquy, and they were respected by the courts and by those who are faithful to the idea of the rule of law.

But beginning around the mid-1980s, this attitude began to change. Death penalty lawyers came to be viewed as accomplices of murderers instead of as defenders of the rule of law. They came to be regarded as something akin to mafia lawyers: people with sympathy for what their debased clients had done. It is difficult to explain precisely how or why this shift occurred, but that it did is incontestable. Thus, writing in the case of a death row inmate named Walter Bell, a federal judge wrote that "the veil of civility that must protect us in society has been twice torn here": first by the murderer himself, and second by the murderer's lawyer, who, in the judge's view, had waited too long to file his appellate papers.

I should perhaps confess that I was also chastised, in print, by a federal judge who rebuked me for filing a habeas petition forty-five minutes later than I had said I would.[32] (In fact, the first page of the petition was sent via facsimile at the exact time I promised, but it takes some time to fax a fifty-page document.) This attitude of hostility toward death row lawyers runs all the way up the chain of command. During one argument before the Supreme Court, Justice Antonin Scalia lambasted the lawyer representing the death row inmate, complaining that she had waited to file her petition for a stay of execution until just five days before the scheduled execution. The lawyer explained that she had filed it as soon as she was permitted to do so—on the very day that she was denied relief by the lower court. Justice Scalia interrupted her and told her not to waste any more of his time. (The inmate, by a 5 to 4 vote, with Justice Scalia in the minority, prevailed.)

When the Supreme Court struck down the death penalty in 1972, it did so because the sentence was arbitrary. When race and wealth continue to matter as much as they do, it is difficult to gainsay that the arbitrariness still runs rampant. Further, this arbitrariness takes more subtle forms as well. In early 1999, Missouri governor Mel Carnahan commuted the death sentence of Darrel J. Mease to a sentence of life in prison following a brief conversation with Pope John Paul II, who asked Governor Carnahan to show mercy toward Mease. Mease is a triple murderer who was convicted in 1988 of killing Lloyd Lawrence and his wife Frankie, along with their disabled grandson William. It would take an uncommon measure of churlishness for a death penalty foe to begrudge Darrell Mease his victory, but the simple truth is that he got lucky because the pope mentioned him by name and Governor Carnahan, for whatever reason, was moved by the pope's appeal. Webster's dictionary defines *arbitrary* as unprincipled or capricious. To the hundreds of men (and the handful of women) on death row in America whose names the pope does not know, that is the perfect word to describe why they will die at the hands of the state even though Mease will not.

Beginning in 1972, the Supreme Court and the lower federal courts took seriously their duty to ameliorate this arbitrariness. And indeed, through the early 1980s, somewhat more than half of all death penalty cases were reversed by federal courts (often the sentence alone, and not the underlying conviction was set aside). These were not primarily cases where the person sentenced to death was subsequently found to be innocent, although a handful of such cases were. Rather, these were cases where basic constitutional norms were violated by state authorities, and the federal courts stepped in and held that even when the defendant is a suspected murderer, the states must still act in accordance with the Constitution. The United States may be like China in its stubborn refusal to jettison the death penalty, but, these federal courts insured, we will not be like China in ignoring our fundamental rules and values.

All that has changed. Since the late 1980s, the reversal rate in death penalty cases has declined precipitously. The reversal rate now is well under 10 percent. It is not that states have become suddenly solicitous of the rules; it is instead that courts have stopped caring. Judges at every level, state and federal, seem to have grown weary of death penalty appeals, with the consequence that executions proceed apace even in the face of egregious constitutional violations.

The single most important factor that explains this turn of events is the contemporary obsession with what is known as "finality." Finality refers to the notion that once the state has conducted a trial and permitted the death row inmate his direct appeal, the case ought not to be disturbed, and the state should be free to carry out the execution.

One illustration of the obeisance that the norm of finality now compels is the federal habeas corpus statute itself. The current statute restricts the power of federal courts in both procedural and substantive aspects. Procedurally, it bars federal courts from granting habeas relief unless, absent limited exceptions, the petitioner has exhausted state remedies.[33] Further, if a petitioner has any available procedure at all under state law, then he will be deemed not to have exhausted state procedures.[34] There is nothing inherently problematic about forcing an inmate to go initially to the state courts; the problem is that the conclusion of the state court must be presumed to be correct when the petitioner finally arrives at federal court, and the burden is on the petitioner to overcome that presumption by clear and convincing evidence.[35]

Substantively, the federal statute restricts the power of a federal court by limiting the grounds for relief. That is, it is not enough for the inmate to show a constitutional violation. Instead, if the state court reached the merits of the petitioner's claim (as opposed to disposing of it on procedural grounds—a distinction that will be discussed below), the federal court cannot grant relief unless the state court's decision was in violation of "clearly established federal law"; in other words, if the state court got it wrong, but its decision was not "clearly" wrong, the petitioner is not entitled to relief in federal court.[36]

Much of the federal habeas statute is actually based on language and principles developed by the Supreme Court, and then embraced by Congress. For when it comes to preferring finality over and above the enforcement of constitutional values, Congress and the courts have marched hand in hand. The case of Roger Coleman, who was executed in 1992, epitomizes the Supreme Court's deference to the icon of finality at the expense of an examination of the merits of a death row inmate's claims. Making this point clearly will require a somewhat detailed recitation of the history of Coleman's desperate attempt to have a federal court consider the merits of his case.

Coleman was arrested and executed for the murder of Wanda McCoy. He was executed despite the fact that a different person confessed to the murder, despite the fact that the physical evidence did not point to him, and despite the fact that the state suppressed evidence. Lawyers representing Coleman had filed a habeas petition in state court in Virginia, raising more than a half dozen constitutional violations, but focusing especially on whether Coleman received effective assistance of counsel, as required by the Sixth Amendment. The Washington, D.C., lawyers who wrote the petition hired local counsel for assistance in conducting the evidentiary hearing, which was held in late 1985. The following June, the presiding judge informed the parties that he intended to rule against Coleman, and he asked the State to prepare an appropriate order. The judge signed the order on September 4, 1986. At that time, the judge who had presided over the evidentiary hearing was out of the county where the trial had been conducted (and where the evidentiary hearing had been held), but Virginia law required that the order be filed in the county where the trial had taken place. The judge therefore mailed the order to the appropriate county clerk, who entered the order on September 9. The clerk's office mailed certified copies of the order to the lawyers, and the date on both the clerk's transmittal letter as well as the certified order was September 9.

Under Virginia law, a notice of appeal must be filed no more than thirty days after entry of the judgment from which appeal is to be taken. Coleman's Washington, D.C., lawyers prepared the notice and sent it to local counsel, who in turn mailed it to the county clerk on October 6. Because the notice was sent by ordinary mail (as opposed to certified or registered mail), it was effective when received by the clerk. Had it been sent by certified or registered mail, it would have been effective on dispatch. The clerk received the notice on October 7.

The attorney general's office decided that it would contest Coleman's appeal on procedural grounds, by arguing that his notice of appeal had not been timely filed. The attorney general took the position that the relevant date for purposes of calculating the time for filing the notice was the date on which the judge signed the order, rather than the date on which it was filed. In other words, the attorney general maintained that the thirty-day period began on September 4, not September 9.

If the attorney general was correct, it meant that Coleman had until October 4 to file his notice of appeal. But October 4 was a Saturday, and under Virginia law, if the thirtieth day to file a notice fell on either a Saturday or Sunday, the party filing the notice of appeal had until the following Monday. According to the Virginia attorney general, in other words, Coleman was required to file his notice of appeal by Monday, October 6. In point of fact, Coleman's lawyer did *mail* the notice on October 6; it was not received until October 7, however, and because the notice was sent by regular mail, it was not effective until received. Coleman's notice of appeal, under this theory, was one day late. For want of the price of a registered letter, the state was able to take the position that Coleman's appeal should not be heard.

Coleman's brief on the merits was filed with the Virginia Supreme Court in December 1986, and less than a week later, the state moved to dismiss the appeal on the sole ground that the notice of appeal had not been timely filed. The Virginia Supreme Court, however, ordered the state to brief the merits of the issues raised in Coleman's petition. But the following April, it issued an order granting the state's motion to dismiss.

One of the doctrines developed by the Supreme Court that make it difficult for death row inmates to have their claims heard by federal courts is known as the "independent and adequate state ground" doctrine; this doctrine precludes federal review of a state court judgment pertaining to federal law if the state court bases its judgment on a state law ground that is adequate to support the judgment and is independent of the federal question.[37] The rule applies regardless of whether the state court's decision rests on substantive or procedural grounds.[38] For example, if a state procedural rule bars the introduction of newly discovered evidence unless it is discovered within, say, thirty days of the date of the trial verdict, and if the state applies this bar regularly, then, if a state court refuses to entertain new evidence introduced six months or a year later, no matter how compelling that evidence happens to be, the IASG doctrine bars a federal court from doing so. The U.S. Supreme Court had previously held that the independent and adequate state ground doctrine applies in habeas corpus proceedings where the state court's decision rests on a consistently applied procedural bar.[39]

Although the doctrine has great potency, its applicability is not supposed to be automatic; it is not supposed to be triggered just because an issue of state law is subsumed in a case. Thus, in *Harris v. Reed*,[40] the Supreme Court made clear when this powerful doctrine applies. In *Reed*, a state court had denied postconviction relief to a state prisoner, but a fair reading of the state court opinion did not make clear whether the judgment rested on state or federal grounds. The Supreme Court held that federal jurisdiction to reach the merits of the petitioner's habeas petition existed unless the state court "clearly and expressly states that its judgment rests on a state procedural bar."[41] In other words, the court ruled that this doctrine will apply only when the state court makes it clear that its decision rests on a procedural bar.[42] Nevertheless, in Coleman's case, the Court determined that even though the Virginia Supreme Court did not expressly state the basis for its decision, its judgment granting the state's motion to dismiss manifestly indicated that Coleman's case was being disposed of for failure to adhere to a state procedural rule; accordingly, the U.S. Supreme Court held that there was an adequate and independent state ground for the Virginia Supreme Court's decision. It would not reach the merits of Coleman's constitutional claims.

There is an exception in federal habeas corpus law to the adequate and independent state ground doctrine. If a petitioner can show cause for failing to adhere to the state law procedure as well as actual prejudice resulting from a putative failure to adhere to federal law, the federal court will reach the merits of the petitioner's action.[43] The actual prejudice prong is exceedingly difficult to meet, for it requires that a petitioner prove that the result of his trial or sentence would probably have been different had the error not occurred. This standard is almost never satisfied, and there is no reason to think Coleman could have satisfied it, either, but the Court did not reach the issue because it concluded that he could not meet the first prong of the test and show cause for the failure to satisfy the state's procedural rule.[44] Attorney error in missing a filing deadline "is not 'cause' because the attorney is the petitioner's agent when acting, or failing to act."[45] Even so, Coleman suggested, might not attorney error in missing a deadline constitute ineffective assistance of counsel? It might in some contexts, the Court conceded, but not on collateral review, because there is no right to counsel at all on collateral review, and, a fortiori, no right to effective habeas counsel.[46]

Justice Sandra Day O'Connor began her opinion in Coleman's case with the striking observation, "This is a case about federalism." To be sure, every challenge to the constitutionality of a death sentence is, in some measure, a case about federalism insofar as a federal right is being deployed by a prisoner as a shield against a criminal sentence that a state is seeking to carry out. But what Coleman's case really was was a case about whether the state could put someone to death without hearing the inmate's appeal simply because the lawyer had been, at most, one day late in filing the notice of appeal. One value of federalism is to avoid federal interference with state sovereignty, but one equally important federal value is to vindicate individual constitutional rights. Moreover, it seems far from extreme to suggest that one constitutional value is that innocent citizens not be executed.

One could argue that Coleman had an "appeal" to the Supreme Court, but what that appeal consisted of was a futile effort to have the Court pass on whether his attorney's performance had been inadequate. As Justice Blackmun observed in his dissent, "one searches the majority's opinion in vain ... for any mention of ... Coleman's right to a criminal proceeding free from constitutional defect or his interest in finding a forum for his constitutional challenge to his conviction and sentence of death."

The Supreme Court's hostility to claims brought by death row inmates has emboldened the lower courts as well to treat them cavalierly.[47] Two recent pairs of cases from Texas illustrate the phenomenon. The first involved Troy Farris, who was sentenced to death in 1983 for killing a police officer. In his appeal to the Texas Court of Criminal Appeals (CCA), he complained that the prosecutors unconstitutionally excluded from the jury a woman who was opposed to the death penalty. Under the *Witherspoon v. Illinois* line of Supreme Court cases,[48] prosecutors are permitted to exclude a potential juror who says it would be impossible for him or her to impose the death penalty, but it is not permissible to strike a juror just because he or she is in principle against capital punishment. If the juror swears that she would be able to carry out her legal duty, she cannot legally be excluded. The sound idea of the *Witherspoon* line is that prosecutors cannot be permitted to empanel a jury that is predisposed toward death.

In Farris's case, the court ruled that the exclusion of a certain juror was permissible because she had "vacillated" on the question of whether she could adhere to her oath.[49] Four years later, however, Michael Riley raised the same *Witherspoon* issue in the CCA, complaining that prosecutors had wrongfully excluded a juror. This time the Texas court realized that it had previously misapprehended federal law, and the court granted Riley relief;[50] moreover, the court in *Riley v. State* expressly overruled its decision in *Farris v. State.*[51]

As it turned out, Farris had not yet been executed. So he went back to court—first state and then federal—and argued that the CCA had acknowledged that it had been wrong in his case and that he should therefore obtain the same relief that Riley received. His appeal was rejected, and he was executed in 1998.[52]

Whereas the Farris debacle was perpetrated by state courts, the federal courts are behaving just as lawlessly. In 1999, two Texas inmates were set to be executed on consecutive days: Danny Barber was set to die on a Tuesday, and Stan Faulder was scheduled for execution on Wednesday, the very next day. Barber's lawyers, believing that they had exhausted their legal claims, were bidding their client goodbye. Faulder's lawyers, in the meantime, were persuading a federal judge in Austin that the state's clemency proceedings are constitutionally defective, and the judge therefore granted Faulder a stay.[53] Faulder's lawyers contacted Barber's lawyers and Barber authorized the identical issue to be raised in his case. He, too, received a stay from the same federal judge.[54]

The state appealed both cases. On Tuesday afternoon the Court of Appeals for the Fifth Circuit refused to disturb the stay in Barber's case. Yet the next day, a different panel of judges from the same court of appeals did dissolve the stay in Faulder's case. Both inmates had raised the identical legal claim; indeed, the exact same pleadings were used by both sets of lawyers—all that differed was the name of the party seeking relief. The court of appeals added a footnote to its opinion in the *Faulder v. Texas Board of Pardons and Parole* case acknowledging that it was aware that a different group of judges had, on the previous day, halted an execution on the same grounds; but the panel did not explain why it was pursuing a different course.[55] (The Supreme Court did eventually stay Faulder's execution, though the legal basis for its decision remains unclear.)

So Michael Riley obtained relief when his lawyers persuaded the CCA to overrule the decision in *Farris*, whereas Troy Farris was struck by lightning. And Danny Barber, who was alerted to the existence of a legal issue by Faulder, had his legal victory upheld on appeal while Stan Faulder's was set aside. (Both Faulder and Barder have since been executed.) The phrase *death penalty law* might not quite be an oxymoron, but Justice Stewart would notice no difference between the system we have today and the regime he condemned twenty-five years ago. Indeed, it is for this very reason that Justice Blackmun, who voted in favor of the state in death penalty cases throughout the 1970s and 1980s, finally announced in *Callins v. Collins* that he would "no longer...tinker with the machinery of death."[56]

The weariness that federal judges seem to have with death penalty appeals has manifested itself in two ways. The first, as I have suggested, is that judges will occasionally direct angry exasperation toward lawyers representing condemned men.[57] This is unpleasant for the lawyers, but not terribly meaningful otherwise. The second manifestation of weariness is more troubling legally; it consists of the systematic narrowing of the universe of claims that death row inmates are even permitted to bring. For example, the Court has indicated that a claim of actual innocence is not, standing alone, a cognizable claim on habeas review.[58] It has held that death row inmates are not entitled to counsel in order to pursue collateral (i.e., habeas) relief[59]—meaning that the Court has sanctioned the execution of men who, at the time of execution, are unrepresented by counsel. Justice Scalia has even referred to lawyers who represent death row inmates in their collateral proceedings as "guerillas," bent on subverting the will of the majority.[60] What is extraordinary about Justice Scalia's tirade—aside from the fact of the tirade itself—is that he delivered it in a case where the death row inmate argued simply that he was entitled to have the sentencing jury know that he would be ineligible for parole under state law should he be sentenced to life in prison (rather than death).[61] Seven Justices, all but Scalia and Justice Clarence Thomas, agreed on the result. As Justice Blackmun put it for the plurality, "The State may not create a false dilemma by advancing generalized arguments regarding the defendant's future dangerousness while, at the same time, preventing the jury from learning that the defendant will never be released on parole."[62] That such a result could prompt Justice Scalia's outburst is stunning.

Of course, there has long been a strain of popular opinion that cares not a whit about constitutional rights if the guilt of the defendant is not in question. This very attitude is what animates lynch mobs. When Justices of the Supreme Court direct such venomous fury against lawyers even in a case where the death row inmate prevails by a lopsided vote, they sanction and even participate in this lynch-mob mentality.[63] Death penalty lawyers are as opposed to violent crime as even the most ardent law-and-order judge or politician. But being against crime does not justify ignoring constitutional rights and values just because the person who stands to be injured by this is a suspected wrongdoer.

A society that ignores the rights of a suspected murderer may not be committing as large an evil as the murderer did, but it is an evil all the same. Ironically, it is this point that the ancient sages, commenting on the *lex talionis* rule of the Old Testament, made so eloquently. Commenting on the biblical reference to the death penalty, Rabbi Meir, who lived at the time of Jesus, told this parable:

> Once upon a time there lived in the same city a pair of twin brothers. One grew up and was made king. The other became a robber. So the king ordered his brother's execution. The passers-by who saw him hanging would thereupon exclaim, "There hangs the king." And so the king gave the order to take him down.

NOTES

1. 408 U.S. 238 (1972).
2. 408 U.S. at 309 (opinion of Stewart, J.).
3. 428 U.S. 153 (1976).
4. 433 U.S. 584 (1977).
5. *Woodson v. North Carolina*, 428 U.S. 280 (1976); *Roberts v. Louisiana*, 428 U.S. 325 (1976).
6. 428 U.S. 153, 188 (1976).
7. See the chapter in this volume by Phyllis Crocker.
8. Audrey Duff, "The Deadly DA," *Texas Monthly*, February 1994.
9. *Murray v. Giarratano*, 492 U.S. 1 (1989).
10. 506 U.S. 390 (1993).
11. 501 U.S. 722 (1991). *Coleman* is discussed below in greater detail.
12. *Perillo v. Johnson*, 205 F.3d 775, 786 (5th Cir. 2000).
13. *Houston Chronicle Pub. Co. v. McMaster*, 598 S.W.2d 864 (Tex.Cr.App. 1980).
14. See *Beets v. Scott*, 65 F.3d 1258 (5th Cir.1995), cert. denied, 517 U.S. 1157 (1996).
15. See *New York Times*, November 3, 1988, A20.
16. *Bass v. Estelle*, 696 F.2d 1154 (5th Cir. 1983).
17. *Romero v. Collins*, 884 F.2d 871, 875 (5th Cir. 1989).
18. *Ex parte Duffy*, 607 S.W.2d 507 (Tex.Cr.App. 1980).
19. See, e.g., *Ex parte Earvin*, 816 S.W.2d 379 (Tex.Cr.App. 1991).
20. *Russell v. Collins*, 892 F.2d 1205, 1213 (5th Cir. 1989).
21. *Ex parte Guzmon*, 730 S.W.2d 724 (Tex.Cr.App. 1987).
22. See Stephen B. Bright, *Counsel for the Poor*, 103 Yale L.J. 1835 (1994).
23. *Nichols v. Collins*, 802 F.Supp. 66 (S.D.Tex. 1992), aff'd in part and rev'd in part, 69 F.3d 1255 (5th Cir. 1995).
24. Bright, *Counsel for the Poor*, 1860–61.
25. *Martinez-Macias v. Collins*, 979 F.2d 1067 (5th Cir. 1992).
26. These data are on file with the author. Moreover, of the twenty-two judges, twenty-one are former prosecutors.
27. See David C. Baldus, *Racial Discrimination and the Death Penalty*, 83 Cornell L. Rev. 1638 (1998); John H. Blume, *Post-McClesky Racial Discrimination Claims in Capital Cases*, 83 Cornell L. Rev. 1771 (1998); see also U.S. Gen. Acc't Office, *Death Penalty Sentencing* 6 (1996) (summarizing data from more than twenty studies); Stephen P. Garvey, *The Emotional Economy of Capital Sentencing*, 75 N.Y.U.L. Rev. 26 (2000).

28. Current statistics, as well as links to death penalty sites, both pro and con, can be found at the website of the Death Penalty Information Center, www.essential.org/dpic.
29. See, e.g., John C. McAdams, *Racial Disparity and the Death Penalty*, 61 Law & Contemp. Problems 153 (1998).
30. 481 U.S. 279 (1987).
31. Lon L. Fuller, *The Case of the Speluncean Explorers*, 62 Harv. L. Rev. 616 (1949).
32. *Ellis v. Collins*, 788 F.Supp. 317 (S.D. Tex. 1992).
33. 28 U.S.C. § 2254 (b)(1)(A).
34. 28 U.S.C. § 2254 (c).
35. 28 U.S.C. § 2254 (e)(1).
36. 28 U.S.C. § 2254(d)(1).
37. The doctrine can be traced to *Murdock v. City of Memphis*, 87 U.S. 590 (1875). The case ordinarily cited for the modern statement of the doctrine is *Fox Film Corp. v. Muller*, 296 U.S. 207, 210 (1935). In recent years, the Supreme Court has treated the rule as jurisdictional. See, e.g., *Ake v. Oklahoma*, 470 U.S. 68, 75 (1985).
38. See, e.g., *Herndon v. Georgia*, 295 U.S. 441 (1935).
39. *Wainwright v. Sykes*, 433 U.S. 72 (1977).
40. 489 U.S. 255 (1989).
41. Ibid., 263.
42. In *Michigan v. Long*, 463 U.S. 1032 (1983), the Court held that it would assume that a state court decision does not rest on an independent and adequate state ground unless the state court decision "indicates clearly and expressly" that federal law plays no role (1040–41). It is difficult to fathom how the Virginia Supreme Court satisfied the "expressly" component of the test.
43. *Coleman v. Thompson*, 501 U.S. 722 (1991); *Murray v. Carrier*, 477 U.S. 478 (1986).
44. 501 U.S. 752.
45. Ibid., at 752–54.
46. Ibid., 754–56.
47. Even former death row inmates fare poorly in the Supreme Court. In *McMillian v. Monroe County, Ala*, 520 U.S. 781 (1997), the Supreme Court used an expansive construction of the Eleventh amendment to preclude a federal suit for damages brought by a former death row inmate against the sheriff whose decision to suppress exculpatory evidence resulted in the former inmate's conviction and six-year stay on death row.
48. *Witherspoon v. Illinois*, 391 U.S. 510 (1968); *Adams v. Texas*, 448 U.S. 38 (1980); *Wainwright v. Witt*, 469 U.S. 412 (1985).
49. *Farris v. State*, 819 S.W.2d 490 (Tex.Cr.App. 1991). The "vacillating juror" problem is associated with *Wainright v. Witt*, supra.
50. *Riley v. State*, 889 S.W.2d 290 (Tex.Cr.App. 1994).
51. Ibid., 299.
52. *Farris v. Johnson*, 144 F.3d 50 (5th Cir.), cert. denied, 525 U.S. 1004 (1998).
53. See *Faulder v. Tx. Bd. of Pardons & Parole*, 178 F.3d 344 (5th Cir.), cert. denied, 119 S.Ct. 2362 (1999) (recounting procedural history).
54. None of the opinions relating to the clemency issue in the *Barber* litigation is published. The Supreme Court's denial of relief is located at 525 U.S. 1132 (1999). I have previously criticized the refusal of the courts—both state and federal—to publish their opinions in death penalty cases. See Dow, *The State, the Death Penalty, and Carl Johnson*, 37 Boston College L. Rev. 691 (1996). The details in the text are based on my firsthand knowledge of the cases.
55. The opinion is unpublished.
56. *Callins v. Collins*, 510 U.S. 1141, 1143 (1994) (Blackmun, J., dissenting from denial of certiorari).
57. See, e.g., David R. Dow, "Frontiers of Justice," *The Texas Observer* 80 (November 25, 1988), 9–10 (concerning former death row inmate Walter Bell); *McFarland v. Scott*, 512 U.S. 849 (1994).
58. *Herrera v. Collins*, 506 U.S. 390 (1993).
59. *Murray v. Giarratano*, 492 U.S. 1 (1989).
60. *Simmons v. South Carolina*, 512 U.S. 154, 185 (1994) (Scalia, J., dissenting).
61. Ibid., at 156.
62. Ibid., at 171.
63. *Simmons* is not the only case where Justice Scalia has expressed this antipathy toward death penalty lawyers. See *McFarland v. Scott*, 512 U.S. 849 (1994) (transcript of oral argument).

THE EXECUTION
OF IVON RAY STANLEY

ince this country's last public execution in 1936, all U.S. executions have been carried out solely in front of state-selected witnesses. Members of the media have tried to bring their cameras and tape recorders into execution chambers but courts have consistently ruled against them. In 1998, however, audiotapes of twenty-two Georgia executions (tapes created by members of the state's Department of Corrections as their own procedural archive) entered the court record when Atlanta capital defender Michael Mears subpoenaed the tapes in a lawsuit challenging the humaneness of the electric chair. This is an edited transcription of one of these tapes: the execution of Ivon Ray Stanley, carried out on July 12, 1984. Stanley's execution was broadcast on May 2, 2001, on public radio stations across the country as a part of *The Execution Tapes: A Public Radio Special Report*, produced by Sound Portraits Productions and WNYC.

Ralph Kemp: This is a recording of the execution of Ivon Ray Stanley EF103603. July the twelfth, 1984.

Willis Marable: Colonel Lowe, Mickey?

Lowe: Yes?

Marable: The witnesses are now entering the witness room.

Lowe: Okay.

Marable: The state witnesses have entered the witness room and have seated themselves on the front row. At this time, the news media witnesses are entering. All witnesses have arrived and have seated.

Mickey: Let's proceed.

Lowe: We can proceed if you're ready.

Marable: Colonel Lowe, Mickey? The warden has entered the execution chamber at this time, approaching the microphone and is in the process of briefing all witnesses to remain quiet and to avoid any unnecessary movements. He also advised them that medical assistance is available if needed (*sound of warden in background*). The warden at this time is in the process of confirming all witnesses. All witness have been confirmed. The warden is in the process of advising all witnesses that we will now proceed with the court-ordered execution of Ivon Stanley. Mickey, Colonel Lowe?

Lowe: Yes.

Marable: We're still waiting for the execution team members to bring him into the execution chamber. (*Voice unintelligible.*) Colonel Lowe, Mickey? The execution team is now in the process of escorting the condemned into the execution chamber. He is walking, unassisted, walked straight to the chair, and has seated himself in it. One of the execution team members is now in the process of securing the back strap. The other members are in the process of securing the arm straps and leg straps.

The back strap is secure at this time.

Both arm straps are secure at this time. They are still in the process of securing the leg straps. At this time the condemned has been secured in the chair. He is not moving, he is just sitting there very passively, staring out at the witnesses.

The superintendent has afforded the condemned an opportunity to make a last statement. He has declined to make a last statement.

He is afforded the opportunity for prayer. He declined this also.

The warden is now in the process of reading the essential court order to the witnesses and to the condemned.

(*Sound of warden in background.*)

The condemned is still sitting there very passively, no movement, staring out at the witnesses.

The superintendent is still in the process of reading the court order to the condemned.

At this time, the superintendent has completed reading the essential court order. The execution team members are now entering the execution chamber with the headset and the leg band. One member is in the process of securing the leg band to the fleshy part of the inmate's right leg. Two members of the execution team is [sic] in the process of securing the headset to the condemned.

The condemned has offered no resistance throughout. He is just sitting there very passively, not moving. The leg band has been secured to the condemned's right leg, and also the headset has been secured to his head. Perspiration is now being wiped from the forehead of the condemned. And he is secure and ready for execution with the exception of the hood being placed over his head and the wires being attached to the leg band and to the headset.

The electrician now has entered the execution chamber and is in the process of securing the wire to the headset.

Lowe: They're moving very well. It's a good time to do it now. Marable, stand still. Mickey, put William Hill on.

William Hill: Hello.

Lowe: William, the attorney general is here.

Michael Bowers: Hill, this is Mike. Have you got any reason why execution shouldn't be carried out?

Hill: No, I don't.

Bowers: Thank you.

Hill: All right.

Marable: Colonel Hill—Colonel Lowe, Mickey? The wires have been attached and secured to the headset and to the leg band. The perspiration has been wiped again from the condemned's forehead and the hood is being placed on at this time. The face hood has been secured. The warden and all the execution team members have departed the execution chamber. Stand by for the warden's last telephone check.

Lowe: Ralph, this is commissioner.

Kemp: Yes.

Lowe: There are no stays. You can proceed to carry out the official order of the court.

Kemp: Very well. At my count of three, press your buttons. One. Two. Three.

Marable: Colonel Lowe? Mickey? The execution is now in progress. When the first surge entered his body he stiffened and I heard a pop, as if one of the straps broke. But I can't tell from this vantage point. He is still at this time sitting there with clenched fists, with no other movements. He is slowly relaxing at this time. The first phase of the execution is completed, we are now into the second phase. The second phase is completed at this time, we are now into the third and final stage. From my vantage point it seems that the inmate has relaxed somewhat. His fists are still clenched, but there is no movement from the condemned. There is still no movement from the individual, he's still just sitting there.

Lowe: Is the third phase completed?

Marable: We're still into the third phase. Third phase and the execution is completed. We're now into the five minutes lapse time. It appeared that when the execution was completed and the power was off, he relaxed somewhat more than he was. It was pretty visible that he relaxed even more than what it seemed before.

Lowe: Any reaction from the witnesses?

Marable: They're sitting very still, just observing. No, uh—I see one or two of the media writing notes, taking notes. But other than that they are just sitting staring into the execution chamber.

We have completed one minute of the five minutes lapse time.

Unknown voice, off-mike: I never drink after ten o'clock at night.

Marable: Colonel Lowe, Mickey? We have now completed two minutes of the five minutes lapse time. There's still no—very little, no movement from the witnesses—no one's even taking notes at this time. They're just sitting there staring into the execution chamber. (*Other voices, unintelligible.*) We have now completed four minutes. One minute remaining.

Unknown voice #1, off-mike: Are they ready to go in?

Unknown voice #2, off-mike: We've got a few more seconds.

Marable: Colonel Lowe, Mickey? We have now completed five minutes lapse time. Stand by. For the—the doctors are now preparing to enter the execution chamber to check for life signs.

One of the physicians is now in the process of doing this.

The first physician has completed his examination, the second physcician is now in the process of making his check. The second doctor has now completed his examination. The third and final doctor is in the process of making his check.

The examination is completed. Stand by for the superintendent's time of death and confirmation of death. (*Superintendent can be heard in background.*)

The superintendent has advised all witnesses that death did occur at 12:24 this date. He has instructed all witnesses to depart the witness room and to be transported back to the front of the institution. Curtains are drawn at this time. Colonel Lowe, Mickey? That completes it.

Lowe: Marable, see if you could find what that snap pop [was] that you were talking about a while ago.

Marable: I think it was just the electricity arc. I don't think any strap broke [or] anything. He just jerked real hard and caused the electricity to arc.

Lowe: Okay.

Marable: They have removed the face hood. The execution team members are now in the process now of removing the straps. The electrical wire has been removed from the condemned's right leg. He is being removed from the electric chair at this time and being placed on the stretcher. He is being removed from the execution chamber at this time and the execution team members are taking him to the autopsy room. And that's all I can see, Colonel Lowe.

Lowe: Is the warden available?

Marable: Just a minute.

Kemp: Hello?

Lowe: You and your staff did an excellent job. We appreciate it very much.

Kemp: OK. We had a little bit of a scare—I don't know if they relayed that to you or not.

Lowe: Pop.

Kemp: The popping sound. We were thinking that what happened because he sat there for that three minutes, that the water in the sponge on his leg ran out right there by his foot, and we were thinking that it was like a little bolt of lightning.

Lowe: Did you see anything?

Kemp: No. They said—Colonel Hardison and the other people in the witness room said they didn't see anything like that. Now, I still feel good about it.

Lowe: It ran too smooth, Ralph, but don't screw it up next time.

Kemp: (*laughing*) Okay.

Lowe: Mike Bowers wants to say something.

Kemp: Okay.

Bowers: Ralph, I second what Dave said. Very smooth job.

Kemp: Okay, we appreciate it. Just give us another one.

Bowers: Thank you, Ralph.

Kemp: Okay, thank you.

Lowe: Marable?

Kemp: Here he is. Just a second, Colonel.

Marable: Colonel Lowe?

Lowe: Marable?

Marable: Yes, sir.

Lowe: I want to thank you.

Marable: You're quite welcome, sir. Any time.

Lowe: Goodnight.

Marable: Goodnight, sir.

PART II

LEGACIES OF LYNCHING

3

DISCRIMINATION, DEATH, AND DENIAL: RACE AND THE DEATH PENALTY

STEPHEN B. BRIGHT

INTRODUCTION

The death penalty is a direct descendant of lynching and other forms of racial violence and racial oppression in America. From colonial times until the Civil War, the criminal law in many states expressly differentiated between crimes committed by and against blacks and whites.[1] For example, Georgia law provided that the rape of a white female by a black man was punishable by death, while the rape of a white female by anyone else was punishable by a prison term not less than two nor more than twenty years.[2] The rape of a black woman was punishable "by fine and imprisonment, at the discretion of the court."[3]

Disparate punishments—exacted by the courts and by the mob—based upon both the race of the victim and the race of the defendant continued in practice after the abolition of slavery. At least 4,743 people were killed by lynch mobs.[4] More than 90 percent of the lynchings took place in the south, and three-fourths of the victims were African Americans.[5] The threat that Congress might pass an anti-lynching statute in the early 1920s led Southern states to "replace lynchings with a more '[humane]...method of racial control'—the judgment and imposition of capital sentences by all-white juries."[6] As one historian observed, "Southerners...discovered that lynchings were untidy and created a bad press.... [L]ynchings were increasingly replaced by situations in which the Southern legal system prostituted itself to the mob's demand. Responsible officials begged would-be lynchers to 'let the law take its course,' thus tacitly promising that there would be a quick trial and the death penalty.... [S]uch proceedings 'retained the essence of mob murder, shedding only its outward forms.'" The process of "legal lynchings" was so successful that in the 1930s, two-thirds of those executed were black.[8]

Powell v. Alabama,[9] decided by the U.S. Supreme Court in 1932, involved nine young African Americans who were charged in Scottsboro, Alabama, with the rape of two white women, the classic case for a lynching or the death penalty. The youths were tried in groups in three trials while mobs outside the courtroom demanded the death penalty. The accused were represented by two lawyers; one was a drunk and the other was senile. All-white, all-male juries sentenced the accused to death. When there was a national outcry about the injustice of such summary trials with only perfunctory legal representation, the people of Scottsboro did not understand the reaction. After all, they felt, they had not lynched the accused; they gave them a trial.[10]

In one of many examples of legal lynchings, a man was hanged immediately after a trial in Kentucky that lasted less than an hour.[11] The *Louisville Courier-Journal* "tried to put the best light on the execution," saying that although it was a little hasty, at least there was not a lynching.[12] The paper also observed that since a "Negro" had raped a white woman, "no other result could have been reached, however prolonged the trial."[13] As racial violence was achieved increasingly through the criminal courts, Georgia became the nation's primary executioner, carrying out the most executions in the twentieth century before the death penalty was declared unconstitutional in 1972.[14] Between 1924 and 1972, Georgia executed 337 black people and 75 white people.[15]

Similarly, a study in 1994 of death sentences in Harris County, Texas, which has carried out more executions and sentenced more people to death than all but one of the other forty-nine states, found that "Harris County has sent blacks to death row nearly twice as often as whites during the last ten years, a growing imbalance that eclipses the pre-civil rights days of 'Old Sparky' the notorious Texas electric chair."[16] And in Florida, which has the nation's third largest death row,[17] the Racial and Ethnic Bias Commission of the Florida Supreme Court found that "the application of the death penalty in Florida is not color-blind."[18] A congressional study found stark disparities in the use of the federal death penalty.[19] Racial disparities have been documented by other observers.[20]

The death penalty was held unconstitutional in *Furman v. Georgia* because of discrimination and arbitrariness in its infliction; new death penalty statutes were enacted almost immediately by a number of states. Some of those statutes were upheld by the Supreme Court in 1976. However, the new statutes have failed to end the influence of racial prejudice in the use of the death penalty.

RACIAL DISCRIMINATION AFTER FURMAN

Most death penalty schemes adopted by the states after *Furman v. Georgia* provide for the death penalty in most first degree and felony murders. Any murder involving a robbery, arson, burglary, rape, or kidnapping may be prosecuted as a capital case.[21] In addition, death may be imposed for any other "heinous, atrocious or cruel"[22] or "horrible" murders,[22] which of course describe almost all murders. But no crime—no matter how heinous—*must* be punished by death. In most states, the sentence is determined by the imprecise and wholly subjective consideration of aggravating and mitigating factors. The breadth of the death penalty statutes and the unfettered discretion given to prosecutors and juries provide ample room for racial prejudice to influence whether death is sought or imposed.[23] As the Supreme Court noted in one case, "[b]ecause of the range of discretion entrusted to a jury in a capital sentencing hearing, there is a unique opportunity for racial prejudice to operate. . . ." As a result, "[R]ace plays an especially influential role in capital sentencing decisions."[24]

The criminal courts are the institutions in the United States least affected by the civil rights movement that brought changes to many American institutions in the last forty years. Judges and prosecutors are still elected in judicial circuits that are drawn to dilute the voting strength of racial minorities.[25] Thus, even in many areas with substantial minority populations, all of the judges and prosecutors are white.[26] In Georgia, for example, all of the elected district attorneys are white.[27] Many other states also have no or very few African Americans as prosecutors.[28] Members of racial minorities are often underrepresented in jury pools and excluded in the jury selection process;[29] often, the only member of a racial minority who participates in the process is the accused. Racial disparities are still apparent in all types of sentencing.[30] The perfunctory capital trial—the legal lynching—is not a thing of the past. Those facing the death penalty still receive token representation by court-appointed lawyers in cases infected by racism. This racism manifests itself in numerous ways.

Tolerance of Racial Discrimination in the Criminal Courts
Wilburn Dobbs, an African American who was sentenced to death in Georgia for the murder of a white man, was referred to at his trial as "colored" and "colored boy" by the judge and defense lawyer and called by his first name by the prosecutor.[31] Two of the jurors who sentenced Dobbs to death for the murder admitted after trial to using the racial slur "nigger."[32] Dobbs was tried only two weeks after being indicted for murder and four

other offenses, and he was assigned a court-appointed lawyer who did not know for certain until the day of trial that he was going to represent Dobbs.[33] The lawyer filed only one motion, a demand for a copy of the accusation and a list of witnesses.[34] Counsel sought a continuance on the morning of trial,[35] stating to the trial court that he was "not prepared to go to trial" and that he was "in a better position to prosecute the case than defend it."[36] Nevertheless, the trial court denied the motion and the case proceeded to trial.[37] The federal district court described the defense lawyer's attitude toward African Americans as follows:

> Dobbs' trial attorney was outspoken about his views. He said that many blacks are uneducated and would not make good teachers, but do make good basketball players. He opined that blacks are less educated and less intelligent than whites either because of their nature or because "my granddaddy had slaves." He said that integration has led to deteriorating neighborhoods and schools and referred to the black community in Chattanooga as "black boy jungle." He strongly implied that blacks have inferior morals by relating a story about sex in a classroom. He also said that when he was young, a maid was hired with the understanding that she would steal some items. He said that blacks in Chattanooga are more troublesome than blacks in Walker County [Georgia]....
> The attorney stated that he uses the word "nigger" jokingly.[38]

Dobbs was convicted and sentenced to death in a trial that lasted only three days. During the penalty phase of Dobbs's trial, when the jury could have heard anything about his life, background, and any reasons Dobbs should not have been sentenced to death,[39] the lawyer presented no evidence.[40] For a closing argument he read part of Justice William Brennan's concurring opinion in *Furman v. Georgia*,[41] which expressed the view that the death penalty was unconstitutional and could not be carried out.[42] Thus, rather than emphasizing to the jury the enormous decision it had to make about whether Dobbs was going to live or die, the lawyer suggested that because the death penalty would never be carried out, the jury's decision was not important.[43]

Dobbs is only one of many cases that starkly illustrate that racial discrimination not acceptable in any other area of American life today is tolerated in criminal courts. The use of a racial slur may cost a sports announcer his job,[44] but there have been capital cases in which judges, jurors, and defense counsel have called an African American defendant a "nigger" with no repercussions for anyone except the accused. For example, parents of an African American defendant were referred to as the "nigger mom and dad" by the judge in a Florida case.[45] The judge did not lose his job; the Florida Supreme Court merely suggested that judges should avoid the "appearance" of impropriety in the future.[46]

Similarly, a death sentence was upheld in a Georgia case where jurors used racial slurs during their deliberations.[47] The court reasoned that the evidence "shows only that two of the twelve jurors possessed some racial prejudice and does not establish that racial prejudice caused those two jurors to vote to convict [the defendant] and sentence him to die."[48] No state or federal court so much as held a hearing on the racial prejudice that infected the sentencing of William Henry Hance before he was executed by Georgia in 1994, even though jurors signed affidavits swearing racial slurs had been used during deliberations.[49] In at least five capital cases in Georgia, the accused were referred to with racial slurs by their own lawyers at some time during the court proceedings.[50]

It is the publicly announced policy of Ed Peters, the district attorney of Jackson, Mississippi, to "get rid of as many" black citizens as possible when exercising his peremptory strikes to select a jury.[51] As a result of this "policy" by a government official, Leo Edwards, an African American, was sentenced to death by an all-white jury, even though he was tried in a community that was 34 percent African American.[52] The federal courts rejected Edwards' challenge to Peters' discrimination,[53] and Edwards was executed in 1989.[54] In what other area of American life may a public official openly espouse and carry out a policy of "getting rid of" people based upon their race and have it approved by the courts?

The practice of total exclusion from jury service on the basis of race is not limited to the district attorney in Jackson. A prosecutor in Chambers County, Alabama, used twenty-six jury strikes against twenty-six African Americans who were qualified for jury duty in order to get three all-white juries in a case involving Albert Jefferson, a mentally retarded African American, accused of a crime against a white victim.[55] At the time of Jefferson's trial, marriage records at the courthouse in Chambers County were kept in books engraved "white" and "colored."[56] During state postconviction proceedings, lawyers representing Jefferson discovered lists that had been made by the prosecutor prior to jury selection in which the prosecutor divided prospective jurors into four lists—"strong," "medium," "weak," and "black."[57] A state circuit judge in Chambers County ruled that no racial discrimination had occurred in the selection of the juries.[58]

Some courts are indifferent to even the most blatant appearances of racial bias. African Americans facing the death penalty in Georgia usually appear before a white judge sitting in front of the Confederate battle flag. Georgia adopted its state flag in 1956 to symbolize its defiance of the Supreme Court's decision in *Brown v. Board of Education*.[59] As observed one federal district court in Georgia, The predominant part of the 1956 flag is the Confederate battle flag, which is historically associated with the Ku Klux Klan. The legislators who voted for the 1956 bill knew that the new flag would be interpreted as a statement of defiance against federal desegregation mandates and an expression of anti-black feelings."[60] The new flag was designed to carry the message that Georgia "intend[s] to uphold what [it] stood for, will stand for, and will fight for"—namely, state-sponsored commitment to black subordination and the denial of equal protection of the laws to Georgia's African-American school children."[61] Although it is well recognized that the flag serves as "a visual focal point for racial tensions"[62] and symbolizes defiance of the principle of equal protection under law, it is displayed in most Georgia courtrooms."

Discrimination in the Exercise of Discretion
Members of racial minorities have long been excluded from being prosecutors, judges, jurors, lawyers, and from holding prominent positions in law enforcement. As one scene in a Georgia courtroom has been described, Four black men stood before a Cobb County judge recently asking for bond to be set in their cases, all involving drug charges. After reviewing each case, the judge ordered them all held without bond until trial. Virtually everyone else in the courtroom—the judge, two prosecutors, five defense lawyers, law clerks and bailiff—were white people. "If [my son] had been white, he'd be coming home," said the mother of one defendant. "You saw what happened in there. It resembled some kind of Klan meeting." While the Cobb judge's handling of the case was not unusual, neither was the mother's reaction."[63]

Things are no different in many other courtrooms throughout the nation. The criminal justice system in Jacksonville, Florida, has been described as follows:

> Often the only black faces involved in Jacksonville murder cases belong to the victim and the killer.
> In a city where most murders are committed by blacks against other blacks, the faces of law and order are overwhelmingly white.
> There are:
> No black felony judges, the only circuit judges to handle homicides.
> No black members of the Public Defender Office homicide team.
> Two black prosecutors out of 14 homicide-team members and supervisors at the State Attorney's Office.
> Four black homicide detectives and supervisors out of 26 at the Jacksonville's Sheriff's Office.[64]

Thus, members of racial minorities often do not participate in the highly subjective decisions that lead to the imposition of the death penalty. Such decisions are frequently made by persons who are hostile to, or at the very least indifferent or insensitive to, the minority community.

The most important decisions that may determine whether the accused is sentenced to die are those made by the prosecutor. It is the prosecutor who decides whether to seek the death penalty, and whether to resolve the case with a plea bargain for a sentence less than death. In many jurisdictions, these critical decisions are made by one white man, the elected district attorney, with no input from the community. Even where more than one person decides, there may be no representation for the minority community. For example, in Orange County, the jurisdiction that ranks third in sending people to California's death row, a panel of prosecutors composed exclusively of white men decides whether the death sentence will be sought in a case.[65] Some prosecutors seek the death penalty frequently; some hardly ever seek it. There are no statewide standards to govern when the death penalty is sought; each local district attorney sets his or her own policy in deciding which cases will be prosecuted as death cases.

In most jurisdictions with the death penalty, all murders accompanied by another felony, as well as all murders considered "heinous, atrocious or cruel" or "outrageously and wantonly vile, horrible and inhuman" may be prosecuted as capital cases.[66] From among the many cases where death could be sought, the local district attorney decides which few will actually be prosecuted as capital cases. For the white men who usually make these decisions in judicial districts all over the country, the crime may seem more heinous or horrible if the victim is a prominent white citizen. As one scholar has observed, "The life-and-death decision is made on trivial grounds, and tends to reflect the community's prejudices."[67]

Race may also influence the decision to seek the death sentence in more subtle ways. Prosecutors make the decision whether to seek the death penalty based in part on the strength of the evidence brought to them by law enforcement in each case. Often, the amount of available evidence differs because the local sheriffs and police departments investigate crime in the white community much more aggressively than crime in the black community.[68] While massive searches involving the police, army units, and even the Boy Scouts may occur when there is a crime against a white person,[69] nothing more than a missing person report may be completed when a black citizen disappears.[70] This disparity in the investigative treatment of cases results in a disparity of evidence available to prosecute the cases. Thus, racial discrimination against crime victims by police departments results in the prosecutor having stronger evidence with which to justify seeking the death penalty in white victim cases and not seeking it in cases where the victim is a minority.

As a result of these influences, many cases in which prosecutors decide to seek the death penalty are indistinguishable from hundreds of other murder cases in which the death penalty is not sought. For example, most tragically, there are many convenience-store robberies that result in loss of life. Only a handful are prosecuted as death cases. A case involving a battered woman with no criminal record who kills her abusive spouse is typically not a death penalty case in most parts of the country. However, the prosecutor in Talladega, Alabama, has obtained death sentences for at least two battered women for their roles in killing their abusers.[71] Of course, there are many other examples of cases that are eligible for the death penalty but are seldom prosecuted as capital cases.

An investigation into why some cases are treated as capital cases when other similar cases are not will almost always reveal the influence of race, class, and politics. Often, there is more publicity and greater outrage in the community over an interracial crime than other crimes. Community outrage, the need to avenge the murder because of the prominence of the victim in the community, the insistence of the victim's family on the death penalty, the social and political clout of the family in the community, and the amount of publicity regarding the crime are often far more important in determining whether death is sought than the facts of the crime or the defendant's record and background.

For example, an investigation of all murder cases prosecuted in Georgia's Chattahoochee Judicial Circuit from 1973 to 1990 revealed that in cases involving the murder of a white person, prosecutors often met with the victim's family and discussed whether to seek the death penalty.[72] In a case involving the murder of the daughter of a prominent white contractor, the prosecutor contacted the contractor and asked him if he wanted to seek the death penalty.[73] When the contractor replied in the affirmative, the prosecutor said that was all he needed to know.[74] He obtained the death penalty at trial.[75] He was rewarded with a contribution of $5,000 from the contractor when he successfully ran for judge in the next election.[76] The contribution was at the time the largest ever received by the district attorney.[77] There were other cases in which the district attorney issued press releases announcing that he was seeking the death penalty after meeting with the family of a white victim.[78] But prosecutors failed to meet with African Americans whose family members had been murdered to determine what sentence they wanted. Most were not even notified that the case had been resolved.[79] As a result of these practices, although African Americans were the victims of 65 percent of the homicides in the Chattahoochee Judicial Circuit, 85 percent of the capital cases in that circuit were white-victim cases.[80]

The prosecutor's decision to seek the death penalty may never be reviewed by a minority juror. Many capital cases are tried in white-flight suburban communities where there are so few minority persons in the community that there is little likelihood the minority community will be represented on the jury. Counties like Baltimore County, Maryland, and Cobb County, Georgia, account for a disproportionately high number of persons sentenced to death in those states.[81] But even in communities where there is a substantial minority population, prosecutors are often successful in preventing or minimizing participation by minorities.

During jury selection for a capital trial, the judge or prosecutor asks potential jurors if they are conscientiously opposed to the death penalty. If they are opposed to the death penalty and cannot put their views aside, the state is entitled to have those people removed for cause.[82] Although this process results in a more conviction-prone jury, it has been upheld by the U.S. Supreme Court.[83] This "death qualification" process often results in the removal of more prospective jurors who are members of minority groups than those who are white. The minority jurors may have reservations about the death penalty because it has been used in a racially discriminatory manner. This is one of many ways in which past discrimination in the application of the death penalty perpetuates continued discrimination.

Often the death qualification process reduces the number of minority jurors to few enough that those remaining can be eliminated by the prosecutor with peremptory strikes. Even when jurors who express reservations about the death penalty indicate they can put aside their personal views and consider it, the prosecutor may justify his strikes with the hesitancy of those jurors to impose the death penalty. For example, in *Lingo v. State*,[84] a Georgia prosecutor used all eleven of his jury strikes against African Americans to obtain an all white jury in a capital case.[85] In a challenge to those strikes under *Batson v. Kentucky*,[86] the Georgia Supreme Court—over the dissent of its two African-American justices—upheld the strikes based on the "race neutral" reasons articulated by the prosecutor, many of which had to do with the jurors' answers to the death qualification questions.[87]

A federal court in Alabama found the "standard operating procedure of the Tuscaloosa County District Attorney's Office" was "to use the peremptory challenges to strike as many blacks as possible from the venires in cases involving serious crimes."[88] The district court also found that prosecutors "manipulated the trial docket in their effort to preserve the racial purity of criminal juries. Inasmuch as they actually set the criminal trial dockets until 1982, they implemented a scheme in which juries with fewer black venirepersons would be called for the serious cases."[89]

In Georgia's Chattahoochee Judicial Circuit, which has sent more people to death row than any other circuit in the state,[90] prosecutors have used 83 percent of their opportunities to use peremptory jury strikes against African Americans, even though black people constitute thirty-four percent of the population in the circuit.[91] As a result, six

African American defendants were tried by all-white juries.[92] Two of them have been executed.[93]

William Henry Hance was the first black defendant tried in a Chattahoochee Circuit capital case after *Furman* to have a member of his race on his jury.[94] During jury selection at Hance's first trial, the prosecutor used nine of his ten peremptory strikes against African Americans, leaving one black person on the jury.[95] The death penalty was imposed. However, it was later set aside because the prosecutor made a lynch-mob type appeal to the jury for the death penalty in closing argument, which the United States Court of Appeals characterized as a "dramatic appeal to gut emotion" that "has no place in a courtroom."[96] These words from a federal court had no impact on the prosecutor. After the reversal, he called a press conference, insisted that he had done nothing wrong, and announced he would once again seek the death penalty against Hance.[97] At the second trial, he used seven of eight strikes against blacks, again eliminating all but one member of Hance's race from jury service.[98] Hance was again sentenced to death and this death sentence was carried out.[99]

The judicial circuit second only to Chattahoochee in sending people to Georgia's death row is the Ocmulgee Judicial Circuit in central Georgia.[100] Joseph Briley tried thirty-three death penalty cases in his tenure as district attorney in the circuit between 1974 and 1994;[101] of these, twenty-four were against African-American defendants.[102] It was discovered that Briley had instructed jury commissioners in one county in the circuit to underrepresent black citizens on the master jury lists from which grand and trial juries were selected.[103] Additionally, the African Americans who were summoned for jury duty in the circuit were often sent back home after Briley used his peremptory jury strikes against them. In the cases in which the defendants were black and the victims were white, Briley used 94 percent of his jury challenges—96 out of 103—against black citizens.[104]

When a prosecutor uses the overwhelming majority of his jury strikes against a racial minority, that minority is prohibited from participating in the process. A jury does not represent "the conscience of the community on the ultimate question of life or death" when one-fourth or more of the community is not represented on it.[105]

African Americans and other minorities continue to be excluded from jury service, even after the Supreme Court's decision in *Batson v. Kentucky*,[106] which changed the standard of proof for establishing a prima facie case of discrimination.[107] *Batson* required trial judges—most of whom are popularly elected—to assess the district attorney's reasons in order to determine whether the prosecutor intended to discriminate.[108] Many judges are former prosecutors who may have hired the district attorneys appearing before them. Even if the judge is not personally close to the prosecutor, he or she may be dependent upon the prosecutor's support in the election to remain in office.[109] Thus, in the many jurisdictions where judges are elected, it may be politically impossible and personally difficult for the judge to reject a reason proffered by the prosecutor for striking a minority juror. Courts routinely uphold convictions and death sentences even where a grossly disproportionate number of African Americans have been excluded from jury service by the prosecutor's peremptory jury strikes.[110]

Racial diversity on juries makes a difference in capital trials. Juries selected through discriminatory practices often bring to the jury box, either consciously or subconsciously, "racial stereotypes and assumptions" that influence them "in the direction of findings of black culpability and white victimization,. . . black immorality and white virtue,. . . blacks as social problems and whites as valued citizens."[111] Experience has taught that the death penalty is much more likely to be imposed in cases tried with all-white juries than in cases tried with more racially diverse juries.[112] Decisions made by all-white juries do not receive the respect of other racial groups that have been denied participation. On the other hand, more diverse juries bring to their decision making a broader perspective gained through varied life experiences. An African-American member of the Georgia Supreme Court has observed, "When it comes to grappling with racial issues in the criminal justice system today, often white Americans find one reality while African-Americans see another."[113] The decisions of representative juries are seen as more legitimate and are accorded greater respect by all segments of the community.

Discrimination by Racially Prejudiced Defense Counsel
In rejecting a challenge to the effectiveness of a defense lawyer who expressed racist sentiments in *Dobbs v. Zant*, both the district court and the court of appeals reasoned that since the defense lawyer did not decide the sentence, the claim should be rejected.[114] But there are numerous other ways in which the racial prejudice of defense counsel may affect the sentencing decision.

A lawyer defending the accused in a capital case has the obligation to investigate the life and background of the client in order to introduce mitigating evidence.[115] To fulfill this constitutional and ethical obligation, a lawyer must be comfortable working with the client, the client's family, and the client's friends. If the appointed lawyer regards the client, his family, or his friends in a demeaning way, the lawyer cannot possibly obtain and present the needed information and fulfill the role as an advocate for the client's life. In addition, the defendant who is assigned a lawyer who shares the racial prejudices of the jurors, judge, and prosecutor is left without an advocate to expose and challenge such biases.

For example, a federal district court in Alabama described the representation provided to an African-American woman whose court-appointed lawyers had assumed she would not be sentenced to death for the "shothouse killing" of another black woman:

> Petitioner's counsel did not prepare for the sentencing hearing....
>
> Roughly one hour after her conviction, petitioner and her counsel appeared before the jury again for the sentencing hearing. [Counsel] testified at the habeas hearing that he told the judge the [capital murder] verdict was so shocking to him that he was not prepared to go forward with sentencing.
>
> Between the time of petitioner's indictment and sentencing, her lawyers did no work on the sentencing aspects of her case....
>
> No social history of petitioner was undertaken prior to either of the sentencing hearings [one before the jury and the second before a judge]. No family members or friends were contacted and informed of either the sentencing hearing before the jury or the trial judge. Therefore, no evidence of mitigation was adduced....
>
> ...At the onset of petitioner's trial, when they clearly should have challenged the prosecutor's intentional and racially-motivated utilization of peremptory challenge to exclude all blacks from the jury chosen to try their black client, petitioner's counsel inexplicably failed to do so.[116]

One reason for the inadequate representation that Melvin Wade received before being sentenced to death by a California jury may have been the racial attitudes of his attorney. The attorney, who used racial slurs to refer to African Americans, including Wade, failed to adequately present evidence of Wade's abuse as a child. The attorney also gave harmful closing arguments, including a penalty phase argument that asked the jury to impose the death sentence on his client. Kim Taylor, professor at New York University Law School and former director of the public defender's office for the District of Columbia, has described the relationship between counsel's racial attitudes and his performance. Taylor writes, "From the evidence before me, it seems clear that race played a significant and insidious role in Mr. Wade's trial.... Mr. Wade was represented by a man who viewed blacks with contempt, and this evidence is supported by the manner in which that attorney conducted himself at trial. Trial counsel failed to take any steps to impeach the state's injection of racial stereotyping and race-based misinformation into the case... and counsel comported himself in his argument to the jury in a manner as to convey his race-based contempt.[117]

Such performances by defense counsel make it impossible for jurors to perform their constitutional obligation to impose a sentence based on "a reasoned moral response to the defendant's background, character, and crime."[118] Nor can courts discharge their responsibility to protect the constitutional rights of the accused, including the right to a trial not infected by racial discrimination, when court-appointed lawyers fail to raise issues of discrimination out of ignorance or indifference.

Disparities in Imposition of Death Sentences in the State and Federal Courts

Sentencing patterns confirm that racial prejudice plays a role in the imposition of the death penalty. Although African Americans make up only 12 percent of the total population of the United States, they have been the victims in about half of the total homicides in this country in the last twenty-five years.[119] In some states in the south, where capital punishment is often imposed, African Americans are the victims of over 60 percent of the murders. Yet 85 percent of the cases in which the death penalty has been carried out have involved white victims.[120]

In Georgia, for example, although African Americans were the victims of 63.5 percent of the murders between 1976 and 1980, 82 percent of the cases in which death was imposed during that period involved murders of whites.[121] David Baldus and his associates conducted two studies of the influence of race in the application of the death penalty, examining over two thousand murder cases that occurred in Georgia during the 1970s.[122] They found that prosecutors are more likely to seek the death penalty where the victim is white, and that juries are more likely to impose the death penalty in such cases. Defendants charged with murders of white persons received the death penalty in 11 percent of the cases, while defendants charged with murders of blacks received the death penalty in only 1 percent of the cases. Defendants charged with killing white victims were over four times more likely to receive a death sentence than defendants charged with killing blacks.[123]

By August 31, 1995, Georgia had carried out twenty executions under the death penalty statute upheld by the U.S. Supreme Court in 1976.[124] Twelve of those executed were African Americans; in eighteen of the cases, the victims were white.[125] Six of the African Americans executed were sentenced to death by all-white juries.[126] These patterns are not limited to Georgia. Nine of the first twelve persons executed in Alabama were African American.[127] The General Accounting Office, in its analysis of twenty-eight studies of the death penalty, summarizes, "In 82 percent of the studies, race of the victim was found to influence the likelihood of being charged with capital murder or receiving the death penalty, i.e., those who murdered whites were found to be more likely to be sentenced to death than those who murdered blacks. This finding was remarkably consistent across data sets, states, data collection methods, and analytic techniques."[128]

These data, showing the role of race, have been replicated in every state where the issue has been examined, including California, Colorado,

Kentucky, Mississippi, New Jersey, North Carolina, Pennsylvania, and South Carolina.[129]

The U.S. Supreme Court permitted such racial disparities in the imposition of the death penalty in *McCleskey v. Kemp*.[130] By a 5 to 4 vote, the Court allowed Georgia to carry out its death penalty law despite racial disparities that would not be officially tolerated in any other area of the law. The Court rejected challenges based on equal protection and the Eighth Amendment's cruel and unusual clause; it found that the studies established "at most . . . a discrepancy that appears to correlate with race" and declined "to assume that that which is unexplained is invidious," thus holding the disparities insufficient even to raise a prima facie case of racial discrimination. The Court also expressed its concern that "McCleskey's claim, taken to its logical conclusion, throws into serious question the principles that underlie our entire criminal justice system."[131] Justice Brennan, in dissent, characterized this concern as "a fear of too much justice."[132]

The Court's fear of too much justice may result in no justice at all. The decision in *McCleskey* has been employed by lower federal and state courts to avoid dealing with issues of racial discrimination. Its crippling standard of proof, discussed more fully below, is so formidable that many courts have denied even a hearing on gross racial disparities.[133] Such an unwillingness to confront racial issues allows discrimination to go unchecked.

The federal government in pursuing death sentences authorized by the Anti–Drug Abuse Act of 1988 has an even worse record of discrimination than the states.[134] The act authorizes the death penalty for murders committed by "kingpins" involved in drug trafficking "enterprises."[135] Federal prosecutors are given wide discretion in deciding whether to seek the death penalty. One congressional committee observed: "The drug trafficking 'enterprise' can consist of as few as five individuals, and even a low-ranking 'foot soldier' in the organization can be charged with the death penalty if involved in a killing."[136]

Although three-fourths of those convicted of participating in a drug enterprise under the general provisions of 21 U.S.C. § 848 are white,[137] the death penalty provisions of the act have been used almost exclusively against minorities. Of the first thirty-seven federal death penalty prosecutions, all but four were against people from minority groups.[138] Nevertheless, in 1994, Congress provided the death penalty for over fifty additional crimes and refused to enact the Racial Justice Act.[139]

Those accused of federal capital crimes are supposedly protected from racial discrimination by the requirements that juries be instructed not to discriminate, and all jurors sign certificates guaranteeing they did not discriminate.[140] But this almost laughable provision is hardly a protection against racial discrimination. By the time the jury is selected, racial prejudice may have already influenced the prosecutor's decisions to seek the death penalty, to refuse a plea bargain for a noncapital sentence, and to strike minority jurors. Moreover, the most pernicious racial discrimination that occurs today is that perpetrated by those who have the sophistication not to admit their biases. Those who live in racially exclusive neighborhoods, are members of racially exclusive social organizations, send their children to segregated academies, and refuse to rent to black citizens may be more than happy to listen to jury instructions and sign the certificate of nondiscrimination before sending some black person off to his death. Of course, many others may not even be aware of their unconscious racism.

Despite the pronounced racial disparities in the infliction of the death penalty in both state and federal capital cases, Congress refused to include the Racial Justice Act as part of the crime bill in 1994, just as it had refused to enact the Racial Justice Act in previous years.[141] The Racial Justice Act was a modest proposal that would have required courts to hold hearings on racial disparities in the imposition of the death penalty and look behind the disparities to determine whether they were related to race or some other factor.[142]

It is not unreasonable to require publicly elected prosecutors to justify racial disparities in capital prosecutions. If there is an underrepresentation of black citizens in a jury pool, jury commissioners are required to explain the disparity.[143] A prosecutor who rules out a disproportionate number of black citizens when selecting a jury is required to rebut the inference of discrimination by showing race-neutral reasons for his strikes.[144] If there are valid race-neutral explanations for the disparities in capital prosecutions, they should be presented to the courts and the public. Prosecutors, like other public officials, should be accountable for their actions. The bases for critical decisions about whether to seek the death penalty and whether to agree to a sentence less than death in exchange for a guilty plea should not be shrouded in secrecy, but should be openly set out, defended, and evaluated.

The likelihood is not that it would be too difficult for prosecutors to rebut the inference of discrimination, but that it would be too easy. The task of rebutting an inference of racial discrimination under *Batson* has proven to be remarkably easy for prosecutors, even when they have used all of their jury strikes against minorities. Nevertheless, the Racial Justice Act presented the threat of "too much justice" to the U.S. Senate and was defeated.

It is not surprising that Congress failed to pass the Racial Justice Act; it had, after all, steadfastly refused to pass an antilynching law when African Americans and other minorities were being lynched.[145] Instead, the federal government put much of its law enforcement efforts into pursuing moonshiners. Today the federal government commits ample resources for questionable and expensive efforts to demonstrate that it is "tough on crime"—the "war on drugs," the pursuit of federal death sentences for many crimes that could be prosecuted in the state courts, and the housing of ever increasing numbers of people in federal prisons for longer periods of time. But few resources are devoted to the constitutional commitment of equality for racial minorities and the poor.

The U.S. Department of Justice, which might be expected to be concerned about racial discrimination in the courts and its impact on public confidence in the courts, is now one of the worst offenders in the discriminatory use of the death penalty. There is no large or powerful constituency concerned about racial discrimination in capital cases. The Republican Party's Contract with America for the 1994 elections promised greater use of the death penalty and even greater utilization of prisons—not passage of the Racial Justice Act. Thus, there is no reason to expect solutions or even leadership from the executive or legislative branches of the federal government with regard to racial discrimination in capital cases.

THE TOLERANCE OF RACIAL DISCRIMINATION IN THE MODERN CRIMINAL JUSTICE SYSTEM

Despite extraordinary competition among politicians to be tough on crime, prosecutors and the judicial system remain remarkably soft on the crime of racial discrimination. Those who discriminate are seldom disciplined or punished. Appellate courts that normally publish long opinions on minor issues often do not even mention the extraordinary racial discrimination that comes before them, finding ways to dispose of cases on other grounds. And when racial discrimination is recognized, the remedies are often woefully inadequate.

Jury officials in Alabama, in an attempt to defeat a challenge to the exclusion of black citizens from jury service in 1933, forged the names of six black citizens on the jury rolls.[146] The local trial judge rejected the assertion of fraud, saying he "would not be authorized to presume that somebody had committed a crime" or had been "unfaithful to their duties and allowed the books to be tampered with."[147] The U.S. Supreme Court generously observed that "the evidence did not justify that conclusion."[148] Although the case was reversed, no action was taken against those responsible for the forgery.[149]

In 1988, the Supreme Court found that a Georgia prosecutor instructed jury commissioners to underrepresent African Americans in jury pools in such a way as to avoid detection and defeat a prima facie case of discrimination.[150] No action was taken against the prosecutor, and he remained in office until 1994, when he resigned while under investigation for sexual harassment.[151]

In Columbus, Muscogee County, Georgia, black citizens were excluded for years and then underrepresented in the jury pools. In 1966, the Fifth Circuit Court of Appeals held that this discrimination violated the Constitution.[152] In 1972, the Supreme Court reached the same conclusion in another case from the county, and three justices even went so far as to point out that the way in which juries were being selected in the county violated 18 U.S.C. § 243, which makes it a criminal offense to exclude persons from jury service on the basis of race.[153]

Despite these court decisions, the unconstitutional, systematic underrepresentation continued throughout the 1970s. This underrepresentation was made possible in part because one public defender, appointed by white judges in Columbus, would not, as a matter of "policy," file challenges to the underrepresentation of blacks in the jury pool for fear of incurring hostility from the community.[154]

As a result, at the capital trial of a black man in Columbus, Georgia, in 1977—eleven years after the Fifth Circuit decision and five years after the Supreme Court warned that the exclusion of black citizens violated federal criminal statutes—there were only 8 black citizens in a venire of 160 persons.[155] A venire that fairly represented the community would have included 50 black citizens. That case was tried by an all-white jury.[156] The death penalty was imposed.[157]

There are people awaiting execution on Georgia's death row who were sentenced to death in Columbus by juries chosen in defiance of the Supreme Court's decision requiring an end to discrimination. Yet those who defied the federal courts and the Constitution were never prosecuted or disciplined. Some are still presiding as judges in the local courts there.

It simply cannot be said that courts are engaging in "unceasing efforts" to eliminate racial discrimination from the criminal justice system when prosecutors can rig juries on the basis of race with impunity, when decisions from the Supreme Court and the U.S. Courts of Appeals regarding discrimination in jury selection can be ignored for years with impunity, and a prosecutor may remain in office and death sentences are carried out even though juries are selected pursuant to the prosecutor's practice of striking from juries as many African Americans as possible. Judicial tolerance of such discrimination sends the unmistakable message that the "war on crime" need not be fought according to the Constitution, and racial discrimination will be tolerated when it is perceived as necessary to obtain convictions and death sentences.

Despite the racial discrimination that has been a major aspect of the death penalty throughout American history, the Supreme Court and lower federal and state courts have been reluctant to face racial issues presented by capital cases. The courts have simply been in a state of denial instead of confronting and dealing with the difficult and sensitive issue of race.

After declaring racially discriminatory jury selection practices in one Georgia county unconstitutional,[158] the United States Supreme Court remanded to the Georgia Supreme Court a capital case in which the jury had been selected by the same illegal means in the same county.[159] However, when the Georgia Supreme Court refused to reconsider its previous holding that the issue had been waived,[160] the United States Supreme Court backed down, denied certiorari, and allowed the execution to be carried out.[161] It appears that the Court, already encountering resistance to its decision in *Brown v. Board of Education*,[162] was anxious to avoid a confrontation with southern state courts over racial discrimination in the criminal courts.[163]

Over ten years later, the United States Supreme Court appeared willing to review the role of racial prejudice in capital cases when it granted certiorari in *Maxwell v. Bishop*,[164] a case in which the Eighth Circuit rejected a challenge based upon the pronounced disparity in the number of African Americans sentenced to death for rape in Arkansas and other parts of the south.[165] However, after twice hearing oral argument devoted mostly to the issue of racial discrimination, the Court vacated the death sentence and remanded the case based upon a jury qualification issue which had not even been raised in the Court of Appeals.[166]

Although the specter of race discrimination was acknowledged by justices in both the majority and the dissent in *Furman v. Georgia*,[167] only Justice Thurgood Marshall discussed racial discrimination at length.[168] Justice Potter Stewart found it unnecessary to decide the issue, while acknowledging that "if any basis can be discerned for the selection of these few to be sentenced to die, it is the constitutionally impermissibly basis of race."[169]

Despite the extraordinary history of discrimination with regard to the infliction of the death penalty upon African Americans for the rape of white women,[170] the Court did not even mention race in striking down the death penalty for the crime of rape in *Coker v. Georgia*.[171]

It is impossible to know how many state courts have found ways to avoid the issue of race in deciding capital cases. The Georgia Supreme Court frequently discusses every issue presented to it, even those that need not be addressed for a decision.[172] But in holding that a trial judge should be recused from a case because of his involvement in opposing a motion to disqualify him, the court never mentioned the motion was based on the judge's long history of racial discrimination.[173] Evidence presented in the trial court established that the judge regularly appointed jury commissions that underrepresented African Americans, tolerated gross underrepresentation of blacks in the grand and trial juries, mistreated black attorneys in court, used racial slurs, and practiced discrimination in his personal life.[174]

The Missouri Supreme Court summarily reversed two capital cases without mentioning evidence that prosecutors in Kansas City used racial slurs to refer to black citizens, systematically excluded black citizens from juries, and refused to plea bargain with African Americans charged with murders of whites while offering plea bargains in all other potential capital cases, including a case of murderers who killed four generations of African Americans.[175]

The Alabama Court of Criminal Appeals similarly failed to acknowledge or discuss disturbing evidence of racial discrimination in setting aside a capital conviction and sentence;[176] the court did not mention that the prosecutor had used twenty-six peremptory jury strikes against African Americans after dividing potential jurors into four lists under the headings "strong," "medium," "weak," and "black," or that the trial court had held there was no discrimination.[177]

Apparently, many courts believe it is best to avoid the sensitive issue of race. Why else did the courts not denounce these outrageous examples of racial discrimination in the strongest terms? While the failure of the appellate courts to mention the race issues in these cases may have been coincidence, it is more likely that courts are defensive about the racial discrimination that takes place in what is supposed to be a system of equal justice. Their opinions leave those who read them without any hint that the cases involved racial discrimination and thus provide trial courts with no guidance in considering those issues. In addition, lawyers reading appellate opinions are less likely to realize the importance of race and search out and challenge discrimination. The failure of the courts to discuss and condemn racial discrimination only fosters more discrimination.

In 1965, in the midst of the Warren Court decisions applying the Bill of Rights to state criminal procedure, the Court upheld a capital conviction in *Swain v. Alabama*,[178] despite evidence that due to peremptory challenges, no black person had ever served on a jury in either a criminal or civil case in Talladega County, Alabama, where African Americans constituted 26 percent of the population. While reiterating its prior pronouncements that "a State's purposeful or deliberate denial to Negroes on account of race of participation as jurors in the administration of justice violates the Equal Protection Clause,"[179] the Court set an almost impossible burden of proof, holding that to establish discrimination by a prosecutor in the use of peremptory strikes, a defendant must prove the prosecutor engaged in a practice of striking black citizens from juries "in case after case, whatever the circumstances, whatever the crime and whoever the defendant or the victim may be...with the result that no Negroes ever serve on petit juries."[180] The decision, disapproving of racial discrimination but allowing it to continue by setting a virtually impossible standard of proof, was subject to "almost universal and often scathing criticism,"[181] but remained the law for twenty years before the standard was changed in *Batson v. Kentucky.*[182]

The Supreme Court has created an equally difficult barrier to sustaining claims of racial discrimination in the infliction of the death penalty. In *McCleskey v. Kemp,*[183] the Court accepted the racial disparities in the imposition of the death penalty as "an inevitable part of our criminal justice system."[184] The Court held that to prevail under the Equal Protection Clause the defendant must present "exceptionally clear proof" that "the decision makers in his case acted with discriminatory purpose."[185] As in *Swain,* the Court found the evidence insufficient to overcome a presumption of propriety with regard to the exercise of discretion by prosecutors.[186] Yet while requiring exceptionally clear proof of discrimination, the Court made it almost impossible to obtain it, concluding that "the policy considerations behind a prosecutor's traditionally 'wide discretion' suggest the impropriety of our requiring prosecutors to defend their decisions to seek death penalties, 'often years after they are made.'"[187]

In rejecting McCleskey's claim under the Eighth Amendment, the Court, while acknowledging the risk of racial prejudice influencing the capital sentencing decision,[188] held that evidence that blacks who kill whites are sentenced to death at nearly twenty-two times the rate of blacks who kill blacks did not "demonstrate a constitutionally significant risk of racial bias affecting the Georgia capital sentencing process." Thus, the Court held the risk of racial discrimination was not "constitutionally unacceptable" under the Eighth Amendment.[189]

This disgraceful decision is more consistent with the Court's decisions in *Swain, Dred Scott v. Sandford,* and *Plessy v. Ferguson* than its more recent decisions recognizing racial discrimination in other areas of life.[190] The Court could have concluded that racial disparities were "inevitable" or not "constitutionally unacceptable" in education, housing, employment, or so many other areas of life where minorities have experienced racial discrimination. Justice Lewis Powell, who cast the deciding vote and authored the majority's opinion in the 5 to 4 decision in *McCleskey,* expressed his regret, after leaving the Court, at his vote in the case.[191]

Other courts have followed the Supreme Court's head-in-the-sand approach. The Florida Supreme Court, by a 4 to 3 vote, refused to require

a hearing on racial disparities in the infliction of the death penalty.[192] The
Georgia Supreme Court upheld the denial of a hearing on racial discrimination in a capital prosecution against an African American accused of
the murder of a white person in Cobb County, a county with a long history of racial discrimination.[193] Some criminal defense lawyers in Cobb
County have stated that they have never had the opportunity to accept or
rule out an African-American juror due to the regular practice of the district attorney's office of striking from juries all African Americans.[194] To
deny even a hearing on racial discrimination in Cobb County is simply to
run from the truth instead of confronting it.[195]

The willingness of courts to tolerate racial discrimination in order to
carry out the death penalty has a corrupting effect not just on capital
cases, but throughout the criminal justice system. For example, the
Georgia Supreme Court, under immense political pressure from
Georgia's attorney general, district attorneys, and dire warnings that the
death penalty was in danger, did a complete about-face in only thirteen
days in a case regarding gross racial disparities in sentencing for drug
offenses.[196] The court first held, by a 4 to 3 vote, that a prima facie case of
racial discrimination was established by evidence that 98.4 percent of
those serving life sentences for certain narcotics offenses were black.[197]
All of the discretion in pursuing life sentences for the offenses was
entrusted to district attorneys.[198] Statistics from the Georgia Department
of Corrections established that less than 1 percent of the whites eligible
for life sentence for narcotics offenses—just 1 in 168—received it, while
16.6 percent of African Americans—202 of 1,219—received it.[199]

The attorney general of Georgia, joined by all of the forty-six district
attorneys in the state (all of whom are white), filed a petition for rehearing, with the court arguing that its decision took a "substantial step
toward invalidating" the state's death penalty law and would "paralyze
the criminal justice system."[200] In response, one member of the court
switched his vote and the court adopted the position of what had previously been the dissent, that the proper governing standard was
McCleskey v. Kemp and, therefore, no prima facie case had been established.[201] The only way a more compelling showing could have been
made would have been if all 100 percent of those serving life sentences
for a second narcotics offense were black, instead of just 98.4 percent.
Yet the Georgia Supreme Court chose to erect an impossible standard of
proof based on its interpretation of *McCleskey* in order to avoid even a
hearing on the reasons for the remarkable racial disparities in sentencing for narcotics offenses.

The U.S. Supreme Court based its decision in *McCleskey* in part on
the "safeguards designed to minimize racial bias in the process."[202] Those
safeguards include the right to a representative jury, the prohibition of

use of peremptory challenges by prosecutors on the basis of race, and the right in cases involving interracial crimes to question potential jurors about racial bias.[203] But in many cases, such safeguards are either nonexistent or inadequate.

The stages of the process that allow the greatest room for racial prejudice are the prosecutorial decision to seek the death penalty and the plea bargaining process. There are no effective safeguards to prevent discrimination at either of these stages. As previously noted, many courts that rely on *McCleskey* do not even allow hearings on the influence of race at these critical stages. Minorities remain woefully underrepresented in decision-making positions within the criminal justice system. Courts have been increasingly hostile to challenges to the exclusion of minorities from state judicial systems, even when it is apparent that the minority vote has been diluted in order to preserve a primarily white judiciary.[204]

The "safeguards" relied upon by the Court in *McCleskey* are also inadequate because issues of discrimination usually focus on the intent of the decision maker, which is exceptionally difficult to prove, instead of the results of their actions. Nor do courts consider unconscious or subtle racial biases of decision makers. As previously discussed, courts allow prosecutors to use even 100 percent of their peremptory jury strikes based on assertions of "race neutral" reasons. The Supreme Court in *McCleskey* found that racial disparities did not sufficiently prove racial discrimination, but it failed to examine the role that racial stereotypes and other attitudes may have played in the results.[205]

Although the Supreme Court in *Turner v. Murray* acknowledged the potential impact that the unconscious racism of jurors might have on the capital sentencing decision, *Turner* is limited to interracial crimes.[206] Thus, an accused who is charged with the murder of a member of his own race is not entitled to ask prospective jurors about their racial attitudes. Even in interracial crimes, trial courts may limit voir dire so that it does not disclose subtle racial attitudes that may come into play.[207]

The failure of courts to provide poor defendants with adequate legal representation may leave the accused without any ability to utilize what limited protections are available. Those accused of crimes in Jefferson County, Georgia, were tried for years before patently unconstitutional juries because local lawyers appointed by local judges failed to challenge the severe underrepresentation of African Americans in the jury pools. It was shown in one capital case in which the accused was represented by pro bono lawyers from outside the judicial circuit that although African Americans made up 54.5 percent of the population of the county, they made up only 21.6 percent of the jury pool, an underrepresentation of over 50 percent.[208] However, when this evidence was presented in a postconviction challenge to the conviction and sentence, the federal courts held that the defendant was barred from raising the issue because no challenge had been made by the local court-appointed lawyer prior to trial.[209] The defendant had the misfortune of being represented—over his protests—by a court-appointed lawyer who, when later asked to name the criminal law decisions from any court with which he was familiar, could name only two: *Miranda* and *Dred Scott*.[210]

In Columbus, Georgia, even after the United States Supreme Court declared that jury officials were unconstitutionally and illegally excluding African Americans from jury service, the practice continued because of the "policy" of the local court-appointed indigent defender of not challenging racial discrimination for fear of incurring hostility from the community.[211] These are not isolated examples regarding a single case. The failure of lawyers to challenge clearly unconstitutional racial discrimination in the composition of jury pools affected every criminal case in these judicial circuits over decades.

In the case of an African American tried before an all-white jury after the prosecutor ruled out four black jurors, the United States Court of Appeals for the Eighth Circuit refused to review a prosecutor's emphasis on the difference in race between the "attractive" white victim and "this black man" because no objection had been made at the time of the argument.[212]

The right to question jurors about race in an interracial crime was utilized as follows by defense counsel in an Alabama case tried in 1993:

> Mr. NELSON [Defense counsel]: I have just a couple of more questions and I promise I will quit. We are talking about this case and not some fictional case. In this case this is a black man and Mrs. Hargrove's son was a young white man. I will ask you this and it's not—it's like Bob said. I'm not asking you this to embarrass you, but do any of you belong to any organizations such as the Klan or have close family members that belong to the Klan or an organization known as the Skinheads, Nazi groups or anything like that who believe that a race is inferior or a religion is inferior? Do any of you belong to any of those things? (No response)
>
> MR. NELSON: Do any of you believe any of that stuff? Is there anybody that believes in that stuff on this jury?
>
> JUROR BARTLETT: The Klan has a lot of stuff that they stand for that is good.
>
> MR. NELSON: I'm sorry, Mr. Bartlett?
>
> JUROR BARTLETT: The Klan has lot of things they stand for that is good. I have read some of their literature.
>
> MR. NELSON: You believe in some of the doctrine that the Klan has in their literature?
>
> JUROR BARTLETT: I guess it would be called doctrine. I don't know.
>
> MR. NELSON: Would you tell me what it is that you believe in that you have read?

JUROR BARTLETT: Well, there are just certain things about the way things are going, the way the law is going about a lot of this stuff.

MR. NELSON: Let me ask you this. The fact that this is a black man over here, do you think you could be fair to him even if—

JUROR BARTLETT: Yeah.

MR. NELSON: Even if the man that was killed was a young white man?

JUROR BARTLETT: I would be as fair to him as anybody else.[213]

No further questions were asked of juror Bartlett or any other member of the panel regarding the issue of race.[214] Such a voir dire is hardly adequate to reveal the "[m]ore subtle, less consciously held racial attitudes" that the Supreme Court described in *Turner v. Murray*.[215]

Despite the limitations of *Batson v. Kentucky* and *Turner v. Murray* in preventing racial discrimination, the Supreme Court in *McCleskey* indulged in the remarkable presumption that the mere existence of these limited procedural safeguards in jury selection were sufficient to prevent racial discrimination in every capital case. At the same time, the Court discounted evidence that established that in reality the race of the victim and the race of the defendant actually influenced the sentence in McCleskey's case and other cases despite the safeguards.

The Supreme Court decision in *McCleskey v. Kemp* is a badge of shame upon American's system of justice. It is a manifestation of indifference on the part of the Court to secure justice for racial minorities in cases in which there is a long history of discrimination and there is every indication that racial prejudice influences the vast discretion exercised in making the highly charged, emotional decisions about who is to die. The *McCleskey* decision is worthy of the universal and scathing criticism visited upon *Swain v. Alabama*.

CONCLUSION

There is enormous public support for the death penalty in the United States, but little honest discussion of the inequities involved in its imposition. Many public officials continue to peddle the preposterous notion that we may ignore over two centuries of history in race relations as easily as we may ignore yesterday's weather. They readily admit racial discrimination up until 1964, or 1972, or even until yesterday, but argue that it suddenly, magically just ended. Unfortunately, this does not square with the reality of race relations in the United States today. As Justice William Brennan observed in his dissent in *McCleskey v. Kemp*, "[I]t has been scarcely a generation since this Court's first decision striking down racial segregation, and barely two decades since the legislative prohibition of racial discrimination in major domains of national life. These have been honorable steps, but we cannot pretend that in three decades we have completely escaped the grip of a historical legacy spanning centuries.... [W]e remain imprisoned by the past as long as we deny its influence on the present."[216]

The courts and legislatures have made a tragic mistake by substituting a notion of what the criminal justice should be for what it is. Citizens, judges, the bar, and the press would like to believe we have a system that equally and fairly dispenses justice. But neither legal presumptions nor legal fictions will make it so. As Justice Thurgood Marshall said in another context, "constitutionalizing [the] wishful thinking" that "racial discrimination is largely a phenomenon of the past" does a "grave disservice... to those victims of past and present racial discrimination."[217]

The criminal justice systems in many parts of the country have suffered from years of neglect, inadequate funding, and other problems. Often they have been entrusted to persons with neither the ability nor the inclination to carry out their high functions. Members of racial minorities continue to be underrepresented in all positions in the criminal justice system. It should not surprise anyone that the problems of racial exclusion and racial discrimination are greater there than in other parts of our society.

The price paid for the denial of racial discrimination by courts, legislatures, and the bar is considerable. Courts cannot deliver justice when they tolerate racial prejudice and racial exclusion. Courts lose respect and credibility when they refuse to acknowledge and remedy racial discrimination that is apparent to everyone else. Responding to the public clamor for executions is not justification for ignoring racial discrimination in the court system. Courts of vengeance are not courts of justice.

There is debate over whether racial discrimination in the infliction of the death penalty can be detected and remedied. Some think racial discrimination is inevitable and impossible to prevent; others think the influence of race can be eliminated.[218] This question must be answered, not avoided. If racial discrimination cannot be prevented, the death penalty should not be carried out.[219] If discrimination can be eliminated, then it should be the highest priority of the courts. But to pretend it does not exist, to deny a remedy, to deny even a hearing, is to give up on achieving the goal of equal justice under law. Tragically, that is what the state and federal courts have done.

In *McCleskey v. Kemp*, the Supreme Court asserted that evidence of racial discrimination should be taken to the legislatures.[220] But legislators respond to powerful interests. The poor person accused of a crime has no political action committee, no lobby, and often no effective advocate even in the court where his life is at stake. The crime debate in the

United States has become increasingly demagogic and irresponsible. There is little reason for hope in the legislatures.

The constitutional buck of equal protection under law stops with the Supreme Court and with judges on lower courts throughout the land who have taken oaths to uphold the Constitution and the Bill of Rights even against the passions of the moment and the prejudices that have endured for centuries. So long as racial discrimination remains a prominent feature of the imposition of the death penalty in the state and federal courts, the challenge of meeting the immense burden established in *McCleskey* for proving racial discrimination must be accepted. Other instances of discrimination must be identified and challenged. State constitutional guarantees must be asserted as a basis for challenging discrimination in the infliction of the death penalty.[221]

Silence about racial discrimination in capital cases will only allow it to continue to fester. Wishful thinking cannot take the place of dealing with reality. Decisions tolerating racial discrimination must be assailed until, like *Swain v. Alabama*, they are rejected and replaced with standards that acknowledge and respond to the influence of racial prejudice in the criminal courts in general and in capital cases in particular.

NOTES

1. A. Leon Higginbotham Jr., *In the Matter of Color: Race in the American Legal Process* (Oxford Univ. Press: New York 1978), 256.
2. Ibid.
3. Ibid. See also *McCleskey v. Kemp*, 481 U.S. 279 (1987), at 329–32 (Brennan, J., dissenting).
4. These numbers come from the archives at Tuskegee University, where lynchings have been documented since 1882. Mark Curriden, "The Legacy of Lynching," *Atlanta Journal and Constitution*, January 15, 1995, M1.
5. Ibid.
6. Douglas L. Colbert, *Challenging the Challenge: Thirteenth Amendment as a Prohibition against the Racial Use of Peremptory Challenges*, 76 Cornell L. Rev. 1, 80 (1990), quoting Michael Belknap, *Federal Law and Southern Order* 22–26 (Athens: University of Georgia Press, 1987).
7. Dan T. Carter, *Scottsboro: A Tragedy of the American South*, (Baton Rouge: Louisiana State University Press, rev. ed. 1992), 115
8. Colbert, Challenging, 80.
9. *Powell v. Alabama*, 287 U.S. 45 (1932).
10. Carter, *Scottsboro*, 104–16; James Goodman, *Stories of Scottsboro* (New York: Random House 1995, 47–50, 297–98.
11. George C. Wright, *Racial Violence in Kentucky 1865–1940* (Baton Rouge: Louisiana State University Press, 1990), 252.
12. Ibid. 253., The editorial read as follows: "The fact, however, that Kentucky was saved the mortification of a lynching by an indignant multitude, bent upon avenging the innocent victim of the crime, is a matter for special congratulation."
13. Ibid. Wright describes other legal lynchings in Kentucky; see 251–305.
14. "The Pace of Executions: Since 1976 . . . and through History," *New York Times*, December 4, 1994, sec. 4, p. 3. Georgia carried out 673 executions between 1900 and the end of 1994, the most of any state during this period.
15. Prentice Palmer and Jim Galloway, "Georgia Electric Chair Spans 5 Decades," *The Atlanta Journal*, December 15, 1983, 15A. After adopting electrocution as a means of execution in 1924, Georgia put more people to death than any state and "set national records for executions over a 20-year period in the 1940s and 1950s."

16. Bryan Denson, "Death Penalty: Equal Justice?" *Houston Post*, October 16, 1994, A1.

17. "Death Row U.S.A." (New York: NAACP Legal Defense Fund, 1999), 18 (stating there are 341 people on Florida's death row).

18. *Report and Recommendation of the Florida Supreme Court Racial and Ethnic Bias Study Commission*, xvi (December 11, 1991). See also Michael L. Radelet and Glenn L. Pierce, *Choosing Those Who Will Die: Race and the Death Penalty in Florida*, 43 U. Fla. L. Rev. 1 (1991); *Foster v. State*, 614 So. 2d 455 (Fla. 1992) (affirming refusal to hold hearing on claim of racial discrimination where evidence proffered showed prosecutors in Bay County State Attorney's office were four times more likely to charge first-degree murder in cases involving white victims than cases involving black victims; that of such cases that went to trial, first-degree murder convictions were twenty-six times more likely in cases with white victims; and that even though blacks constituted 40 percent of the murder victims in Bay County between 1975 and 1987, all seventeen death sentences that were imposed were for homicides involving white victims).

19. Staff Report by the Subcommittee on Civil and Constitutional Rights of the Committee of the Judiciary, U.S. House of Representatives, *Racial Disparities in Federal Death Penalty Prosecutions 1988–1994*, H.R. 458, 103d Cong. 2d Sess., 2 (March 1994); hereafter House Subcommittee, *Racial Disparities*.

20. In addition to the studies cited by the General Accounting Office in its report, (see note 128), see David C. Baldus, George Woodsworth, and Charles A. Pulaski, Jr., *Equal Justice and the Death Penalty* (1990); Samuel R. Gross and Robert Mauro, *Death & Discrimination: Racial Disparities in Capital Sentencing* (Boston: Northeastern University Press, 1989); Bob Levenson and Debbie Salamore, "Prosecutors See Death Penalty in Black and White," *Orlando Sentinel*, May 24, 1992, A1 (reporting that "[j]ustice . . . is not colorblind in Central Florida when it comes to the prosecution of first degree murder cases"); Jim Henderson and Jack Taylor, "Killers of Dallas Blacks Escape the Death Penalty," *Dallas Times Herald*, November 17, 1985, 1 (accompanied by other stories and charts demonstrating the relationship between race and imposition of the death sentence); David Margolick, "In the Land of Death Penalty, Accusations of Racial Bias," *New York Times*, July 10, 1991, A1 (describing racial disparities in the infliction of the death penalty in Georgia's Chattahoochee Judicial Circuit, which includes the city of Columbus); Paul Pinkham and Robin Lowenthal, "The Color of Justice in Jacksonville: Killers of Blacks get off Easier than Killers of Whites," *Florida Times-Union*, December 8, 1991, D1; Thomas J. Keil and Gennaro F. Vito, "Race and the Death Penalty in Kentucky Murder Trials: 1976–1991," paper presented to Academy of Criminal Justice Sciences, Chicago, 1994 (finding that blacks accused of killing whites had a higher than average probability of being charged with a capital crime by the prosecutor and being sentenced to death by the jury).

21. See, e.g., Ga. Code Ann. ss 16-5-1, 17-10-30 (Michie 1994); Fla. Stat. Ann. s 921.141 (West 1985 and Supp. 1994); Ala. Code s 13A-5-40 (1994). For a summary of capital offenses by state, see Bureau of Justice Statistics, *Capital Punishment 1993*, table 1, p. 5 (December 1994). Under many capital statutes, the death penalty may also be imposed for the murder of a police or correctional officer, contract murders, murders related to drug offenses, and murders committed by persons with a previous conviction for a violent crime.

22. Fla. Stat. Ann. s 921.141(5)(h) (West 1985 and Supp. 1994). Ga. Code Ann. §17-10-30(b)(7) (Michie 1994).

23. *Turner v. Murray*, 476 U.S. 28, 35 (1985).

24. *Blair v. Armontrout*, 916 F.2d 1310, 1351 (8th Cir. 1990) (Heaney, J., concurring and dissenting).

25. *Nipper v. Smith*, 39 F.3d 1484, 1537–41 (11th Cir. 1994) (en banc); *League of United Latin American Citizens, Counsel No. 434 v. Clements*, 999 F.2d 831, 904–18 (5th Cir. 1993) (en banc) (King, J., dissenting), cert. denied, 114 S. Ct. 878 (1994). Ruth Marcus, "Does Voting Rights Law Cover Judicial Elections?" *Washington Post*, April 21, 1991, A4.

26. Mark Curriden, "Racism Mars Justice in U.S. Panel Reports," *Atlanta Journal and Constitution*, August 11, 1991, D1, D3 (observing that only 6 of Georgia's 134 Superior Court judges were African American, and those 6 were in three judicial circuits); Associated Press, "Second Black Alabama Supreme Court Justice Sworn In," *Columbus Ledger-Enquirer*, November 2, 1993, B2 (noting that there was only 1 African American among Alabama's 17 appellate court judges and only 12 blacks among the state's 255 circuit and district court judges); Rorie Sherman, *Is Mississippi Turning?*, Nat'l. L. J., February 20, 1989, 1, 24 (only 2.6 percent of all state court judges in the United States are black).

27. Mark Curriden, "Racism Mars Justice," D3.

28. Jesse Smith and Robert Johns, eds., *Statistical Record of Black America* 774–75 (Detroit:

Gole Research, 3d ed. 1995), listing the number of African Americans as judges, magistrates and justices of the peace and showing no African American for "other judicial officials" for Arkansas, Connecticut, Florida, Illinois, Indiana, Michigan, Oklahoma, South Carolina, and Texas.

29. American Bar Association Task Force on Minorities and the Justice System, *Achieving Justice in a Diverse America* (Washington, D.C.: American Bar Association, 1992), 15.

30. See, e.g., *State v. Russell*, 477 N.W.2d 886 (Minn. 1991) (finding equal protection violation due to more severe sentences imposed for possession of crack cocaine than for powdered cocaine where 96.6 percent of those charged with possession of crack cocaine are black and 79.6 percent of those charged with possession of powdered cocaine are white); *Stephens v. State*, No S94A1854, 1995 WL 116292 (Ga. S. Ct. Mar. 17, 1995), withdrawn and superseded, *Stephens v. State*, 456 S.E.2d 560 (Ga. 1995) (stating that of 375 persons serving life sentences for a second conviction for sale or possession with intent to distribute certain narcotics, 98.4 percent are African American). See, e.g., Samuel Myers Jr., *Racial Disparity in Sentencing: Can Sentencing Reforms Reduce Discrimination in Punishment?* 64 U. Colo. L. Rev. 781 (1993); Gary Kleck, *Racial Discrimination in Criminal Sentencing*, 46 Am. Sociological Rev. 783 (1981); Dennis Cauchon, "Sentences for Crack Called Racist," *USA Today*, May 26, 1993, 1A; Curriden, "Racism Mars Justice," D1; Ruth Marcus, "Racial Bias Widely Seen in Criminal Justice System," *Washington Post*, May 12, 1992, A4; Richard A. Berk and Alec Campbell, *Preliminary Data on Race and Crack Charging Practices in Los Angeles*, 6 Fed. Sent. R. 36 (1993); Douglas C. McDonald and Kenneth E. Carlson, *Why Did Racial/Ethnic Sentencing Differences in Federal District Courts Grow Larger under the Guidelines?* 6 Fed. Sent. R. 223 (1994); Charles J. Ogletree, *The Significance of Race in Federal Sentencing*, 6 Fed. Sent. R. 229 (1994); Rhonda Cook, "Sentence Disparities are the Rule in Ga.," *Atlanta Journal and Constitution*, December 3, 1990, A1; Tracy Thompson, "Blacks Sent to Jail More Than Whites for Same Crimes," *Atlanta Journal and Constitution*, April 30, 1989, 1A (with related stories and charts); Tracy Thompson, "Justice in Toombs Circuit not Colorblind, Some Say," *Atlanta Journal and Constitution*, December 13, 1987, 1A (three other articles appeared on the following days).

31. *Dobbs v. Zant*, 720 F. Supp. 1566, 1578 (N.D. Ga. 1989), aff 'd, 963 F.2d 1403 (11th Cir. 1991), rev'd, 113 S. Ct. 835 (1993).

32. Ibid., 1576.

33. Trial counsel testified, "There was uncertainty all the way up until the trial began as to whether or not I would represent him." Transcript of State Habeas Corpus Hearing of Sept. 28, 1977, 55, included in Record on Appeal, *Dobbs v. Zant*, 963 F.2d 1403 (11th Cir. 1991), rev'd and remanded, 113 S. Ct. 835 (1993). Defense counsel testified before the federal court, "As a matter of fact, I didn't know for sure what he was going to be tried for." Transcript of trial at 85, included as part of the Record on Appeal in *Dobbs*, 963 F.2d 1403.

34. Record on Appeal to Georgia Supreme Court at 24, included in the Record on Appeal in *Dobbs*, 963 F.2d 1403.

35. Transcript of trial at 2, included in the Record on Appeal in *Dobbs*, 963 F.2d 1403 (11th Cir. 1991).

36. Ibid., 7, 5.

37. Ibid., 10.

38. Ibid., 1577.

39. Any aspect of the life and background of the accused may be considered by the sentencer as a reason to impose a sentence less than death. *Penry v. Lynaugh*, 492 U.S. 302 (1989); *Eddings v. Oklahoma*, 455 U.S. 104, 110 (1982); *Lockett v. Ohio*, 438 U.S. 586, 604 (1978).

40. Transcript of trial at 503–5, included as part of the Record on Appeal in *Dobbs*, 963 F.2d 1403.

41. *Furman v. Georgia*, 408 U.S. 238, 257–306 (1972).

42. Transcript of Closing Argument, included as part of the Record on Appeal in *Dobbs*, 963 F.2d 1403 (11th Cir. 1991).

43. A prosecutor is not allowed to make an argument that would diminish the jury's sense of responsibility for its life and death decision. See *Caldwell v. Mississippi*, 472 U.S. 320, 328–30 (1985).

44. See "CBS Drops Commentator," *New York Times*, January 17, 1988, A1. See also Richard Harwood, "Pressure from the 'Isms,'" *Washington Post*, February 11, 1990, C6; "Racial Remarks Cost Dodger Official His Job," *New York Times*, April 9, 1987, A1.

45. *Peek v. Florida*, 488 So. 2d 52, 56 (Fla. 1986).

46. Ibid.

47. *Spencer v. State*, 398 S.E.2d 179 (Ga. 1990), cert. denied, 500 U.S. 960 (1991).
48. Ibid., 185.
49. *Hance v. Zant*, Super. Ct. of Butts Co., Ga., No. 93-V-172 (affidavits of juror Patricia LeMay and Gayle Lewis Daniels). See also *Hance v. Zant*, 696 F.2d 940 (11th Cir. 1983), cert. denied, 463 U.S. 1210 (1994) (Blackmun, J., dissenting from denial of certiorari); Bob Herbert, "Mr. Hance's 'Perfect Punishment,'" *New York Times*, March 27, 1994, D17; Bob Herbert, "Jury Room Injustice," *New York Times*, March 30, 1994, A15.
50. Charlie Young, Curfew Davis, George Dungee, Terry Lee Goodwin, and Eddie Lee Ross were all referred to as "niggers" by their defense lawyers at some point in the trials during which they were sentenced to death. Transcript of Opening and Closing Arguments, *Dungee v. Kemp*, 778 F.2d 1482 (11th Cir 1985), decided sub nom. *Isaacs v. Kemp*, 778 F.2d 1482 (11th Cir. 1985), cert. denied, 476 U.S. 1164 (1986); *Goodwin v. Balkcom*, 684 F.2d 794, 805 n.13 (11th Cir. 1982). See also *Ex parte Guzmon*, 730 S.W.2d 724, 736 (Tex. Crim. App. 1987) (defense counsel referred to his own client, a Salvadoran man, as a "wetback" in front of an all-white jury).
51. *Edwards v. Scroggy*, 849 F.2d 204, 207 (5th Cir. 1988).
52. Ibid.
53. Ibid., 208.
54. "Death Row U.S.A.," 6.
55. *Alabama v. Jefferson*, Cir. Ct. Chambers County No. CC-81-77 (Order of Oct. 2, 1992). One jury was for a hearing on Jefferson's mental competence to stand trial, another was for guilt and the third was for sentencing.
56. "Alabama County Still Records Marriages by Race," *Atlanta Journal and Constitution*, July 21, 1991, A2.
57. *Alabama v. Jefferson*, Order of Oct. 2, 1992.
58. Ibid.; the court held that there were race-neutral reasons for each of the strikes of African Americans.
59. Ga. Code Ann. §50-3-1 (Michie 1994); 347 U.S. 483 (1954) (holding that racial segregation in the public schools violates the Equal Protection Clause); *Brown v. Board of Education*, 349 U.S. 294, 300 (1955) (requiring that desegregation of the public schools proceed "with all deliberate speed").
60. *Coleman v. Miller*, 885 F. Supp. 1561, 1569 (N.D. Ga. 1995). See also Julius Chambers, *Protection of Civil Rights: A Constitutional Mandate for the Federal Government*, 87 Mich. L. Rev. 1599, 1601 n.9 (1989).
61. Jim Auchmutey, "Unraveling the Flag: A Guide to Rebel Colors," *Atlanta Journal and Constitution*, September 29, 1991, M1, M8 (quoting state representative Denmark Groover). See also "Miller Throws in Towel on Flag," *Columbus Ledger-Enquirer*, March 10, 1993, A1. Governor Marvin Griffin delivered the same message of defiance during his State of the State address in 1956, stating, "All attempts to mix the races whether they be in the classrooms, on the playgrounds, in public conveyances, [or] in any other area of close contact imperil the mores of the South." Mark Sherman, "Pledging Allegiances at Flag Forum," *Atlanta Journal and Constitution*, January 29, 1993, G1, G6.
62. *Augustus v. School Board of Escambia County*, 507 F.2d 152, 155 (5th Cir. 1975). As one court observed, "To some, [the flag] represents the undeniable fact that Georgia was a member of the Confederacy and did secede from the Union. The flag may also represent southern heritage, the old South, or values of independence. Undeniably, to others it represents white supremacy, rebellion, segregation, and discrimination. The court is not prepared to say that any of these perspectives are incorrect. The only thing that is clear is what the flag is not: a symbol of unity for Georgians." *Coleman*, 1569.
63. Curriden, "Racism Mars Justice," D1, D3.
64. See generally Paul Pinkham and Robin Lowenthal, "Getting more Minorities Involved... Fosters Respect for the System," *Florida Times Union*, December 10, 1991, A1.
65. Rene Lynch, "Deciding Life or Death for O.C.'s Worst Murderers," *Los Angeles Times*, February 23, 1994, A1.
66. See, e.g., Ga. Code Crim. Proc. §17-10-30; Miss Code Crim. Proc. §99-19-101; North Carol. Gen. Stat. §15A-2000; Tenn Code Ann §39-13-204; Va. Code Crim. Proc. §19.2-264.2. See generally Nina Rivkind and Steven F. Shatz, *The Death Penalty* (St. Paul: Nest, 2001), 147–66.
67. Rick Bragg, "Two Crimes, Two Punishments," *New York Times*, January 22, 1995, 1 (quoting Franklin Zimring, Director of the Earl Warren Legal Institute at the University of California at Berkeley).
68. Studies and cases documenting discriminatory practices by police against racial minorities are collected and discussed by Charles J. Ogletree, "Does Race Matter in

Criminal Prosecutions?" *Champion,* July 1991, 7, 10–12. Even before the notorious Rodney King case and the Mark Fuhrman tapes, there was concern about the racial attitudes of the police department in Los Angeles. See *Los Angeles v. Lyons,* 461 U.S. 95, 116 n.3 (1983) (Marshall, J., dissenting) (noting that although only 9 percent of the residents of Los Angeles are black men, they have accounted for 75 percent of the deaths resulting from chokeholds by police).

69. See, e.g., Carl Cannon, "Abducted Girl Found Slain Near her Columbus Home," *Columbus Ledger-Enquirer,* July 17, 1977, 1 (describing search for missing white victim by police officers, "truckloads of Military Policemen, trained dogs, an Army helicopter, and troops of Boy Scouts").

70. For example, after an African-American youth disappeared in Columbus, Georgia, he was first reported missing. Later his father was told a body had been found but it could not be identified because it was so badly decomposed. Two weeks later, the police told the father the body was definitely that of his son, who had been stabbed to death. Transcript of hearing held on Sept. 1–14, 1991, Sept. 12, 1991, 176–77, *State v. Brooks,* Indictment Nos. 3888, 54606, on appeal, 415 S.E.2d 903 (Super. Ct. of Muscogee Co., Ga. 1992), hereafter Hearing on Racial Discrimination.

71. *Ex parte Haney,* 603 So. 2d 412 (Ala. 1992); *Walker v. State,* 586 So. 2d 49 (Ala. Crim. App. 1991), after remand, 611 So. 2d 1133 (Ala. Crim. App. 1992).

72. Hearing on Racial Discrimination, Transcript of Sept. 12, 1991, 67–69. The evidence is described in Margolick, "In Land of Death Penalty," A1; and Death Penalty Information Center., http://www.deathpenaltyinfo.org/dpic. rll.html. Chattahoochee Judicial District: *The Buckle of the Death Belt* (1991), 10.

73. Transcript of Hearing at 38, *Davis v. Kemp,* Super. Ct. of Butts Co., Ga., (1988) (No. 86-V-865) (testimony of James Isham, father of the victim).

74. Ibid.

75. *Davis v. State,* 340 S.E.2d 869, cert. denied, 479 U.S. 871 (1986).

76. Clint Claybrook, "Slain Girl's Father Top Campaign Contributor," *Columbus Ledger-Enquirer,* August 7, 1988, B1.

77. Ibid.

78. See, e.g., Phil Gast, "District Attorney Criticizes Court for Rejecting Sentence," *Ledger-Enquirer,* September 17, 1983, A1, A2.

79. Hearing on Racial Discrimination, transcript of Sept. 12, 1991, 178, 184–85, 192–93, 197, 199–200.

80. See Defense exhibit 1A, admitted at Hearing on Racial Discrimination.

81. See *Report of the Governor's Commission on the Death Penalty: An Analysis of Capital Punishment in Maryland: 1978 to 1993* (November 1993) at 91, 92, 119 (although the city of Baltimore has well over ten times as many murders as Baltimore County each year, of forty-one death sentences imposed in Maryland under its current death penalty statute, twenty-two were imposed in Baltimore County; of the fifteen death sentences in effect on June 30, 1993, all but four were from Baltimore County; only five death sentences were imposed in the city of Baltimore and only two of the sentences in effect on June 30, 1993, were from the city of Baltimore). This author is aware of seventeen death sentences imposed in Cobb County, Georgia, under the death penalty statute adopted by Georgia in 1973. This is among the highest number of death sentences for a Georgia county.

82. See *Wainwright v. Witt,* 469 U.S. 412 (1985); *Witherspoon v. Illinois,* 391 U.S. 510 (1968).

83. *Lockhart v. McCree,* 476 U.S. 162, 173 (1986).

84. *Lingo v. State,* 437 S.E.2d 463 (Ga. 1993).

85. Ibid., 465.

86. *Boston v. Kentucky,* 476 U.S. 79 (1986).

87. *Lingo,* 437 S.E.2d at 466–67.

88. *Jackson v. Thigpen,* 752 F. Supp. 1551, 1554 (N.D. Ala. 1990), rev'd in part and aff'd in part, sub nom. *Jackson v. Herring,* 42 F.3d 1350 (11th Cir. 1995).

89. Ibid., 1555.

90. By this author's count, the death sentence has been imposed twenty-two times in the Chattahoochee Judicial Circuit, more than any other judicial circuit in Georgia. Four of those death sentences have been carried out. Three of the four persons executed were African Americans.

91. Defense Exhibit 2A, admitted at Hearing on Racial Discrimination.

92. Ibid.

93. Joseph Mulligan and Jerome Bowden, both sentenced to death by all-white juries, have been executed. "Death Row U.S.A.," 5.

94. See Defense Exhibit 1A, admitted in Hearing on Racial Discrimination.

95. Ibid.
96. *Hance v. Zant*, 696 F.2d 940, 952 (11th Cir. 1983), cert. denied, 463 U.S. 1210 (1983).
97. Hearing on Racial Discrimination, transcript of Sept. 12, 1991, 144–46 (testimony of William J. Smith, the prosecutor in *Hance*).
98. Defense Exhibit 2A, admitted in Hearing on Racial Discrimination.
99. Hance was executed on March 31, 1994. "Death Row USA," 8.
100. By this author's count, eighteen persons have been sentenced to death in the Ocmulgee Judicial Circuit since 1973.
101. Charts showing most of the prosecutor's capital trials are included in *Horton v. Zant*, 941 F.2d 1449, 1468–70 (11th Cir. 1991), cert. denied, 117 L.Ed.2d 652 (1992). Two other capital cases were tried against white defendants before the prosecutor left office. *Tharpe v. State*, 416 S.E.2d 78 (Ga. 1992); *Fugate v. State*, 431 S.E.2d 104 (Ga. 1993).
102. *Horton*, 941 F.2d, 1468–70.
103. *Amadeo v. Zant*, 486 U.S. 214 (1988).
104. *Horton*, 941 F.2d, 1458.
105. *Witherspoon v. Illinois*, 391 U.S. 510, 519 (1968).
106. 476 U.S. 79 (1986).
107. Ibid. After years of criticism about the crippling and virtually impossible burden of proof established in *Swain v. Alabama*, 380 U.S. 202 (1965), the Supreme Court held that a prima facie case of racial discrimination could be established by disparate strikes against minority jurors in a particular case. *Batson v. Kentucky*, 476 U.S. 79 (1986). *Swain* had required the defendant to prove that the prosecutor struck black citizens from juries in general. *Swain* is discussed further in notes 225–28 and accompanying text.
108. See *Batson*, 476 U.S., 98.
109. See, e.g., Mark Ballard, *Gunning for a Judge; Houston's Lanford Blames DA's Office For His Downfall*, Tex. Law., April 13, 1992, at 1 (describing how Houston District Attorney John B. Holmes, unhappy with rulings by a Republican judge in two murder cases, helped cause the judge's defeat by running one of his assistants against the judge and causing congestion in his docket).
110. See Kenneth B. Nunn, *Rights Held Hostage: Race, Ideology and the Peremptory Challenge*, 28 Harv. C.R.-C.L. L. Rev. 63 (1993); Michael J. Raphael and Edward J. Ungvarsky, *Excuses, Excuses: Neutral Explanations under* Batson v. Kentucky, 27 U. Mich. J.L. Ref. 229 (1993).
111. Peggy C. Davis, *Popular Legal Culture: Law as Microaggression*, 98 Yale L.J. 1559, 1571 (1989).
112. The psychological tendency of predominantly white decision makers to sympathize more with whites than blacks is described in Samuel H. Pillsbury, *Emotional Justice: Moralizing the Passions of Criminal Punishment*, 74 Cornell L. Rev. 655, 708 (1989); Francis C. Dane and Laurence S. Wrightsman, "Effects of Defendants' and Victims' Characteristics on Jurors' Verdicts," in *The Psychology of the Courtroom*, Norbert L. Kerr and Robert M. Bray, eds. (New York: Academic Press, 1982), 104–6. The effect is particularly pronounced and results in the most severe sentences where the victim is of the same race and the defendant is of a different race from that of the jurors.
113. *Lingo v. State*, 437 S.E.2d 463, 468 (Ga. 1993) (Sears-Collins, J., dissenting).
114. *Dobbs v. Zant*, 720 F. Supp. 1566, 1578 (N.D. Ga. 1989), aff'd, 963 F.2d 1403, 1407 (11th Cir. 1991), rev'd and remanded, 113 S. Ct. 835 (1993).
115. Any aspect of the life and background of the accused may be considered by the sentencer as a reason to impose a sentence less than death. For a discussion of the special demands upon defense counsel in properly preparing for the defense of a capital trial see Welsh S. White, *Effective Assistance of Counsel in Capital Cases: The Evolving Standard of Care*, 1993 U. Ill. L. Rev. 323 (1993). See also Gary Goodpaster, *The Trial for Life: Effective Assistance of Counsel in Death Penalty Cases*, 58 N.Y.U. L. Rev. 299, 303–04 (1983).
116. *Jackson v. Thigpen*, 752 F. Supp. 1551, 1555, 1556, 1562 (N.D. Ala. 1990), rev'd in part and aff'd in part, sub nom. *Jackson v. Herring*, 42 F.2d 1350 (11th Cir. 1995).
117. Declaration of Kim Antoinette Taylor, Sept. 30, 1991, filed in *Wade v. Calderon*, 29 F.3d 1312 (9th Cir. 1994), cert. denied, 130 L. Ed. 2d 802 (1995).
118. *Penry v. Lynaugh*, 492 U.S. 302, 319 (1989) (quoting *California v. Brown*, 479 U.S. 538, 545 (1987) (O'Connor, J., concurring).
119. Erik Eckholm, "Studies Find Death Penalty Often Tied to Victim's Race," *New York Times*, February 24, 1995, A1; see also Kathleen Maguire and Ann L. Pastore, eds., Bureau of Justice Statistics, U.S. Dep't of Justice, *Sourcebook of Criminal Justice Statistics 1993* (Washington, D.C.: Government Accounting Office, 1993), 384, table 3.128 1993).
120. "Death Row U.S.A.", 3.
121. Gross and Mauro, *Death and Discrimination*, 43–44.

122. The studies are discussed extensively in Baldus et al., *Equal Justice*, and in the Supreme Court's decision in *McCleskey v. Kemp*, 481 U.S. 279, 286–87 (1987); see also 325–28 (Brennan, J., dissenting).
123. Baldus et al., *Equal Justice*, 316; *McCleskey*, 481 U.S., 287.
124. "Death Row U.S.A.," 9.
125. Ibid., 4–9.
126. This author has made this determination from the trial judge's reports to the Georgia Supreme Court in the six cases that indicate that no member of the defendant's race was on the jury that sentenced him to death.
127. Ibid.
128. U.S. General Accounting Office, *Death Penalty Sentencing: Research Indicates Pattern of Racial Disparities* (February 1990), 5.
129. Ibid.
130. *McCleskey v. Kemp*, 481 U.S. 279 (1987).
131. Ibid., 306, 312, 313, 314–15.
132. Ibid., 279, 339 (Brennan, J., dissenting).
133. See notes 190–95 and accompanying text.
134. Anti–Drug Abuse Act, 21 U.S.C. § 848 (1988).
135. House Subcommittee, Racial Disparities, 2.
136. Ibid.
137. Ibid.
138. Ibid., 3.
139. See The Violent Crime Control and Law Enforcement Act of 1994, Pub. L. No. 103-322, 108 Stat. 1796 (1994). There is no reason to expect that the federal government will be more successful in preventing discrimination under the Violent Crime Control Act than it has been with the Anti–Drug Abuse Act.
140. 21 U.S.C. §848(o)(1) (1988).
141. The Racial Justice Act was adopted in a version of the crime bill that passed the House of Representatives in April 1994. See David Cole, "Fear of Too Much Justice," *Legal Times*, May 9, 1994, 26. However, due to opposition in the Senate, it was not included in the final bill reported by the conference committee and adopted by both the Senate and the House later in the summer.
142. See Cole, "Fear of Too Much Justice," 26.
143. See, e.g., *Castaneda v. Partida*, 430 U.S. 482 (1977); *Gibson v. Zant*, 705 F.2d 1543 (11th Cir. 1983). Once it is shown that there is substantial underrepresentation, jury officials must demonstrate that it was not the result of discrimination.
144. *Batson v. Kentucky*, 476 U.S. 79 (1986).
145. See W. Fitzhugh Brundage, *Lynchings in the New South; Georgia and Virginia, 1880–1930* (Urbana: University of Illinois Press, 1993); see also, generally, Wright, *Racial Violence in Kentucky*.
146. *Norris v. Alabama*, 294 U.S. 587, 592 (1935). Expert testimony established that the names of the six black citizens were added by the clerk at the direction of a jury commissioner.
147. Ibid., 593.
148. Ibid.
149. Norris was again sentenced to death. See Carter, *Scottsboro*, 370.
150. *Amadeo v. Zant*, 486 U.S. 214 (1988).
151. "The Briley File," *Fulton County Daily Report*, November 7, 1994, 1. The district attorney was not prosecuted for either racial discrimination or sexual harassment and was allowed to retire with a pension after twenty years in office.
152. *Vanleeward v. Rutledge*, 369 F.2d 584 (5th Cir. 1966).
153. *Peters v. Kiff*, 407 U.S. 493, 505–7 (1972) (White, J., concurring).
154. *Gates v. Zant*, 863 F.2d 1492, 1498 (11th Cir.), rehearing denied, 880 F.2d 293, 293–97 (Clark, J., dissenting from denial of rehearing), cert. denied, 493 U.S. 945 (1989).
155. Challenge to the Petit Jury Array filed in *State v. Brooks*, Indictment No. 3888 (Nov. 1977), on appeal, 261 S.E.2d 379 (1979), vacated and remanded, 446 U.S. 961 (1980), on remand, 271 S.E.2d 172 (Ga. 1980), cert. denied, 451 U.S. 921 (1981), conviction and death sentence vacated sub nom. *Brooks v. Kemp*, 762 F.2d 1383 (11th Cir. 1985) (en banc), vacated and remanded, 478 U.S. 1016 (1986), decision adhered to on remand, 809 F.2d 700 (11th Cir. 1987) (en banc), cert. denied, 483 U.S. 1010 (1987).
156. Trial Judge's Report to the Georgia Supreme Court in *State v. Brooks*, 6, §E(4).
157. Ibid.
158. *Avery v. Georgia*, 345 U.S. 559, 562 (1953).
159. *Williams v. Georgia*, 349 U.S. 375, 391 (1955).

160. *Williams v. State*, 88 S.E.2d 376, 377 (Ga. 1955), cert. denied, 350 U.S. 950 (1956).
161. *Williams v. Georgia*, 350 U.S. 950 (1956).
162. *Brown v. Board of Education*, (Brown I) 347 U.S. 483 (1954); *Brown v. Board of Education*, (Brown II), 349 U.S. 294 (1955).
163. Del Dickson, *State Court Defiance and the Limits of Supreme Court Authority:* Williams v. Georgia *Revisited*, 103 Yale L.J. 1423, 1425–26 (1994).
164. *Maxwell v. Bishop*, 398 F.2d 138 (8th Cir. 1968), vacated and remanded on other grounds, 398 U.S. 262 (1970).
165. Ibid., 147.
166. *Maxwell v. Bishop*, 398 U.S. 262, 262 (1970). Michael Meltsner, *Cruel and Unusual: The Supreme Court and Capital Punishment* (New York: Random House, 1973), 163–67, 199–211.
167. *Furman v. Georgia*, 408 U.S. 238 (1972). See 408 U.S. 257 (Douglas, J., concurring) (describing the statutes before the Court as "pregnant with discrimination"); 310 (Stewart, J., concurring); 364–65 (Marshall, J., concurring); 389, n.12 (Burger, C.J., dissenting); and 449–50 (Powell, J., dissenting).
168. Ibid., 364–65 (Stewart, J., concurring.).
169. Ibid., 310. Justice Douglas concluded there was an unacceptable risk of discrimination. (257).
170. As Justice Marshall pointed out in *Furman*, of the 455 persons executed for the crime of rape after the Justice Department began compiling statistics, 405 were African Americans. Ibid., 364.
171. *Coker v. Georgia*, 433 U.S. 584 (1977).
172. See, e.g., *Thornton v. State*, 449 S.E.2d 98 (Ga. 1994).
173. *Isaacs v. State*, 355 S.E.2d 644 (Ga. 1987), cert denied, 497 U.S. 1032 (1990).
174. See ibid., transcript of hearing on motion to recuse held Oct. 6–8, 1986.
175. See *State v. Taylor*, Mo. S. Ct. No. 74220 (Order of June 19, 1993); *State v. Nunley*, Mo. S. Ct. No. 76104 (Order of June 29, 1993) (both orders vacate the judgments in the two cases and remand for a new penalty hearing without opinion or further elaboration). The evidence of racial discrimination was presented in an evidentiary hearing before the Circuit Court of Jackson County, Missouri, in 1992.
176. *Jefferson v. State*, 645 So. 2d 313 (Ala. Crim. App. 1994).
177. Ibid.
178. *Swain v. Alabama*, 380 U.S. 202 (1965).
179. Ibid., 203–4.
180. Ibid., 223.
181. *McCray v. New York*, 461 U.S. 961, 964 (1983) (Marshall, J., dissenting from denial of certiorari).
182. *Batson v. Kentucky*, 476 U.S. 79 (1986).
183. *McCleskey v. Kemp*, 481 U.S. 279 (1987).
184. Ibid., 312.
185. Ibid., 312, 292.
186. Ibid., 296.
187. Ibid.
188. Ibid., 279, 308.
189. Ibid., 327 (Brennan, J., dissenting), 313, 309.
190. *Dred Scott v. Sanford*, 60 U.S. 393, 407 (1857), (holding that African Americans were "altogether unfit to associate with the white race, either in social or political relations; and so far inferior, that they had no rights which the white man was bound to respect"). *Plessy v. Ferguson*, 163 U.S. 537, 552 (1896) (holding that "[i]f one race be inferior to the other socially, the Constitution of the United States cannot put them upon the same plane").
191. John C. Jeffries Jr., *Justice Lewis F. Powell Jr.: A Biography* (New York: Charles Scribner's Sons, 1994), 451.
192. *Foster v. State*, 614 So. 2d 455 (Fla. 1992), cert. denied, 114 S. Ct. 398 (1993).
193. *Jones v. State*, 440 S.E.2d 161 (Ga. 1994).
194. Affidavit of Darrell Green, introduced at hearing, *Hill v. Zant*, Super. Ct. of Butts Co., Ga., No. CV 85–105(RC), Tr. of Hearing of Dec. 9, 1990, 39–42, 51–52, of Dec. 9, on appeal, 425 S.E.2d 858 (Ga. 1993), cert. denied, 114 S. Ct. 342 (1993). The extraordinary efforts of officials of Cobb County to keep African Americans out of their community by refusing to join the Metropolitan Atlanta Rapid Transit Authority and other means is described in the affidavit of Brian Sherman, Ph.D., filed in *Hill v. Zant*.
195. See also *Griffin v. Dugger*, 874 F.2d 1397 (11th Cir. 1989), cert. denied, 493 U.S. 1051 (1990) (upholding denial of a hearing on racial discrimination).
196. *Stephens v. State*, No S94A1854, 1995 WL 116292 (Ga. S. Ct. Mar. 17, 1995), withdrawn and superseded, *Stephens v. State*, 456 S.E.2d 560 (Ga. 1995).

197. Ibid.
198. Ibid.
199. Ibid.
200. *Stephens v. State*, 456 S.E.2d 560 (Ga. 1995); Emily Heller, "Second Thoughts on Second-Offense Law," *Fulton County Daily Report*, April 3, 1995, 1, 10.
201. Emily Heller, "Racial Test Put to the Test," *Fulton County Daily Report*, March 30, 1995, 1, 5.
202. *McCleskey v. Kemp*, 481 U.S. 279, 309, 313 (1987).
203. Ibid., 309 n.30.
204. See, e.g., *Nipper v. Smith*, 39 F.3d 1494 (11th Cir. 1994), petition for cert. filed (Mar. 2, 1995); *League of United Latin American Citizens v. Clements*, 999 F.2d 831 (5th Cir. 1993) (en banc), cert. denied, 114 S. Ct. 878 (1994).
205. For a discussion of the relationship of unconscious racism to the decisions in *McCleskey v. Kemp, Turner v. Murray,* and *Batson v. Kentucky,* see Sheri Lynn Johnson, *Comment, Unconscious Racism and the Criminal Law,* 73 Cornell L. Rev. 1016 (1988).
206. *Turner v. Murray*, 476 U.S. 28, 35, 36 (1986).
207. The Supreme Court's decision in *Turner* gives trial judges discretion to limit the form and number of questions and even allows collective questioning of the jurors. *Turner*, 476 U.S. at 37.
208. *Birt v. Montgomery*, 725 F.2d 587, 598 n.25 (11th Cir. 1984), cert. denied, 469 U.S. 874 (1984).
209. Ibid., 600–601.
210. Transcript of Hearing of Apr. 25–27, 1988, 231, *State v. Birt* (Super. Ct. Jefferson Co., Ga. No. 2360, 1988). The lawyer was referring to *Miranda v. Arizona*, 384 U.S. 436 (1966), and *Dred Scott v. Sandford*, 60 U.S. 393 (1857); *Dred Scott* was not a criminal case.
211. See notes 151–55 and accompanying text. See also *Barrow v. State*, 236 S.E.2d 257, 259 (Ga. 1977) (defense attorney did not challenge underrepresentation of blacks on the jury because "he felt adverse community pressure would insure to him personally" if he did so); *Goodwin v. Balkom*, 684 F.2d 794, 806 (11th Cir. 1982) (discussing how lawyer's concerns over "community ostracism" not only inhibited his performance at trial, but "every facet of counsel's functions").
212. *Blair v. Armontrout*, 916 F.2d 1310, 1333, 1351–52 (8th Cir. 1990) (Heaney, J., concurring in part and dissenting in part); also 1325 n.15.
213. Record at 593–94, *State v. Pace*, Cir. Court of Morgan County, Decatur, Alabama, No. CC-92-609 (Nov. 9, 1993).
214. Ibid.
215. *Turner v. Murray*, 476 U.S. 28, 35 (1976).
216. *McCleskey v. Kemp*, 481 U.S. 279, 344 (1987) (Brennan, J., dissenting.).
217. *Richmond v. J. A. Croson Co.*, 488 U.S. 469, 552–53 (1989) (Marshall, J., dissenting).
218. See David C. Baldus, George Woodworth, and Charles A. Pulaski Jr., *Reflections on the "Inevitability" of Racial Discrimination in Capital Sentencing and the "Impossibility" of Its Prevention, Detection and Correction*, 51 Wash. & Lee L. Rev. 359 (1994); *McCleskey*, 481 U.S. at 367 (Stevens, J., dissenting) (expressing the view that the death penalty could be constitutionally imposed if limited to the upper range of cases where prosecutors consistently seek death and juries consistently impose it).
219. *Callins v. Collins*, 114 S. Ct. 1127 (1994) (Blackmun, J., dissenting from the denial of certiorari) (expressing the view that the death penalty is unconstitutional because of the racial disparities in its infliction); *McCleskey v. Kemp*, 481 U.S. 279, 367 (1987) (Stevens, J., dissenting) ("If society were indeed forced to choose between a racially discriminatory death penalty...and no death penalty at all, the choice mandated by the Constitution would be plain" since racial disparities influenced by race would flagrantly violate[ ] the Court's prior "insistence that capital punishment be imposed fairly, and with reasonable consistency, or not at all." Quoting *Eddings v. Oklahoma*, 455 U.S. 104, 112 [1982]); *Godfrey v. Georgia*, 446 U.S. 420, 442 (1980) (Marshall, J., concurring in judgment) ("the effort to eliminate arbitrariness in the infliction of that ultimate sanction is so plainly doomed to failure that it—and the death penalty—must be abandoned altogether").
220. *McCleskey*, 481 U.S. at 319.
221. See, e.g., *Foster v. State*, 614 So. 2d 455, 465–68 (Fla. 1992) (Barkett, J., dissenting) (suggesting a standard for analyzing claims of racial discrimination in the infliction of the death penalty under the equal protection clause of the Florida Constitution); *Livingston v. State*, 444 S.E.2d 748, 757–61 (Ga. 1994) (Benham, J., dissenting) (asserting that admission of victim impact evidence violates various provisions of the Georgia Constitution).

4

KEN SILVERSTEIN

As any student of the death penalty in America knows, the chance that a person charged with a capital crime will live or die depends greatly on race, social class, and—perhaps most important—where the alleged crime was committed. First and foremost is the question of whether the defendant comes to court in one of the thirty-eight states where capital punishment is on the books. If he (or occasionally she) does, the outcome will differ greatly state by state and county by county, depending chiefly on the quality of the local defense bar, the trial judge, and the district attorney, who alone decides whether to seek capital punishment. For all these reasons, the odds on death are particularly high in Alabama, especially in the port town of Mobile, and most of all in the courtroom of Judge Ferrill McRae.

Though rarely mentioned in the national media's treatment of the death penalty, Alabama has the largest number of people per capita on death row. Its criminal defense system is the worst in the country, as rated by the American Bar Association (ABA). And Alabama is one of only a few states where judges can ignore a jury's recommendation of life without parole and unilaterally impose the death penalty. Thirty-two individuals, about one-sixth of the current population of Alabama's death row, were sent there by judges who overruled the jury. Judges can also reduce a jury's death sentence to life without parole, but in a state where capital punishment is hugely popular and judges run for office, that rarely happens.

Ferrill McRae sentenced his first man to die in 1981 and has sent many others to the electric chair since then. In six cases, more than any other Alabama magistrate, he's employed "override"—six times he has, as the quaint local lexicon has it, "enhanced" a jury's call for life without parole.

On a brutally hot morning in September 2000, I passed through the metal detectors in the lobby of Government Center, a huge, modern building in downtown Mobile, and rode the elevator to Judge McRae's chambers on the sixth floor. The courtroom is lined by seven rows of benches for spectators, who on this day are exclusively African Americans. So, too, are the defendants. All the lawyers and prosecutors—as well as the judge—are white.

The first case on today's docket involves a young woman seeking a restraining order against her estranged husband, who recently beat her up. "Why didn't you pick up something and hit him in the head?" McRae asks, nodding toward her short, stocky husband, who's also standing before the bench.

"He's too big," she replies weakly.

"He doesn't look too big to me," says McRae. "He looks like he's been drinking a case of Budweiser every night." Using, at length, the metaphor of King Solomon, he lectures the two about the division of marital property before granting the restraining order.

Next up is a young mother caught stealing $2,000 worth of goods from a Target store where she worked. The district attorney is willing to plead her out, reducing a ten-year sentence to thirty days for time served. McRae tells the woman she's getting off easy but ratifies the proposal. "Be good and be gone," the judge admonishes. "You don't want to see me again. If you do, bring your toothbrush." Now comes a teenager charged with robbery, who arrives in the company of his court-appointed attorney. McRae notes that the accused has previously been busted for smoking marijuana, which, in McRae's view is "the worst drug you can put in your system—worse than heroin. . . . Marijuana will eat away your brain, like termites to wood." McRae accepts a plea bargain that lets the teen off for time served but sets up a periodic drug testing schedule. One slipup, he warns, and "you are gone."

This is the kind of folksy moralism that might earn the sixty-six-year-old judge his own TV show. Yet according to local attorneys, this is Ferrill McRae on his very best behavior. When an African American in his courtroom wears a noticeable cologne, Judge McRae has been known to sniff the air and exclaim, "Ahhhh, evening in Prichard"—the name of a poor, predominantly black city outside of Mobile. One young attorney, who didn't want to be identified for fear of incurring McRae's wrath, recalled needing the judge's signature on a client's bail-reduction application. McRae first wanted to know the client's "color." When informed that he was black, McRae supposedly told the attorney that he "shouldn't try too hard because we need more niggers in jail." According to another

Mobile trial judge, Joseph Johnston, McRae once queried Johnston's court reporter on the matter of whom she'd "been fucking lately," and asked a female attorney in his own courtroom if she was wearing her "trial tits." In newspaper accounts, McCrae has denied making such comments; but Johnston and others stand by their stories and locals, both friend and foe, say the judge is famous for his salty language.

All this would be bad enough in probate or small-claims court; in this criminal courtroom, where the stakes can be life or death, Judge McRae's views are especially alarming. And legal authorities in Alabama are well aware of McRae's antics: the state's Judicial Inquiry Commission has been investigating the judge since the summer of 2000—but has thus far taken no action against him.

At 11:15 A.M., McRae adjourns, as he needs to attend a friend's funeral. When I approach the bench and introduce myself, the judge is affable. He orders three courtroom employees to stick around for our conversation and then starts talking before I can pull a list of questions from my back pocket. "If I were you," he begins, "I'd ask why one person should be able to override what twelve citizens do. The answer to that question is rather simple. Judges are better able to determine if everyone is being treated fairly. Do you know anything about fixing a transmission? Neither do I—but I do know something about criminal law. If the defendant shows no remorse, I see that over the course of two or five or ten days."

During the next thirty minutes, Judge McRae expounds on everything from historical precedents for the death penalty ("Throughout the Bible it states that death is permissible") to Alabama's status as one of just a few states to conduct executions using the electric chair exclusively ("I'm not sure lethal injection is more humane. With 7,000 volts of electricity, you're dead that quick"). On the subject of judicial override, McRae might be mistaken for a bleeding-heart liberal. "Let's say twelve rednecks find somebody guilty and give him death that quick," he says. "Shouldn't the judge have the power to reduce the sentence if it's not appropriate? If anybody thinks it's easy to tell a man that he'll get death by electrocution, it is not. It's a traumatic experience, one any judge would like to leave in the jury's hands. When a judge reduces it from death to life, I guarantee you he's happy."

McRae sounds fair, racially impartial, above politics—all of which is inconsistent with his record. Five of the six men the judge has sentenced to die via override are African American, and he's never substituted a life sentence for a jury verdict of death—even when an all-white jury condemned a retarded black man who couldn't read the confession that he signed. And despite his insistence to the contrary, McRae's colleagues seem far happier to override for death (which has occurred seventy times) than for life (eight times). Indeed, Alabama judges have overruled juries to condemn the deranged, the young, the retarded, and dozens of others—including the innocent—to die in the arms of "Yellow Mama," the state's garish yellow electric chair.

LIFE IN THE DEATH BELT

In 1972 the U.S. Supreme Court ruled in *Furman v. Georgia* that the death penalty was unconstitutional because sentencing discretion given to juries and judges in imposing capital punishment made the entire process arbitrary and irrational. Four years later, after a number of states prepared new statutes designed to reduce such discretion, the Court reinstated capital punishment. Since then, as of this writing, 705 individuals have been executed nationally—392 of them in the past five years.

Popular and political support for capital punishment is strongest in the south—defense attorneys call the region the "death belt"—where more than 80 percent of all executions are carried out. In Alabama, 188 inmates are awaiting execution and, according to the Alabama Prison Project, an anti–death penalty group based in Montgomery, some 300 defendants have capital cases pending in the state's courts. Twenty-three individuals have been executed in Alabama since the reinstatement of capital punishment—as many or more than in all but six states—and the pace of killing is likely to increase: in the summer of 2000, the state's supreme court gave itself the prerogative of passing on what was previously an automatic review of all death sentences.

As elsewhere, Alabama's death row occupants are overwhelmingly poor—95 percent are indigent—and they are in the racial minority. Blacks make up 26 percent of Alabama's population, but 46 percent of death row, just higher than the national average of 43 percent. In the United States, about two-thirds of all murders involve victims who are black—yet more than 80 percent of those who are executed are sentenced for killing whites. Of the 23 persons executed in Alabama since 1976, 17 murdered whites. And the lingering effects of Jim Crow attitudes on the state judiciary are obvious: there are few black trial judges in Alabama, the court of criminal appeals is all white, and the only two African Americans on the Alabama Supreme Court were both voted out in November 2000.

Alabama's criminal defense system is abysmal. Those who face the death penalty are often saddled with incompetent lawyers who expend little energy pursuing their cases. To take just one of the worst examples: Judy Haney was convicted in 1988 for hiring a hit man to kill her husband, who routinely beat her and her children. It's rare for women who kill an abusive spouse to get the death penalty, but Haney's attorney came to court so drunk that the judge halted the proceedings and sent him to jail overnight to dry out. When the trial resumed the next day, Haney was sentenced to die. Bad lawyering is a primary reason that capital trials are so swift in Alabama, frequently running just a few days. In many states, jury selection alone can take weeks.

States have no obligation to provide counsel during the appeals process, and many don't. In Alabama, judges can choose to appoint an attorney during the appeals process, but only after the condemned files a petition claiming to have found new evidence or procedural flaws at trial—a step beyond the ability of most death row inmates. Alabama caps pay for defense counsel at the appeals level to $2,000, which—given that a properly handled case requires about five hundred hours of pretrial preparation—works out to four dollars per hour. Defendants can also seek help from the Equal Justice Initiative in Montgomery or the ABA's pro bono death penalty project. Demand, though, far outstrips supply. Currently, thirty individuals on Alabama's death row are watching the clock tick down to their execution date without the aid of lawyers.

Even if defendants do have lawyers, they face one of the nation's toughest capital statutes. While jurors must vote unanimously to convict, only ten of twelve must agree on a death sentence. Even worse is the provision that allows judges to ignore the jury's sentence altogether, a power shared only by their colleagues in Delaware, Florida, and Indiana.

Yet Delaware judges are appointed, not elected, which is probably why they overwhelmingly use override to spare a life rather than take it. In Florida, judicial overrides for death outnumber those for life, but not nearly as dramatically as in Alabama's nine-to-one ratio. Indiana judges have overridden nineteen jury verdicts, ten for death and nine for life. Indeed, override is rarely employed anymore in Indiana or Florida, because the supreme courts in those states frequently reject its application—something that has never happened in Alabama. Indiana and Florida also require a judge to meet formal, written standards to set aside a jury's sentence, which is to be "given great weight." Alabama judges are supposed to balance aggravating circumstances, such as a prior record of violent crime, against mitigating ones—a history of mental illness, for example—but are otherwise free to do as they please. In ten cases, a judge has overridden a twelve-person jury's unanimous recommendation for a sentence of life in prison.

MAX BRAX AND THE BLACK DEATH

Defense attorneys complain that a number of Alabama judges appear to have a predisposition toward the death penalty. Recently retired Mobile judge Braxton Kittrell, who meted out five death overrides, was known by insiders as "Max Brax" owing to his tendency to impose the maximum sentence. Over baked salmon and spinach au gratin one Sunday evening, Kittrell told me that when he killed a leopard during a safari in Zimbabwe, "It broke my heart." He spoke more easily of sentencing prisoners to death, saying of one of the men he sent to the electric chair, "You could look in his eyes and see he was evil incarnate."

Judge Charles Price, an African American from Montgomery, portrays himself as a prudent advocate of capital punishment. "I'm a product of the civil rights movement and the era of unfairness of the system," Price, a big man with a bushy mustache, told me in his chambers. "I look for examples of unfairness." That would come as a shock to defense attorneys, who have nicknamed Price "the Black Death." Judge Price overrode a jury's life sentence in the case of William Knotts, a white teenager who murdered a black woman, and then rejected Knotts's appeal, including the assertion that his defense had been incompetent. In this he ignored that Knotts's two lawyers did not call a single witness during the guilt phase, and that during his closing argument cocounsel Paul Lowery—who slept through part of the trial—said, "I'll have to compliment the prosecution.... They certainly have an abundance of evidence."

Death penalty opponents have long sought to do away with override, arguing, among other things, that judges who run for elected office feel undue pressure to impose capital punishment. In 1995 lawyers with the Equal Justice Initiative convinced the U.S. Supreme Court to review override in the case of *Harris v. Alabama*. The appellant, Louise Harris, had been convicted of conspiring to kill her husband. The jury spared her life—Harris was a churchgoing mother of seven who held down three jobs—but the judge overruled the verdict and ordered her death. In an 8 to 1 decision, the Supreme Court ruled for the state and remanded Harris to death row, where she currently awaits execution. "Judges who covet higher office—or who merely wish to remain judges—must constantly profess their fealty to the death penalty," Justice John Paul Stevens wrote in dissent. "The absence of any rudder on a judge's free-floating power to negate the community's will... renders Alabama's capital sentencing scheme fundamentally unfair."

By now, professing fealty to the death penalty is a well-established feature of judicial elections in Alabama. A few years ago, Alabama Supreme Court candidate Claud Neilson boasted in a campaign ad that he'd "looked into the eyes of murderers and sentenced them to death." Another candidate for the state's highest court, incumbent Kenneth Ingram, ran a TV ad that opened with grainy videotape footage from inside a convenience store where, twenty years earlier, a teenager had murdered the owner. Here, said the ad's narrator, "a sixty-eight-year-old woman, working alone, was robbed, raped, stabbed seventeen times, and murdered. Without blinking an eye, Judge Kenneth Ingram sentenced the killer to die." The victim's daughter then appears on screen to give her personal endorsement. "It was my mother who was killed, and Judge Ingram gave us justice. Thank heaven Judge Ingram is on the supreme court."

LESS APT TO RULE ON SYMPATHY

The State Building in downtown Montgomery lies a few blocks away from the King Memorial Baptist Church, on Dexter Avenue, where Martin Luther King Jr. once preached. There, in a fourth-floor office, Clay Crenshaw currently heads the attorney general's capital litigation division. His secretary's office door is covered with *Far Side*–style cartoons. In one, two guards stand watch over a man in an electric chair, which sits in the prison yard during a rainstorm. As the guards wait for a bolt of lightning to hit the chair, one says to the other, "These darn cutbacks have gone too far." Upon spotting me reading the cartoons, Crenshaw, a tall, balding man, chuckles and says, "We've got a little gallows humor here. Whatever helps you do a better job." But Crenshaw doesn't seem to need much help getting up for his job. Speaking about the case of James Harvey Callahan, who raped and strangled a college student, Crenshaw says, "She was a person who would have contributed to society, and this piece of trash kills her. He deserves to die."

Crenshaw expresses the same certainty when it comes to the question of deterrence. "If criminals know that if they go to a 7-Eleven store and kill the woman there for fifty dollars, that they are going to forfeit their life—they aren't going to do that as often," he says. Even if that's true, I say, what's the justification for override? After all, anyone who opposes the death penalty is summarily dismissed from the jury pool for capital cases, a practice that results in especially conservative panels. If a "death-qualified" jury comes back with a life sentence, it surely had good reasons. Not so, replies Crenshaw. "A jury may base its decision on emotion, a crying mother or sister. A trial judge will rule on the law and is less apt to rule on sympathy."

In preparation for my visit, Crenshaw had printed out summaries of some of the most gruesome murders in Alabama's recent history. One he hands me concerns Judy Neelley, who helped her husband kidnap and sexually brutalize a thirteen-year-old girl. When they finished, Judy—who was eighteen at the time—tried to kill the girl by injecting her with Drano and, when that failed, shot her in the back. On his last day in office in 1999, Governor Fob James commuted Neelley's sentence to life without parole—the only commutation given by an Alabama governor since the death penalty was reinstated.

Crenshaw's summaries don't mention the testimony and evidence that can lead juries to opt for life sentences. To learn about that, I drove a mile across town to the old pink Victorian that houses the Alabama Prison Project, where I spent the afternoon sitting on the floor examining a stack of files on former and current death row inmates. Since Crenshaw had flagged the Neelley case, I made sure to examine Neelley's dossier. According to her clemency petition, Neelley's father died when she was nine and the family fell into poverty. She had no encounters with the law until she met her husband, who was eleven years her senior, when she was fifteen. During the trial, it emerged that Neelley's husband regularly beat her. He told her that if she ever left him he'd kill her family. Once, after accusing her of infidelity, he raped her with a plunger handle and urinated in her mouth. Yet Crenshaw labeled Governor James's commutation of Neelley's death sentence "a travesty of justice and a great disservice to the state of Alabama."

Neelley's story is one of hundreds stored in five battered filing cabinets that occupy nearly an entire wall. Another Prison Project file tells the story of Walter McMillian, one of two men sentenced to die by judicial override only to be exonerated later, before they were put to death. McMillian, sentenced to life imprisonment by a jury for the alleged murder of a white teenage girl, had no prior felony record and produced twelve alibi witnesses. Judge Robert E. Lee Key Jr. condemned McMillian to the electric chair, citing the "vicious and brutal killing of a young lady in the first full flower of adulthood." After McMillian had spent six years on death row, his attorney discovered that the state's principal witness, a career criminal, had avoided a capital murder charge by falsely testifying against him.

Over the course of the afternoon, I found a number of cases in which judicial override was implemented in a manner that's hard to see as anything but arbitrary. Robert Lee Tarver was sentenced to die for the murder of a storekeeper. The only evidence against him came from codefendant Andrew Lee Richardson, who secretly got a break from the prosecution in exchange for testifying. Tarver denied committing the crime, and an appeals court would later concede that "very little evidence made Tarver a better candidate than Richardson to be found to be the actual killer."

Whatever the issues with his conviction, Tarver had a compelling case at sentencing. For instance, his grandparents had taken him in after his mother abandoned him, and years later he returned the favor when they were too feeble to care for themselves. But none of his good deeds was introduced at trial, because Tarver's attorney spent just four hours preparing for the penalty phase. Judge Wayne Johnson—who overrode the jury's life sentence—learned of Tarver's better side five years later, when an out-of-state lawyer recruited by the ABA presented it on appeal. Johnson promptly ruled that Tarver's original defense had been constitutionally deficient, said he'd never have ordered him to the electric chair if he'd known all the evidence, and scheduled a new sentencing hearing. The state went to the Alabama Court of Criminal Appeals, which ruled that Tarver's defense had been sufficiently capable and that it was too late for Johnson to change his mind.

At the bottom of Tarver's file, I found a letter sent by his daughter, Clissie Rogers, to Alabama governor Don Siegelman. "Is life without parole possible for the father and grandfather of those pictured above?" she asked in words typed below a photo of herself and her two beaming kids. Alas, it wasn't: Tarver was executed April 14, 2001.

Taurus Carroll is one of fourteen Alabama inmates sent to death row as a juvenile and one of four sent there via override. Carroll, along with a teenage companion, robbed a Birmingham dry cleaning store in 1995, when he was seventeen. Before fleeing with ninety dollars, Carroll shot—the gun went off accidentally, he claimed, and there was no direct evidence to show the contrary—and killed the store's owner, Betty Long. The jury at Carroll's trial found him guilty of capital murder. During the penalty phase, the panel heard that Carroll's mother had kicked him out of the house at the insistence of her drug-abusing husband and that his grandmother raised him in one of Birmingham's worst slums. Several members of Betty Long's family asked that Carroll's life be spared. "When he took Betty's life, he destroyed mine," her mother testified. "[But I] do not want to see him dead, because if Betty was standing here instead of me, she would say the same thing, 'Don't kill him, but make him pay for the suffering that he has caused me.'" The jury voted 10 to 2 for life, but Judge Alfred Bahakel ordered Carroll to the electric chair.

DEATH IN MOBILE

Capital-defense attorneys hate to end up in court in Mobile, partly because death penalty zealots have frequently occupied the local district attorney's office. Charlie Graddick, who served during the 1970s, pledged that on his watch he would "fry murderers until their eyeballs pop out." After the court of criminal appeals tossed out a death sentence that District Attorney Chris Galanos had won at trial, Galanos, who served until 1994, described its members as "the five dumbest white men in the universe."

Mobile judges tend to be cut from the same cloth. Ferrill McRae, one of five locals who has employed override, was born in Irvine, Kentucky, a railroad town in the foothills of Appalachia. His parents moved to Mobile when he was a child, taking along Ferrill and his nine siblings, including the judge's twin brother, Merrill.

McRae's judicial career dates to 1965, when Governor George Wallace—still in his "Segregation forever!" phase—appointed McRae to the bench just four years after he graduated from the University of Alabama's law school. McRae heard domestic cases during his first five years on the bench, but he's been handling criminal cases ever since. He's lost track of the number of capital trials he's presided at, other than to say there have been "a lot."

In at least six death penalty cases, McRae has issued findings that were ghostwritten by the attorney general's office. He's also pursued an open-door policy with a number of local district attorneys, especially Chris Galanos. Mike Odom, a lawyer who formerly worked on Galanos's staff, recalls two unspoken rules worked out between the DA and McRae. "The first was that there should always be at least one pretty woman on the jury so that the judge had something nice to look at during trial. The second was never to strike a juror who came from the 36608 zip code, because that's where the rich white locals live."

Like the rest of the South, Alabama turned increasingly Republican after Lyndon Johnson introduced civil rights legislation in 1964. Last year, a local lawyer named Charles Miller filed to run against McRae as a Republican, and the judge, a lifelong Democrat, deftly switched party affiliation so he could face him in the GOP primary. Miller crushed McRae in a preelection poll conducted by the Mobile Bar Association— it was the first time an incumbent had failed to win the local bar's endorsement—but the judge eked out a narrow victory on primary day.

Though his views on the subject are well known, McRae ran TV ads to highlight his support for capital punishment. In one he is shown on the bench while an announcer notes that the judge has "presided over more than 9,000 cases, including some of the most heinous murder trials in our history." Meanwhile, the names of notorious convicted murderers whom McRae sentenced to death flash on the screen: "Singleton, Murdered Catholic Nun" and "State Trooper Martin, Murdered and Burned Wife."

Cornelius Singleton, a mentally retarded black man, got death from an all-white jury. He signed a confession—with an X—that he couldn't read; later he said he thought he was admitting to stealing laundry off a neighbor's clothesline. The confession was extracted before Singleton had a lawyer and after the police told him that the murder charge carried a maximum sentence of life in prison and allowed his girlfriend to sit on his lap in exchange for waiving his right to silence. Singleton's court-appointed attorney refused to meet with him and didn't tell the jury that his client was retarded. McRae allowed prosecutors to make inflammatory final arguments to the jury—one called the defendant a "creature [that] I can't refer to as a person or a human being"—and at sentencing dismissed the testimony of four defense psychologists while crediting a prosecution expert who said that Singleton was intellectually limited but not retarded. Singleton went to the electric chair in 1992. His IQ—in the range of 55 to 67—was lower than that of anyone executed in the United States during the past quarter-century.

George Martin, a former state trooper, was convicted, in the spring of 2000, of killing his wife for insurance money. His attorney, Dennis Knizley—who has handled a score of capital cases and has only two men on death row, both McRae overrides—feared that with the primary election against Miller coming up, the judge would exploit Martin's case. "He'd given plenty of continuances to me in the past, but this time he refused" to extend the May 1 trial date, Knizley said over drinks at a local hotel. "I don't know if he was politically motivated, but I do know that he had the opportunity to be on TV and in the newspapers every day." What's especially noteworthy is that when the campaign ad ran, the jury had convicted Martin but voted to spare his life. McRae had not yet rendered his decision, though the ad all but announced that he planned to give Martin death—which he soon did.

When asked about such cases, McRae isn't the least bit defensive. "I never enter into a decision hurriedly—I always put it off at least five or six days," he told me in his courtroom. "After I've imposed it, I've never felt like I made a mistake." And what about Singleton, I asked a few months later, after learning details of the case. McRae faxed back, "Do I think Singleton received a fair trial? The answer is yes. There is no such thing as a perfect trial, but his comes close to it."

McRae disputes that race is a factor in the imposition of the death penalty. "It's the most overrated thing in the world," he lectures me from the bench when I mention *Batson v. Kentucky*, the 1986 Supreme Court ruling that prevents prosecutors from striking African Americans from the jury on the basis of race. "I'm taking up for blacks now, I'm not speaking badly of them. The idea that a black will stick up for a defendant just because he's black ought to offend every black. I would be offended by the attitude I hear from the lily-whites, that blacks are softer on crime."

Meanwhile, McRae's override of the Martin verdict sparked a small backlash. The conservative *Mobile Register* editorialized soon afterward that "no one man should be empowered, on his own, to sentence another to death." Last December, Hank Sanders, an African-American state senator from Selma, called for a three-year moratorium on executions, saying that override is one of his chief concerns. It's doubtful, though, that any significant change is on the horizon. Sanders's appeal was greeted with a chorus of catcalls from top state officials. "I'm not interested in a moratorium," Governor Siegelman replied. "That's another way of saying let's look at an alternative to the death penalty, and that's not a discussion I'm willing to engage in."

Judge McRae doesn't believe lawmakers will heed Sanders's call—nor that they should. "Some say some judges are more prone to give the death penalty than others," he tells me in his courtroom before departing for his friend's funeral. "There's no question about that. But if it's based on what's fair in the case, I have no problem with that."

5

"FROM MY VANTAGE-DISADVANTAGE POINT": SAMUEL B. JOHNSON IN THE NEW SOUTH

MARK DOW

"Each of us knows, though we do not like this knowledge, that a courtroom is a visceral Roman circus. No one in this contest is, or can be, impartial. . . . For to suspend judgment demands that one dismiss one's perceptions at the very moment that one is most crucially—and cruelly—dependent on them. We perceive by means of the kaleidoscopic mirror of this life. . . . The light is always changing in that mirror. This light will not permit us to forget that we are mortal: which means that we are all connected—which complicates the judgment."

—James Baldwin, *The Evidence of Things Not Seen*

The police report reads: "On 31 December 1981, at approximately 1350 hours, Mississippi Highway Patrol Officer BILLY LANGHAM, Badge J-52, stopped a vehicle, occupied by four (4) black males. Patrol Officer Langham was stabbed in the back with a large butcher knife and then shot with his own service revolver."

One of the four black men received a death sentence; two were sentenced to life; and the fourth, on whose testimony the other convictions were based, got five years.

Eleven years after the murder, one of the eyewitnesses told an investigator, "The only mistake the great State of Mississippi made is not to shoot the son-of-a-bitch niggers at the roadblock. . . . They should kill all of them, then we know that we killed the right one, too." There is a certain logic to that suggestion: exercise power and eliminate complications. But then power has its own complications. The same man tells the investigator—this is in 1992—"A nigger can't make it in life if he doesn't have a white man, and a white man can't make it if he doesn't have himself a nigger." He was apparently talking about an employment situation; but he was talking about a system of justice, too.

Samuel Bice Johnson, the man who was sentenced to death for the murder of officer Billy Langham, would later write, after the state of Mississippi executed an African-American man in a separate case, of "the 'racists' who, either openly or in secret, perhaps with pride and perhaps without, say: 'He was: A Nigger, A Nigra, A Coon, A Shoe, A Scobe, A Pickaninny (or whatever), and HE KILLED (no doubts about it) a: White Man, Superior Being, God, Member of the MASTER RACE, Master (or whatever), and we should kill him again because we must make the rest of them fear and respect us as the Divine Beings that we are.'"[1]

Officer Billy Langham was white; we know this because no mention is made in the records of his race.

"JUST COMMON THREATS"

"Scholars have long debated the relationship between lynchings and executions," writes historian David M. Oshinsky in "Worse Than Slavery": Parchman Farm and the Ordeal of Jim Crow Justice, a book that Sam Johnson first recommended to me in a letter from his own Parchman cell. Data from 1882 to 1930 suggest, Oshinksy writes, "that both lynchings and legal executions rose dramatically in times of racial stress. Lethal punishment signaled social control."[2]

Photos of the crime scene show Officer Langham's blue-gray highway patrol hat on the brownish December grass by the roadside. Another photo shows a butcher knife, and another the officer's service revolver. The cars in the photos help one to go back in time. The patrol car, parked along the then-unpaved shoulder of Highway 49, is a Dodge sedan with a single blue light on the roof. A police investigator's drawing adds the nearby pecan trees. A group of men appears in some of the photos, standing at the scene of the crime. Almost all have their hands in their pockets, as if they don't know what they should do.

Did someone come along and tell them what they should do? Or were they not among the crowd that would soon gather at the jail? The four black men had been taken to the county jail in Collins. A police investigator himself wrote in a report that "a large crowd of citizens and Law Enforcement Officers gathered. It was obvious that there was going to be trouble there; so the four (4) subjects were moved to the Simpson County Jail at Mendenhall." A second investigator would later testify that a group of "'concerned citizens'" followed the officers and the four men they had arrested into the jail itself; these citizens wanted "'to kill them, hang them, shoot them,'" the investigator said, according to a *Jackson*

Advocate account; "'you know, just common threats.'"[3] One of the defendants was sent through a "gauntlet" of citizens as part of his interrogation and then beaten.

And so the four were moved for their safety to the nearby Simpson
County jail, where they were fingerprinted and beaten again. Johnson
would later tell his friend and correspondent Cliff Williams, "I was
beaten almost to death eight straight days and held incommunicado for
those eight days. I didn't see a lawyer, judge, or anyone but the police and
the rest of those who beat on me." He wouldn't have an attorney for
about another month. Meanwhile he refused to sign the Waiver of
Rights, as the others had been persuaded to do, that read, "I have read
this statement of my rights and I understand what my rights are. I am
willing to make a statement and answer questions. I do not want a lawyer
at this time. I understand and know what I am doing. No promises or
threats have been made to me and no pressure or coercion of any kind
has been used against me."

Writing about the coerced confession that had implicated Edward
Earl Johnson in a separate case, Sam Johnson observed that his friend,
never having been involved with the law, "never knew of his right to
counsel or any other rights except the 'right hand' of the sheriff." The
"right hand" in Sam Johnson's case was that of notorious Simpson
County Sheriff Lloyd Jones. "The federal courts upheld a charge that
Jones threatened to whip Johnson and his co-defendants with a bicycle
chain when they were in his jail. Jones also allegedly attempted to have
them killed."[4]

Jackson Advocate publisher Charles Tisdale cut through a large
swath of civil rights history when he summarized the life of Sheriff Jones
in a 1995 obituary headlined "Lloyd 'Goon' Jones dead: Simpson County
sheriff's reign of terror finally over":

> Loved by the state's segregationists, Jones had a long history of racial
> confrontations....
>
> As the Roman empire had its centurians to enforce its edicts on its
> near-slave population in what is now the Middle East during biblical
> times, Mississippi has its own enforcers; its own racist epic
> heroes—Simpson County's Lloyd Jones was among the best or worst of
> them.
>
> "He was a legend in his own time," Davis Smith, a former Jackson
> newsman recalled. "He was known as 'tough on niggers.' Everybody
> knew Lloyd Jones wasn't going to take no sh— from no niggers"....

Tisdale notes that Jones didn't mind being called "Goon," saying once
that it was something African Americans "'have been calling me since
Freedom Rider days.'" Jones had the explicit support of the Ku Klux
Klan; was present "when Ben Brown was shot in the back by a law

enforcement officer"; was "on hand to lead" when two Jackson State University students were gunned down by law enforcement officers; and was implicated in the suspicious 1992 death in his jail of a nonviolent eighteen-year-old man.

Jones's role in twentieth-century Mississippi is memorialized in a 1972 court decision. As a Highway Patrol inspector, he was involved in the "surveillance" of civil rights activists. Reverend John Perkins and others were arrested—supposedly for traffic infractions—as they drove along Highway 49 after a demonstration demanding desegregation in the town of Mendenhall. Jones was among the officers making "the Highway 49 arrests," in the court's phrase, and who forced the activists to shout their list of demands as they were mocked; who shaved their heads and poured moonshine over them; and "who got up and stomped" Perkins after another officer had forced Perkins to mop up his own blood and also pushed a fork into his nose and down his throat.[5]

Oshinsky writes that in the 1960s, Parchman Farm became a weapon in the civil rights struggle: "Mississippi officials used the Delta prison to house—and break down—those who challenged its racist customs and segregation laws."[6] Now Sam Johnson—born in 1942 in Alabama but at home most of his life in Rochester, New York—was not driving down Highway 49 as a Freedom Rider; he was on his way to cash some bad checks. But Mississippi's living history and its lockups, and of course Parchman Farm itself (just off a western stretch of Highway 49) transformed Johnson into "that New York nigger," as the local authorities liked to call him. "Their survival depends on my remaining enslaved and what better way to keep me enslaved than by enslaving my mind?" he would write. So he worked to clarify a few things for himself and for others, at least as he saw them "from my vantage-disadvantage point," as he put it in a poem.

From Parchman's death row, Johnson wrote to the prison's director of educational programming three times without receiving an answer. "I know for a fact that they don't want any of us to get any type of an education program here but I have been trying to get them to look at us as humans and change their minds.... The only thing that they are interested in is keeping us locked into these cells 23 3/4 hours each day. Lately we haven't been getting any yard call.... Each day the authorities try to instill a deeper sense of guilt into a person and take away their will to be an individual. I've had them tell me...'You're alive, aren't you? Be thankful for that.'...I've spoken to the unit administrator about starting the school program (he's black) and he told me 'NIGGER, you ain't runnin' shit here!'...I guess that I was supposed to be terrified when he called me a nigger. ha-ha-ha- I'm getting 'sidetracked' again...."

Oshinsky tells of a turn-of-the-century Mississippi governor who opposed all spending on "Negro" education because "[t]he only effect of educating him... is to spoil a good field hand and make an insolent cook."[7] In Paul Hamann's 1987 BBC documentary *Fourteen Days in May*, Sam Johnson looks up from his chess game with Edward Johnson, and, indicating the inmate field workers visible through the fence, explains, "It's slavery *modified* into today's world... instead of calling it a planta- tion they call it a farm. But there is no difference." And in a letter written around the same time: "Racism is prevalent from the top to the bottom and all of the way in between.... The black officers are tolerated... in basically the same sense that 'house niggers' were tolerated by 'massa' during pre-civil war days. The only difference between now and 1787 is two hundred years."

Sam sent me a copy of the *Advocate*'s obituary on Sheriff Jones. On the back of it he wrote: "Here's the scoop on the ol' sheriff. He brought me to death row in 1982 and before handing me over to these prison guards told me: 'This is your home. I'll be back shortly to watch them execute your black ass.' I told him: 'Don't bet the farm on it.'" Sheriff Jones was murdered in an unprovoked shooting as he sat in his truck with a jail "trusty." Johnson joked that the worms eating the sheriff were probably taking Maalox. But in another letter he wrote, "For some reason I don't even feel the sense of elation or joy I always thought I would feel if he died or was killed. I hate it that he was killed. He was the TOP DOG in mistreating me while I was in his jail but now that he's dead I don't feel anything but sadness over his death."

"NO SUFFERING"

The old-fashioned lynching thwarted, there was still the matter of the newfangled kind. In his closing statement during the sentencing phase of Johnson's trial, district attorney Bob Evans tried to help jurors dis- tance themselves from what he was asking them to do. Anticipating that the other side would ask for mercy, he told jurors that "forgiveness is not the privilege of this Court. That belongs to the Lord." He also tried to transfer to the jurors some of the comforting diffusion of responsibility that helps to make mob action possible: "You are not the one executing Samuel Johnson. Regardless of what they tell you, you're not the one. He chose that himself...."

But not completely by himself: the defense would learn that when an African-American juror held out for life over death, he was told that the Ku Klux Klan would be sent to burn his house down.

In a closing statement so thin that it took my breath away, even though I knew the ending already as I sat reading it twenty years later in a dusty file room in New Orleans, one of Johnson's trial attorneys said to the jury, "I ask you to think about what it's going to be like if he goes to the gas chamber, what it will be like there, and I ask you to spare his life."[8] District attorney Evans, a friend of the victim, responded, "I can tell you what it's like. It's a gray room all the way around about like this and there's a bench in it and under that bench, there is a pail of water and above that are two pills, and the Sheriff pulls the handle that drops those pills into water. Then Sam Johnson will take a deep breath and in five or ten seconds his life will be ended. There will be no pain, there will be no agony, there will be no suffering...." Apparently Evans couldn't shake the notion that the "ol' sheriff" would exact justice; but in fact, before switching to lethal injection, Mississippi would pay an executioner five hundred dollars to pull, on the warden's order, the lever that dropped the cyanide crystals into the sulfuric acid.[9] And, even as he suggests that the defendant deserves more pain, Evans gives the jurors a version of the death chamber seemingly designed to put them at ease.

The truth is somewhat different: "In 1983, convict Jimmy Lee Gray, convicted of raping and killing a child, died an agonizing death in the gas chamber, his mouth foaming, his eyes rolling, his head slamming into an iron pipe by the chair." Donald Cabana was the Parchman warden when a "headrest" was added to the chair to prevent banging against that pipe. Cabana describes the reality of execution by gas, which helped make him a vocal opponent of capital punishment. Almost as soon as the crystals hit the acid, he writes in an account of the killing of Connie Ray Evans,

> The EKG monitor fluctuated wildly.... With Edward Johnson's execution still fresh in my mind, I knew only too well what to expect.... a cloud of poisonous gas began rising from the floor... [Evans] breathed very deeply several times in rapid succession; then, to my horror, he began holding his breath.... His fingers gripped the arms of the steel chair, and his teeth were clenched.... The veins in his neck were nearly popping... Connie started to inhale in extremely rapid, short bursts. Suddenly his eyes rolled back, revealing nothing but white, then rolled forward again. They grew large, the size of silver dollars, and a wild look of fear engulfed his face.... Connie's muscles strained at every point up and down his body. He was beginning to drool from the corners of his mouth, his face twitching violently. I thanked God that we had installed the device to secure his head. Even strapped firmly as he was, it was a violent, repulsive death. His chest heaved against the leather straps.... Thick, foamy, yellowish saliva began to pour from the corners and bottom of his mouth, and his nose exuded a runny, clear liquid. His eyelids repeatedly fluttered open and shut, as his eyes rolled back out of sight again. His feet strained against the floor, with his toes jerking violently upward.... Somehow it was worse than before, more violent than I had remembered.[10]

A young intern in the district attorney's office had also imagined what the execution of Sam Johnson would be like. After the death sentence was handed down, law student Jeff Weill Sr. wrote a short story remarkable for its melodramatic, soft-core fantasy of a final humiliation of Johnson, with plenty of vomit, piss, and shit, as well as for its pathetic but perhaps earnest blackface: "'No goddamn lawyer gonna get a stay at this time of night,' Sam thought, 'Lazy-ass crackers.'" And, "There was a lot of traffic speeding, but the others were white. That made Sam mad." And, "'White honkey motherfuckers.' Sam clawed at the guard and drew blood.... Two guards sat on him and felt the excrement." The prosecutor's intern mailed the story to one of the defense attorneys.

Twenty years later, I called Weill to ask him what he had had in mind. He was now a private attorney in Jackson, having worked briefly as an assistant district attorney himself. The facts of the case—or rather, the DA's version of them—were fresh in his mind. "I really got spanked" by a judge considering whether the story, first written as a law school class assignment, had constituted evidence of racial bias in the prosecution of the case, he recalled. As for his motivation in writing the piece, "I'm a Christian, and I really wanted to wrestle with the idea of capital punishment—killing somebody—whether or not it was consistent with my faith.... I wanted to put myself in the shoes of somebody on death row." (Most death row inmates "view themselves as normal people caught up in abnormal circumstances," observe Dan Malone and Howard Swindle in their nationwide survey. "Slightly more than half of death row inmates said that except for their death sentences, they consider themselves average people, not much different, in fact, from the jurors who condemned them."[11])

When I asked Weill what had captured his imagination about this one man, he said, among other things, "I'm embarrassed to say it, but I hated him." He recalled his cynicism, which has since waned, that although Johnson had "made a great effort to approach me" at the resentencing hearing, and they did shake hands—"I even remember what it feels like"—he resisted acknowledging Johnson's humanity. "I came down on the side of being in favor of the death penalty," Weill said of his exercise. But "in the last few years, especially in light of the abortion debate, and assisted suicide and other life issues, I've begun to look at life as being much more sacred... I'm fairly ambivalent" on the issue now. He adds that the arguments about lack of deterrence and the arbitrariness of its infliction "are beginning to sway me to your side of the argument. I'm not there yet. God bless your efforts."

"You are not the one executing Samuel Johnson.... He chose that himself when he decided to be a criminal in 1963." The DA's reference was to a felony assault conviction from New York against Sam Johnson. It was the principal aggravating circumstance against Johnson, and Evans mentioned it twenty-two times in his closing statement. That conviction was later thrown out by New York courts, but the Mississippi Supreme Court then ruled that it nevertheless remained a valid basis for imposing death in the Langham case. The issue went to the U.S. Supreme Court, where Mississippi actually argued that the New York conviction provided adequate support for the death penalty *even if it was invalid, since petitioner had served time on the conviction.* In an unusual move, the New York State attorney general filed a brief in support of the prisoner. Mississippi's assistant attorney general Marvin White Jr. told a reporter, "New York doesn't have the death penalty, so I guess they don't understand how the law works."[12]

The U.S. Supreme Court ruled 9 to 0 in Johnson's favor. Justice John Paul Stevens wrote, "Contrary to the opinion expressed by the Mississippi Supreme Court, the fact that the petitioner served time in prison pursuant to an invalid conviction does not make the conviction itself relevant to the sentencing decision.... That petitioner was imprisoned is not proof that he was guilty of the offense; indeed, it would be perverse to treat the imposition of punishment pursuant to an invalid conviction as an aggravating circumstance."[13]

NO SMILING

Samuel Johnson's 1992 resentencing hearing took place in the circuit court in Vicksburg, Mississippi, on a bend of the Mississippi River. The state's case against Johnson had been based largely on the testimony of Anthony Fields, the "black male" who had been sentenced to five years, as an accessory after the fact. Under cross-examination by attorney Clive Stafford-Smith, the state's version of what had happened on Highway 49 unraveled. Several times Fields—whose uncle was a friend of Sheriff Lloyd Jones—was forced to choose between admitting that he had lied at an earlier proceeding and that he was lying at the moment.

But the hearing was not about guilt or innocence; it was about the sentence. Surrounding the high drama of the cross-examination was evidence presented by Stafford-Smith of the racism underlying the prosecution of Johnson. I attended the hearing and spent time with Johnson's family in motel rooms, restaurants, and bars; evidence of continuing racism and dehumanization, some subtle and some shameless, was everywhere. The deputy sheriff who brought Sam Johnson into the courtroom each day instructed the prisoner not to smile at his friends and family in the courtroom, the great majority of whom he had not seen for a decade. Attorney Stafford-Smith was instructed by the same deputy to tell friends and family not to look at or smile at Johnson if they wished to remain in the courtroom. Meanwhile, the prosecutor asked the judge not to allow the jury to see photos of Sam Johnson's family members (his request was denied).

When I attended a parole board hearing for Robert Sawyer at the Louisiana State Penitentiary, I heard a local reporter ask the prosecutor who was arguing against clemency if Sawyer's story had affected her thinking. She responded that everybody has a story, by which she meant that no one's story matters, and continued to argue for killing the brain-damaged man. South Carolina attorney David Bruck has written that "unyielding insistence on the individuality of each condemned man and woman is the heart of the legal struggle against the death penalty. It is also the heart of all democratic feeling and life. Its clearest antithesis is racism. One can thus see why the history of capital punishment should have been, and still is, so inextricably intertwined with race."[14]

One hot afternoon, during what a Dutch filmmaker on the scene called "those long Mississippi minutes," several spectators dozed in the courtroom. The bailiff came over and rapped on the bench to startle one woman out of her slumber, barking, "No sleeping in the courtroom." The woman was wearing jeans, and she was African American; in front of her sat a well-dressed, white woman, whom the bailiff left dozing in peace. Another day, one of Johnson's supporters was stopped at the entrance because he had a soda in his hand; inside the courtroom, a white spectator sat with a drink, undisturbed. Some of Johnson's family were delayed one day on their way to court because troopers had set up a roadblock to check drivers' licenses—just across from the Scottish Inns off Highway 80, where Johnson's family and supporters were staying. The Warren County sheriff came in one day and, while court was in session, walked over to hug Officer Langham's widow, shook hands with each of the five uniformed troopers who sat in a circle around her, shook hands with the prosecutor, slapped and greeted his deputies, then walked past the judge's bench to take his place, foot planted on a railing, and watch the proceedings. The only uniformed officer he failed to acknowledge was the one responsible for transporting the prisoner; that officer was African American.

One of the witnesses hoping to persuade the jurors to resentence Johnson to life was an African-American correctional officer from the Maximum Security Unit at Parchman who had come to know Sam. Another was a white, former police chief of Rochester, New York, who testified that in the 1960s, Johnson had saved his life when his patrol car was overturned during a riot. Sam's sick father was permitted to appear on videotape, holding a photo of his son in military uniform. Jane Schutt, a seventy-nine-year-old white woman, testified that she had come to know Johnson through letters after reading his article about the prosecution and execution of Edward Earl Johnson.[15] Schutt said that the article rang true to her based on her knowledge of race relations in the area. The prosecutor indignantly asked her where she had come by this knowledge. She explained that in the 1960s she had served as Mississippi's representative to the U.S. Commission on Civil Rights. And things haven't changed since then? the prosecutor demanded. *Some* things had, she responded. On a Saturday morning, as we waited for the verdict, I spoke with one of Johnson's pen pals, who recalled how her mother used to cook for the Freedom Riders when they came through town. She also remembered sitting up nights behind her father, at the window with his shotgun, all the lights on, when black homes all over the county were being bombed.

In Mississippi's capital sentencing scheme, death can only be imposed by unanimous vote of the jury. Johnson's resentencing jury voted for death, but the vote was 7 to 5, so he got life. The seven for death were all white; one of the five for life was white, and the other four were African American.

To the chagrin of some, Mississippi has not executed anyone since 1989, though Parchman has over sixty inmates on death row today. A U.S. Supreme Court ruling on acceptable jury instructions concerning the imposition of death and a lack of funding for state-appointed defense attorneys are among the reasons for the slowdown. A year before Sam Johnson's resentencing, assistant attorney general Marvin White Jr., who prosecuted the case, told the House Judiciary Committee that he opposed national standards on competency of defense counsel in capital cases "[a]s a matter of federalism." He called the move for such standards "another back-door attempt to do what will not be done through the front door and that is to abolish the death penalty in this country or so restrict its application as to effectively abolish it."[16] White told me recently that back when he was in law school, he would probably have said he was against the death penalty, as a result of his "liberal education." Today he freely admits that he and other members of the Association of Government Attorneys in Capital Litigation "jokingly" call themselves the "fryers' club."

The editors of the Jackson *Clarion-Ledger* also remain nostalgic for the day when legalities did not get in the way of justice. In an editorial urging victims' families to pressure the legislature to speed up the killing, the editors write, "While Leo Edwards of Hinds County was the last death row inmate legally executed in Mississippi on June 21, 1989, the truth is that the last death row inmate executed was Donald Ray

Evans. He was stabbed to death by fellow death row inmate Jimmy Mack on Jan. 4, 1999. *Even the condemned men waiting to die on death row can expedite the execution process faster than the state of Mississippi.*"[17]

CORRESPONDENCES

Sam Johnson went on a hunger strike after the killing of Leo Edwards. He wrote, "I don't know whether Leo is (was) guilty of the crimes he was convicted of or not...but I do know that he was victimized by Racism and that it was because of Racism he was murdered[18]...They have been killing us since 'day one' and now that they've allegedly 'moved ahead,' instead of outright lynching us as they used to do, they've started taking us into the courtrooms before lynching us...." Meanwhile, Sam continued, the Republicans and Democrats mouth off about the constitutionality of flag burning. Yet, "I've searched my heart and the deepest recesses of my mind, and I don't hate these people even though I hate what they are doing to us here and all across our country."

Sam had also known Jimmy Lee Gray, who was executed in 1983. He had grown close to Edward Earl Johnson, executed in 1987, who lived two cells away, "and this closeness has me kinda mesed up." Three weeks before the killing of Edward Johnson, Sam wrote, "It's May 1st now and the new day has brought the Commissioner (Cabana), the acting warden (Dwight Presley) and three of their flunkies.... Cabana did most of the talking and showed compassion towards Earl. I'm telling you what Earl told me. What strikes me as strange about the whole episode is that NOW they want to treat Earl humanely. All before now they have treated Earl (and the rest of us too) worse than animals...." In *Fourteen Days in May*, Sam Johnson says of Edward Earl Johnson, "I feel as much a part of him as a person could be.... They've kept him here seven years, killing him daily.... Everyone here is dying tonight...I could never be the same after this...we're supposed to be vicious and cruel, but this goes beyond anything that anyone could ever do." Finally words fail him, and he turns away from the camera.

Jan Arriens saw the documentary in England and, taken with Sam Johnson, wrote him a letter. Out of that evolved an organization, called Lifelines, of people who correspond with death row inmates in the United States.[19] My own correspondence with Johnson began after I met him on a visit to Parchman in late 1986; he cultivated a network of correspondents in order to stay alive. Through Arriens, Johnson contacted Donald Cabana after Cabana left his job at the prison, and they too corresponded for several years. After Sam was moved to the prison in

Leakesville, Cabana, who was teaching criminal justice at the University of Southern Mississippi, took one of his classes to Leakesville so that Sam could speak to the students. He wanted his students to see that even after years on death row, Johnson "didn't look any different than anybody else."

Yet certain lines remain too clearly drawn. This is not, it happens, an essay about a death sentence that was carried out, but it is about how individuals can overcome the state's tendency to make some lives worth more than others and even to make some completely invisible.

As Johnson lay dying of cancer, the Mississippi Department of Corrections (DOC) refused to allow family or friends to visit him. In one case, Sam's doctor had already approved the visit, but no matter. A few years before, a relative who came to visit Sam at Parchman was arrested and jailed for having six dollars in her purse when, according to prison regulations, visitors to the prison were to have a maximum of five dollars on them. Even after Johnson's sentence was changed to life in prison, Parchman kept him on maximum security lockdown for three years before moving him to general population—"to be watched," as he angrily wrote. After fourteen years on death row, and almost twenty years in prison, Samuel Bice Johnson died on March 11, 2001. My letter inviting him to contribute to this volume was returned unopened from the Leakesville prison.

Johnson once wrote me about the arbitrary and arbitrarily shifting rules on mail in the prison: his friend Jan Arriens had sent him two books of stamps in an envelope but "two books of stamps in one envelope constitute a package and I wasn't eligible for a package when he sent them. . . . These people are doing everything possible to cut us off from the outside world." (In 1997, Parchman guards were arrested and charged for illegally interfering with inmate mail.) Johnson was buried in the prisoners' cemetery at Parchman, and although a chaplain there had already agreed to accompany me to the grave, the state denied permission. "It was just a value judgment thing," DOC public information officer Ken Jones told me. "I . . . received my instructions." Chain-of-command, distancing, dehumanization, denial.

Back on a Wednesday evening in 1990, Sam had cheerfully begun a letter to me with these words: "Greetings from Mississippi's rectum. Because of its evacuationary problems, I remain locked."

Mississippi's tight DOC also refused to permit me to interview death row inmates who might agree to speak with me, or to see death row itself. Visits are possible, however, when they suit the dehumanization process. Spokesperson Jones claims that the school tours that visit Parchman do not walk the death row tiers. But according to a man who lives on that tier, the tours only stopped a year earlier. And three men living on the state's death row report that such tours were regular events. One says he used to pull a sheet over his head and growl to give the spectators what they came for; another fantasized about hanging out a sign telling the gawkers to bring snacks next time for feeding.

Spokesperson Jones: "All requests are denied.... You will not be allowed to visit the grounds of the Mississippi State Penitentiary.... We do not allow death row interviews and/or visits on death row." Asked to explain, he recounted that the media have been severely restricted from Parchman ever since some foreign reporters got in and were too critical of the death penalty more than a decade earlier. He was referring to the crew that made the film *Fourteen Days in May*. It is noteworthy that Donald Cabana—who was warden at the time the foreigners got in, who is featured in the film, and who led Edward Johnson into the gas chamber—describes the film crew as "professional" and "unobtrusive."[20] Cabana told me that after the documentary aired he received calls from corrections commissioners around the country praising it and his decision to give the filmmakers access. But Jones noted that the film's producers had "turned around and sold" the film to HBO instead of broadcasting it solely in Britain, as he alleges they had promised; that it was to have been an "objective" film, yet turned out to be "most negative" about capital punishment; and that the producer had even dared to call the governor on the night of the execution to request clemency for the condemned Edward Earl Johnson.

In his essay "The Death of a Murderer?" about his friend Edward Earl Johnson and capital punishment, Sam Johnson wrote, "There is the executioner who, under his black cloak-hood (as if we don't know who he is—This is America, Mr. Executioner, STAND UP for what you do . . . are you ashamed???) . . . with his breath smelling like cyanide, will say: 'No comment.'

"We have nothing to hide," DOC spokesperson Jones said.

To dismiss and depend on our perceptions at the same time is to acknowledge that life means change, and that authority's categories cannot contain us. At the start of our correspondence, Sam Johnson wrote:

> Think that we could write a book together? I've given that thought some thought and how does it sound to you? (smile) . . . I truly would enjoy telling people (in an understandable way) just how fucked up this legal system of ours is. A person doesn't realize just how fucked up our system is until they become enmeshed in it and by that time, it's too late for them to do a damn thing about it. A criminal can't change a damn thing. Know what I mean?

NOTES

1. Samuel B. Johnson, "Death of a Murderer?" (unpublished essay); a much shorter version did appear in *The Other Side*, March 1998, 25.
2. David Oshinsky, *"Worse Than Slavery"* (N.Y.: Free Press, 1996), 209.
3. "Lynch Mob Followed Sam Johnson, Others," *Jackson Advocate*, October 29–November 4, 1992.
4. Ann Coleman, "State's Justice System under Fire . . . . . Again!" *Jackson Advocate*, November 7–13, 1991.
5. *Perkins v. Mississippi*, 455 F.2d 7 (5th Cir. 1972).
6. Oshinsky, *"Worse Than Slavery"*, 233.
7. Ibid., 89.
8. To be clear: this quotation is an excerpt, not the attorney's entire closing statement.
9. Donald A. Cabana, *Death at Midnight: The Confession of an Executioner* (Boston: Northeastern University Press, 1996), 17.
10. Description of the Gray execution: Oshinsky, *"Worse Than Slavery"*, 253. Description of the Evans execution: Cabana, *Death at Midnight*, 188.
11. Dan Malone and Howard Swindle, *America's Condemned: Death Row Inmates in Their Own Words* (Kansas City: Andrews McMeel), 9, 11. The survey was based on the "more than 700" responses to a survey mailed to the "approximately 3000" inmates on death rows at the time.
12. Quoted from Rita Ciolli, "Convict, and NY, vs. Mississippi," *New York Newsday*, May 5, 1988, p. 4. See also "Mississippi Lacks Respect," *New York Times*, June 16, 1988, p. A26; Tamar Lewin, "Justices Resolve an Unusual Capital Case," *New York Times*, June 17, 1988, p. B8; and Richard Prince, "Wall St. Lawyers Save Local Man from Execution," Rochester (N.Y.) *Democrat and Chronicle*, January 13, 1990.
13. *Johnson v. Mississippi*, 486 U.S. 578, 585-86 (1988).
14. David I. Bruck, "Does the Death Penalty Matter? Reflections of a Death Row Lawyer," *Reconstruction* 1, no. (1991), 39.
15. Johnson, "Death of a Murderer?"
16. Testimony at Hearing on Habeas Corpus Reform Measures before U.S. House of Representatives Judiciary Committee, Subcommittee on Civil and Constitutional Rights, May 22, 1991.
17. "Death Penalty System is Broken; State Can Fix It," *Clarion-Ledger* (Jackson, Miss.), editorial, June 24, 2001, p. 4H; emphasis added.
18. See Stephen B. Bright, "Discrimination, Death, and Denial" in this volume, on racial issues in Edwards's jury selection.
18. See Jan Arriens, ed., *Welcome to Hell: Letters and Other Writings by Prisoners on Death Row in the United States* (Cambridge, England: Ian Faulkner, 1991). An expanded edition appeared in the U.S. with a foreword by Sister Helen Prejean (Boston: Northeastern University Press, 1997).
20. Cabana, *Death at Midnight*, 157.

PART III

INEVITABILITY
AND INNOCENCE

6

JOUSTING WITH
THE JUGGERNAUT

ANDREW HAMMEL

T he law isn't justice. It's a very imperfect mechanism. If you press exactly the right buttons and are also lucky, justice may show up in the answer.
— Sewell Endicott, in Raymond Chandler's
The Long Goodbye

INTRODUCTION

If the law is a mechanism, Texas death penalty law is a fearfully efficient one. Texas has executed far more convicts than any other American state since the resumption of the death penalty in 1976, and will soon easily outdistance any other American state with a pace of fifty to sixty executions a year. Observers often call Texas a death penalty *juggernaut*, a word that *Webster's Dictionary* defines as "a massive inexorable force, campaign, movement, or object that crushes whatever is in its path."[1] *Massive*, maybe. But Texas doesn't execute people by the dozens after rudimentary trials, as China does; in fact, Texas doesn't execute many more people than can be expected for a state its size.

Inexorable, definitely. The word captures a feature of Texas' death penalty justice system that distinguishes it from that of any other American state: its unique success not only at imposing, but more importantly at defending and carrying out, the death sentences its criminal justice system generates. Texas prosecutors who ask juries for death sentence get their wish about 80 percent of the time, a higher proportion than in any other death penalty state.[2] The state appeals courts are explicitly committed to upholding virtually all death verdicts, the federal courts almost never reverse the state courts, and the parole board and governor never pardon death row inmates or commute their sentences. In almost no other American state—except, perhaps, Virginia—are the inmate's chances of winning so slim *at every stage* of the process.

I don't have a systematic, empirical explanation for this state of affairs. I do know the system pretty well, though, having worked for four years filing appeals for death row inmates in Texas. Texas' numbers are so high, I think, because the success of the Texas death penalty system creates a vicious circle. Every Texas criminal defense attorney knows the statistics. Those statistics suggest that any given capital case is much more likely to end up in a conviction and death sentence than in any other outcome. This oppressive feeling of inevitability, in turn, affects the way some Texas defense lawyers do their jobs. They view their role as passive and reactive: they do their best to calm the client's nerves, explain his choices, and do a respectable, workmanlike job of representing him. They've decided that the odds of saving the client's life or winning on appeal are virtually nil, no matter what they do, so they don't put in the stringent effort required to give the client a real chance at avoiding execution. That's not to say these lawyers put in no effort at all; they just don't put in *enough* effort to begin winning a lot of cases. The numbers thus keep getting grimmer, completing the circle.

In this essay, I will suggest why executions begin to seem inevitable. For my purposes, I'll refer to a hypothetical defense lawyer, an anonymous composite of dozens whose work I have reviewed to a greater or lesser extent. This lawyer starts out reasonably competent and conscientious. He's not a hero (although there are many heroic death penalty defense attorneys in Texas), but neither is he a knave. Texas' criminal justice system spawns many horror stories of corrupt or incompetent lawyering, but not enough to explain the statistics. Most Texas death row inmates were, in fact, represented by decent lawyers who wanted to save their clients, and who may have started out believing that they could. This is what happened to them.

BUILDING INEVITABILITY

Funding: Lack of Money is the Root of All Evil

Properly representing a capital defendant takes an enormous amount of money: money to hire investigators and experts who will thoroughly explore the defendant's background, money to copy and sort thousands of documents, money to find and interview witnesses, money to pay for legal research and office workers, money to pay the rent. In Texas, as in many southern states, a defense lawyer isn't going to get anywhere near enough money or help to do all these things. Until 1995, the entire amount available to a Texas criminal defense lawyer for investigative and expert assistance in any indigent case—including capital cases—was $500.[3] In Alabama and Mississippi, until recently, the cap on all compensation for court-appointed counsel in capital cases was $1000.[4] By now, you could probably fill a small room with articles, studies, and exposés denouncing the niggardly sums southern legislatures spend on lawyers for poor criminal defendants.[5] Even prosecutors admit that the underfunding of indigent defense is a serious problem.[6]

Some state legislatures, usually after prodding and threats from their courts, have grudgingly tossed a few more dollars at the problem. In Texas, the courts have shown almost no concern about this issue. Funding increases have been piecemeal, concentrated in wealthier urban counties, and in any event, inadequate to boost compensation to more than a fraction of what a private attorney would charge in a capital case.[7] In most cases, the defense attorney must beg the judge for each little chunk of money he needs to prepare his case, and the judge in turn has to justify the outlay to county authorities, who have plenty of things they'd rather do with county funds than pay an accused killer's lawyer. Every funding request is picked apart carefully, and the lawyer knows the money will run out at some point. The constant need to pinch pennies is never far from the lawyer's mind.

The appointed lawyer must perform a kind of draining, humiliating triage. She knows she can't do a complete job with what she's been given, so she begins paring away at the ideal defense, choosing which witnesses not to speak to, which experts not to hire, which documents not to copy. She tries to guess how likely it is that a particular lead will turn up something useful, and then weighs how much it will cost to pursue. If it's little trouble, she'll follow it up even if it's likely a dead end. If it's going to be expensive (such as hiring a neuropsychiatrist for a thorough analysis of the defendant's neurological functioning), she'll have to be certain it will blow the case open before she can justify it. The leads in the middle—the expensive ones that hold uncertain but potentially great promise—get sacrificed. Our hypothetical lawyer struggles against the temptation to take the path of least resistance, which is to take what the state pays her and do whatever amount of work will allow her to turn a profit. Not all succeed.

The Community: Sentencing "Slugs" and "Air Stealers"
In Texas, the same jury that convicted the defendant decides whether to sentence him to death or life in prison. Picking a jury in a death penalty case thus involves thoroughly examining jurors about their views on capital punishment one by one, under oath. The process can take weeks (it's usually twice as long as the trial, if not longer), and results in volume

after mind-numbing volume of interview transcripts. I've read hundreds of these, as have all Texas death penalty lawyers. As tedious as they are, they make us experts on public opinion about this issue.

To understand why Texas juries hand down so many death sentences, you must first realize that they are applying one of the narrowest death penalty laws in the nation. Texas' capital sentencing law focuses the jury's attention almost exclusively on whether the defendant, whom the jury has just found guilty of capital murder, will present "a continuing threat to society." As current U.S. Supreme Court Chief Justice William Rehnquist said about the Texas scheme in 1980, "It is hard to imagine a system of capital sentencing that leaves less discretion in the hands of the jury" consistent with minimum constitutional safeguards.[8] However, the narrowness of the law doesn't explain everything. The sentencing scheme was amended in 1991 to allow much broader consideration of mitigating factors, but this fundamental change seems to have yielded only a slight decrease in prosecutors' success rates.[9]

Texans, as you might imagine, think about violent criminals in ways that make a death penalty defender's job difficult. The basic attitude can be summarized without oversimplifying it at all: If you kill someone intentionally, and you didn't have a good reason for it, you should die. This is the "law-and-order view." It's often accompanied by an appropriate Old Testament reference. The law and order view is concrete: it ignores abstract conceptions of social policy or philosophical debate about limits on state power. Law-and-order jurors conceive of a killer's deeds in terms of free moral agency and strict personal accountability, and they're reluctant to blame society for anything. That is, when they think about a "good reason" for killing someone, they are not thinking about child abuse or poverty. They are thinking about traditional provocation: the victim was sleeping with your wife, or pointing a gun at you, or trying to break into your house. In Texan terms, the victim "needed killin'."

The frequency of violent crime in Texas, and the obsessive news coverage it receives, have entrenched the law-and-order view in all social classes. You're just as likely to hear it from an engineer or marketing executive as you are from a cab driver or construction worker. In my experience, in fact, working-class people may be slightly more likely to express doubts about the death penalty. Some cite their belief in one of the earthier and more forgiving varieties of Christianity that flourish in the south; others admit that they could imagine themselves waiting for the gurney if their lives had taken a few wrong turns. Support for the death penalty can also live next to liberal beliefs in Texans' hearts and minds. Texas Democrats running for statewide office often trumpet their law-and-order views more loudly than Republicans.[10] Nobody doubts the Republicans on this issue: their platform, slightly ominously, calls for enforcement of the death penalty to be "swift and unencumbered."[11]

Law-and-order jurors fall into two general camps, which I call *intu-itive* and *defensive*. Ask an intuitive supporter why he supports the death penalty and he'll often say, "Well, I don't know. I've never really thought about it before." Executions have always been a part of the social back-ground for this sort of juror, and he considers them a given. He thinks the legal system handles them well enough, and basically feels that they represent justice being done to killers. He approves of them in the same vague, unexamined, intuitive way he might approve of parades or corpo-rations. If he's pressed for further explanation, he might halfheartedly invoke deterrence, or retribution, or some other reason that seems to fit into a principled view of how society should operate. If you convince him to abandon that rationale, he'll switch to another. If you challenge that one, he might try yet a third. At some point, he'll jettison the rational-sounding justifications, and insist that "it's just the right thing to do" or "we've just got to have it for some crimes." The intuitive supporter some-times expresses a twinge of sympathy for those who await lethal injec-tion, as if they were the hapless victims of some grim but vital ritual: "I wish we didn't have to execute people, but we do. It's the price we pay to keep order."

Defensive supporters, on the other hand, pay attention to arguments against the death penalty and have responses at the ready. To them, the death penalty is anything but a fixture of society—it's a vulnerable insti-tution that must be defended from the softheaded or corrupt forces that oppose it. I call them defensive because that's how they often sound. Their arguments, like the anti–death penalty arguments they respond to, come straight from the letters-to-the-editor page: "They say it doesn't deter people, but if you think about it, executing someone has to have some effect—it just makes common sense"; "Sure, we could lock them up for life, but it costs too much to keep them in prison"; "Plenty of people grew up poor and were abused as kids, and they didn't go out and kill anybody." You can probably fill in some more yourself. Unlike the intu-itive supporters, the defensive supporters will stubbornly defend their arguments if challenged. The death penalty isn't just "there"—it *should* be there.

Their confidence sometimes strays into belligerence. An aide to Florida's governor remarked that his state should be more like Texas, where authorities "put them on a gurney and rock and roll."[12] Florida Attorney General Bob Butterworth, acknowledging that inmates' hair had ignited during executions in his state's electric chair, snickered, "People who wish to commit murder, they better not do it in the state of Florida because we may have a problem with our electric chair."[13] Johnny Holmes, former district attorney of Harris County, Texas, calls murder defendants "slugs" and jokes openly about inducting them into the "silver needle society."[14] (This society, whose full name is the Silver Needle

Society of the Permanently Rehabilitated, is commemorated by a plaque in the Harris County District Attorney's Office bearing the names of executed inmates from that county.) A juror who served on one of the cases handled by our office summed it up nicely. After reassuring inquisitive appellate attorneys that he hadn't lost a second of sleep since sentencing our client to death, he questioned why any society would keep such an "air stealer" alive long enough to appeal his sentence.

There are sometimes apologies or retractions from the politicians ("Sorry about that. I do understand that executions are serious business after all"), but they just highlight the attitude that made the flippant comment possible. Most such talk is probably nothing more than ghoulish posturing. But there's sometimes a deeper purpose to these bits of sanguinary rhetoric: they proclaim that indifference is a perfectly appropriate reaction to these killers. It's an attempt to cut short introspection about whether the death penalty is right. "If you waste any time thinking about whether it's right to execute these slugs and air stealers," the defensive supporter might say, "you've already begun to let them win."

With that introduction, I will sketch what the jury selection process looks like in a typical Texas capital murder case. First, the law allows both sides to remove from the initial pool of jurors anybody who categorically opposes the death penalty in all cases, or who would automatically give it in all cases.[15] After this initial culling, the prosecutor's demographic advantage comes into play: there are so few remaining jurors who have serious doubts about capital punishment that the prosecutor can remove them all with peremptory challenges (which he can use for any reason and doesn't have to explain). That leaves a pool of people who solidly support the death penalty, but who aren't throbbing with retributive fury. The prosecution and defense each try to skew the picks from the remaining pool to their advantage.

The typical Texas jury, thus, will consist about halfway of hard (usually defensive) death penalty supporters who will likely conclude that the defendant deserves to be executed as soon as they find him guilty, and who will largely ignore mitigation.[16] The other half will be softer (usually intuitive) supporters, who may withhold their final decision about the defendant's fate until the punishment phase, and who may pay attention to mitigating evidence, if it's especially convincing. If the soft supporters voice any doubts about executing the defendant during deliberations, one or two of the hard supporters will usually take the lead in debating, cajoling, or even bullying the pro-life "holdouts" until they agree to vote for death. The defendant's hopes for a life sentence rest on the holdouts' ability to withstand the pressure from fellow jurors. The defensive supporters, having given much thought to the death penalty, have rhetorical ammunition at the ready. When that fails, things can become bizarre. In one case our office handled, the rest of the jury gathered around the holdout juror, laid hands on her, and held an impromptu prayer session to convince her that executing the defendant was the only Christian option. It should come as no surprise that holdout jurors invariably later describe jury service as one of the most spiritually taxing experiences of their lives, and frequently report feeling pressured into death verdicts they didn't really support.

The Courts: Virtuosos of Defeat

There's a perennial debate, which I'm about to grossly oversimplify, between legal scholars who think that judges are generally governed by the rule of law and their more skeptical colleagues who believe that the law is flexible enough to permit judges to pretty straightforwardly vote with their ideological preferences. To put it more academically, the skeptics claim that "legal materials and legal reasoning are sufficiently plastic that they can offer an acceptable post hoc rationalization of whatever result the judge favors, and judges are habitual rationalizers."[17] There's no such debate among criminal defense attorneys. A death row lawyer in Texas who does not subscribe to the skeptical view is either suffering a cognitive deficit that his clients should be warned about or is running for judicial office.

The state and federal courts in Texas use the law to foster the atmosphere of inevitability. No juggernaut, after all, can develop suitable momentum if the courts routinely throw it into reverse by overturning death sentences and remanding cases for new trials. At the state court level, it's not hard to see how politics affect Texas capital cases: Texas judges, during their reelection campaigns, explicitly vow to pound criminal defendants. Texas Court of Criminal Appeals Presiding Judge Sharon Keller recently sent a campaign mailing that pictured a criminal languishing in a cell, above the slogan, "He won't be voting for Judge Sharon Keller." Texas' judicial ethics commission recently reprimanded her colleague, Judge Tom Price, for declaring that he "did not believe in leniency" and had "no feelings" for criminals.[18] Stephen Mansfield was voted onto the same court in 1994 despite the revelation, well before the election, that he'd lied about his credentials and had almost no criminal-law experience. What was important to the voters, apparently, was that he was a Republican and that he promised "greater use of the death penalty, greater use of the harmless-error doctrine [to uphold flawed trials], and sanctions for attorneys who file 'frivolous appeals especially in death penalty cases.'"[19]

Judges aren't supposed to suggest bias toward or against one category of litigants during their election campaigns. Although statements like the ones above seem to be doing just that, the judges insist that these little flourishes merely illustrate their "judicial philosophy," which is allowed by ethics rules. As well, the judges usually accompany the rhetoric with obligatory promises to be fair and impartial. Nobody misses the underlying message, which approximates to this: "I may have to overturn a conviction here and there when a clear, binding rule leaves me no choice, but if there's a way to make a particular criminal defendant lose, I'll make it happen."

The candidates have delivered on their campaign promises with zeal. The Texas Court of Criminal Appeals, the state's highest criminal court and the one that all death penalty direct appeals must pass through, reversed only 8 out of 256 death sentences it reviewed between 1995 and 2000. This is the lowest reversal rate, over that period, of any American death penalty state. Florida's rate, for instance, was 50 percent, and Illinois' was 30 percent.[20] When the court does encounter a rule that seems to force a ruling in an inmate's favor, it often scraps the rule rather than grant relief. Thus the court has, in recent years, overturned dozens of previous decisions, almost always upholding an inmate's conviction after replacing the existing rule with one more favorable to the prosecution.[21]

Things get even more lopsided during habeas corpus appeals, which proceed separately from the direct appeal. In a habeas corpus appeal, the defendant gathers evidence to support his unfair-trial claims, and presents it to the same judge who presided over his initial trial. Typical claims include ineffective assistance of counsel or prosecutorial misconduct. The judge may hold a hearing to resolve factual disputes. To finally decide the case, the judge must create a judicial opinion called Findings of Fact and Conclusions of Law. In this opinion, the judge decides what actually happened (Did the lawyer sleep at trial? Did the prosecutor knowingly withhold evidence helpful to the defense?), and, in the "conclusions of law," applies the law to the facts she's found. The law firm I worked for decided to study these rather obscure appeals, which rarely generate published opinions. From across Texas, we picked at random 103 capital cases that had been filed since 1995, and checked the results.

The defendants lost *every single time*. What's more revealing is how they lost. In over 83 percent of the cases, either the prosecution wrote the judge's opinion for him or the judge copied the prosecution's "proposed" findings almost verbatim. In countless cases, we encountered documents entitled "~~State's Proposed~~ Findings of Fact and Conclusions of Law and Order Denying Relief." The judge had crossed out "state's proposed," added a date and signature at the end, and effortlessly moved the defendant one step closer to death, leaving no perceptible sign of having even read the document.[22] When they draft their "proposed" findings, then, Texas prosecutors know that virtually anything they write will be rubber-stamped by the judge and become an official, binding ruling of the court.

They wield the Napoleonic privilege of crowning their own arguments with victory—every lawyer's dream. They become virtuosos of defeat: in their hands, a claim fails not just because the defendant's proof isn't sufficient, but also because his previous lawyer didn't raise the correct argument, *and* because he didn't raise that incorrect argument in the proper forum, *and* because he used the wrong font in his legal brief, *and* because, in any event, the law doesn't even recognize his claim. Judges occasionally cross out blatantly bogus findings or personal attacks, but everything else gets through. The defense is allowed to submit its own findings, of course. It might as well staple a few pages of the phone book together, for all the effect it will have on the outcome. The process is a joke, a sham. For defense lawyers who want to win, it evokes impotent fury. For those who have already accepted inevitability, it is simply further proof that heroic exertions are pointless.

After a death row inmate has lost all of his state-level appeals, he files a federal habeas corpus appeal seeking independent review of his claims of error by a federal court. The federal courts, at least theoretically, act as backstops. They are meant to independently review the case and catch any serious errors that were overlooked or ignored in the state court system. In Texas, where virtually all death row inmates lose all of their state appeals, federal court is generally the only game in town if you think you have a winning constitutional claim and you would like a new trial.

Appointees of Republican presidents now dominate the U.S. Court of Appeals for the Fifth Circuit, which hears all Texas habeas corpus appeals from death row inmates. To put it diplomatically, these judges don't go out of their way to find constitutional error in death penalty cases; they wouldn't be where they are if they'd shown any inclination to that sort of behavior. The case of *Penry v. Lynaugh* illustrates the Fifth Circuit's approach. In 1989, the U.S. Supreme Court identified a constitutional flaw in Texas' death penalty sentencing scheme. The Court held, essentially, that Texas law's single-minded focus on the defendant's future dangerousness didn't give the jury enough leeway to consider mitigating evidence, such as death row inmate Johnny Paul Penry's evidence of severe mental retardation and child abuse.[23] The Texas Court of Criminal Appeals, in a rare move, made the Supreme Court's judgment retroactive by ruling that death row inmates could raise a Penry claim even if they had not raised it during their trials. Consequently, every one of the some 280 inmates on Texas' death row in 1989 could, at least in theory, petition in state or federal court to have his death sentence thrown out.[24] Most did.

Like many of the Supreme Court's death penalty opinions, *Penry* often reads less like a legal judgment than an essay in political science or moral philosophy. There was no handy summary at the end telling lower courts how to interpret it. The most pressing question was how far to extend *Penry's* reasoning. The Court had decided that the sentencing scheme didn't allow juries to properly consider mitigating evidence such as mental retardation and severe child abuse. But what about other forms of mitigation—the defendant's youth, for instance, or a history of mental illness? *Penry's* language was vague enough to conceivably justify granting an inmate a new trial if he had introduced *any* such mitigating evidence at trial, under the theory that the jury had been unconstitutionally forced to ignore it by the unduly restrictive sentencing law. The state of Oregon, whose death sentencing statute was identical to that of Texas, apparently took this view: it concluded that *Penry* left it no choice but to grant new sentencing hearings to all twenty-three of its death row inmates.[25]

The Texas Court of Criminal Appeals and the Fifth Circuit, by contrast, quickly moved to bar the jailhouse door. Together, they chipped away at *Penry* on two fronts. The first was procedural: they erected several hoops that death row inmates had to prove they had already jumped through in order to have their *Penry* claims heard. For instance, if the inmate's trial lawyer had chosen not to present mitigating evidence at his trial years before, he could not now claim the benefit of *Penry*.[26] The second front had to do with the scope of the decision. When an inmate had successfully navigated the procedural obstacles, he found that the courts had progressively restricted the definition of mitigating evidence that qualified him for a new trial.[27] The joke among capital defenders was that the *Penry* decision had been narrowed to the point that a death row inmate could win under it only if his last name was Penry. That's an exaggeration, of course, but not much of one. After the smoke cleared, only about 7 inmates out of a potential pool of 280 managed to obtain new trials because of the *Penry* decision.

And *Penry* is just one case. Texas state and federal courts have seen thousands of death penalty cases presenting every imaginable issue. Every area of death penalty law has, like *Penry*, been tricked out with dozens of deadly little doctrines that provide overlapping ways for death row inmates to lose their appeals. These doctrines have made denying relief to death row inmates quite straightforward. Gone are the heady days of the early 1980s, when Fifth Circuit judges sometimes publicly agonized over death penalty appeals, or used them as occasions to ponder the frailties of mankind, or locked horns with their more liberal clerks over them. Since 1995, according to my informal estimate as a careful court watcher, the Fifth Circuit has denied relief in at least 95 percent of all death penalty cases. Most capital cases heard by the Fifth Circuit are now resolved without oral argument—many by unpublished opinions, which will never be seen by anybody but the parties to the case. When the court does schedule oral argument in a capital case, the lawyer for the state often doesn't even use the full allotment of time. Their thinking, as they've told me, is that the longer they speak, the more they risk inadvertently saying something that will trouble or anger one of the judges, thus possibly derailing the otherwise inevitable victory that awaits them.

Am I being cynical? Absolutely. A death row lawyer who still believes in comforting legal platitudes such as the rule of lenity (the rule of interpretation that requires that a statutory ambiguity be resolved in the manner more favorable to the accused) or the principle that like cases should be treated alike is like a political prisoner hoping to win his freedom by making thoughtful arguments to the proper undersecretary through the official channels. Such a lawyer will find a brutal bushwhacking around every corner, and his client will be marched to the execution chamber in short order. Cynicism aside, though, the picture I've painted of the appeals process is accurate. I ask the doubter to take a look at the numbers. In recent years, the percentage of inmates who prevailed on *any* of their death penalty appeals has dwindled to the low single digits (or to zero) in every appeals forum available to a Texas death row inmate.

It was not always so. From 1974 to 1995, the number of Texas death penalty cases reversed on appeal was much higher: 31 percent in the Texas Court of Criminal Appeals, and 32 percent in the Fifth Circuit Court of Appeals.[28] The present condition of maximum frustration at *all* levels of the process is not only of recent vintage but also unusual among American death penalty states. In other states, a stingy state supreme court will be balanced out by a more generous federal system—or vice versa. Texas inmates, like those in Virginia, simply have nowhere to turn. There are only two possible explanations for the recent radical decline in the number of appellate reversals. The first is that Texas has recently achieved a virtually flawless death penalty justice system, while the rest of the country remains mired in error. The second is that the Texas death penalty system is still generating plenty of errors and injustices, but that the legislators and judges have together devised a body of law permitting the courts to tolerate or ignore virtually all of them. One need be only a realist, not a cynic, to know which explanation is right.

Crying Uncle

At some point, our hypothetical defense lawyer may conclude that all is lost. Perhaps jury selection went poorly, or whatever minimal investigation he was able to perform yielded nothing helpful, or the crime scene photographs were just too horrifying. At this point, he concludes that his client's fate is sealed. However, he must still go through the motions. Usually, the result is lackluster, paint-by-numbers lawyering. The lawyer files a few motions, cross-examines the right witnesses, objects a few times, and delivers a decent but hardly stirring closing argument.

Occasionally, though, the lawyer gives up not with a whimper but with a bang. One state court habeas corpus appeal that came across my desk was filed on behalf of Robert Earl Carter. Well-prepared death penalty appeals usually run hundreds of pages, and are accompanied by volumes of exhibits and documents. This one was three pages long. It consisted of generic claims of the type distributed on computer diskette at lawyers' conferences. It had probably taken the lawyer ten minutes to throw together. I turned to the final page, and noticed that the lawyer hadn't even bothered to sign or date it. After a futile trip through federal court, Carter was executed on May 31, 2000, having spent an unusually short six years on death row. So much for those infamously long and complex death penalty appeals.

The moment of defeat may happen at trial. Take the case of Wayne East, whose appeal several gifted colleagues of mine handled. East stood trial years ago for robbing and killing an elderly oil heiress in a small North Texas town. To make sure East got what was coming to him, the woman's family had hired a seasoned ex-prosecutor to consult with the local district attorney. The state's case looked airtight, in part because it had concealed evidence from the defense.[29] The defense lawyer's closing argument to the jury started out, as it does in many Texas cases, with a somewhat haphazard attack on inconsistencies in the state's evidence. Then it took a strange turn. The lawyer advised the jury that they had an important decision to make. Whenever he was in that situation, he confided, he always sang "Home on the Range" to help settle his nerves. Then he warbled through the whole song, including, if memory serves, the less famous verses about zephyrs and stars.

A middle-aged lawyer, in a dingy North Texas courtroom in the early 1980s, serenading a bewildered jury with an old frontier ditty while his client's life hangs in the balance. Could there be a more poignant picture of capitulation?

GETTING DOWN WITH THE CAUSE

Anti–death penalty lawyers reject the closed, self-perpetuating logic of defeat that produces capitulations like these. Like any self-styled social vanguard, anti–death penalty lawyers have a detailed worldview—the cause—that sustains them. The basic component of the cause, of course, is opposition to the death penalty. Not all anti–death penalty lawyers are committed moral abolitionists, but just about every one at least opposes capital punishment on procedural grounds. (Even if it were abstractly morally permissible, it can't be done fairly.) Merely opposing the death penalty, though, isn't enough. Many death penalty opponents, fortunately for them, have never had seen the large, color crime-scene photographs of the cruel and shocking mayhem the now condemned inmates have caused. Cause lawyers must be able to look at them and say to themselves, "The man who did this deserves the best representation I have to offer."

To get to this point, they have to go beyond simple opposition to the death penalty and construct a worldview consisting of many separate beliefs and assumptions about society, human nature, and the justice system. When I first started doing this work, I sometimes secretly chuckled at things I heard more experienced cause lawyers say. To a child of the 1980s, the more idealistic pronouncements had a whiff of patchouli about them; and the remarks about the death penalty justice system seemed grotesquely cynical to a newly fledged lawyer. But as I threw myself into the work, I experienced several epiphanies in which I realized just how right they were. It would take an entire book to do justice to the cause in all its complexity. Here, at least, are some of the main tenets of the cause that relate directly to the lawyer's job.

Why We Fight: The Right Side of History
The cause lawyer never doubts that he's on the side of the angels. A colleague once told me he enjoyed his job, despite the frustrations, because he was always wearing the white hat. He lost no sleep anxiously staring at the bedroom ceiling, wondering whether his work was morally sound. Whatever he did, he did to preserve human life—not just one life, but potentially thousands. Cause lawyers consciously think of themselves as avatars of social transformation. They probably won't see the United States abolish the death penalty in their lifetimes, but they have to believe it will happen eventually, and there's enough evidence to that effect to sustain them, especially recently.

To put it horribly tritely, they have a dream. The death penalty in 2001, cause lawyers believe, is like racial segregation in 1930, or slavery in 1830. As entrenched as it now seems, the halting-but-inexorable logic of human progress will reject it one day. When that day comes, arguments for the death penalty, like those for slavery or segregation, will be dismissed as a patchwork of expedient half-truths and rationalizations. Society will collectively smack its forehead and say, "What were we thinking?" Those who fought capital punishment—lawyers among them, but certainly not at the front—will be hailed as visionaries, and celebrated in the pages of as-yet-unwritten books. Who cares whether this happens a decade from now, or a century from now? All that matters is the belief that it will happen at some point. Getting rid of the death penalty is like building a cathedral. Each generation completes only a small portion of the job, but nurtures a sustaining vision of the ultimate result.

The Trial: The Myth of the Inevitable Death Sentence
When the punishment phase of a death penalty trial begins, the defense stands at the bottom of a long and tortuous path. Technically, a Texas jury is to assume that the defendant is entitled to a life sentence, and must require the prosecution to prove beyond a reasonable doubt that the defendant instead deserves execution. However, the jury has just concluded that the defendant in fact committed the crime, and the trauma and outrage caused by the crime scene photographs are still fresh. Their outrage at the defendant's actions is completely justified— even hearing descriptions of the kinds of senseless crimes for which prosecutors seek the death penalty will likely revolt and sicken the average person. The jury views the defendant with unmixed fear and loathing, and many of the jurors will already have come to the unalterable conclusion that he should die.

Because jury verdicts must be unanimous, the defense need persuade only one juror to hold out for life in order to spare a defendant. However, the prosecution's case is far from over. In addition to reemphasizing the facts of the capital murder the defendant committed, the state is entitled to bring in any evidence it can find of the defendant's previous wrongdoing, from serious things like prior assaults to more minor matters such as smoking marijuana, abusing prescription drugs, or just plain being a nasty piece of work. The state then often produces a psychiatrist to testify that the defendant is a sociopath who will surely strike again if not eliminated, and finishes up with wrenching testimony from the victim's family about the loss the defendant has inflicted on them.

In many trials I reviewed, this point is precisely where the will of the defense lawyer crumbles. Throughout the trial, she has entertained the furtive fantasy that the jury will not convict her client, despite strong evidence. Having sensed death's inevitability in the event of conviction, she has done little or nothing to prepare a punishment-phase case. She brings in a few family members to testify to the defendant's previous acts of kindness, or to hint at problems with his upbringing. Finally, the defendant's mother almost always troops up to the witness stand and, sobbing, begs the jury not to kill her son. Our hypothetical lawyer hopes against hope that an impassioned plea from a family member, or a keenly eloquent closing argument, might kindle a spark of mercy. But she doesn't really believe that will happen, and has reconciled herself to her client's fate. She may already be thinking of what she'll say when her performance is challenged on appeal.

The cause lawyer, by contrast, rejects the insidious logic of inevitability. No matter how grievous the defendant's crime, no matter how sordid his criminal past, no matter how many damaging statements he's made, there is *always* a way to convince the jury to spare *any* defendant. In any zealous penalty phase defense, the cause lawyer has two themes—*surface* and *background*. The surface theme guides the presentation of the defense. Perhaps the defendant has positive qualities that lay undeveloped; or his history of abuse, brain damage, or poverty partially explains his crime; or he was a passive follower whose participation in the crime was relatively minor; or some combination of the above.

The background theme is very simple—it's that the defendant is an individual human being with a history, a personality, and some potential. The prosecution focuses solely on the crime and the history of wrongdoing. In prosecution's closing arguments, the defendant is a cardboard cutout villain: an alien, or an animal, or a blank, empty psychopath. But it's never that simple, the defense says; the defendant may be capable of great evil, but also perhaps capable of some good, or of some redemption. While filling out the picture of the defendant, the cause lawyer may even reveal some more nasty facts about him. There are likely to be many—out of the crooked timber of humanity, as Immanuel Kant said, nothing straight was ever made. But given a choice between creating a richer portrait of the defendant and a narrower one that omits some seamy details, the cause lawyer usually chooses the richer one, so long as the seamy details aren't too devastating. You can never predict which of the defendant's traumas, quirks, or weaknesses will resonate with any particular juror. After presenting a thorough, reasonably honest biography of the defendant—complete with telling details—the lawyer turns to the jury and asks each individual juror a simple question: "Do you want to kill this man?"

The cause lawyer won't always win. There are some crimes so incomprehensibly gruesome that a jury of anarchists would condemn their perpetrators. But the only chance she has of winning depends on her adopting an inflexible, categorical commitment to the notion that any client can be spared, no matter what he has done. Many cases will tempt even the cause lawyer to give up. But, like a wayward votary struggling to recapture her ebbing faith, the cause lawyer wills herself to believe again. If she puts in the effort, she will be rewarded. Not always, but often enough to continue believing, and sometimes in cases in which the death penalty had seemed inevitable. By winning a decent number of seemingly "inevitable" cases, she and her comrades keep their states from descending into the spiral of fatalism that threatens to claim Texas.

The Appeals: Changing the Picture

Once a defendant has arrived on death row, the atmosphere of inevitability materializes and announces its arrival as the legal doctrine of finality. The U.S. Supreme Court has described the idea, noting, "no effective judicial system can afford to concede the continuing theoretical possibility that there is error in every trial and that every incarceration is unfounded. At some point the law must convey to those in custody that a wrong has been committed, that consequent punishment has been imposed, that one should no longer look back with the view to resurrecting every imaginable basis for further litigation but rather should look forward to rehabilitation and to becoming a constructive citizen."[30] A death row inmate doesn't have a lot to look forward to. But the paragraph does convey the question-settling, docket-clearing appeal of finality, which has become a watchword of the current Court.

This doctrine is in some tension with the informal rule—still generally observed—that every death row inmate should have one full and fair round of appeals. The legal system reconciles these competing ideals by progressively narrowing the focus of appellate review. When a death penalty appeal starts, there is an official story, a story that is strongly presumed to be correct in every salient detail. The defendant has been convicted and sentenced pursuant to sworn testimony and evidence, as affirmed by a unanimous jury verdict. The appeals court, according to the "presumption of regularity," assumes that what was said at trial was true, and that the procedures were tolerably fair. As the appeal progresses through each layer of review, the presumption of regularity becomes more and more entrenched, and later courts give greater and greater deference to the views of earlier courts. The narrowing process decrees certain issues and claims to be correctly resolved—or not worth bothering over any longer—until only one or two remain.

Our hypothetical defense lawyer, who knows the odds and has reconciled himself to defeat, does the standard job. He takes the transcript of the trial testimony, checks it for obvious errors, and patches together a relatively short document pointing them out and adding some boilerplate claims for good measure ("the death penalty offends the dignity of man" and the like). Because he has done no additional investigation, the appeals court can easily resolve the issues by reference to the trial record. The "human dignity" claims are easily swatted aside: the last thing today's judge imagines himself to be is an apostle of human enlightenment. Because the lawyer has raised no complex or troubling questions—which alone can slow the momentum of the narrowing process—the defendant's appeals move to a quick, superficial and fatal conclusion. These appeals, in turn, perpetuate the vicious circle: the court briskly overrules the trivial and generic arguments it has been presented with; the percentage of successful appeals drops even lower; and the process of filing appeals appears all the more pointless to the next attorney.

The cause lawyer can't prevent the narrowing process, but he can try to ensure that the most important issues survive. He wants to "change the picture" of the case, as death penalty appeals lawyers often say. To do this, the cause lawyer needs facts, not law. If a judge is going to reevaluate a case—something the finality doctrine tells him to do rarely, if at all—it will only be because dogged investigation by the appeals lawyer has revealed serious problems specific to that inmate's particular trial. The cause lawyer reinvestigates the defendant's background, revisits the crime scene, speaks to more witnesses, or reinterviews former attorneys. He seeks facts that chip away at the facade of fairness and regularity: something important the jury never heard about, something that undermines seemingly solid physical evidence, some hitherto concealed document that plants doubts about the motives or honesty of government witnesses. Specifics are key: That witness lied, and I can prove it. The defense lawyer never discovered this important fact, and I can prove it. In Texas, where no death penalty case has been exhaustively investigated prior to trial, it is always possible to discover new information. After this, the appeals lawyer's job is to convince the judge that the new information is important enough to justify a new trial.

Even the most jaundiced judge, after all, wants to do justice. My cynicism about the judicial process is considerable, but not complete. The law still plays some role in deciding the fate of death row inmates, and most judges at least try conscientiously to apply it. But the law in this area is so fraught with adverse judgments that it never, by itself, points the judge unambiguously in the direction of granting relief to a death row inmate. Something more is needed to "push" the judge: to get him to *want* to grant relief. If the cause lawyer can trigger a gut reaction in the appeals judge that the defendant got a raw deal, the law is usually flexible enough to permit the court to fashion some remedy. Just as the court can create an exception to a rule in order to deny relief, it can sometimes create an exception to that exception to shepherd a deserving inmate through the minefield of precedent to the promised land of a new trial.

A recent Fifth Circuit case provides an example. The court granted relief to a Texas death row inmate because his confession had been obtained illegally. (The police detective had ignored the suspect's requests for a lawyer.) Once the court had determined that the defendant's confession was illegal, it had only to determine whether its use against him at trial probably contributed to his conviction. This question is a "no-brainer," as juries tend to pay a lot of attention to confessions. The appeals court, though, went to great lengths to demonstrate that the confession was not only illegal but *probably false*.[31] Until the judges write their memoirs, it won't be possible to prove they found the confession illegal in large part because they had become convinced that the defendant might have been innocent. But no seasoned cause lawyer would doubt it. In Sewell Endicott's terms, the appeals lawyer pressed the right buttons, and, most importantly, *got lucky*—another panel of judges could and would have penned an equally plausible opinion denying relief.

Becoming Jesus Christ: The Perils of the Cause

The cause provides armor against attack, and spiritual nourishment during adversity. But it has many dangers. The first, obviously, is burnout. Believing in the cause requires you essentially to harbor false hopes about the fate of each of your clients to enable you to put the required effort into trying to save them. If indeed you work in Texas, the system will bluntly remind you, year after year, just how false those hopes were. Eventually, the lawyer may conclude that there's simply no point to the process anymore, or that his presence actually adds an undeserved veneer of credibility to a game that is clearly rigged from the outset.

Another danger is pomposity. There's a fine line between righteousness and self-righteousness, and it's impossible to believe in the cause without occasionally crossing that line. Death penalty abolitionists are unusually susceptible to smug tut-tutting, naive or sentimental attitudes toward violent criminals, and cringe-worthy rhetorical overkill. One legendary abolitionist lawyer, presenting an oral argument before the Supreme Court in a 1976 death penalty case, reportedly struck the justices as so self-righteous that one privately dismissed him as a "nut" and another declared, "Now I know what it's like to hear Jesus Christ."[32]

The cause can also create divisions among defense lawyers. The stereotypical crusading anti–death penalty attorney comes from somewhere up north. He arrives in town, straps on his armband, dismisses local attorneys as compromised hacks, and gets down to the business of "putting the system on trial." This stereotype, happily, is less and less true. The growth of the death penalty in the United States has drawn talented lawyers to the cause from all over the country. The level of confrontation has also declined since the early days of anti–death penalty lawyering. Sometimes a ferocious posture is the client's only hope, but many attorneys who've tried it have been chastened by defeat and frustration. The best cause lawyers working today—such as my former colleagues in Texas—try as often as possible to build fruitful relationships with local attorneys. The ideal strategy in any death penalty case often blends the technical sophistication developed by the cause lawyer with the local attorney's invaluable knowledge of the legal and social landscape.

But the ideal strategy is often not good enough. When the cause lawyer loses a client, he steps back to try to glean a lesson from the defeat. Sometimes he decides he's just not cut out for it, and departs for other quarters. In another lawyer, though, the cause may be stronger. "There are thousands of inmates out there awaiting trial or execution," he reasons, "and somebody is going to represent them. If it's not me, then it might be someone who's already succumbed to inevitability." The cause lawyer resumes the stance of chastened, forced optimism, and jousts with the juggernaut again. He won't alone transform the United States into a society that doesn't execute its citizens. He may not save the next client—especially in Texas. But even if he doesn't, he can bear witness, and ensure that the law doesn't take another life without confronting the effect executions have on the ideals it claims to honor.

NOTES

1. "Juggernaut," *Merriam Webster's Collegiate Dictionary*, 10th ed. (Springfield, Mass.: Merriam-Webster, 1997), 633.
2. Mike Tolson and Steve Brewer, "Harris County Is a Pipeline to Death Row," *Houston Chronicle*, February 4, 2001, A1 (reporting that prosecutors obtained death penalty verdicts in 75 percent of the cases in which they were sought in Harris County from 1980 to 2001, and that the proportions were even higher in the counties in which Dallas and San Antonio are located).
3. See *Lackey v. State*, 638 S.W.2d 439, 441 (Tex. Crim. App. 1982) (discussing then-Tex. Code Crim. Proc. art. 26.05).
4. Louis D. Bilionis and Richard A. Rosen, *Lawyers, Arbitrariness and the Eighth Amendment*, 75 Tex. L. Rev. 1301, 1371 (1997).
5. See, e.g., Stephen B. Bright, *Neither Equal Nor Just: The Rationing and Denial of Legal Services to the Poor When Life and Liberty Are at Stake*, 1997 Ann. Surv. Am. Law. 783; Douglas W. Vick, *Poorhouse Justice: Underfunded Indigent Defense Services and Arbitrary Death Sentences*, 43 Buff. L. Rev. 329 (1995); David L. Bazelon, *The Defective Assistance of Counsel*, 42 U. Cinn. L. Rev. 1 (1973).
6. Alan Berlow, "Requiem for a Public Defender," *The American Prospect*, June 5, 2000, 28 (reporting that only two percent of all criminal justice funding goes to indigent defense and noting Attorney General Janet Reno's concern that persistent under-funding of indigent defense will "inevitably erode the community's sense of justice").
7. In Harris County, a large county that provides comparatively generous funding for indigent defense, the defense is still limited to an overall expenditure of about $50,000—a small fraction of what a highly qualified attorney in private practice would charge. See Steve Brewer and Mike Tolson, "Court-Appointed Defense: Critics Charge the System is Unfair," *Houston Chronicle*, February 7, 2001, A13.
8. *Adams v . Texas*, 448 U.S. 38, 54 (1980) (dissenting opinion).
9. See Mike Tolson, "Between Life and Death," *Houston Chronicle*, February 5, 2001, A1 (reporting that from 1996 to 2000, Harris County juries returned death penalty verdicts in 68 percent of eligible cases, a slight decrease from the former rate).
10. One, Democratic former governor Mark White, aired an ad in which he strolled about in front of black-and-white photographs of persons whose executions he had overseen during an earlier term as the state's governor, intoning, "I made sure they received the ultimate penalty: death." Richard Cohen, "Playing Politics With the Death Penalty," *Washington Post*, March 20, 1990, A19. Garry Mauro, who ran as a Democrat against Texas governor George W. Bush in 1998, declared that Texas death row inmate Henry Lee Lucas should be executed for a murder he did not commit, because he was generally a nasty person who had been convicted of other murders. The reporter to whom he made this comment asked him, to make sure, whether he was saying that Lucas should be executed for a murder he didn't commit solely because of "what . . . he might have done in other cases," to which the candidate replied, "That's what I said." He later protested, a little bizarrely, that the paper had "quoted what he said but not what he meant." R. G. Ratcliffe, "Mauro: Bush was Wrong to Grant Lucas Clemency," *Houston Chronicle*, July 1, 1998, A17. As the article's title indicates, Texas Governor George W. Bush had granted Lucas clemency.
11. The platform can be viewed at http://www.texasgop.org/library/RPTPlatform 2000.pdf.
12. Laurie Goering, "Florida Lets Speed Govern Executions," *Chicago Tribune*, February 28, 2000, N1.

13. Jenny Staletovich, "The Electric Chair Power Struggle: Florida's 'Old Sparky' Endures Despite Inefficiency," *Palm Beach Post*, January 2, 2000, at 1A.

14. Mike Tolson, "Capital Punishment Deeply Rooted in South," *Houston Chronicle*, February 5, 2001, A12 (reporting "slug" comment and noting Holmes' advocacy of the "cold" but "realistic" view that Texas juries should not be offered the option of sentencing capital murder defendants to life in prison without parole because that policy shift might reduce the number of death sentences).

15. As a practical matter, this technical parity between the prosecution and the defense favors the prosecution somewhat. Jurors who oppose the death penalty usually do so categorically, making them eligible for removal because they simply will not obey the law and hand down a death sentence if the evidence "requires" it. By contrast, very few jurors genuinely believe that all murderers should always be executed, no matter what. Even if they say this initially, a skilled prosecutor can usually get them to imagine a situation in which they might opt for life imprisonment instead of death. This flexibility makes them legally eligible to serve.

16. A recent comprehensive study of jurors who had served in death penalty cases from many different states (including Texas) found that even before the sentencing hearing had begun, "three out of ten jurors had essentially made up their minds [about the defendant's punishment], and another two in ten were leaning one way or the other...." See William J. Bowers, *The Capital Jury Project: Rationale, Design, and Preview of Early Findings*, 70 Ind. L. J. 1043, 1090 (1995). My experience tells me the proportion is even higher in Texas.

17. Duncan Kennedy, *A Critique of Adjudication (Fin de Siècle)* (Cambridge, Mass.: Harvard University Press, 1997), 159.

18. Bruce Hight, "Judge Violated Conduct Code, Panel Decides," *Austin American Statesman*, January 31, 2001, B1. Judge Price accepted the reprimand graciously, admitting that the need to appeal to voters "sometimes...gets us out of whack with what judges are really supposed to be doing."

19. Stephen Bright, *Elected Judges And The Death Penalty in Texas: Why Full Habeas Corpus Review by Independent Federal Judges Is Indispensable to Protecting Constitutional Rights*, 78 Tex. L. Rev. 1805, 1828 (2000).

20. Sara Rimer and Raymond Bonner, "Capital Punishment in Texas: Bush Candidacy Puts Focus on Executions," *New York Times*, May 14, 2000, A1.

21. See Matthew Paul and Dianne Burch Beckham, *Do the Right Thing: Consistency Isn't Always What it's Cracked Up to Be*, Tex. Law., November 8, 1999, at 19. The lead author of this article was the state's prosecuting attorney, who represented law enforcement before the court of criminal appeals. The article argues that the frequent reversals were justified because they eliminated flawed and unworkable precedents.

22. These findings are presented in chapters 7 and 8 of a report my former law firm released in October of 1998 called *State of Denial: Texas Justice and the Death Penalty*. The report is available online in its entirety at justice.policy. net/proactive/newsroom/release.vtml?id=18860.

23. *Penry v. Lynaugh*, 492 U.S. 302, 319 (1989).

24. The number is from the July 1989 Issue of "Death Row U.S.A.," a report issued by the NAACP Legal Defense Fund, Inc.

25. Mark Ballard, *Oregon's* Penry *Woes Mirror Texas'*, Tex. Law., February 12, 1990.

26. *Black v. Collins*, 962 F.2d 394, 407 (5th Cir. 1992).

27. For a detailed account of the treatment of *Penry* in the lower courts, see Deborah Denno, *Testing Penry and its Progeny*, 22 American J. Crim. L. 8–22 (1994).

28. These numbers are taken from appendices A and B of a comprehensive study of death penalty appeals performed by Columbia University law professor James S. Liebman. The appendices are available online at http://justice.policy.net/jpreport/liebapp3.pdf and http://justice.policy.net/jpreport/liebapp 4.pdf.

29. See *East v. Johnson*, 123 F.3d 235 (5th Cir. 1997) (reversing death sentence on grounds that state had withheld information that key punishment-phase witness had severe mental problems).

30. *Schneckloth v. Bustamonte*, 412 U.S. 218, 262 (1972) (Powell, J., concurring).

31. The case is *Soffar v. Johnson*, 237 F.3d 411 (2000).

32. Edward Lazarus, *Closed Chambers: The Rise, Fall and Future of the Modern Supreme Court* (New York: Random House, 1998), 114.

THE POLITICS OF FINALITY AND THE EXECUTION OF THE INNOCENT: THE CASE OF GARY GRAHAM

MANDY WELCH
RICHARD BURR

reality that the condemned, their lawyers, abolitionists, and even courts and prosecutors have known for years is that innocent people have been wrongfully convicted of capital murder and sentenced to death. This reality burst into public consciousness in January 2000, when Governor George Ryan declared a moratorium on executions in Illinois after the thirteenth person had been released from Illinois' death row because of newly discovered evidence of innocence.

Suddenly Americans began to feel uneasy about the death penalty. Innocent people were not just being wrongly convicted but were also being condemned to die. As a people, we shuddered to think that innocent people may have been mistakenly put to death. The system that produced death sentences, long ignored by most people, began to come under public scrutiny. And because this new public attention was emerging as then-Governor George W. Bush was running for president, a great deal of attention was paid to the question of whether Texas had executed an innocent person during Bush's tenure as governor. Proving that someone who was executed was innocent is somewhere between very difficult and impossible. Most capital murder cases do not turn on DNA evidence. Nevertheless, there is overwhelming evidence that Texas did in fact execute an innocent man while George W. Bush was governor; that man's name was Gary Graham.

What is becoming apparent to the public is what has been apparent to lawyers and judges involved in death penalty cases for years: the process by which death sentences are imposed is flawed, prone to mistakes, and very difficult to make less so. For this reason, innocent people get convicted and sentenced to death, and for reasons we will discuss, the law is indifferent to these mistakes.

The law is presently far behind growing public concern about the trustworthiness of the death penalty process. For more than two decades, vigorous enforcement of the death penalty has been perceived by politicians as an essential condition for political success. Prevailing political wisdom has been that one risks being perceived as "soft on crime" if one questions, much less opposes, the use of the death penalty. By the mid-1980s, politicians who wanted to be perceived as even tougher on crime turned their attention to the large proportion of state death sentences that were being successfully challenged on federal constitutional grounds in the federal courts through habeas corpus proceedings. Concerned not that the states were imposing death sentences en masse in violation of the Constitution, but rather that the federal courts were *reversing too many state-imposed death sentences*, members of Congress began to propose ways in which the scope of the federal court review of state-imposed death sentences could be narrowed, if not virtually eliminated. There followed a ten-year process through which the federal courts, then Congress, accomplished these goals.

In a historic and tragic irony, by January 2000, when public awareness about the flawed processes for imposing the death penalty first dawned and began to grow dramatically, the law governing the review of state death penalty cases in the federal courts had so constricted the federal courts' review that the risk of executing innocent people had increased exponentially. No case better illustrates the collision of these conflicting forces than the case of Gary Graham. Graham was convicted of capital murder and sentenced to death in 1981 for a crime that, by 1993, newly discovered evidence showed he did not commit. For seven years following 1993, Graham tried to get a hearing in the state and federal courts—a proceeding in which the newly discovered evidence of innocence could be presented through the testimony of witnesses, and the fairness of his trial, in which his court-appointed lawyer had failed to find and present the evidence of his innocence, could be examined. No hearing was held for Graham, and on June 22, 2000, he was executed.[1]

This chapter examines through the lens of the Graham case how, at a time when public concern about the flaws in the death penalty process was growing in an unprecedented way, the courts could have failed to intervene. The story is one of politically motivated changes in the legal rules and processes governing federal courts' review of state capital convictions through federal habeas corpus proceedings. Those proceedings are now designed to let even innocent people condemned to death be killed if the evidence of their innocence is discovered too late to be considered by the federal courts. New habeas corpus rules give the need for "finality" in capital cases precedence over the prevention of the wrongful execution of an innocent person. These rules are the reason Gary Graham was executed without a hearing. These rules are the reason any person wrongfully convicted and sentenced to death is at greater risk today of being executed than at any previous time in our history, notwithstanding the increasing public outcry against the death penalty for its tendency to wrongfully convict and sentence innocent people to death.

THE GRAHAM CASE

Gary Graham was convicted of capital murder on October 28, 1981, in Harris County, Texas, for a crime that occurred when he was seventeen years old. He was sentenced to death two days later, on October 30, 1981. His conviction and sentence were upheld by the Texas Court of Criminal Appeals on direct appeal in 1984.[2] His first state and federal habeas corpus petitions were ultimately unsuccessful following an extended period of litigation between 1987 and 1993.[3]

Facts showing that the single eyewitness upon whose testimony Graham was convicted was mistaken, and that Graham was innocent, were first discovered thereafter, in an investigation conducted within the first four months of 1993, nearly twelve years after Graham was convicted. These are the facts that Graham tried for the next seven years to have heard in a hearing in state or federal court. The evidence at trial, and the evidence of innocence discovered twelve years after trial, are discussed next.

THE EVIDENCE AT TRIAL

At about 9:30 P.M. on May 13, 1981, Bobby Grant Lambert left a Safeway grocery store in Houston, Texas. As he walked across the parking lot to his van, a young black man approached him from behind. After a brief confrontation, the black man shot Lambert and fled. Lambert had sixty $100 bills in his pocket when his clothing was examined by the police. No one saw the assailant take any money from Lambert.

At trial, the only evidence connecting Graham to the crime was the testimony of one eyewitness, Bernadine Skillern, who saw the killing at a distance of thirty to forty feet through the windshield of her car in the dimly lit parking lot. Ms. Skillern testified that she had a glimpse of the front of the shooter's face twice—once for a "split second" and again for two or three seconds. After a suggestive identification procedure (which we will detail below), Ms. Skillern picked Graham out of a lineup.

Graham, who was seventeen years old at the time and lived nowhere near the Safeway store, was not a suspect until he was arrested nearly two weeks after the Lambert killing for other robberies and assaults that occurred in different parts of Houston. There was no evidence that Graham knew the victim Bobby Lambert. He had none of Lambert's property; none of Graham's fingerprints, blood, DNA, or hair was found on Lambert or at the scene. No physical or circumstantial evidence whatsoever proved that Graham was at the crime scene.

THE EVIDENCE DISCOVERED TWELVE YEARS AFTER TRIAL

Twelve years after Graham's trial, new lawyers assumed the responsibility of representing Graham. Unlike the lawyers who represented Graham at trial, on appeal, and in his first state and federal habeas corpus proceedings, these lawyers undertook a thorough investigation of the evidence of Graham's guilt and innocence. What they found was profoundly disturbing.

Graham's court-appointed trial lawyer, Ron Mock, had undertaken no investigation of Graham's consistent assertions of innocence because he believed Graham was guilty. This belief was not based on any admission or other information he got from Graham concerning the murder, nor on any evidence connecting Graham to the murder—there was no such evidence—but solely on Graham's admissions that he had committed a number of unrelated robberies and assaults that, by coincidence, took place shortly after the date of Lambert's murder. Convinced of his client's guilt, Mock failed to interview or undertake any investigation of the witnesses at the scene of the Lambert murder, many of whom saw the assailant before and after Lambert's shooting and none of whom, other than Ms. Skillern, identified Graham. In addition, Mock failed to present to the jury substantial evidence, known to him because of his review of the police report, that Ms. Skillern's identification was the product of a suggestive identification process rather than her observations at the crime scene, and that the fatal bullet was not fired by the only similar caliber weapon known to be connected to Graham.

EYEWITNESSES

The evidence Mock failed to present to the jury, and about which the jurors were entirely ignorant when they convicted Graham, was rooted in the investigation by the Houston Police Department. Five eyewitnesses were identified by the police as having had the best opportunity to see the shooter—Bernadine Skillern, Daniel Grady, Wilma Amos, Ron Hubbard, and Sherian Etuk. All agreed on the accuracy of the composite drawing made by a police artist with the help of Ms. Skillern. All the eyewitnesses also agreed that the shooter was a young black man, eighteen to twenty-five years old, with a thin face, dark complexion, short "Afro" haircut, and no facial hair, who was wearing a white sport coat and dark pants.

Three of the eyewitnesses, Ms. Skillern, Ms. Amos, and Mr. Grady, were called to testify at Graham's trial. Ms. Skillern described the events she saw and identified Graham as the shooter. Ms. Amos testified about what she saw and said she could not remember what the shooter looked like, but was never asked by either side whether she believed Graham was the shooter. Similarly, Mr. Grady, who had been in a car only a few feet from the shooting, also described only the events he saw, and also testified that he could not describe the shooter, but was not asked whether Graham was the shooter. Clearly, if Amos or Grady *had* identified Graham, the prosecutor would had to have asked them whether Graham was the shooter.

Of more significance is what the jury *did not* hear—and what no judge ever heard in a courtroom under oath, and then evaluated after cross-examination.

Ronald Hubbard, an employee of the grocery store, told the police he had first seen the shooter near the front of the store when he (Hubbard) went out to gather shopping carts prior to the shooting, and then again, as the shooter was fleeing from the parking lot after the shooting; he did not see the actual shooting. At the *very same* lineup where Ms. Skillern picked out Graham, Mr. Hubbard told the police the shooter *was not* in the line-up. Prior to trial, the prosecutor let Ron Mock see the offense report, which included Mr. Hubbard's exclusion of Graham in the lineup.[4] However, no one from the defense ever interviewed Mr. Hubbard, and he never testified in court. Mr. Hubbard is also a long-time employee of the United States Postal Service and is an ordained minister. He has no criminal record.

One of the most compelling eyewitnesses, Sherian Etuk, a female cashier at the store, had seen the shooter just outside the store before he walked into the parking lot. She had observed him only a few feet away for some time. At the moment of the shooting, she was no longer looking out the front of the store, but earlier she had clearly seen the man in the white coat, whom everyone agreed was the shooter. Like the other eyewitnesses, she also told the police that the composite drawing constructed by Ms. Skillern looked like the man she had seen that night. She told Graham's lawyers in 1993 that the shooter's build reminded her of that of her husband, who was 5'3" and weighed 130 pounds. Graham was 5'9" and weighed 150 pounds at the time of the shooting. Ms. Etuk was never interviewed by anyone from the trial defense team and never testified.

When she was shown a photo in 1993 of Graham at age seventeen, Ms. Etuk was certain that Graham *was not* the shooter. As Ms. Etuk explained in her affidavit, "[The shooter's] face was extremely narrow. Just thin from top to bottom. It was not oval shaped. More like oblong. . . . I have been shown four photographs of Gary Graham that I have signed, and they accompany this affidavit. One arrest photo, two photos where Gary is in a lineup with other guys, and one photo where he is dressed nice. None of these photos depict the guy who shot the man out in the parking lot that night. The guy who did it had a thinner face and smaller build."

Ms. Etuk's exclusion of Graham on the basis of his facial features—and even her exclusion on the basis of the shooter's height and weight—were questioned by the prosecution in court papers first filed in 1993. This was the result of a misleading omission in the offense report. In the only passage that describes what Ms. Etuk saw, the report says that *after* the shooting Ms. Etuk looked out the front window into the parking lot to see the shooter backing away from Lambert. On that occasion, Ms. Etuk told the police "she could not see his face due to the glass of the windows and dark parking lot. . . ." The report fails to mention that Ms. Etuk also saw the shooter *prior* to the shooting, up near the front of the store. Her description of this is only in her 1993 affidavit, taken by Graham's counsel. As she explained in that affidavit, on the night of the shooting she had become frustrated with the slowness of payment by a customer and looked out the window at the front of the store, just a few feet away, and "saw a black man dressed really sharply standing by one of the concrete columns outside at the front of the store. He was right up against the window, and appeared to be leaning slightly. I looked at him for quite a while, more than a few seconds. He was looking back in my direction and so I saw him clearly."

Confirmation of the truth of this statement in Ms. Etuk's affidavit—even though this description of seeing the shooter is not in the offense report—comes in two ways. First, the offense report notes that Ms. Etuk was shown a photo array of possible suspects. She excluded everyone in the array but told the police that "the suspect's facial features resembled #207610 but . . . the suspect was much more neat looking than in the photo. . . ." Had she seen the shooter only *after* the shooting—when, according to the offense report, she "could not see his face due to the glass of the windows and the dark parking lot"—Ms. Etuk would not have told the police when she was shown a photo array that "the suspect's facial features resembled" one of the persons depicted in the photo array. She had to have seen the shooter's face as she reports in her affidavit, up close to the store before the shooting, in order to make this observation about the person depicted in the photo array. Second, the police report confirms that the shooter *was* standing in the area where Ms. Etuk saw him just before the shooting. When Ronald Hubbard first saw the man who would later shoot Lambert, Mr. Hubbard told the police, "This man was standing by a concrete column near the [northeast] corner of the front of the store." This is exactly where Ms. Etuk declared in her 1993 affidavit that she first saw the shooter and observed not only his height and weight but also his facial features.

Ms. Etuk was plainly telling the truth in her affidavit. Ms. Etuk is a long-time employee of Harris County Child Protective Services and has no criminal record.

Mr. Hubbard and Ms. Etuk did not know Graham; they were neutral witnesses who willingly gave statements to the police and participated in the investigation. Neither was interviewed by Graham's trial defense team, neither was heard by the jury that convicted Graham, and neither was ever heard by any judge reviewing Graham's case in state and federal habeas corpus proceedings.

The only eyewitness who identified Graham was Bernadine Skillern. Ms. Skillern's opportunity to observe the shooter differed dramatically from the opportunities of Ms. Etuk and Mr. Hubbard. Comparison of the opportunities of these three witnesses to observe the shooter demonstrate that the observations of Ms. Etuk and Mr. Hubbard were more reliable than the observations of Ms. Skillern:

- Ms. Skillern saw the man in the white coat, by her estimate, for a total of a minute or a minute and a half—the time that elapsed from the moment she first saw the shooter approach Lambert, to the end of the incident, when the shooter disappeared into the night. During this time, she had only two brief glimpses of the front of the shooter's face—once for "*a split second*," when she honked her horn to try to prevent the shooting and the shooter glanced at her, and again, for "*two or three seconds*" when the shooter was fleeing and she was following him in her car through the parking lot and he hesitated and glanced at her. During the rest of the time the incident took place, Ms. Skillern had a view of the side of the shooter's face or the back of his head.
- In contrast, Sherian Etuk saw the front of the face of the man in the white coat over a *twenty-to-thirty-minute period* preceding the shooting. Ron Hubbard, though not examining the man in the white coat very long, looked directly into the face of this man as he approached Hubbard on foot just outside the store, as Hubbard said hello to him, and as he walked past Hubbard.

- The lighting conditions in the parking lot where Ms. Skillern observed the shooter were marginal. The shooting took place after 9:00 P.M., and the lot was dark, illuminated only by a few lights.
- In contrast, Ms. Etuk and Mr. Hubbard both saw the shooter in the same place—under the well-lighted overhang immediately in front of the grocery store.
- Ms. Skillern's initial observation of the front of the shooter's face was at a distance of thirty to forty feet through the windshield of her parked car. Ms. Skillern's second observation of the front of the shooter's face was closer—about a car length away—but she was driving and the child who was in the car with her was screaming.
- In contrast, Ms. Etuk's observation of the shooter's face occurred about ten to fifteen feet away through the window glass of the store. Mr. Hubbard, on the other hand, walked within one or two feet of the shooter and saw him unobstructed, face-to-face, as he spoke to the shooter.
- Because she saw the shooter only during the course of the crime, the entire time that Ms. Skillern saw the shooter she was experiencing the trauma of the shooting incident and was under very intense stress.
- In contrast, Ms. Etuk and Mr. Hubbard both observed the shooter without any stressors—no trauma, no negative emotions, no fear of a gun or of being shot, no screaming child in the car. Their observations, for the most part, preceded the shooting.
- Ms. Skillern estimated the shooter's height at between 5'10" and 6'. However, she never expressed any reference point or comparison that she relied on to estimate the shooter's height. She did not, for example, compare the shooter's height to Lambert's height, nor did she compare his height to that of anyone she knew.
- In contrast, Ms. Etuk gauged her estimate of the shooter's height by comparison to her own height, nearly 6', and the height of her husband, who was 5'3". She said that the shooter was about the height of her husband because she could see the crown of his head in the way she could see the crown of her husband's head. Similarly, Mr. Hubbard estimated the shooter's height to be about the same as his mother's, 5'4". Mr. Hubbard developed this impression when he walked right by the shooter and looked at him.[5]

In addition to having had a much poorer opportunity to observe the shooter than Ms. Etuk and Mr. Hubbard, Ms. Skillern was subjected to a highly suggestive identification process. This process likely distorted her memory of the shooter and led her, quite simply, to make a mistaken identification of Graham. Graham's trial counsel also failed to bring out any of this evidence before the jury.

When shown an array of five photos (re-created above), Ms. Skillern saw only one in which the person depicted had a short Afro haircut and no mustache or beard—a photo of Gary Graham. Graham's photo, in the bottom left of the array, was the only photo even close to matching the description of the shooter, with short hair and no facial hair, and his was the only photo that had anything marked out on it. Even then, Ms. Skillern declined to identify Graham as the shooter. She said his photo looked like the shooter, "except the complexion of the suspect she saw on the night of the offense was darker and his face was thinner." Because of this, Ms. Skillern "said she could not say that the man in the photo was the suspect. . . . "

This was a critical observation, because Ms. Skillern's exclusion of Graham when she first saw his photo—on the basis of the shooter's having a thinner face—was consistent with the composite she helped draw of the shooter. A side-by-side comparison of the composite and the booking photo of Gary Graham (illustrated on page 136) shows clearly that the shooter's face, depicted in the composite, was strikingly thinner than Graham's face. Importantly, the composite was constructed long before Graham was ever arrested or became a suspect. Thus, the facial features reflected in the composite are likely to be more accurate than the subsequently seen facial features of Graham.

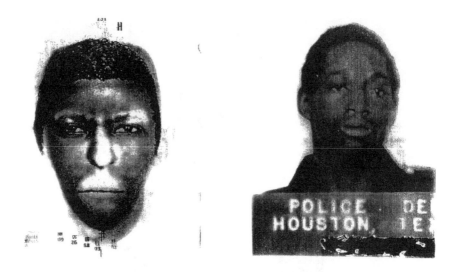

The jury never heard any evidence about Ms. Skillern's exclusion of Graham in the photo array. To the contrary, Ms. Skillern testified—mistakenly—that she did identify Graham from the photo array.[6] The offense report shows that she did not, but Graham's trial counsel failed to bring this to the jury's attention.

On the day after she saw this photo array, Ms. Skillern, along with Ronald Hubbard, viewed a live lineup. The *only* man in the live lineup whose photograph was also in the photo array was Graham. Not surprisingly, she picked him out. Later, she told one of the homicide detectives "that she recognized the suspect she picked out as being in the photo showup she view[ed] the previous night."

Experts say that the likelihood of a false identification under these circumstances is greatly increased, because it is likely that the eyewitness will pick out the person familiar to her because of the recently viewed photograph, not because she had actually seen the person commit the crime. As Elizabeth Loftus, one of the nation's leading experts in eyewitness identification, observed in connection with Ms. Skillern's identification of Gary Graham, "There is no way to determine whether the identification of Graham was based on the photograph or on Skillern's memory of the gunman. However, the risk is substantial that it was based solely on the photograph."

Graham's trial attorneys failed to cross-examine Ms. Skillern in the presence of the jury about the suggestive photo array, her nonidentification of Graham in the photo array, and the suggestive lineup procedure. Nor did they make any other effort to present this information—going to the heart of the reliability of Ms. Skillern's identification of Graham—through any other witnesses.

The composite drawing that Ms. Skillern constructed eleven days before Graham became a suspect—which all the eyewitnesses said was accurate—confirms that Ms. Skillern's identification of Graham was mistaken. Compared to the booking photograph taken when Graham was arrested for an unrelated offense one week after the shooting, the person depicted in the composite is clearly not Graham. The man in the composite has a much thinner face than Graham, just as Ms. Etuk *and* Ms. Skillern said. The jury was not given the opportunity to compare the composite drawing and the booking photo, however, because the composite drawing was not introduced into evidence.

THE FORENSIC EVIDENCE

Bobby Lambert was killed by a .22 caliber bullet. Graham had a .22 caliber pistol when he was arrested several days later. The jury heard the first of these facts in the guilt phase of trial and the second in the penalty phase. However, when deciding whether Graham killed Lambert, the jury did not hear the undisputed conclusion of the Houston Police Department's firearms expert: The fatal bullet could not have been fired from Graham's pistol. As the offense report explained, "The pistol we submitted [taken from Graham upon his arrest] had 8 lands and grooves and the bullet that was submitted from the complainant's [Lambert's] body had only six lands and grooves. Therefor[e] he [the firearms examiner] said it couldn't be the weapon." The only forensic evidence that did exist—a pistol in Graham's possession that was the same caliber as the murder weapon—excluded Graham as the shooter.

MOTIVE EVIDENCE

There was no motive for Graham to kill Lambert; they did not know each other. The state claimed the crime was a robbery gone bad. But Lambert had $6,000 in cash still stuck in his back pocket when the police searched his pants. This was not a robbery.

There *were* people who had a motive to kill Lambert. According to the offense report in Graham's case, before Bobby Lambert's murder, Lambert was facing federal drug trafficking charges in Oklahoma City following his arrest in August, 1980, while "piloting a plane carrying 40,000 Qualudes and several ounces of cocaine" into a small town in

Oklahoma. Investigation conducted by Graham's lawyers in 1999 and 2000 revealed that late in 1980, the drug trafficking charges were dropped against Lambert because Lambert's plane, in which the drugs were found, was searched without a search warrant. Thereafter, the federal prosecutor provided immunity to a reluctant Bobby Lambert to force him to testify before a federal grand jury about the person or persons for whom he was transporting the drugs. Shortly thereafter, Lambert was killed.

In the wake of his death, a Drug Enforcement Administration agent from Oklahoma City called the Houston Police Department about Lambert, noting that "he had a grand jury summons for [Lambert] on a drug related case." The attorney representing Lambert in connection with the federal prosecution in Oklahoma City informed Graham's counsel that he and others involved in this case believed that Lambert was killed by the drug organization for whom he worked to prevent him from testifying before the grand jury. No certain evidence that this was the case had been developed by the time Graham was executed. However, someone plainly had a motive to kill Lambert that Gary Graham did not have.

GRAHAM'S ATTEMPTS TO GAIN A HEARING, 1993–1998

When evidence of innocence that could have been discovered by defense counsel has not been presented at trial, a wrongfully convicted person can attempt to show in state or federal habeas corpus proceedings that his trial counsel provided ineffective assistance in failing to discover and present such evidence.[7] This did not occur in Graham's first state and federal habeas corpus proceedings, however, because the lawyer representing Graham in those proceedings, which took place between 1988 and 1993, also failed to undertake an adequate investigation. That attorney failed, as trial counsel had, to discover and interview the crime scene witnesses whose names were contained in the Houston police offense report, failed to realize the significance of the firearms analysis contained in the police report, and failed to investigate the motive of others to kill Lambert, the seed of which was contained in the police report. Only in connection with a second round of state and federal habeas corpus proceedings in 1993 was the evidence of innocence discovered and presented in papers filed in the state and federal courts.

When this evidence was presented in the 1993 state habeas application, the state courts refused to reexamine their previous conclusions concerning Graham's guilt and denied the application without holding a hearing to evaluate the credibility of the numerous crime scene witnesses, or any of the other evidence that would have exonerated Graham and shown that his trial lawyers provided ineffective assistance.[8] Significantly, as well, the state courts refused to stay Graham's scheduled execution and continue the state habeas proceeding even though Graham was first getting access to the police report on the day the state trial court denied his habeas application. After the state courts had already ruled against Graham, his access to the police report produced more evidence corroborative of his innocence—two more crime scene witnesses who would have exonerated him had they testified at trial, and extensive corroboration of the already-discovered crime scene witnesses' observations that exonerated Graham.

Thereafter, in July 1993, Graham filed a second petition for writ of habeas corpus in the federal district court, one that included the evidence his lawyers had discovered after the state courts had already ruled against him. To be able to have the claims presented in a second federal habeas petition considered, Graham had to show "cause" for failing to raise these claims in his first petition,[9] and "prejudice" or actual harm to his defense at trial because of the constitutional violations underlying his claims. In 1993, the law permitted the claims in a subsequent petition to be considered even if the prisoner could not show "cause" for failing to present the claims in the first petition, if he could show an extraordinary degree of prejudice—that he was convicted even though he was "probably actually innocent."[10]

Graham could not show "cause," because ineffective representation by prior counsel, at trial, on appeal, or in prior habeas corpus proceedings, cannot constitute cause for failing to raise an issue in the first habeas petition—such a factor not being considered "external to the defense." Therefore, his entitlement to have his claims heard in federal habeas proceedings rested on his ability to show that he was convicted even though he was probably actually innocent.

Graham made such a showing—on paper—in his federal habeas petition. The federal district court agreed that he had made the necessary showing, but rejected his claim that his lawyer provided ineffective assistance because of the deference that it believed it had to give to the state habeas court's decision denying the claim.[11] Again, like the state courts, the federal district court refused to hold an evidentiary hearing at which the evidence of Graham's innocence could have been fairly considered.

On appeal to the United States Court of Appeals for the Fifth Circuit, the district court's decision was overturned and its deference to the state court's decision was set aside. In its decision in August, 1996, the Fifth Circuit explained that the facts showing that Graham was innocent and that his trial lawyers provided ineffective assistance were not sufficiently resolved for it to decide the merits of Graham's case—precisely because there had been no evidentiary hearing concerning these issues. The court noted, "The issues in this case are almost exclusively factual, and the relevant factual scenario is complex, highly controverted, and in many respects unresolved. The district court denied the petition without an evidentiary hearing. There is a large body of relevant evidence that has not been presented to the state court. It is doubtful that the record before us allows review of the underlying issues on a fully informed basis."[12]

Because of its view that "a large body of relevant evidence... has not been presented to the state court," the Fifth Circuit decided that the federal habeas proceeding should be dismissed to permit the state courts a further opportunity to resolve the factual questions concerning Graham's innocence. This further opportunity was provided to the state courts in 1998 when Graham filed his third state habeas corpus application. Rather than reconsidering Graham's claims, however, the Court of Criminal Appeals simply decided that the application failed to satisfy the statutory criteria for bringing a subsequent state habeas corpus application and dismissed the application without any hearing.[13] Despite the Fifth Circuit's dismissal of the federal case so that the state courts could hold the sorely needed evidentiary hearing, again no evidentiary hearing was held in which Graham's witnesses' testimony could be heard and evaluated.

GRAHAM'S ATTEMPTS TO GAIN A HEARING, 1998–2000

Immediately after the Texas court's refusal to hold a hearing, Graham returned to federal court—this time to be met with a new, insurmountable barrier to the consideration of his claim of ineffective assistance of counsel and innocence. During the three-year period while the appeal of the denial of the 1993 federal habeas petition was pending (1993–1996), Congress enacted the Anti-Terrorism and Effective Death Penalty Act of 1996 (AEDPA). Among other things, the AEDPA included substantial amendments to the federal habeas corpus statute, all of which were designed to reduce the number of cases in which federal courts could grant relief to prisoners convicted and sentenced in the state courts. One of the changes effected by this legislation was to require federal habeas petitioners who were returning to federal court on a second or subsequent federal habeas petition to show not only what they had to show in 1993—a probability that they were innocent—but also to require a showing of "cause" *even where the prisoner could also show innocence.* To meet this requirement of "cause," the prisoner had to show that the evidence of innocence underlying the claims in the subsequent petition could not have been discovered in connection with a previous federal habeas proceeding by the exercise of "due diligence." In other words, Graham had to prove not only that he was innocent, but also that his original lawyers could not have discovered this evidence of his innocence. Of course, he could not prove that; his original lawyers could have discovered the evidence had they done their job properly, and that is precisely the point.

This new cause requirement precluded any consideration of Graham's claims, for he was unable to show that the evidence of innocence could not have been discovered earlier through the exercise of due diligence. Clearly it could have been, for the leads to all the evidence of innocence were contained in the police report. Indeed, Graham's claim was that trial counsel should have discovered this evidence in connection with trial, because the prosecutor made the offense report available to them. Because of these changes in federal habeas corpus law, the federal district court and the United States Court of Appeals for the Fifth Circuit held that Graham's claims could not be considered at all.[14] On May 1, 2000, the Supreme Court refused to review these decisions.[15]

Shortly thereafter, an execution date of June 22, 2000, was set for Graham. He filed an original habeas petition directly with the U.S. Supreme Court, but the Court denied review and a stay of execution by a 5-to-4 vote. Over waves of protest in Texas and around the country, Governor Bush and the Texas Board of Pardons and Paroles refused to intervene, and Graham was executed.

CONVENTIONAL DEATH PENALTY POLITICS AND THE GROWING PUBLIC DISCOMFORT WITH THE DEATH PENALTY

Gary Graham's execution signals a dramatic milestone in the evolution of conventional death penalty politics. As a result of nearly two decades of political pressure to constrict the federal courts' ability to remedy constitutional violations that occur in state capital trials, Congress has now so misshaped federal habeas corpus law that the federal courts frequently cannot intervene even to stop the execution of a person who is plainly innocent and wrongly convicted. If evidence of innocence is discovered after the condemned prisoner has already been through a first round of federal habeas corpus review, and the evidence could, with due diligence, have been discovered by the lawyers representing the prisoner in the first round of habeas corpus, that evidence cannot be considered by the federal courts in determining whether to stay an execution or remedy a constitutional violation in the prisoner's trial. This is true no matter how strong the evidence of innocence. What matters most is not innocence, but when the evidence of innocence is discovered and whether it is some lawyer's fault for not having discovered it before. If the lawyer is at fault, the innocent prisoner is put to death, just as Gary Graham was. The premium is on finality—on being sure that a condemned prisoner cannot delay his execution by coming into court a second or subsequent time on a claim that should have been brought on his behalf the first time—not on preventing what the Supreme Court recognized as "[t]he quintessential miscarriage of justice... the execution of a person who is entirely innocent."[16]

The tragic irony for the innocent victims of the death penalty, such as Gary Graham, is that the public, in increasing numbers, finds a system of law that permits the execution of the innocent unbelievable and intolerable. At a time when the politics of the death penalty is changing, when conventional politics giving supremacy to finality is beginning to yield to a new politics questioning the death penalty, the federal courts are still manacled to the law that conventional politics produced. There will be changes in the law that reflect the newly emerging politics of the death penalty. There will be a time when it would be not only unthinkable, but illegal, to execute a Gary Graham. But before that time comes, there will be others like Gary Graham, who will be put to death despite clear evidence that they are innocent, because the governing law reflects the view that the need to carry out executions expeditiously is more important than the need to be sure the people being executed are guilty.

NOTES

1. In 1994, Graham changed his name to Shaka Sankofa to reflect and honor his African heritage. He continued to be known as Gary Graham in his case, however, and most people who supported him over the years knew him as Gary Graham. For these reasons, he is referred to here by that name.

2. *Graham v. State*, 675 S.W.2d 529 (Tex.Crim.App. 1984) (table referring to unpublished opinion). The "direct appeal" is the appeal immediately following trial to Texas' highest appellate court with jurisdiction to review criminal cases, the Court of Criminal Appeals. The issues raised in the direct appeal are based solely on the trial court record and must have been somehow "preserved" at trial—by the filing of a motion or other request by defense counsel, or by the making of an objection by defense counsel, which were denied by the trial judge. Any issue based upon facts or evidence not made a part of the trial record, for example, because defense counsel failed to present the testimony of a witness or several witnesses, cannot be raised on direct appeal. That issue must be raised in state habeas corpus proceedings where a record can be made of what the witnesses would have said had they been called.

3. See *Graham v. Johnson*, 168 F.3d 762, 764-767 (5th Cir. 1999) (recounting procedural history of case).

4. The offense report minimizes the significance of Hubbard's exclusion of Graham by noting that Hubbard "indicated to [Detective] Ellis prior to the showup that he did not get a look at the suspect's face at the time of the offense."

   However, Hubbard had been quite specific in describing to the police the shooter's height and build—"5'5", 120–130 lbs"—and it was on the basis of the lineup suspects' build that Mr. Hubbard excluded Graham and all the others in the lineup. In an affidavit provided by Mr. Hubbard in 1993, he explained, "I was unable to pick anyone out of that group that reminded me physically of the guy that shot Mr. Lambert."

Mr. Graham was 5'9" and weighed 150 pounds at the time of his arrest and appearance in the lineup. All the participants in the lineup were approximately the same height and weight. Having estimated the shooter's height as 5'5" and weight as 120–130 pounds, Mr. Hubbard was correct in excluding everyone in the lineup.

5. The other eyewitnesses who in 1993 gave height estimates of the shooter to counsel for Graham, and who made their estimates in relation to their own height or Lambert's height—Wilma Amos and Leodis Wilkerson—estimated, consistent with Ms. Etuk and Mr. Hubbard, that the shooter was shorter than Lambert, who was, according to the autopsy, 5'6".

6. Her testimony was unequivocal:

    Q: Okay, did you again have an occasion to see any photographic displays?
    A: Yes, on the 26th of May two detectives came and brought some pictures to me.
    Q: Did you make an identification at that time?
    A: Yes.

7. The Sixth Amendment to the United States Constitution entitles a person accused in a criminal prosecution to the effective assistance of counsel. The Fourteenth Amendment makes this protection applicable to state criminal prosecutions.

8. *Ex parte Graham*, 853 S.W.2d 564 (Tex.Crim.App. 1993).

9. Cause is defined as "some objective factor external to the defense [that] impeded counsel's efforts to comply with the [rule requiring that all claims be raised in the first petition]." *Murray v. Carrier*, 477 U.S. 478, 488 (1986).

10. See *Kuhlmann v. Wilson*, 477 U.S. 436, 444 n.6, 454 (1986); *McCleskey v. Zant*, 499 U.S. 467, 494 (1991).

11. *Graham v. Collins*, 829 F.Supp. 204 (S.D.Tex. 1993).

12. *Graham v. Johnson*, 94 F.3d 958, 971 (5th Cir. 1996).

13. The Court declared only the following, without explanation: "We have examined the application and find it fails to satisfy Art. 11.071, § 5, and accordingly dismiss the application as an abuse of the writ." *Ex parte Graham*, No. 17, 568-05 (November 18, 1998). Article 11.071 of the Texas Code of Criminal Procedure provides, in pertinent part, as follows:

    (a) If a subsequent application for a writ of habeas corpus is filed after filing an initial application, a court may not consider the merits of or grant relief based on the subsequent application unless the application contains sufficient specific facts establishing that: (1) the current claims and issues have not been and could not have been presented previously....

14. *Graham v. Johnson*, 45 F.Supp.2d 555 (S.D.Tex. 1999). *Graham v. Johnson*, 168 F.3d 762 (5th Cir. 1999).

15. *Graham v. Johnson*, 120 S.Ct. 1830 (2000).

16. *Schlup v. Delo*, 513 U.S. 298, 324–325 (1995).

8

BOB BURTMAN

The State of Texas executed Odell Barnes on March 1, 2000. Except for a smattering of news briefs in big-city dailies, his death went largely unnoticed in the United States. At first glance, Odell's case offered nothing unusual to a public already numbed by the pace of lethal injections in the Lone Star state, which had already dispatched 208 inmates since the death penalty was reinstated there in 1976. Odell would be but one of forty death row inmates executed in the year 2000, an average of one every nine days.

Convicted of a brutal 1989 murder after only three hours of jury deliberations, Odell seemed but another faceless killer with nothing to argue for special attention from the media. Though he had always professed his innocence, he had other felony convictions for rape and robbery that weakened his claim; reporters and editors prefer innocence stories without such shades of gray to confuse the issue. Even an eleventh-hour clemency plea from French prime minister Lionel Jospin to Governor George W. Bush was mentioned in but a few accounts, and then only in passing.

I knew a lot about Odell, having written a lengthy piece about him for the *Houston Press*, an alternative newsweekly. I'd interviewed him in prison, reviewed a dozen boxes of court files and other documents, spoken at length with the attorneys and investigators battling to save his life, and gone to the north Texas city of Wichita Falls to visit the crime scene and talk to the district attorney who had prosecuted him. I'd immersed myself in Odell's life for more than two months.

I was also supposed to watch his execution. Many of those working on Odell's behalf believed he'd at least get a temporary reprieve while the courts considered new evidence, but that was wishful thinking. His execution date fell during Bush's presidential campaign, and the candidates were typically trying to outgun each other on the crime front. No political advantage from a stay of execution would accrue to Bush. No political advantage, no reprieve—it doesn't seem to work any other way in Texas.

Or in many other states. In 1984, North Carolina grandmother Velma Barfield became the first woman executed in the U.S. since the Supreme Court ruled the death penalty constitutional eight years earlier. Convicted of poisoning her fiancé and accused of killing several others to get money for her drug habit, Barfield had turned her life around and become a beloved role model for women inmates throughout the state prison system.

The Democratic governor, Jim Hunt, was in a tight battle for the U.S. Senate seat held by Republican Jesse Helms, and the usual tough-on-crime rhetoric was flying. A Republican judge scheduled Barfield's execution for November 2—the day before the election. Despite support from religious and civic leaders to commute her sentence to life, Hunt declined to intervene and gave the go-ahead. He still lost to Helms.

The *Press* story ran about a month before Odell's date with death, and he had asked me to be there when the deadly chemicals started flowing. But the state said no. Only three categories of witnesses are permitted by law: family members of the victim, friends and family of the condemned, and the media. The slots reserved for the media were already filled, and even though Odell had put me on his personal witness list, prison officials said I couldn't "switch roles"—once a reporter, always a reporter. I was disappointed, but not surprised; it was the typically random, ad-hoc rule making for which the Texas Department of Criminal Justice is notorious.

I've asked myself many times since about that disappointment—where it came from. Partly it was out of deference for the man's last wishes, which seemed reasonable enough to accommodate. I was also intensely curious, both to feel the effects of watching someone die and to compare my reactions with others'. But more than that, I felt it was my responsibility as a journalist to see the execution process. Over the years I've written about the death penalty and debated countless people about its consequences, but I'm not sure anyone can have a complete understanding of what it really means without witnessing the act itself.

Mike Charlton, one of Odell's lawyers, did watch the execution. It was Charlton who had first told me about Odell. He and fellow attorneys Gary Taylor and Philip Wischkaemper had put countless pro bono hours into the effort to save Odell's life—and raised substantial evidence that a miscarriage of justice had occurred. As he described Odell's final hours to me over the telephone, he sounded defeated, as though he somehow hadn't done enough to save his client.

We'd previously worked together on the case of Roy Criner, who had been imprisoned for life for a crime he didn't commit (Charlton eventually helped win Criner's release). While covering that story, I asked Mike to let me know if he ever came across a death row case that had a strong innocence claim. One afternoon late in 1999 he called with not one, but three. The list included Gary Graham, who had already been under the media microscope when his scheduled execution had been postponed earlier that year; Michael Blair, a paroled child molester whose alleged murder of a West Texas six-year-old spurred passage of more than a dozen new laws aimed at sex offenders; and Odell.

The issues surrounding Graham had been thoroughly picked apart as various execution dates had approached and been postponed, and Blair's case was not yet ripe (his attorney was still in the preliminary stages of getting DNA tests that would later cast doubt on his guilt). Odell's case seemed to offer the best opportunity for breaking new ground, and the quickly draining sand in his hourglass added an element of urgency. In addition to the innocence issue, all the classic flaws of the death penalty system were glaringly apparent: a throwaway, indigent defendant; prosecutorial and police ineptitude (and possibly misconduct); inadequate, court-appointed defense counsel; and weak access to the courts on appeal—no matter the evidence.

When Helen Bass didn't show up for work on November 30, 1989, her colleagues grew worried. Bass, a vocational nurse at the state hospital in Wichita Falls, rarely missed a day and always called if a problem arose. Mary Barnes, a friend who often carpooled with Bass and had dropped her off at home the night before, called a neighbor and asked her to drop by the house, a small wood-frame place on Harding Street. The neighbor found the front door open and walked in. She then called the police.

Bass was lying face down on her bed in a pool of blood; an autopsy would later reveal she'd been shot, stabbed, and clubbed with a heavy object. The house was trashed, and blood was smeared throughout the bedroom and elsewhere. Police arrived and began cataloging the evidence, which included a bloody knife, a shoe print on a kicked-in door, cigarette butts, a bloody towel found on the ground outside. Semen in the victim's body indicated she'd been sexually assaulted.

Within a day police had a suspect: Odell Barnes, Mary's son. He had been linked to the crime by an anonymous telephone tipster. A witness interviewed by investigators placed him at the Bass residence the night of the murder. Odell had recently been paroled for armed robbery, and other violent crimes in the same neighborhood—including a murder and rape just five days earlier—were reason enough to suspect him.

Odell was arrested and charged with the killing. Further investigation yielded more evidence: a partial bloody sneaker print (on a checkbook) that might have come from one of his shoes; a fingerprint on a lamp that may have been used to beat the victim; another witness who stated that he'd seen Odell with a gun similar to the murder weapon; lab tests that indicated the semen in the victim may have come from Odell (though DNA testing had not yet advanced enough to prove it conclusively). Moreover, a drop of blood found on the coveralls Odell was wearing when detained matched the victim's blood type. The evidence was circumstantial, but damning on its face.

Since Odell had no money for his defense, his case was assigned to the Wichita County Public Defender's Office. But the staff there had no experience with capital murder defense and begged off, claiming that forcing them to represent Barnes at trial would constitute malpractice. Instead, the judge appointed local defense attorneys Marty Cannedy and Reggie Wilson. Each had tried but one capital case—Wilson as a prosecutor several years earlier. Though Wilson told me the pair hired an investigator and interviewed several witnesses before trial, he couldn't remember any of the particulars. And their rather sketchy notes and presentation at trial offered little to confirm anything but the most superficial of efforts.

During my research, I spoke with investigator Dana Rice of the public defender's office, who had looked into Odell's case as part of the post-conviction appeals process. Though she remains unsure to this day of his guilt or innocence, Rice said she was dismayed by the apparent lack of effort on the part of his defense team. "Probably the most disturbing thing was that his attorneys did not do an investigation," she told me. "I had never seen a case where the defense didn't do anything at all."

The trial lasted two weeks. Prosecutor Barry Macha presented witness Robert Brooks, who testified that while driving home from his girlfriend's house the night of the murder he had seen Odell jump the victim's fence and run off. During cross-examination, defense attorney Cannedy noted that the testimony contradicted the statement Brooks made to police two days after Bass was killed. In the revised version, Brooks was much closer to the fence (making the difficult night-time identification more believable) and was traveling in the opposite direction. But Cannedy failed to drive home a more important point. Brooks was quite sure precisely when he had seen the defendant make his leap: Odell had left the scene forty-five minutes before Helen Bass had arrived home from work.

Pat Williams and Johnny Ray Humphrey, neighborhood residents with long rap sheets for drug and other offenses, also testified for the prosecution. Both were former buddies of Odell, though friendships in their world might more accurately be called alliances of convenience. Williams said he'd seen Odell brandish the gun that night during a drug dispute, and Humphrey said he'd gotten the gun from Odell the next day, after which he'd traded it to Williams for crack. Defense witness Marquita Mackey, herself no stranger to the criminal justice system, told the jury that Humphrey had given her the gun, wrapped in a bloody rag, sometime after the murder, and that she later sold it to Williams.

Macha's case consisted of little beyond that. But it was enough for the jurors, who deliberated only three hours before issuing a guilty verdict. A few days later they meted out the death sentence.

Ordinarily, that would have been that. Had his case been typical, a predictable series of events would have ensued. Odell's court-appointed attorney(s) would file a string of state and federal appeals that would be dismissed without comment. With new federal "fast-track" legislation that restricts death-penalty appeals and hastens the process, he would have faced execution within a decade, and probably much sooner. An execution date would be set, and he'd be put to death.

In 1998, however, U.S. District Judge Sam Cummings appointed attorneys Philip Wischkaemper and Gary Taylor to represent Odell in his habeas corpus appeals. The pool of competent, committed postconviction appellate lawyers in Texas willing to defend death row inmates is small, and Odell lucked into two of the best. They hired a private investigator, Lisa Milstein, who began to dig beneath the surface that had merely been scratched by previous examinations. They recruited Mike Charlton, a seasoned criminal defense lawyer, who joined the fray. Experts were hired to review the evidence.

Though many death row inmates deny their guilt, innocence among that population is not so common. The attorneys I've met who take on the thankless task of representing capital defendants do so in part because they believe the principal that even the guilty are entitled to a defense. At the same time, they know that most of their clients should remain incarcerated for a long time, if not forever.

But as an increasing number of cases around the country have proven, the system is prone to error. And the more the lawyers and investigators learned, the more they became convinced that Odell was one of these mistakes.

Mike Ward, a former police officer, took the job of dissecting the forensic evidence. Unfortunately, as Ward discovered when he traveled to the Wichita County Sheriff's Deptartment, very little of the forensic evidence remained to be dissected. Key items identified in police reports, including the kicked-in entryway door, fingerprint-laden closet doors from the victim's bedroom, and a blood-stained washcloth, had disappeared. The entryway door was eventually discovered, unlabeled, lying in a garage used for storage. The footprint noted on the police report had been wiped clean.

Ward also discovered that blood samples collected from inside and outside the house had never been tested; that the victim's broken fingernails hadn't been scraped to see if she'd scratched her attacker(s), which is standard procedure in homicide cases; that the videotape and still photos of the crime scene were of such poor quality as to be practically worthless. Fingerprints lifted from the scene were never compared to those of anyone other than Odell, and only the lamp print matched his. "It appears to be a less-than-diligent effort," Ward told me diplomatically. "It's the McDonald's style of burger-flipping police work."

The Wichita County authorities might try and discredit Ward for having a stake in the outcome, but they'd have a tougher time with Wichita Falls police detective Bill Pursley, whose assessment was harsher than Ward's. Interviewed by telephone, Pursley said he was especially surprised at the lack of fingerprint comparisons and the improper handling of the evidence. "There were parts of that crime scene that if you read the books today," he said, "you could look back and say, 'Boy, did we do that wrong.'"

Lisa Milstein also went to Wichita Falls and worked the neighborhood, interviewing as many people as she could find who knew the cast of characters. Though none of Milstein's sources would state flatly they knew who had killed Helen Bass, she found plenty of residents who felt strongly that Odell had not taken part in the crime. Even those who suspected his involvement thought he must have had accomplices.

And the evidence strongly suggested multiple perpetrators. It made no sense, for example, that one person would have used three different weapons (a gun, a knife, and a bludgeon), even in a fit of overkill. The fact that blood could have been spattered all over the house without Odell getting more than two nickel-sized drops on his coveralls also defied logic. Why he would have had to smash down the victim's door to gain entry in the first place provided yet another mystery—Bass knew both Odell and his mother well. It was established at trial that Odell had done work on her house on several occasions, which not only meant that he had easy access to the house, but also could explain the fingerprint on the lamp.

Despite the incongruities, the defense team couldn't get past two crucial bits of evidence against him: For one, the semen found in Bass's body, which the state had retested in 1998, belonged to Odell. And DNA tests also proved that one of the blood spots on his coveralls was hers.

Odell had an answer for the first hurdle, claiming that he and Bass had had an ongoing sexual relationship. While prosecutors scoffed that the story was invented years after the crime to explain the conclusive

DNA link, Odell had been telling the same story from the beginning. Two days after he was arrested and jailed, in fact, he told a Wichita County Public Defender's attorney about the tryst, and had written of it in subsequent letters.

An independent forensic scientist, Libby Johnson, further bolstered Odell's version. Johnson analyzed the sperm sample and, by virtue of several biological indicators, concluded that Barnes most likely had sex with the victim at least twenty-four hours prior to her murder. "If they're claiming that he raped her and killed her right away," she told me, "the findings are not consistent with that."

That left the bloodstain on the coveralls. Acting on a hunch, Odell's attorneys sent the sample to blood-preservative expert Kevin Ballard, whose credentials included working on the O. J. Simpson case. Ballard's report shocked even the the most fervent believer in Odell's innocence: Because the stain was loaded with a preservative not found in the human body at such high concentrations, he wrote, the blood had either been accidentally spilled from a sample taken from the victim, or had been planted there.

Scientists are not prone to hyperbole, but Ballard didn't mince words when I asked him about his findings. "This is the most blatant case of tainted evidence I've ever seen," he said.

Odell Barnes tried to con me the moment we started talking. I'd traveled to Huntsville to interview him; it would be our first and last meeting. Odell was smooth and engaging in a way that showed a good deal of street smarts as well as an ability to manipulate people to his advantage. At first he wanted me to think that he was an angel framed by a corrupt system, as he had convinced some of his supporters outside the legal system, including an undetermined number of women with whom he'd corresponded over the years. Some of those women had helped fund his appeals and rallied support for his cause; they thought he'd done nothing worse then smoke a little crack and rip off a convenience store or two.

But Odell had done worse, as Wichita County DA Barry Macha proved in court. His crimes included two armed robberies and rapes he had committed while out on parole, and the testimony of his victims left little room for compassion. Yet as he spoke of his life, stuffed into the interview cage at Ellis Unit, Odell's downward spiral seemed sadly predictable, a fixed-track ride with a prison cell the only possible destination.

It starts in Wichita Falls, a city of 120,000 near the Oklahoma border, unbearably hot in the summer and as frigid in wintertime as anywhere in Texas. Odell came from the East Side, the lower-income part of town where most of the blacks live. The housing stock is crumbling; one of the few successful business ventures is crack dealing. It would not be a stretch to say that the majority of East Side residents have intersected with the criminal justice system at some point in their lives. Escape from the vicious cycle requires a monumental effort of will.

Odell didn't make much of an effort to escape. He didn't have to fall in with the wrong crowd, because the wrong crowd was all he ever knew. When he was in his early teens, his father attacked his mother and Odell shot him in the leg. In high school, he played on the football team, started doing drugs and stealing. Except for the occasional odd job, he had no way to support himself beyond subsistence level.

Eventually he graduated to armed robbery and earned the nickname "Freezer Bandit" for his habit of locking convenience store and restaurant employees in coolers after robbing them. Eventually—inevitably— he was arrested, charged in a pair of holdups, convicted and sentenced to eight years in the state penitentiary. After he had served less than twenty months the state pushed him back onto the streets. He received no treatment or counseling while in prison, but did learn more criminal skills from his fellow inmates. Within days he was back to his old routine.

The police in Wichita Falls have a maintenance program for drug dealers. They know where the crack houses are, but rarely bust them. The locations are no secret—while I was interviewing a source at the restaurant where she worked, an addict walked up and tried to bum money. The addict staggered less than a block to her hangout, a house where people were openly sitting outside in a crack-induced daze while a stream of others pulled up in front, went inside, then exited minutes later and drove off.

Instead, the police allow the status quo to prevail, as long as it stays within the 'hood. When someone gets out of line, they use a network of informants to help remove the offender from society. The informants are often controlled by the threat of probation revocation or other legal troubles if they fail to cooperate. Everyone knows the rules, one of which is: Don't talk to outsiders.

Odell, the police felt certain, had gotten way out of line. Whether they used snitches to pad their case remains a matter of speculation, but two of the key witnesses against him had significant legal problems of their own. Pat Williams, a drug dealer, faced two felony drug charges while Odell awaited trial. Two months before he appeared in court, Williams accepted a plea bargain and got ten years' probation—contrary to the district attorney's policy at the time, which was not to accept plea bargains in any felony drug case, according to sources in his office.

The leniency continued after Odell was sentenced to death. Parole officer Jolene Whitten referred four violation notices against Williams to the DA in the first two years of his probation, where they died. According to written guidelines, the violations should have been passed to a judge for a possible revocation. His probation was eventually cut in half, a privilege usually reserved for those with spotless records. The entire time, neighbors told me, Williams dealt drugs out of his house.

Johnny Ray Humphrey, though under no official sanction at the time of trial, had previously been convicted of drug possession, assault and other assorted crimes. Known to be fond of intoxicants, it would not have taken much to get him under the law enforcement thumb.

It was difficult to find any reliable sources in the incestuous East Side. Reporters come and go, but the residents and police aren't going anywhere, and the disincentive to making waves is high. They might chat with the press, but their stories often conflict, and their distrust of strangers is palpable. After a day in the trenches, I knew one thing for certain: A lot of people knew much more than what they were saying, but I would never hear a word of it.

One of them was Pat Williams, who denied he'd cut a deal with the DA, denied dealing drugs, denied everything. But he did say that he wasn't sure what kind of gun he saw Odell brandish the night of the murder; could have been a .38, could have been a .32. At trial, on the other hand, he was quite sure. As the weapon he bought from Humphrey the day after the killing was displayed in the courtroom, he told the prosecutor, "This is the same gun I seen Odell with."

Seven weeks before Odell's execution, someone did talk. I had found, buried in one of the files, a couple of letters written in 1995 by inmates at the women's prison in Gatesville. Odell did not commit the murder, the letters stated. One of them identified a woman who claimed to be an eye-witness, Felita McKinney. Investigator Lisa Milstein tracked McKinney down. The night Bass died, she told Milstein, she was sleeping in a car that served as home to her ex-boyfriend, Randy Harper. She awoke to see Harper standing outside, covered in blood and holding a gun. She heard another man, who she believes was Johnny Ray Humphrey, ask "Why did you have to shoot her?" Harper then got in the car and warned her to keep quiet about the gun and what she'd seen.

McKinney also said she had never come forward because she feared for her life. Harper had beaten her frequently, she told Milstein, and was capable of extreme violence. Her fears were not idle: Harper had been spent years in prison for various crimes, including assault and armed robbery. He had been most recently paroled in 1999 and was believed to be living near San Antonio, though we couldn't locate him. Police had even tried to interview Harper, but he refused to come to the station, instead conversing by phone with a detective who only asked about his knowledge of Odell's movements before and after the murder.

But McKinney's statement made no difference to the courts, nor did the allegation of evidence-tampering or other leads that pointed away from Odell. One by one, they denied his appeals without comment. Despite the frantic, all-night efforts of the defense team, the freight train had no brakes. Once he was convicted, Odell never had a chance.

A month after Odell's death, I was invited to Paris to discuss his case (and the death penalty in general) with various lawyers, elected officials, and human rights groups. The meetings were arranged by Colette Berthes, an activist who had created an organization focused on Odell. My first meeting was with Robert Badinter, the former minister of justice who had played a pivotal role when France abolished the death penalty in the early 1980s. Badinter also successfully pushed for adoption of an anti–death penalty provision in the European Union charter, which means that any nation wanting to reinstate the death penalty will have to leave the EU, and anyone wishing to join will have to ban executions.

Badinter couldn't understand the bloodlust that seemed to consume so many Americans. For him, killing an innocent person is an intolerable miscarriage of justice, and he will be forever convinced that such a result is unavoidable no matter how diligent the system.

I had similar conversations with dozens of others; almost everyone I spoke with had heard of Odell Barnes. At a gathering of about two hundred students from a university in the south of France, I asked who was familiar with his case; the room filled with waving hands. It would be safe to say that more people in that auditorium knew of Odell's case than in the entire United States outside of Houston and Wichita Falls. That was the media's doing: The French dailies all ran comprehensive stories about Odell, before and after his death, and his face appeared regularly on every television network. Other executions in the United States have received similarly thorough treatment in the European press.

In June 2001, hundreds of delegates from around the world gathered in Strasbourg, France, for an international conference against the death penalty. Badinter gave the keynote address, and the secretary general of the European Union as well as many other luminaries participated. The conference got front-page treatment throughout Europe and as far away as Japan; in the American press, there was no mention.

Clearly, the silence of the media in the United States has contributed to the desensitization of the public to capital punishment. By the time Gary Gilmore went before the firing squad in 1977 and became the first person executed in this country since 1968, he had been immortalized in hundreds of stories and countless hours of videotape about his life and death. Coverage of executions in subsequent years became steadily more superficial and devoid of context.

The 2000 presidential election saw a resurgence of media interest in the death penalty. The *New York Times, Chicago Tribune, Newsweek*, and others wrote lengthy pieces about innocence cases and the flaws of the criminal justice system in Texas and elsewhere. Others followed suit. As a consequence, public opinion began to shift away from unequivocal support for the death penalty. State legislatures considered moratoriums and passed laws expanding inmate access to DNA tests and restricting the execution of the mentally ill.

Though the efforts of the mainstream media were both sincere and effective, the spate of coverage had more to do with the election than some sudden awareness of the system's defects. The death penalty became a hot topic by virtue of George W. Bush's track record in Texas, and the media opportunistically exploited it. Since then, media interest in death penalty issues has waned considerably, though the number of problematic cases offers no shortage of material.

Though the seeds of doubt about the essential fairness of the death penalty have been sown, without continued media scrutiny, the old myths will continue to flourish: that it's a deterrent, that defendants get adequate representation, that the appeals process provides necessary safeguards, that innocent people have never been executed. And that if systemic problems do exist, they can be fixed with a simple tweak here or there.

That ignorance isn't limited to the unwashed masses. After Illinois Governor George Ryan declared a moratorium on the death penalty in 2000, former Texas Attorney General John Cornyn wrote a bizarre op-ed piece defending his own state's record. Illinois and other states may execute innocent people, he opined, but not here, because this is Texas, and we have appeals and other safeguards to prevent it. That every other state had the same mechanisms in place apparently escaped his notice. Several newspapers printed the piece without challenge.

Was Odell Barnes innocent? After my investigation, I was 90 percent sure he did not kill Helen Bass. The other 10 percent has doubts. I found Gary Graham's case more convincing, as well as that of David Spence, executed in 1997 despite the recantings of the witnesses who put him on death row. We'll probably never know, but I have no doubts that more than a few innocent people have died at the hands of the state. And now that the wheels are greased to hasten executions and eliminate appeals in Texas, the certainty that more innocent people will be victims of the death penalty is unavoidable.

Few people want to admit the state makes mistakes, especially one as dramatic as executing an innocent man. Those who participate in the process are understandably among the most rigid in its defense. Barry Macha, the Wichita County DA who prosecuted Odell, told me he had real ethical reservations about the death penalty and used it sparingly, in only the most egregious cases. One was a case in which a man had killed an entire family (whose photos Macha had framed on his office wall). Another was Odell. Macha was quite cordial and forthcoming, promising to rebut the bloodstain report and answer other questions about the case that couldn't be addressed during the initial interview, but he never did.

Odell Barnes grasped the politics of death. When I interviewed him, he seemed remarkably relaxed, almost cheerful, though his execution date was less than two months away. Odell was philosophical about his tiny sliver of a chance for a reprieve and the flood of executions in Texas: "A lot of us understand why it's happening," he said. "I feel that the courts are not reviewing these cases thoroughly. What good does it do to have adequate lawyers if you're not gonna let 'em present what they find? It's more or less a rush process on human lives."

9

CHANCE AND THE EXONERATION OF ANTHONY PORTER

SHAWN ARMBRUST

nthony Porter shuffled into the room and sat across the table from us, clad in the Cook County Jail's khaki prison uniform, handcuffs, and shackles. His cuffed hands pushed four Jolly Rancher candies across the table to his attorney, my investigative journalism professor, a classmate, and me—a college senior at Northwestern University's Medill School of Journalism.

"I'm innocent," he said. "I didn't do this crime."

We told him that we believed him, and the forty-three-year-old death row inmate started sobbing. He apologized to me for "crying in front of the lady," but said we were the first people in seventeen years to believe in his innocence. As we left the jail, Porter lifted his cuffed arms over his head and threw them over each of us, in his best attempt at a hug.

The next time I saw Anthony Porter was seven weeks later, also at the Cook County Jail. This time, Porter ran outside. The next thing I knew, he lifted my professor off the ground in a huge bear hug. I was next, followed by three classmates. A mob of reporters snapped pictures and filmed the release.

Anthony was the tenth inmate since 1977 released from Illinois death row due to a finding of innocence, and the story became particularly newsworthy because I—along with four classmates, our investigative journalism professor and a private investigator—had uncovered the evidence that proved his innocence and led to his release.

That's right. As a twenty-one-year-old undergraduate journalism student, I had the incredible opportunity not only to investigate an old murder case, but to help secure the release of an innocent man from death row. For the next two years, all I heard—from journalists, from politicians, from lawyers, from friends, from everyone—was how inspiring, amazing and wonderful it is that college kids were able to make that kind of impact.

But I just can't look at it that way. The idea that I—at least in some small part—was as a college senior responsible for the life of the crying, shackled man I met in the Cook County Jail is terrifying. It's terrifying because I know that—despite the hard work of my classmates, my professor, our private investigator, and his lawyer—so much of it was sheer luck. Without it, Porter could just as easily have been executed, despite his innocence.

That might sound strange. The idea that approximately 100 innocent persons have been exonerated from U.S. death rows since the death penalty was reinstated has heightened people's sensitivity to the problems in the death penalty system. But it also is oddly comforting that so many have been saved. The perception among much of the public and among most public officials is that the high number of exonerations is proof that "the system works," and that there are adequate safeguards to prevent the execution of the innocent.

That sounds logical, and a few years ago I might have agreed. But the opportunity to work on the case of Anthony Porter changed all of that. From the moment I started reading about the case, it was obvious that the system hadn't done its job. Police officers zeroed in too quickly on one suspect, Porter's trial attorney failed to adequately represent his client, and appeals courts weren't concerned about these blatant injustices. It was up to students—people completely outside the system—to right those wrongs. And the more we investigated, the more it also became obvious that chance was playing a far greater role than it ever should when a person's life is at stake.

On September 28, 1998, I attended my first Media and Capital Punishment class with the journalism school's semi-legendary professor David Protess. I signed up for the class to learn more about the death penalty. It also was unlike any other class at Northwestern—a class in which students were able to investigate old murder cases to determine whether or not prisoners had been wrongfully convicted of the crimes.

As Protess described the first three cases we could choose to work on that semester, I couldn't decide which one sounded the most interesting. The cases of Aaron Patterson, Leamon Jordan, and Nancy Risch all sounded like clear cases of innocence, and I didn't know which one would be best for me. But when he got to the fourth case, I immediately knew what I wanted to do.

It was the case of Anthony Porter, who had been scheduled for execution in Illinois on September 23, five days before that first class. He had received a stay fifty hours before the sentence was to be carried out, after he had been fitted for his burial suit and had ordered his last meal. But Porter hadn't received a stay because anyone thought he was innocent. The Illinois Supreme Court granted it because of his IQ, which had been assessed at 51. His lawyer argued—and the justices agreed—that a hearing should be held to determine whether Porter was mentally competent to be executed, whether he really could understand his punishment.

That's where Protess came in. Porter's lawyer, Daniel R. Sanders, thought his client might be innocent, but he was focused on preparations for the upcoming competency hearing. On a whim, he called Protess and asked if Protess's students could help investigate the case. Luckily, Protess was looking for a new case to take for his class that semester.

He told us on that first day that he had no idea whether Porter was innocent, but that it would be our job to find out. He said there was a lack of physical evidence connecting Porter to the crime, an eyewitness whose story seemed shaky, and a possible alternative suspect named by one of the victim's mothers.

Intrigued by the idea of starting an investigation from scratch, and drawn to the case of a man who needed lots of help in a hurry, I immediately signed up to work on the Porter case. Shortly thereafter, I was joined by three other students, and we immediately started learning all we could about the case—reading transcripts, police reports, appellate briefs, and decisions. Not only did I learn about his case, but I learned about the harsh realities of our death penalty system.

Marilyn Green, nineteen, and Jerry Hilliard, eighteen, were shot to death in the bleachers overlooking a swimming pool in Washington Park on Chicago's South Side shortly after 1:00 A.M. on August 15, 1982. Immediately after the shooting, police interviewed William Taylor, who had been swimming in the park pool when the murders occurred. Taylor at first said he had not seen the person who committed the crime. Later at the station, he said he had seen Anthony Porter—whom he knew from the neighborhood—run by right after he heard the shots. After another seventeen hours of interrogation, Taylor told police that he actually had seen Porter shoot the victims.

When police contacted Marilyn Green's mother, she implicated a man named Alstory Simon, whom she had seen with her daughter and the other victim that night. But it was Porter who interested the police. A gang member, he already had served time for committing a robbery in that same set of Washington Park bleachers. He also was known for mugging people in the neighborhood.

After hearing that his name had been mentioned in connection with the double murder, Anthony Porter went to the police station. Despite his protestations of innocence and the lack of physical evidence connecting him with the murders, he was arrested and charged with the two murders, one count of armed robbery, one count of unlawful restraint, and two counts of unlawful use of weapons.

Porter qualified for representation by the Cook County Public Defender's Office, but his family thought he would be better off with a private lawyer. They retained Chicago attorney Akim Gursel, agreeing to pay him $10,000; later, however, they only could pay him $3,000. Due to lack of funds, Gursel stopped investigating.

In September of 1983, Porter went on trial in Cook County Circuit Court. During the trial, Gursel once fell asleep; the transcript shows that the judge awakened him. After the prosecution rested, Gursel called only two alibi witnesses and a photographer who had taken aerial shots of Washington Park. The jury deliberated nine hours before convicting Porter on all counts.

The next day, Gursel waived Porter's right to a jury for sentencing, and a bench sentencing hearing began. After Porter had been determined eligible for the death penalty, and the judge had determined that there were no sufficient mitigating factors, the judge sentenced Porter to death, calling him "a perverse shark."

In February of 1986, a sharply divided Illinois Supreme Court denied Porter's direct appeal. The principal issue was whether Porter had been denied a fair trial before an impartial jury—one of the jurors knew the female victim's mother. Though three justices argued that Porter should be granted a new trial on these grounds, the four-member majority voted to uphold the conviction—arguing that, when the error was discovered, the trial judge adequately questioned the juror about her potential bias.

Porter then filed a postconviction petition alleging he had been denied effective assistance of counsel by Gursel's failure to locate and call four witnesses from the neighborhood who could have suggested that Alstory Simon and Inez Jackson actually committed the murders. The trial court denied the petition, and the Illinois Supreme Court unanimously affirmed that denial.

In a petition for a federal writ of habeas corpus, Porter asserted essentially the same errors that he had raised in the state courts. A U.S. District Court judge denied relief in 1996. The following year, the denial was unanimously affirmed by the U.S. Court of Appeals for the Seventh Circuit. The U.S. Supreme Court denied certiorari on March 23, 1998, and Porter's execution was set for September 23.

At this point, a volunteer Chicago lawyer, Dan Sanders, took the case and had Porter's IQ tested. His IQ of 51 saved him from being the twelfth person in Illinois executed since the death penalty was reinstated in 1977. It wasn't his obviously inadequate trial counsel, the lack of credible evidence against him or the alternative suspect that saved him. As Sanders put it, "Anthony didn't die because he was dumb."

After studying my first ever death penalty case, I couldn't believe it was handled so poorly. It didn't convince my fellow students and me that Porter was innocent, but it left us angry enough to try to find out.

Once we learned about the case, Professor Protess sent us out on our first real job, reenacting the crime. We set out on a cold November afternoon for Washington Park, a dangerous South Side area that is a far cry from the huge lakefront homes near Northwestern. As we roamed around the park trying to find the pool, we groused that we looked ridiculous and probably weren't going to find anything useful.

When we finally found the pool area and bleachers, we stood around for a while—with huge gusts of wind blowing trial testimony and other papers into the pool—trying to reconstruct where the crime had taken place and where the eyewitness had been. Once we figured it out, I stood in the northwest corner of the bleachers, where the murder had taken place, and my classmates stood at the south end of the pool. I thought I was much too far away for them to see me in the middle of the day, and the crime had occurred at 1:00 A.M.

When I went back to them, they agreed that it was too far away, but they also pointed out that a wrought-iron fence separating the pool and the bleachers kept them from seeing anything at all. As they stood where the eyewitness said he stood, all they could see when looking into the bleachers was a wall of black. So the eyewitness couldn't have seen what he said he saw.

The next task was to interview the eyewitness, William Taylor, who had been interviewed countless times—by police, by earlier defense investigators, and by Porter's current attorney. That job went to Tom McCann—the only man in the group—and Paul Ciolino, a private investigator who helped Protess with his cases.

Paul—a huge man with a Chicago accent straight out of *Saturday Night Live*—was exactly the right guy to accompany the genial, mild-mannered Tom. Together, they found William Taylor in a seedy residence motel on the North Side of Chicago and grilled him. He said he didn't want to get involved or talk at all—that he had been interviewed about this case too many times. But they kept at him, pointing out the inconsistencies in his testimony and telling him what we had seen in the park.

Eventually, Taylor broke down. He said that he had lied—that he hadn't seen Porter in the park that night and had been pressured by the police into naming him. He signed an affidavit a few days later, on December 14, thereby destroying the bulk of the state's case against Anthony Porter.

According to Protess, that wasn't enough. Courts don't really trust witness recantations, and our main job was going to be solving the crime. Luckily, we had an alternative suspect—Alstory Simon—who had fled to Milwaukee soon after the murders. We also were at this point heading home for winter break, and my home happened to be the suburbs of Milwaukee. I spent much of my winter break trying to find information about Simon and trying to find out where his former wife—Inez Jackson—was.

By the time we returned from break, at the beginning of January, 1999, I hadn't had any luck finding Inez Jackson, though I had, with my brother, talked to a few women with the same name.

We decided to try interviewing her nephew, Walter Jackson, who was mentioned in one of the affidavits from Porter's 1995 postconviction petition. Jackson allegedly had lived with Alstory Simon and Inez Jackson at the time of the crime, and we heard that he was in an Illinois prison for committing murder or some other serious crime.

I looked up Walter Jackson on the Illinois Department of Corrections website and found ten men. Protess and I guessed, based on the crime and the age, which was the correct one, and Protess wrote him a letter. We guessed right, and he responded right away.

I went with two female members of our group to visit him the second week in January. With guards standing plastered outside the door of a small room in the prison, we started to interview Jackson, not sure if he'd be willing to talk. He definitely hadn't been willing to talk to Porter's investigator for his postconviction petition.

But he got to the point as soon as we mentioned the murders, telling us that "Alstory's your man." Jackson told us that he was sixteen at the time of the crime and living with his aunt and uncle. His uncle, Simon, was a drug supplier, and Jerry Hilliard was one of his dealers—one who owed Simon a lot of money. When Simon came home that night, he told Jackson that Jerry Hilliard had been "taken care of," and then made Jackson stand guard at the door of the apartment with a gun. The family left the neighborhood a few days later, eventually ending up in Milwaukee.

Jackson signed an affidavit for us two weeks later, and also gave us something much more valuable—a list of relatives who lived in Milwaukee and possibly could help us find Inez Jackson. She was the key to the case, as we thought she had been with Simon at the time of the shootings and possibly could be the only real eyewitness to the crime.

With Jackson's list, I went to Milwaukee for the day with three other group members. We said we weren't going to come back until we found Inez Jackson. I wandered with one student, Cara Rubinsky, around Jackson's former neighborhood, asking for people who knew her; two other students went to the Milwaukee County Courthouse to find addresses for the relatives Walter had given us. They had the most luck, finding addresses for two of the relatives on the list, both nieces. We drove to the first address, and Rubinsky and I got out of my car at a house with boarded-up windows. No one was there. But at the second house, Rubinsky and I went right inside and told the niece that we were looking for Inez Jackson. She immediately gave us an address, and we raced over there.

A young woman answered the door, and Rubinsky and I explained that we were students at Northwestern University and that we were looking for Inez Jackson. A few seconds later, a tiny black woman in a big orange turban emerged from a bedroom.

We weren't supposed to talk about the case—Protess wanted to be there for major interviews. So we gave her our names and gave her the message we had been told to deliver if we found her—that we were Northwestern students here to set up an appointment for her with our professor, who had a message to deliver from a male relative who was incarcerated. She agreed to see us two days later, on January 29.

We arrived again in Milwaukee on the 29th—Protess, Ciolino, Rubinsky, and me—and headed to Jackson's house. We had decided in advance that the best way to talk to her would be to take her to a restaurant, and we took her to John Hawk's Pub, a faux-British pub on the Milwaukee River. The waitress seated us in a huge corner booth, and we started talking. Not about Porter, but about Jackson—her kids, her health (she was HIV-positive) and eventually her ex-husband. As she stared right at me, she told us that Simon used to beat her, that he once took a coathanger to her, and that she often thought he'd kill her. She got progressively more angry, and then Protess suddenly interjected, "Inez, we know what happened that night in Washington Park, so why don't you just tell us?"

Her eyes dropped, and she didn't say anything for a few moments. When she finally looked up again, she didn't look right at any of us as she talked. She gazed off and told the story of that night—that she was sitting next to her husband and two friends, Hilliard and Green, in the bleachers of Washington Park. She and Green were watching the people in the swimming pool, and Hilliard and Simon started to argue about something. She wasn't paying attention, but then she suddenly heard six gunshots. As she screamed, she looked up to see Green and Hilliard slumped over and Simon stuffing the gun down his pants. Simon grabbed her by the arm and dragged her out of the bleachers, telling her to shut up or he'd kill her, too.

Simon watched her like a hawk for the rest of the night, making sure she didn't say a word. And—despite being interviewed numerous times—

she hadn't said a word for seventeen years, until now. She had left him five years ago, and that finally made it possible for her to tell the story.

As she talked, Ciolino fired questions at her and crafted a four-page affidavit at the table. She signed it, and then we took her to my parents' house, where we videotaped her statement in my parents' dining room for CBS News, which had agreed to produce stories on any compelling new evidence we found in the case.

On February 2, a story about Anthony Porter's case ran on the *CBS Evening News*. The next morning, Ciolino decided that he would go to Milwaukee to bring Inez Jackson to Chicago, to keep her safe from Simon. He also said he was going to interview Simon—whose address we had found in the Milwaukee phone book and verified with Inez Jackson—and get him to confess. We didn't think it would happen, but he wanted to try.

But it did. As Ciolino started interviewing Simon, Simon wasn't willing to talk. He insisted that he had nothing to do with the crime and that Ciolino should leave. The interview wasn't going anywhere.

That's when Ciolino heard something in the next room. Though we didn't know it, the *CBS Morning News* was rebroadcasting the story about Porter from the night before—in only five markets in the United States. Believe it or not, Simon's television was turned to CBS, and Ciolino heard the story begin.

Ciolino told Simon to get in there, that there was something he should hear. Simon walked into the next room to see his ex-wife implicating him in a seventeen-year-old murder on national television. Within ten minutes, he was in front of Ciolino's video camera confessing to the crime, saying that he shot the victims in self-defense.

That unbelievable confession added to what already was a media frenzy in Chicago. Thanks to the confession and to the media coverage, Porter was released two days later, on February 5, at the state's request.

So that's it. Yes, the investigation of the Porter case required investigative and strategic skills on the part of Protess and Ciolino, and it required my fellow students and me not to screw anything up. But the bottom line is that we only interviewed four people in our entire investigation, and all of those people had been interviewed before, either by the police or for Porter's 1995 postconviction petition. Two of those people— Inez Jackson and Walter Jackson—admitted that they wanted to talk earlier, but they were both too afraid of Simon to take the risk. And Simon's confession resulted from the bizarre coincidence of the *CBS Morning News* running a story about Porter while Ciolino happened to be in his house.

And that's why the story of Anthony Porter, rather than making me feel ecstatic about a life saved, scares me. If it weren't for an IQ test and some genuinely lucky investigative breaks, Porter would have been executed, and he probably would have been cited as an example of "how the system works" to execute heinous murderers.

Since I learned that lesson in the Porter case, I've had the opportunity to work as the case coordinator at the Center on Wrongful Convictions at the Northwestern University School of Law. I've studied and worked on numerous cases of wrongfully convicted people on death row, and I've learned that the element of chance so apparent in the Porter case is evident in most cases like his.

In the majority of these cases—those of Darby Tillis and Perry Cobb, Dennis Williams and Verneal Jimerson, Kirk Bloodsworth, and many more—the criminal justice system failed them. Police officers, trial attorneys, prosecutors, appellate courts didn't do their fundamental job of protecting the rights of the accused and convicting the guilty. It was actors outside the criminal justice system and a series of lucky coincidences that proved the innocence of these men, thus sparing them from execution.

On the flip side, I, along with the Center on Wrongful Convictions, got involved in the case of Gary Graham, a man who was sentenced to death based on the testimony of a single eyewitness, even though six eyewitnesses said Graham was not the perpetrator. The identification was far more unreliable than William Taylor's identification of Porter, as Taylor actually knew Porter. But Graham never was granted any sort of relief in the courts, and his execution was scheduled for June 22, 2000. Although the Center on Wrongful Convictions and a host of other organizations got involved in publicizing the case, and although it garnered intense media scrutiny, Graham was executed on his scheduled date. Despite obvious questions about Graham's guilt, the Texas Board of Pardons and Paroles and Governor George W. Bush decided that a reprieve was unnecessary.

The totality of this work has left me more convinced than ever that the death penalty system in America is irreparably broken. Proponents of the death penalty will argue that there is no proof that an innocent person has ever been executed in the United States, and that the exoneration of 100 men proves that our current safeguards save the lives of the innocent. Some will even say that there are so many safeguards in place that executions don't happen fast enough.

But those proponents are just plain wrong. My experiences with the Porter case, as well as the Graham case, have proved to me that there are not enough safeguards in the system, and that it requires actors outside the system and some lucky breaks to prove your innocence once you have been sentenced to death.

Regardless of how one feels about the death penalty, I don't think anyone but the most ardent supporter of the practice could be comfortable with a system in which chance—not order or fairness—rules the day. The death penalty—intended to result in the deaths of horrible murderers—could, and probably has, resulted in the deaths of other innocent victims. I don't think the life of Anthony Porter or any other innocent person sentenced to death is worth that risk.

PART IV

INSIDE THE WALLS

10

THE STOPPING POINT: INTERVIEW WITH A TIE-DOWN OFFICER

STACY ABRAMSON
DAVID ISAY

This transcript is taken from a two-hour interview with Fred Allen, former Texas Department of Criminal Justice tie-down officer. Excerpts of this interview, conducted at Allen's home by Sound Portraits producers Abramson and Isay, were used in *Witness to an Execution*, a Peabody Award–winning radio documentary about the men and women who witness and carry out executions in Huntsville, Texas.

Can you tell us a little bit about what your role in executions was?

I started out really early in my career, so I had different job responsibilities. When I was just a correctional officer, I would stay back in the death house with the condemned inmate. They would bring him over from Ellis and as soon as they'd get there we'd make sure that everything was secure.[1] I was for the security, but also to make the individual comfortable. If the inmate was curious about the process, we would tell 'em. We didn't want any secrets back there. We wanted that individual to know that everything would be done professionally, with integrity. Whatever he would ask—within reason—we would accommodate him.

Later on, after you were promoted, you were on the tie-down squad. Can you tell us what that entailed?

The majority of the time I stood on the right side of the cell door. The warden would walk in and tell the individual, "It's time." Another guard would unlock the door and I would tell the individual "Just follow me." We would walk into the death house. I'd tell him, "Sit right down here. Put your head down. Put your feet over here." Then just as soon as he'd sit down we would start strapping him down. I would make sure that all the straps and everything was taken care of, make sure that none of the straps were too loose or too tight. That wouldn't be right. I would take care of those adjustments then exit the death house. I would be one of the last individuals to leave. Lots of times I would exit and go into the witness chamber, on the inmate's family side, because usually if we have family members—you can understand, seeing an individual that's being executed in front of you, as a family member—there's lots of individuals that would break down, would fight. And I would be there just to make sure that we could get them out, that we could get some medical attention if we needed to.

How many executions did you witness?

Over 120. It could be 130. I didn't care to count. I didn't care to keep track of people's names or what they did. All I knew was that I had the final part of the law to carry out. And I wanted to be the person to make sure that everything was being done right. That was my main reason, and then I quit.

Why did you quit?

It was two days after Karla Faye [Tucker] and something triggered within me. I don't know what it was. I was very grateful that Chaplain Pickett was right around the corner because he immediately came over.[2] He knew exactly what I was going through. What it was—all these executions all of a sudden all sprung forward. Something triggered within and everybody—every thought, everything—all the pictures just came rolling through my mind again. I told my warden at that time, "I can't participate no more." I don't want to go back. I don't care to see it on television, in the paper. I just want that part of my life over with. That's all there is to it.

What exactly happened to you?

I was just working in my shop. It was right around six o'clock that all of a sudden I started crying, shaking uncontrollably. I walked back in the house and my wife asked, "What's the matter?" I said, "I don't feel good." I was shaking and tears, uncontrollable tears, were coming out of my eyes. I told her I just thought about that execution that I did two days ago and everybody else's that I was involved with. I said "I need to call Chaplain Pickett." I got him on the phone and he talked to me. It was good, just for him to talk to me. Thirty minutes later I felt anxiety again. I called Chaplain Brazzil.[3] He was real good to talk to also. He even volunteered to come over then and it was already getting late in the evening—eight, nine o'clock. I told him no, I'll be okay. And we talked a good forty-five minutes, maybe closer to an hour, until I called Chaplain Pickett back and asked if he would have some time tomorrow.

He was there as soon as I got off work. We sat on my back porch swing, listened to the roosters and the doves, and we just kind of talked about it. He explained it to the point of—you take a vase and you put a drop of water in it. Every time you put a drop of water in it, it fills up. One last drop of water, it overfills. He said that's how you might want to look at the way you did the executions: you did so much your vase is full now and you're done. You're spilling over and it's over with.

I don't know if it was mental breakdown. I don't know if probably it would be classified as more of a traumatic stress, similar to what individuals in war had. When they come back from war it might be two months, it might be two years, it might be five years, and then all of a sudden one day they're reliving it. All that has to come out. The best thing Chaplain Pickett says is to talk about it, get it out. For the longest time I didn't want to talk about it. I'd rather just put it behind me. I would still rather just rather leave it behind me. Even if I do get it all out, I don't know if it would ever be over with. Some of it is always going to be within me. My main concern right now is these other individuals, the ones who do this procedure now. I hope this doesn't happen to them. And I believe very sincerely that somewhere down the line something will.

How are you feeling right now?

Now I am starting to get—I apologize—now I'm really starting to think of more and more stuff I'd rather keep behind me—I'd rather keep it buried. It's too much to try to bring it back up. There is a certain line that I can express myself with this, and then when I see myself get deeper I see myself withdrawing faster from it. [*Long pause.*] My heart is racing because I'm thinking more and more of it. I really just want to withdraw from it at this point.

Are there other executions that stick in your mind?

I remember some telling jokes all day. I remember one walking the floor—asking him if he needed anything, a cup of coffee, punch, if he wanted a cinnamon roll. Remembering individuals that all they wanted to talk about was Dallas Cowboy football, you know, and he's glad he's going beyond and he's glad that the Dallas stadium has an open roof so that he can still watch 'em. There are so many of them. It's like you take a projector and you got those little slides and you sit there and you just keep hitting a button. Every once in a while you could stop and I can see a picture. But there's just so many of 'em, I just choose to keep my projector unplugged. Everybody says that you can bury it within your mind, but you always have memory. And once it happened it's just like pushing a button and watching it over and over: him, him, him, him.

When you had your breakdown, what was going on? Was it that slide projector going around?

I was seeing pictures of what would happen after the execution. After it was over, we had to go back inside to take the individual off the gurney, and there were a lot of times when you'd go back in there and the individual's eyes are still half open. After you remove 100 or so individuals that you stay back there with a certain length of time in the death house and they're executed, and then you remove them—that's what all came out.

And before Karla Faye Tucker you never had any problems?

No. I was pro–death penalty. I knew that what I was doing was according to the law. I did it sincerely, professionally, with integrity. But my wife would tell you that she could definitely tell afterwards because I would toss and turn at night. She's caught me sleepwalking before. She woke me up a couple of times because I was walking around. She told me that I talk in my sleep, but I sleep so soundly that I don't remember it. She does. She can recall every one of them. She would tell you, two years ago when I quit, how much more relaxed I was.

What do you think it would feel like to go back there?

Oh, just asking that question—even having the little bit of thought of walking back there—you see—I can barely even talk. Right now, I barely know what to tell you. I can feel my heart beating a little faster—the anxiety growing up. The thought of it—no. As soon as I say "no" I can retreat. And when I can retreat I'm better off. I don't want anybody to feel sorry for me or anything like that. I went through this. It's over with now. I am just going to adjust. I was messed up and I'm still going to be messed up. Every time I talk about it, it's going to mess with me. But I'm going to get over it. What kind of help can they give me? If I talk to a psychologist, he's going to tell me that I had a mental relapse. I know this already. Are you going to give me some kind of antidepressive drugs? I'm not a depressed person. I don't need medication. I need life.

Are you aware that there are executions tomorrow, Wednesday and Thursday?

I hear about 'em, just like you tell me now, but like I said before I don't want any part of it. I want to say I don't care, but if you push my buttons,

I'm going to tell you yeah, I do care. But I am not going to go out and pro-claim that it's wrong. I am just a thirty-eight-year-old man that has a family. It's just me and my family. That's the only people I am going to take care of. I'm not going to go out and proclaim right and wrong, make a stand. I am not an individual that—what right do I have to give a mes-sage to anybody?

The main reason I am doing an interview is that it's very easy for the law—for the judge, for the jury—to convict an individual. It's very easy to sentence him and put him over on death row and keep track of him until his date comes. But then you have to carry out that execution. There are individuals that I know of personally who have had trouble with it after so many of 'em, and they choose not to say anything. I don't know if it's because they're still within the system. Somewhere down the line some-thing is going to trigger. Everybody has a stopping point. Everyone has a certain level. That's all there is to it.

NOTES

1. The Ellis Unit, where Texas's death row was housed until 1999, was twelve miles from the death house at the Hunstville "Walls" Unit. Death row is now housed at the Terrell Unit in Livingston, Texas, forty-five miles away.
2. Carroll Pickett was the death-house chaplain from 1980 until his retirement in 1995. He oversaw ninety-five executions.
3. Jim Brazzil is the current death-house chaplain. He had overseen 114 executions at the time of this interview.

11

"THE LINE BETWEEN US AND THEM": INTERVIEW WITH WARDEN DONALD CABANA

MARK DOW

onald A. Cabana is the author of *Death at Midnight: The Confession of an Executioner* (Northeastern University Press, 1996), in which he recounts his role in the executions of Edward Earl Johnson and Connie Ray Evans. Cabana's career in corrections began with a student internship at the Massachusetts Correctional Institution at Bridgewater, the "hospital for the criminally insane," which became the subject of Frederick Wiseman's long-banned cinema verité documentary *Titicut Follies*. He went on to become warden of the Missouri State Penitentiary and of the Mississippi State Penitentiary at Parchman, where Johnson and Evans were killed.

Cabana teaches in the Department of Criminal Justice at the University of Southern Mississippi at Hattiesburg. On the morning I visited his corrections class, he walked in, took attendance, and began preaching. Before moving on to the day's lecture topic (the history of county jails), he read his students an article from the previous day's paper about Jerry Townsend, a mentally retarded man who spent twenty-two years in a Florida prison before DNA evidence exonerated him. "Jeb Bush would say it proves the system works," Cabana told his class, holding up the paper with its small photo of the forty-nine-year-old Townsend. "Tell that to him."

After class, we spoke in Cabana's office. This is an edited transcript of that conversation.

THE SHOES SHE WALKED IN

In this book, readers can see the backgrounds of several prisoners by way of "mitigating evidence" presented by their attorneys. Can you tell us about your family and how you got onto the path that you're on?

What little I know about my biological parents is that my father was an Italian immigrant, and my mother was probably the same. She was a very colorful person, apparently. She had, I think, ten children—the last two born while she was in prison. She was a heroin addict, a hooker, convicted of armed robbery, doing time in New Jersey. She did a lot of other time for checks and stuff like that. She was an interesting person, but I never wanted to know anything about her when I was growing up. I knew I had siblings, but I didn't know anything about them. My parents took care of me since I was placed in foster care when I was six months old, but it took nine years for them to adopt me because my mother was always on the run and couldn't be found, or else she wouldn't agree to terminate her parental rights. All of us were removed from her custody.

I was born in Lowell, Massachusetts, which is a nasty old former mill town, in 1945, literally in one of those typical northeastern, large city rowhouses. I was one of the younger ones, so I heard things from the others—they have lots of recollections, and they have a lot of things to deal with in terms of baggage. They watched the johns being brought home, and they watched the heroin being cooked and shot up, they put up with the sexual abuse from both her and the johns.

At some point—and this sounds like it was almost Dickensian—it was in the winter time, and my sister had no socks, so she put on a pair of shoes that didn't fit, and she tromped through the snow to a neighborhood tavern. She went in and asked the tavern owner if he would give her some milk because I was crying constantly, hadn't been fed in three days. So the tavern owner called the Society for the Prevention of Cruelty to Children, and they in turn contacted—I don't know what they called it then—something like the Massachusetts Division of Child Guardianship—and they came to investigate and removed all of us. They proceeded to start terminating parental rights. I was the only one that was ever adopted. All the others lived in foster care, except my sister—when we were split up, she was put in a state-run orphanage where she remained until she was twenty-one or twenty-two.

My freshman year in college—I was going to Northeastern University in Boston—I cut a class one afternoon and hopped on the subway downtown to the state headquarters of the welfare department. As luck would have it, the lady who had been my caseworker for the nine years that my parents had me in foster care was working there in an administrative position. In the course of the conversation, she said, once you find one of your siblings, I think you are going to find most all of them. It may get down to whether you want to find the youngest one, whose name is Joseph, because that may mean having to have contact with your biological mother, because he may still be with her. How would you feel about that? I said, Well, I don't have any desire to see my mother. She had ten kids, she abandoned each and every one of them. And she said, I can understand that, but I knew your mother better than anybody else, probably. Let me tell you a strange thing.

She said, I am not Catholic, but I know a little about the Catholic religion. I know infant baptism is terribly important in the Catholic religion. She said, When you all were physically removed from that house and put into foster care, she was entitled to a hearing. So I go to serve the papers which notified her that the hearing to terminate her parental rights was going to be on a date three weeks later. In that three-week time period, she called and asked for permission to have you brought from the foster home so she could take you to Immaculate Conception church in Lowell to have you baptized. The caseworker said, I wondered about that over the years. Here's a woman who's a prostitute, a pretty tough broad—a convicted felon, heroin addict, well-known to the police—as amoral an individual as you could ask for, and yet she made sure that you were baptized. And she said, you know as we research the records, every one of you had been baptized. Over the years I have thought that maybe that was the only gift she had to give you, other than life itself. If that's the case, then it seems to me she gave you the two most important gifts there are, and perhaps you might not ought to be quite so judgmental until you know a little bit more about the shoes she walked in.

It turned out I did have the opportunity to meet her and I elected not to. I just couldn't bring myself to meet her. She passed away in the mid-seventies, and I have had regrets since then that I did not meet her, because I think I would like to have looked her in the eye and asked her why. But my siblings assure me that she wouldn't have had an answer, and that she might not have even wanted to see me or talk to me.

She was colorful to the very end. When I was running Parchman, I had a good friend in the New Jersey prison system who did some digging. She had spent some time there in the late forties up through the fifties. He said, Man oh man, I tell you one thing, she was a tough broad even inside the joint. She spent a lot of time in segregation, you know, she was assaultive and stuff.

So I was extremely fortunate in the sense that I avoided what my older brothers and sisters could not avoid. They have the emotional baggage and scars that I don't have.

My parents adopted me, and I grew up in a solid, dirt-poor, working-class family. There were seven of us kids. My father was a textile mill foreman, and after supper, in order to make more money, he ran a Texaco service station. Did what he had to do. We were not rich. We were pretty rich in love, though. We were a very close family. The Catholic religion had a big part in that. My parents did a remarkable job. My father was proof that there are still genuine heroes in America. His parents immigrated from Quebec, first to Rhode Island and then to Massachusetts, to follow the textile industry. My grandfather was foreman of the textile mill before my daddy. They had eleven boys, and they all worked in the mill. The only thing that interrupted that was World War II. None of them ever finished school. My grandfather let them go through the fifth grade, then they had to go to work. And the northern mill town was very much like the southern plantation. I mean, my father grew up in a company mill house. When he and Mama first got married, they lived in a company house and shopped at the company store. And as the song says, the company literally owned their souls.

There was no question that my father was the product of the tail end of the Industrial Revolution. Kids worked in factories. My grandfather was a stern, unloving kind of disciplinarian—which surprisingly made my father the most gentle human being you could ask for. It would pain him to raise a hand to his children. And he would never talk about his own childhood, which I always found sad. He was a strong person, and he felt very strongly that you ought to be involved in government stuff. He would have been very comfortable as a revolutionary. He was a voracious reader, and that replaced his formal education. He used to tell me, Folks try to make this business so complex, but there are only two kinds of people. There are leaders, and there are followers. You've got to know which kind of person you are, and then do the best at it you can.

He insisted that I go to college. I was the first one in the family to go to college. He wasn't going to have me working in the mill or working at General Motors like my brothers. I could make more money, frankly, working on the line at General Motors with a high school diploma, but that wasn't the point to daddy. I was going to have an education, and my parents gave me the foundation that you see has served me well. And so it turns out rough beginnings allowed me to have a really great childhood. Good childhood.

THE ULTIMATE RESPECT

In your book, you mention being accused of having ice in your veins, of being a stern disciplinarian. You also tell the story of how at Parchman you were once accused of being a "nigger-lover" for intervening on behalf of an inmate to stop a lynching by correctional officers. Then you spend a lot of time on how you broke a prisoners' work strike. And finally, you write of corrections being a "narcotic"—you were "enamored of little Alcatraz," the max unit at Parchman, and you call it "exhilarating."

My wife would say you have to be a sick person to find pleasure in that. She says that lovingly.

Tell me about that pleasure.

In the corrections field, there are a number of subplots that go on. First of all, corrections has to pretty much fend alone in the criminal justice arena. The courts don't particularly like it, cops don't respect us, the public doesn't respect us. So we always feel like we're out there left to our own devices. You find yourself not being a full member of the criminal justice fraternity sometimes. That gives you a sense of independence and a kind of, Hey I'll show you.

Within the institutions there is also a traditional kind of pecking order. When I went to Florida, I was superintendent of a correctional institution. Florida has bunches of correctional institutions, but they only have one state prison. Well, a prison by any other name is still a prison, except in the prison industry. And that one prison has a warden, not a superintendent. *Warden* and *superintendent* are interchangeable, they mean the same damn thing. But in the business, for whatever reason, particularly coming out of the old school that I started out in in the late sixties, "warden" is a title that just carried the ultimate respect. So when you get to a system like Missouri, and there's fifteen institutions— fourteen correctional institutions and the Missouri state penitentiary— and you're a warden at the Missouri State Penitentiary, that's something different than being a superintendent at the medium security prison over in Forbland.

I was probably brainwashed. The first warden I ever worked for told me, There's nothing else in the correctional business that comes close to this. He told me one day, I sit up here and I look out on the prison yard, I've got 4,000 convicts and they're all in my custody. They're all within these four walls. He said, I've got every kind of cut-throat murderer. I've had the Boston strangler. I've got people in here who have done the worst kind of deeds imaginable, and I'm responsible for all of them. He said, Not everybody can do this and do well at it. It takes a special breed.

And it does. What I've discovered over the years, of course, is that what it takes largely is that the warden has to be schizophrenic. As I pointed out in the book, you have to be able to point a shotgun at some inmate's head in the morning and say, I'm going to blow that shit all over my wall, and then in the afternoon you have to be able to put your arm around an inmate and console him because his mother passed away. I don't know of anything more schizophrenic than that.

When you call that schizophrenic, do you feel that it's a kind of role-playing or that it's different parts of you that are both real?

When I say "schizophrenic"—you have to play all kinds of different roles. I liken it very much to being a drill instructor in the military. They give you the standard speech: I am your mother, your father, your doctor, your lawyer, your preacher. A police officer is a cop, he's a psychologist, he's a social worker. So a warden has to play all those different kinds of roles. In a max unit, some of those roles are much more sharply defined than they would be in a less secure institution. But nevertheless, yeah, it's role-playing. You've got to be able to shift gears and do it kind of fluidly. Walk out of a hostage situation, come down from that, and when an inmate comes up to you, and here's this grown man with ugly-ass home-made prison tattoos from head to foot, and he's crying because he's just got ten divorce papers from the old lady, you know, you can't say, Get out of my damn face because I've just dealt with a couple of wackos who wanted to kill some people on the staff. You can't do that, you've got to be able to shift gears.

Why do you have an autographed picture of Tammy Wynette in a collage with the Missouri penitentiary on your wall?

She came to the institution to do a concert for us. She and her husband George were really enamored with weird stuff, and she said, Have you ever had anyone to escape from here? And I said yeah. The first person to ever actually escape by scaling the wall or tunneling out, something like that à la Hollywood, was Pretty Boy Floyd. And of course the other most infamous one was James Earl Ray. And she said, Oh, could I have pictures of them? She just asked us if we'd do that little collage. We had an old linotype photograph of Frank James that we were going to put on there, but it wouldn't work. Neither he nor his brother ever did time there, but there wasn't a jail in Missouri that could hold them, so they ended up doing some time there waiting on court stuff.

FORGIVENESS FOR DOING MY JOB

In Death at Midnight, *you write, "Executions strip away the veneer of life for both warden and prisoner. Connie Ray Evans and I transcended our environment and the roles in which we had been cast. The two of us had somehow managed to become real people to each other. There were no more titles or social barriers behind which either of us could hide. I was no longer a prison warden, and he had become someone other than a condemned prisoner. We were just two ordinary human beings caught up in a vortex of events that neither of us could control." Certainly the power of your memoir is in the way you frame it with the life and death of Connie Evans. But to say that both of you, at that moment, were equally not in control—is that a fair analogy?*

I think so. He certainly didn't have any control over the fact that he was going to be executed. He had run out of ways to stop it, and there wasn't any way that I could stop it, despite my personal feelings. I tried, I tried to create a way, I tried to plead with the governor for executive clemency. So I think what happens is that you decide—I can't stop it, so what I'm left with is to try and walk with this guy through this process as far as I can go. I couldn't die with him, but I can be there for him, I can try to comfort him, I can try to console him, I can try to do what one human being ought do for another human being. And perhaps at the same time I can make up for the way the victim died.

It has always struck me that being a murder victim must be the most lonesome of ways to die. I just can't imagine the feeling of loneliness when one is confronting being murdered. What a horribly, lonely way to die. And I've always regretted, frankly—I mean, I place a great value on my faith, and I truly believe that we're given certain gifts, and that we're expected to do what we can with those gifts. But I also think that at least the God I worship has a certain plan in mind for our lives. And I have frequently wished that God's plan for my life, rather than having me in the execution chamber, had been to allow me to be there for the victims of these crimes. That is not to suggest that I would have stepped in front of the bullet or plunging dagger. I don't think that we can know if we have that kind of courage or not. But I think that I would like to have been able to be there to comfort those victims even if I couldn't have prevented their deaths. To at least not let them die alone.

So the execution in some respects afforded me the opportunity to kind of make up for that, in the sense that this guy didn't have to die alone. And that I had an opportunity to carry these things out from a different perspective, not as a representative of a vengeful state but as somebody who was doing a job but nevertheless was sincerely touched by the humanity that I found in the chamber, in the execution room. And I think you do find it.

You write that Connie Evans had forgiven you.

I think that's absolutely essential to most wardens. We'll never know what [Timothy] McVeigh said, if anything, in the final minutes, or in the days leading up to his execution, to the warden out there. His case was so different it might not have unfolded the way most do. But I think most wardens—and I've certainly heard others say it, and I've read it—I think most wardens look for absolution. It seems to me probably that if you don't get it from the prisoner, then you are left feeling pretty empty. You know, Evans forgave me, Johnson forgave me, I never ran into problems of not being forgiven.

How many executions did you administer?

Four. I carried out two in the gas chamber in Parchman, I witnessed one in the gas chamber there, and I was part of a team in Florida for one in the electric chair. And I think you have to walk away from those things — whether you're the warden, or one of the guys who pulls the lever, or pushes the button, or mixes the chemicals, or whatever that function is — I think you have to do that hoping like hell that the inmate doesn't take it personally.

You know, there is a bit of gallows humor that I purposely chose not to put in the book. People would not have understood it. Abolitionists in particular would have just gone bonkers over it. But we used to have a bit of gallows humor that allowed us to deal with that issue. I remember one of my execution team members who said, Well warden, the inmate understands that there is nothing personal, it's just business. There's a large grain of truth in that. That's how you have to pursue it. That's certainly how I explained things to these guys. I'm not doing this as a matter of choice. They'd say, I know warden, you're just doing your job.

That phrase "doing your job" comes up several times in your book. Did it ever cross your mind, in even the remotest way, that you had a choice not to carry out than execution?

I think it crossed my mind, but I don't think it was ever serious. Where Connie was concerned, the afternoon before his execution, my wife Miriam and I were fixing to leave the chapel after mass, and I looked at my Catholic chaplain, Art Kerwin, and I said, I don't know if I can do this. And of course he lectured me. He said, You *can* do it, and you *have* to do it. I said, Look, I know what my job is, you don't have to tell me that. Art said, That's not what I'm talking about. You have to do it because you have an obligation to be there for that inmate. Because if you're not there, if you're not there to care a little bit about him, who the hell else will? And you have an obligation to be there for the victim who has been crying out from the grave, and for the victim's family. And you have an obligation to this inmate's family, so you can look them in the eye later and assure them that his final moments were as peaceful as one can expect them to be under these kinds of circumstances. He said, You've got too many responsibilities, you can't walk away from it.

Now would I have said that if I had not have been so intimately involved with Evans? Probably not, although I certainly had the same kinds of feelings about Johnson. But I had the opportunity. The governor gave me the opportunity. We were good personal friends, and once he came to Parchman, and we drove around one night just talking. We weren't even talking about executions, but out of the blue the governor said, There's a conference coming up that I'm supposed to attend. It's the same time as this next execution. I could send you as my representative, and then you wouldn't have to be here to do it.

And I thought, What a remarkable offering, for a politician, and of course I knew Billy [Allain] was more than a politician. But he was Catholic. And so he and the bishop and I had frequent conversations. I recall looking at him and I said, Well, are you going to be out of the state so that the lieutenant governor has to be the person who makes any last minute decisions about it, and he said no. He said, That's my responsibility. And I said, Well I'm not going to ask my deputy warden to do something that's my responsibility. So I never seriously considered that.

I've been assailed about that point a number of times. A young lady in Chicago, after I gave a speech, came up and said, I've read your book, I loved the book and I admire you for speaking out, but I deplored the lack of courage you showed when it would have counted most. And I said, Let me guess; that would have been in the execution chamber—I should have turned around and walked out and refused to do it? She said yes. And I said, Well, that's not how it is.

What did that woman not understand?

I don't think she understood, frankly, that, especially in terms of the relationship I had with Evans, that for me to turn around and walk out—I mean hell, *he* couldn't walk away, you know, and I'd have been turning my back on a friendship that had formed. And I'd be deserting him when he was going to most need me, even though I was the one fixing to kill him.

The other thing she didn't understand—I really did emphasize this more because I thought it would kind of shock her more, since she was feeling rather negative about me anyhow—I said, Besides that, I'm a very pragmatic bureaucrat. She said, What do you mean? I said, I've got a wife and six kids, at that time, all at home. I said, What is it you would have me do—come home at midnight and look my wife in the eye and say, Honey, I did the morally right thing just now, I refused to execute him, and oh by the way, the governor fired my ass, we've got to be off this farm and out of the house in thirty days? I said, That's not how life is. That's not the real world.

You know, I owed something to them. Connie Evans had given me enough in our relationship, friendship-wise, that I wouldn't have done that to him. And he wouldn't have done it to me, I don't think. It wouldn't have stopped the execution, except he would have died a little more alone. And despite the respect I had for my deputy wardens, he would have died with a little less dignity and sense of compassion.

And again, back to the pragmatic thing, in a conservative state like Mississippi, to have a warden who refused to carry out his duties would not have been a very smart thing politically. Frankly, even though many corrections people *privately* are very ambivalent about the death penalty, I would have had a hard time finding a job anywhere in the United States unless I wanted to restrict myself to those dozen or so states that didn't have a death penalty.

Is there a difference between you as one person in that role—past tense—with your doubts, and a whole body of correctional people who could conceivably speak out against capital punishment? What does this mean for the abolitionist movement?

I think most wardens that have had to execute people oppose the death penalty, or at least are very ambivalent about it. If you look at San Quentin's Clinton Duffy, or Sing Sing's Lewis Lawes, out of the 1930s and '40s, those two guys alone executed over five hundred folks in their career. They were outspoken opponents of the death penalty from different perspectives. Duffy became famous in corrections circles for uttering the phrase, "It seems to me the death penalty is a privilege reserved for the poor." Lewis Lawes, in his book *20,000 Years in Sing Sing*, talks about the utter futility of executions because they don't make anything better. He wasn't necessary morally opposed to them, he was just pragmatically saying, It doesn't work, so why bother? Whereas Duffy, I think, was coming at it from a different perspective.

But whatever their perspective, you get into abolitionist meetings and sometimes these folks do themselves a terrible injustice. They'll say things like, We shouldn't be discussing whether or not innocence is a problem. The *hell* we shouldn't. If that's how you win the battle, then that's what you use. Don't give me this high-ground bullshit about we have to eradicate the death penalty because it's morally objectionable. That's okay, I understand that, but if that's not going to win the day and the innocence problem is—I mean, I hope there are some abolitionists who are paying attention to the fact that the reasons the numbers are coming down in the polls supporting the death penalty is because of the kind of thing I read this morning in class. Americans are never going to abolish the death penalty because they are morally objecting to it. They are going to abolish it because we have an innate sense of fairness.

When I was giving a speech in Boston several years ago, there's this lawyer from Texas who represents Gary Graham, and she's up there talking about Gary and she uses a phrase, and my instant reaction was just so negative, but I didn't say anything. Now of course, as it turns out, by the time Graham was executed, everybody in the country probably thought he was innocent, as he claimed to be. But anyhow, she said, Gary is such a sweet guy. Fortunately, an ACLU attorney responded first. He said, That is the biggest disservice that these folks can do to this process.

Americans already think that abolitionists are left-field wackos whose elevators don't go to the top. You don't describe a death row convict as a "sweet guy." In Graham's case, of course, he had a criminal record, he had done a lot of damn things—he wasn't a damn angel. And there probably wasn't any question that his ass belonged in prison, it just didn't belong on death row for that particular murder. I think it's a disservice to the abolitionist community to do that sort of stuff.

PRAGMATISM AND FAITH

Give me the short answers to (a) why were you were in favor of the death penalty, and (b) why are you opposed to it now?

(A) because I thought it was a necessay evil for the worst few people, and (b) because my Catholic faith weighed in more and more with me, and (b-2) because it doesn't work. It doesn't work. I'm probably much more comfortable, frankly, saying it doesn't work, than saying it's morally objectionable. But it doesn't. It doesn't work.

Can you say something else about it being morally objectionable?

I just think there has to be a better way to solve our worst problems than for the state to employ killing. I was doing a call-in television show the other night on Mississippi TV, and this lady who lost her daughter and her in-laws in Oklahoma City was on the telephone line with us, and she started quoting scripture. That's a dangerous thing to do with the death penalty, as my students find out the hard way. She said that Jesus himself was a supporter of the death penalty. I've only heard one other person say this, and that was Jerry Falwell. She must have heard him, too. I said, I want to know how Jesus would support the death penalty. He was an execution victim himself—an unjust execution victim. And she went so far as to say, That's how you explain, horrible as it is, innocent people being executed. I said, Well, I guess it all depends on how you interpret things.

It doesn't matter whether it's the Catholic Bible or the King James Bible, this little quote's the same, as he's being executed, he says something like, Father, forgive them—and I presume "them" means his executioners—for they don't know what they're doing. That speaks volumes. And she says, Well, what about the eye for an eye? And I said, When I give that to my students, I caution them to read the whole damn passage, because if you read the whole passage, it's been taken out of context so badly, because what the writer is really talking about is that justice should be a level playing field for the poor and powerless as well as the rich and powerful. It takes on a different meaning.

Here we're talking about these competing biblical interpretations—it seems that in organized religion as well as in a prison system, there's a chain of command and necessary authority. You enjoy being a maverick, and you also accept the necessity of a chain of command.

Part of that is because I spent time in the military, where you're thoroughly indoctrinated in the chain of command. And then the prison business is very semi-military in terms of its hierarchy. So over the course of a career, the chain of command becomes much more important to you than you realize. When you're running prison systems for a living, there has to be a so-called orderly, systemic kind of process, just to keep your head above water. The left hand has to know what the right hand is doing, so the chain of command becomes important.

I did a television show not long ago, and the interviewer said, If you were to go back into corrections today, would you avoid going to work in a prison in a death penalty state? I said, Most states have more than one prison, I wouldn't necessarily have to be working at the state prison that has the death row. He said, Would you avoid that? I said no. He said, What would you do then? I said, Let me put it this way: When I say I wouldn't avoid it, what I mean is, if Texas said we want you to come run the Walls in Huntsville, obviously I'd have to make a decision about that, knowing that that's where they hold death row and that's where they do their executions. If I decided to take the job, I would do it with my eyes wide open, just like I did early in my career. You don't go into the business of running prisons wthout understanding that you may just end up having to play an executioner some day. If you don't want to do that, then you have no business taking that job. Do something else. I said, You can be a reluctant suitor and still do the job.

You know, part of the problem I would have—if you were the governor of Mississippi and you said, I want you to go to Parchman and take the superintendant's job—well, it's going to be hard for me to look you in the eye and say, Well, Governor, I would but I can't because you know how I feel about executions. That would be hard for me to do. It really would. It would be hard for me to walk away from what I would see as a larger responsibility of which executions are a very small, occasional, fortunately infrequent part.

If I understand you right, you're saying an astonishing thing—

Would I execute anybody again?

Right.

I wouldn't take a job in an execution state unless I had decided, squared away with the fact that I might have to execute somebody. I wouldn't do that to the state. I wouldn't take the job if I was convinced that I would not carry out all the responsibilities. *Privately*, I don't think I would ever go do it again. But I would not respond by categorically rejecting such a prospect. Probably what I'd say is, Governor, let me think about it, there are some things to weigh in on it. And then I'd probably say no.

VIETNAM AND MAXIMUM SECURITY

When we first spoke, you said that writing Death at Midnight *was cathartic for you in the same way that returning to Vietnam was. Can you tell us about your time during the war?*

I was an Air Force paramedic, and I spent most of my time flying around on Hueys getting shot at, trying to get folks out. It was a tough job to stay alive in. I think that helped me, frankly, in the prison business later on, in the sense that I felt like I was a survivor.

I was there in '68 and '69. The life expectancy of an Air Force paramedic—when you had a lull during the monsoons, things slowed down, you might have a life expectancy of three days, but most of the time it was more like three hours. It was a live-on-the-edge job. You took certain risks, and you'd find yourself volunteering to do things that you had to be crazy to do—to dash across the DMZ into North Vietnam or over into Cambodia trying to get a pilot out, when you could be safe in a place like Denang or Camp Bonday at that particular moment. And I think ultimately—I didn't realize it in Vietnam, of course—the thing that angered me and made me bitter about Vietnam was something I had no control over. Paramedics were expected to play God. People died. You had no control over that like a doctor's supposed to. That came charging home to me when my best friend died in my arms.

Years later, I had a psychologist who worked for me at a prison. We'd had a serious disturbance, inmates tried to take hostages. Finally, when things had settled down, we kicked back in my office, and I uncharacteristically—because I'm not a drinker—I pulled out a bottle of confiscated whiskey and took a damn good slug, and so did my psychologist. He looked at me and said, You know, I've known you a good while, and I've tried to figure out what in the hell it is about you that makes you love this kind of environment so much, and I've finally decided what it is. You're a Vietnam vet. It's the closest thing you'll ever have to combat for the rest of your life.

And I think that there's a lot of truth to that. The military and Vietnam really prepared me well for that kind of environment, although it didn't prepare me for the execution process. I don't think there's anything that can. I thought I was prepared—I really thought, Shit, after some of the things I've done in Vietnam, and participated in, and some of the things I've seen, this won't be all that difficult. But that's different. You're shooting at some guy two hundred yards away across a rice paddy or from a chopper, they're shooting back at you—that's kind of a level playing field. That's different from executing somebody.

We have an interview with Fred Allen in the book.

I thought it was absurd that any state asks somebody to participate in something like 130 executions. That's insane, in whatever minor form it might be, and being on the strap-down team is not a minor thing. Everybody has their threshhold and their breaking point. I'm amazed that he was able to get through that many of them.

Even in his interview you can see him fighting against talking about it.

Sure. Corrections is a macho business, and any sign of humanity or compassion is a sign of weakness.

THE EXECUTION PROTOCOL

What about the ritual of last meals? The media fascination with it is almost obscene, as if, after making someone into a monster in our minds, we need this perverse kind of rehumanizing.

Well, exactly; if we humanize them in the final hours or moments, then we can feel good about ourselves a little bit in terms of carrying out the process. So much of what goes on in this execution business is built upon what caters to public feelings. Let me give you an example in answering that question. Execution methods: Why bother to go to the trouble of inserting a needle in somebody's vein and injecting drugs into him, as harmless and painless as that is compared to the electric chair and gas chamber, when in fact all you have to do is put him in a room and pipe some carbon monoxide poison into it? It is colorless, odorless, painless, you just fall asleep, gently. My theory is the reason that we don't do this is because the appearance of a person who dies by carbon monoxide poison would be disconcerting to the public. They look bad, you know, they turn that bright cherry red, and so on. And that would not make the public feel very good, we'd be kind of queasy about it.

What's the perspective on last meals from inside the prison?

I have always marveled that they even bother to ask for their last meals. I wouldn't be able to eat, and I've never seen very many who do except to push the food around. It's all part of the larger thing called the execution protocol, developed over the years. I suspect that not many people understand that what is important about the execution protocol is that it helps the warden and the prison staff get on through the damn execution process because you've got things you have to tend to. It is not something that any individual designed. It's kind of come together over centuries, and I think every country that's practiced executions has had a certain kind of protocol.

But I would feel very much like Evans did, frankly. I would say, What the hell do you really care what I want for a last meal? Do you think I really want to eat anything anyway? Get out of my face with that bullshit. But when you are dealing with that, in those moments, you are not thinking about—you're not seeing the images of—and it takes your mind away from it. I think it's a necessary part of the process, from the warden's perspective. I think you'd feel somewhat naked walking out and there was no last meal issue to talk about. Even if he doesn't want a last meal, you still have to talk to him about that. That takes time. That takes time away from thinking. It allows you to try to convince yourself that you are still operating in normal parameters. There is enough minute, detail stuff to deal with that you wouldn't think you'd have time to think about the actual execution itself, but you do.

REDEMPTION IS THE KEY

In addition to the sections on Edward Earl Johnson and Connie Evans in your book, you describe two other events apparently just as transformative for you. One is the suicide of an inmate at Parchman, and the other is the death of your friend Wayne Fleming. These make it seem that your feelings about the death penalty have less to do with politics and ideology than with the interconnections of life and death and people and love.

You know, I've chided my church from time to time on this issue of the death penalty, from the perspective that while the Catholic Church's doctrine has been very clear—this pope in particular clearly states what the Church's perspective is, just as he does on abortion—you have not seen the same kind of vigor put into this as you have on abortion. Every year on the anniversary of *Roe v. Wade*, I can count on going to mass and the homily will beat me over the head about the evils of abortion. Make no mistake about it: I don't like abortion. In this day and age, I think abortion-on-demand as a birth control process is just unnecessary. I do struggle with the fact that maybe it ought to be between that woman and her God, but not like abortion-on-demand.

When I gave a speech before the Massachusetts Legislature a few years ago, Cardinal Law also spoke. He was seen as a liberal on this issue in Mississippi, but up there he's seen as a conservative. So folks up there were just delirious that he came out and spoke against the death penalty. And I thought, What the hell do you expect a Cardinal to do? He and I conversed afterwards, and I said, Cardinal, what you did today is important, it's a good start. He kind of looked at me, and he said, What do you mean a *start*? I said, well, as a cradle Catholic, let me tell you. I have heard about *Roe v. Wade* for twenty-five years, and rightfully so. That is absolutely appropriate. But I am still waiting for the first homily that talks about the Church's teaching on capital punishment.

The problem I have is that as a Catholic, I believe that when I die, if I go to heaven, in theory I should not be surprised if I find Hitler there. In theory, I have no way of knowing if Hitler, in the final moment before he pulled the trigger, didn't asked for forgiveness. And ultimately for Christians, forgiveness is what it's all about. I don't expect to see him there, I may be surprised to find *myself* there, but, I mean, in theory, at least—should I be surprised if I get there and find Tim McVeigh there? I would be, because he didn't show any signs of remorse, any more than Hitler did, but I do not know what his private thoughts were.

Redemption is the key, redemption is the key. A part of my argument to the governor in each of these cases was, Look, you and I spend a lot of time sitting in mass, reading scripture, getting ready to teach these various lessons, and one of the messages is that you never give up on life, never give up on a person's ability to achieve redemption in God. And when we execute somebody, we cut them off from that possibility. There may be people like McVeigh or Hitler who never would have done it anyhow, but how do you know? And maybe the guy I execute was going to achieve redemption in his life tomorrow or the next month or next year. Maybe never, but you don't know that.

So for me, part of it is just a reverence for life. True enough, there is not much good to say about a McVeigh, I suppose, or a Ted Bundy. But I was opposed to Bundy's execution, simply because, number one, there is so much to learn from these guys that might help us prevent the next predator from exploding, and, number two, they say a picture is worth a thousand words. I have found pictures of some of these guys in grammar school. You say what the hell went so wrong? What goes so wrong? They got the cowlicks, and they got the freckles, they got the missing teeth. They look like I did. And you did. The kid next door. Our kids. I try to remind myself—I envision a Ted Bundy in his mama's arms, as the same kind of helpless, defenseless infant that any of us are. We all started out in the same condition. The complexity of life leaves us with few answers in terms of why some of us end up on death row while others don't. It's a pretty confusing journey.

I have no idea how I would have turned out if I had not been taken out of that environment in Lowell, Massachusetts. I have two brothers who are alcoholics—one's a highly successful, upper-class alcoholic, and the other is a skid-row bum who eats literally out of soup kitchens and sleeps on park benches. So when I look at Connie Evanses, Edward Johnsons, I think it's not such a wide line between us and them. When I look at the Ted Bundies, I think there is a big difference between me and Ted Bundy, but the bottom line for me is that my faith just makes it damn uncomfortable for me to live in a society where the state says that executing people is okay. Lock 'em up and throw the key away for the rest of their damn lives, but, as the abolitionists say, how do you teach kids that killing's wrong by killing?

PART V

LIVES INTERTWINED

IS THE DEATH PENALTY GOOD FOR WOMEN?[1]

PHYLLIS L. CROCKER

From 1989 to 1994, I was a staff attorney at the Texas Resource Center in Austin, Texas, where I represented men on death row in their postconviction appeals. Representing one of my clients, in particular, proved to be a significant challenge for me. This man was severely mentally disabled, and he had committed a brutal murder: neither factor distinguished him from many on death row. What disturbed me was that he had a history of physically abusing women, and he had raped and murdered his wife and niece. I came to the practice of criminal law as a feminist and encountered some difficulties squaring my feminist politics with who some of my clients were and what they had done. With this client, for example, my sympathies lay with the women who were abused, yet I was representing the man who killed one of those women.

In a law review article, I wrote about how I could reconcile my anger at my client with my anger that this mentally disabled man had been sentenced to death. I concluded that we must consider, simultaneously, the individual circumstances of the man—he was severely abused as a child, mentally retarded, and brain damaged—and the broader societal context in which the murder occurred: one in which we spend more money on death row cases than on shelters for battered women. We could not blame the man for who he was and what he had done without taking responsibility ourselves for the conditions that led to this tragedy.

Aside from the history of abuse, however, I was still troubled by the murder my client committed. He was eligible for the death penalty because he raped his wife and niece. He did not just kill; he raped them and then he killed them. If he had just killed them he would not have been eligible for the death penalty because killing more than one person was not a capital murder at the time. So, I wanted to consider what difference the rape made to the imposition of the death penalty. This essay reflects some of my thinking about that issue.

In recent years, the death penalty has begun to undergo a profound reexamination in this country. I suggest a different and particularly feminist reason for reexamining, and rejecting, the death penalty. The death penalty perverts society's response to the tragedy of a woman being raped and murdered by relying on a form of racism that is gendered in nature and by making the horrific nature of the crime of rape-murder a more important consideration in determining punishment than the individual characteristics of the person who committed it.

The death penalty is not good for women. In the case of rape-murder, it is used most often to vindicate the honor of white women, not women of color. This has been true historically for rape and continues to be true today for rape-murder. The racial and sexual biases about rape continue to infuse how it is treated in the criminal justice system: the State is able to rely on sexual and racial myths about African-American men and white women, and discount the rape-murder of African-American women. Moreover, the overly high representation of men convicted and sentenced to death for rape-murder in Ohio, Florida, Colorado, and Oregon attests to the potency of this emotionally laden crime. Outrage at rape-murder distracts sentencers, and us as a society, from adequately considering the individual defendant's background and probable mental impairments. The application of the death penalty to a defendant may act as a salve in an individual case, but it is a ruse that allows us to ignore the deep social problems that contributed to who the individual defendant is and to his raping and murdering a woman.

Rape-murder is an emotionally charged crime. It combines two terrifying violent crimes: rape, which the U.S. Supreme Court characterized as "[s]hort of homicide, . . . the ultimate violation of self,"[2] and murder, which the Court again observed could always be "fairly characterize[d] . . . as 'outrageously or wantonly vile, horrible and inhuman.'"[3] As such, it is a crime that "cries out for punishment."[4] But it behooves us to ask whether the death penalty is the proper punishment.

In every state that has the death penalty, a defendant who commits a murder contemporaneous to a rape may be eligible for the death penalty.[5] This is also true of murder that occurs during the course of other types of felonies, such as robbery or kidnapping. Even when a murder is statutorily eligible for the death penalty, prosecutors have broad discretion in deciding whether to seek the death penalty in a particular case.[6] Yet, the emotional outrage that rape-murder evokes makes it more susceptible to assessment as an appropriate death penalty case.

Prosecutors are effective at taking advantage of the emotional aspects of rape-murder.[7] My analysis shows that in several states across the country the percentage of men on death row for rape-murder is remarkably high compared to the percentage of murders that are rape-murders in each of the states and nationwide.

Integral, however, to rape-murder appearing as the kind of crime that typifies the appropriateness of the death penalty are two features that reveal the death penalty's inherent flaws. First, rape-murder death penalty cases perpetuate a particularly gendered form of racism, one in which the overwhelming percentage of victims are white women, and African-American women victims are discounted.[8] Second, these cases underscore the inability of death penalty schemes to ensure that the death penalty is appropriate for the individual defendant, not just the crime.

I examine both of these flaws by analyzing how the criminal justice systems treat these cases in four states: Ohio, Florida, Colorado, and Oregon. Rape-murder is, most often, a vicious attack by a man against a woman.[9] My analysis shows that in each of the four states the women about whom the state is most concerned are white. In none of these states is a white man on death row for the rape-murder of an African-American woman, and very few white men have been sentenced to death for the rape-murder of a woman of color.

This statistical information reveals gendered racism. Historically, African-American men were sentenced to death for the rape of white women far more often than white men were. Today, rape itself is no longer punishable by death,[10] but rape-murder is. While the race of the defendants sentenced to death has changed somewhat, the race of the victims has not: the state still seeks to defend the honor of white women, not all women. This entrenched gendered racism alone should cause feminists to conclude that the death penalty is not good for women.

More generally, the overrepresentation of rape-murder cases on death row demonstrates how the facts of the crime overwhelm proper consideration of whether the death penalty is appropriate for the individual defendant. This problem is not unique to rape-murder cases, but these cases help to illuminate the issue. By emphasizing the facts of the crime over the character and background of the defendant, the jury is encouraged to ignore factors such as a defendant's own mental and emotional impairments that may make the death penalty improper. Moreover, focusing on the crime allows us, as a society, to ignore the myriad forces, ranging from the defendant's own upbringing and development to societal attitudes about women, that contribute to his becoming a man who raped and murdered a woman.

The judicial system's treatment of rape, murder, and the death penalty allows us to consider important issues about the relationship between violent crimes against women and punishment for such crimes. This is an area that has not received much critical analysis by feminists. Most often, it has meant seeking harsher punishments for those who commit crimes of violence against women.[11] As Martha Minow remarked:

> To put it bluntly, feminists have pushed for greater retribution, including criminal prosecutions, for violence done to women and more caring, empathic responses to women who risk criminal charges for their own conduct. This pattern smacks not only of inconsistency but also of unreflective desires simply to advance what is good for women.[12]

As I argue, however, this is one area where the greatest retribution is not good for women: using the death penalty to punish the crime of rape-murder reinforces gendered racism and masks our inability to address effectively some of the profound ills that plague our society.

TAKING ADVANTAGE OF RAPE-MURDER

Rape-murders comprise only 1.1 percent of murders nationwide.[13] Yet, in several states, rape-murders comprise a disproportionately large segment of the crimes for which men are on death row.[14] Moreover, identifying who the defendants and victims are in these rape-murder death row cases[15] shows disparities based on their race and relationship, especially when we consider the rape-murder percentages in these states and nationwide. Statistical information on rape-murder cases suggests that the state takes advantage of societal prejudices and fears, especially with the emotionally laden crime of rape-murder, in seeking and obtaining the death penalty.

I first examined death row rape-murder cases in the state of Ohio.[16] My analysis showed that the proportion of men on death row for rape-murder in Ohio was much greater than the proportion of sexual-assault murders to all murders nationwide and in Ohio.[17] Within the category of rape-murder itself, the race and relationship percentages also showed skewed patterns. The proportion of African-American defendants on Ohio's death row was larger than the proportion of African-American offenders in sexual assault murders nationwide and within the state, and no white men were on death row in Ohio for the rape of an African-American woman.[18] Finally, rape-murders where the defendant and victim were strangers to each other were overrepresented when we consider the national and state percentages.[19] Thus, at each turn, the data on who was on death row in Ohio for what kinds of rape-murders did not reflect the reality of rape-murder, but rather racial inequities and fear of strangers. Despite the small numbers involved in the sample, these data began to show how the state misused the crime of rape-murder to obtain death sentences.

My continued investigation into rape-murder death row cases in other states supports what I observed in Ohio. An analysis of rape-murder cases in Florida, Colorado, and Oregon[20] shows that the crime of rape-murder is vastly overrepresented on each death row and that within the category of rape-murder racial and relational biases persist.[21] What emerges from this examination is a pattern, even if not an intentional one,[22] of the pernicious perversion of the crime of rape-murder into an easy mark for the State to use to seek and obtain death sentences.

Rape-Murder in the State of Florida

The death penalty is a thriving enterprise in Florida, which has the third largest death row in the country and the third highest rate of executions.[23] The crime of rape-murder plays a major role in the state's death penalty activity.[24] The numbers show similar disparities to those in Ohio with one important difference: The percentage of men on death row for rape-murder as a percentage of all men on death row is substantially greater than in Ohio. The most apparent reason for this difference is the breadth of aggravating circumstances that Florida prosecutors may present to the jury as it decides whether to recommend a sentence of life or death.

Race and Relationship

Race plays a disturbing role in the application of the death penalty in Florida,[25] especially for African-American victims in rape-murder cases. In Florida, rape-murders constitute 0.9 percent of all murders with known circumstances from 1976 to 1994.[26] The percentages for race of offender and victim, where known, are: 60 percent, white offender/ white victim; 18 percent, African-American offender/African-American victim; 21 percent, African-American offender/white victim; and 1 percent white offender/African-American victim.[27] 20 percent of all men on death row in Florida have been convicted of rape-murder. The percentages for race of defendant and victim in these rape-murder death row cases are: 58 percent, white offender/white victim; 13 percent, African-American offender/ African-American victim; 20 percent, African-American offender/white victim; and 0 percent, white offender/ African-American victim.[28]

The most noteworthy difference is the low representation of African-American victims: 19 percent of rape-murders across the state, 1976–1994,[29] but only 13 percent of those on death row for rape-murder.[30] The overall state percentage of African-American victims is composed of both white and African-American offenders (1 percent and 18 percent respectively), while the death row percentage of African-American victims is composed of only African-American offenders because not a single white defendant is on death row in Florida for the rape-murder of an African-American victim. When we consider the sex of the victims and defendants, this means no white man is on Florida's death row for the rape-murder of an African-American woman.[31] Ohio also had no white men on death row for the rape-murder of a African-American woman. But in Florida it is even more striking because the available data cover all men who have been sentenced to death since 1972, including those who were later sentenced to life, acquitted or otherwise freed, died or were executed. Of that group, not one white man received the death sentence for raping and murdering a African-American woman.[32] In a southern state, the similarities to the era of slavery are palpable.[33]

The relationship between the defendant and the victim for Florida death row rape-murder cases is also skewed. Rape-murders in Florida, where the relationship is known, fall into the following categories: 4 percent, family/intimate; 50 percent, acquaintance; and 46 percent, stranger.[34] The percentages for Florida death row rape-murder cases are different: 6 percent, family/intimate; 29 percent, acquaintance; and 65 percent, stranger.[35] The most striking difference is between acquaintance and stranger rape-murders: The percentage of Florida rape-murder death row cases involving an acquaintance is about one half of the state and nationwide percentages, and the stranger percentage is larger by nearly 50 percent. This is a graphic demonstration of what others have noted about death penalty cases generally: They reflect our fear of strangers, not of those who actually harm us the most.[36] So too, the overrepresentation of stranger rape-murders, and underrepresentation of acquaintance rape-murders, suggests the tenacious misconception that "real rape" is committed by a stranger,[37] and thus is the kind we should most severely punish.

Aggravating Circumstances
Apart from the racial and relational biases present in the Florida rape-murder cases, the most remarkable feature of these cases is their sheer number. Of the 393 men currently on death row in Florida, 80 are there for a crime that included rape and murder.[38] That is 20 percent—greater than the percentage in Ohio (12 percent) and greater by far than the Florida percentage of rape-murders among all murders (0.9 percent). It is slightly higher (23 percent) if we include those on death row for whom the underlying murder did not involve rape, but the state presented evidence of the rape of another woman at another time as an aggravating

circumstance at the punishment phase.[39] Comparing the role rape plays in a rape-murder death penalty case in Ohio and Florida sheds light on the difference death penalty statutes make on what jurors may consider and how they may exercise their discretion when making their punishment decision.

In Ohio a defendant must be convicted of an aggravated murder with a death penalty specification in order to be eligible to be sentenced to death.[40] Both the aggravated murder and the specification must be proved beyond a reasonable doubt. [41] The aggravated murder may either be premeditated murder or murder in the course of an enumerated felony, including rape.[42] The death penalty specifications are limited to facts directly related to the murder, including a rape that is concurrent to the murder.[43] At the punishment phase the jury must weigh the death penalty specification it found at the guilt phase against the mitigating circumstances presented by the defendant.[44] The nature and circumstances of the murder itself may be considered by the jury only if they are mitigating.[45]

The jury may consider the rape of the murder victim as a factor at punishment only if the state charged rape as a death specification in the indictment and the jury found that the prosecution proved rape beyond a reasonable doubt at the guilt phase.[46] Evidence of rape of someone other than the victim of the rape-murder may come in at the guilt phase only if the state joined a separate rape charge with the rape-murder charge[47] or if it is relevant to establish a pattern or distinctive characteristic of the rape.[48] In either situation, the evidence of other rapes cannot be an aggravating circumstance that the jury may consider at the punishment phase.

In contrast, in Florida, the breadth of aggravating circumstances that the state may present as the basis for a jury to recommend a sentence of death allows for the presentation of a wealth of rape-related evidence. That evidence may play a significant role in explaining why a defendant is sentenced to death.

At the guilt phase the state must prove the defendant guilty of a capital felony which may be premeditated murder or felony murder, including the felony of sexual battery.[49] At the punishment phase, the jury renders an advisory sentencing opinion as to whether the defendant should be sentenced to life or death based on considering "whether sufficient mitigating circumstances exist which outweigh the aggravating circumstances found to exist."[50] The judge, "[n]otwithstanding the recommendation of a majority of the jury," must then weigh the aggravating and mitigating circumstances and decide whether to sentence the defendant to life or death.[51]

The aggravating circumstances that the jury and judge may consider are much broader than those permitted in Ohio. Two aggravating circumstances allow the state to present evidence of rape that the jury did not consider at the guilt phase: prior violent felony convictions and that the murder was "heinous, atrocious, or cruel."[52]

A prior felony conviction must "involv[e] the use or threat of violence to the person."[53] This allows evidence of a rape to factor in the punishment decision in a variety of ways. The state may present evidence of a prior rape conviction unrelated to the rape-murder for which the defendant was convicted.[54] Or, the "prior felony conviction" may be a contemporaneous sexual battery of a separate victim in the same criminal episode as the murder.[55] Even if the defendant was not convicted of rape-murder, the state may introduce evidence of prior rape convictions.[56] This may include cases in which some suggestion, but apparently no charge, of sexual battery was made at the guilt phase, but prior rape convictions then serve to legitimate the unproven yet suspected, rape.[57]

Most broadly, the jury may find the aggravating circumstance that the murder was "heinous, atrocious, or cruel."[58] Florida juries are instructed that:

> Heinous means extremely wicked or shockingly evil. Atrocious means outrageously wicked and vile. Cruel means that designed to inflict a high degree of pain with utter indifference to, or even enjoyment of the suffering of others. The kind of crime intended to be included as heinous, atrocious or cruel is one accompanied by additional acts that show that the crime was conscienceless or pitiless and was unnecessarily tortuous to the victim.[59]

Rape-murder may readily fit this description either because of the manner of death or the facts of the rape.[60] For example, over one-third of the rape-murders involved strangling the victim to death.[61] As the Florida Supreme Court has consistently recognized, one may "infer that strangulation, when perpetrated upon a conscious victim, involves foreknowledge of death, extreme anxiety and fear, and that this method of killing is one to which the factor of heinousness is applicable."[62] The details of the concurrent rape are also subject to classification as heinous, atrocious, or cruel. For example, in one case the trial court found that "the evidence showed that the Defendant with his penis literally ripped [the victim's] vagina apart while he raped her."[63] The trial court concluded that "if any crime meets the definition of heinous atrocious or cruel, it is this case."[64] Indeed, in approximately one-quarter of rape-murder cases, the Florida Supreme Court specifically relied on the facts of the sexual battery when discussing just how heinous, atrocious, or cruel the murder was.[65]

The broad range of Florida's aggravating circumstances affords the state a multitude of ways to introduce evidence of rape for the jurors and judge to consider in making their decision about whether the defendant should live or die. Unlike Ohio's death penalty statute, which keeps the jury focused on the aggravating circumstances it found beyond a reasonable doubt, the Florida statute allows the sentencers to consider the incendiary nature of the rape for which the defendant was convicted, or evidence of other rapes that may be far afield from the rape-murder. The breadth of the Florida aggravating circumstances permits jurors' emotional responses to rape, and their racial biases, especially those connected to rape,[66] to influence, consciously or not,[67] their punishment phase decision.

Rape-Murder in Colorado and Oregon

Colorado and Oregon have distinctly smaller death rows than do Florida and Ohio, but in some ways they provide the starkest evidence of the ways the state exploits the crime of rape-murder. In both states the common wisdom is that it is "hard" to get on death row; therefore, the crime must be truly egregious.[68] Rape-murder appears to embody this description.

Colorado has only six men on death row.[69] Four of them, 66 percent, were convicted and sentenced to death for a first-degree murder that included raping the victim.[70] Yet, in Colorado, rape-murders are only 1.5 percent of all murders with known circumstances from 1976 to 1994.[71] The very high representation on Colorado's death row suggests that the state is not only aware of, but correct about, the outrage the crime of rape-murder engenders. Indeed, in the first six months after Colorado changed from jury to judge sentencing in death penalty cases, the state sought the death penalty in six cases, all of which involved a defendant who had committed a rape either contemporaneous to the murder or previously.[72] Two of the six defendants were sentenced to death, both of whom were convicted of a rape that occurred as part of the same criminal episode as the murder.[73]

The demographics of the victims and the four men convicted and sentenced to death for rape-murder are no less disturbing than those of Ohio and Florida. Every single one of the victims was a white woman.[74] The defendants are of different races: two hispanic, one African American, and one white.[75] In three of the cases the defendant and victim were strangers, and in the fourth, the three murder victims were former girlfriends of the defendant.[76] It begins to look like the death penalty is an available punishment for raping and murdering white women, stranger or not, regardless of the defendant's race.[77]

Similar results are present in Oregon. Twenty-seven men are on death row in Oregon,[78] thirteen of them for rape-murder.[79] They are 48 percent of Oregon's death row; not as high as the percentage of rape-murders on Colorado's death row, but still extraordinarily high when we consider that of all murders with known circumstances in Oregon, 1976–1994, only 2.5 percent were rape-murders.[80] Of the thirteen, all but one of the defendants are white,[81] and all of the victims are white.[82] Given the relatively high rates of death sentences for African-American men who raped and murdered white women in Ohio and Florida, it is surprising that none are on death row in Oregon.[83] But it is not surprising that all of the victims are white women.[84] That bias has appeared in each of the four state's death row rape-murder cases.

Relational biases are also evident in Oregon's rape-murder death row cases. As in all three other states, cases in which the defendant and victim were strangers are overrepresented when we consider state rape-murder figures: 46 percent of Oregon rape-murder death row cases, 26 percent of Oregon's rape-murders, 1976–1994. Oregon rape-murder cases are also underrepresented where the defendant and victim were acquaintances: 39 percent of death row cases, 63 percent of rape-murders, 1976–1994.[85] At the least, these numbers confirm the proclivity to subject strangers to the harsher punishment of death, even though they are not the greatest threat.

REJECTING THE DEATH PENALTY FOR RAPE-MURDER

The racist application of the death penalty and the inability of the system to ensure proper evaluation of the appropriateness of the death penalty for each individual defendant are two of the many problems cited as reasons to oppose the death penalty. Both are issues that have special resonance for feminism in light of how the state manipulates the death penalty as a punishment for rape-murder. The significance of the racial disparities in rape-murder death row cases that I have identified leads to the conclusion that when the State has been able to seek the death penalty for a crime involving rape, it has done so in ways that discount African-American women and rely on sexual myths about African-American men. Moreover, throughout the last one hundred years, women have identified the interaction of racial and sexual biases about rape as reasons to oppose the lethal punishment of men, be it in the form of lynching or the death penalty. Finally, the strikingly high rate at which the death penalty is sought and imposed in rape-murder cases shows how the state effectively maintains focus on the crime. This prevents proper consideration of the appropriate punishment for the particular defendant, and it distracts us from acknowledging broader issues, such as mental illness, sexism, and racism, that are inexorably part of these cases.

The Interaction of the Death Penalty, Rape, and Racism

Prior to 1977, when the death penalty was still an available punishment for the crime of rape,[86] the death penalty was used overwhelmingly against African-American men convicted of raping white women. This was true as a legal matter in the criminal justice system as well as outside of the legal system where African-American men were often lynched under the pretext of having raped a white woman. Lynching African-American men for the rape of white women no longer occurs as it once did[87] and rape is no longer punishable by death, but the gendered and racist use of the death penalty when rape is present, persists in modern times.

Rape is a crime of sexual violence that is intimately connected with myths about race. Dorothy Roberts noted that the criminal law enforces a racial construction of rape, one that focuses on the rape of white women by African-American men, and devalues the rape of African-American women, especially by white men.[88] She observed that this construction of rape relies on a "racialized sexual mythology arising from slavery" where African-American women were sexual objects and African-American men were predators who threatened the virtue of white women.

The application of the death penalty to the crime of rape reflected and reinforced these racial and sexual myths. In a comprehensive study of racial discrimination in the imposition of the death penalty in rape cases in the south from 1945 to 1965, Marvin E. Wolfgang and Marc Riedel documented the disproportionate application of death to African-American defendants for the rape of white women.[89] They found that while 36 percent of African-American defendants convicted of raping white women were sentenced to death, only 2 percent of defendants in all other racial combinations were sentenced to death.[90] Thus African-American defendants who were convicted of raping white women were sentenced to death approximately eighteen times more often than any other racial combination. By examining a series of nonracial variables Wolfgang and Riedel analyzed whether this disparity was attributable to race. They concluded that "in none of the seven states carefully analyzed can it be said that any of the nonracial factors account for the statistically significant and disproportionate number of blacks sentenced to death for rape."[91] Thus, for rape, the death penalty was applied overwhelmingly to condemn African-American men for violating white women.

The statistics on those sentenced to death in Florida, Ohio, Colorado, and Oregon for rape-murder echo some of the racial disparities Wolfgang and Riedel found for rape. In the Wolfgang and Riedel study, African-American defendant/white victim cases comprise 86 percent of the rape cases in which the death penalty was imposed. The Florida figures show that African-American defendants convicted of the rape-murder of white women are approximately 20 percent of those sentenced to death.[92] The rates are similar in two of the other states: in Ohio 27 percent of the rape-murder death row cases are African-American defendant/white victims; in Colorado, 25 percent;[93] but in Oregon, 0 percent.[94] These percentages show a sizable drop from the Wolfgang and Riedel findings. The apparent overt racism against African-American defendants in cases involving rape has diminished but not vanished.

Even though the percentage of African-American men sentenced to death for the rape-murder of a white women is lower today than it was, issues of racism persist in the cases. For example, in a Florida case, an all-white jury convicted Johnny L. Robinson, an African American, of the sexual battery, kidnapping, robbery, and murder of a white woman.[95] At the punishment phase the prosecutor elicited testimony from the defendant's medical expert that Robinson told him he had sexual encounters with several other white individuals.[96] The trial court denied the defense attorney's objection to this line of questioning, but the Florida Supreme Court vacated the death sentence, finding that this was a deliberate attempt to inject racial bias and prejudice into the case.[97] The court acknowledged that discrimination based on race exists in our culture and concluded:

> The situation presented here, involving a black man who is charged with kidnapping, raping, and murdering a white woman, is fertile soil for the seeds of racial prejudice. We find the risk that racial prejudice may have influenced the sentencing decision unacceptable in light of the trial court's failure to give a cautionary instruction.[98]

Conversely, concern about appealing to racial bias in rape-murder cases may not be sufficient to exclude racist imagery from being presented, or alluded to, at trial. In Robert Harlan's case, the Colorado Supreme Court acknowledged that it was troubled by the apparent racial dimensions of the trial.[99] Harlan, an African American, had kidnapped, raped, and murdered a white woman. In rebuttal at the punishment phase, the state called five women, each of whom testified to sexual misconduct by Harlan. Each woman was white. The Colorado Supreme Court conceded that, especially with a jury that had no African-American members, this "may have echoed a subconscious and pernicious racist image of African-American males as sexual predators preying on Caucasian women."[100] Nonetheless, the court concluded that because the jury was instructed not to consider race, the prosecution did not rely on a racially based argument, and the killing was brutal, no error occurred.[101] The court affirmed Harlan's death sentence.

In both cases, the prosecution sought to bolster its argument that the defendant should be sentenced to death by appealing to the presumed racial prejudices of the juries. In each case it was not just a generalized racial bias that the State invoked, but one specifically steeped in our American history, the "racialized sexual mythology arising from slavery"[102] in which African-American men are an ever-present threat to white women. The Florida and Colorado Supreme Courts each recognized that this racial prejudice could improperly infect the defendant's trial. Regrettably, however, each also thought that a jury instruction to disregard the issue of race would be sufficient to protect the defendant's rights. Given the tenacity of racial prejudice, especially in the context of an African-American man convicted of raping and murdering a white woman, it seems implausible that jurors could so readily dismiss the personal biases that the prosecution had called to the fore.[103]

Gendered racism is apparent not only in the prosecution of African-American men charged with the rape-murder of white women, but also in the overall percentage of men of all races on death row for crimes involving the rape of white women. In Florida, 78 percent of the victims of defendants on death row for rape-murder are white women.[104] The Ohio percentage of white women victims is similar: 72 percent. Colorado and Oregon are much higher; in both states 100 percent of the victims of men on death row for rape-murder were white women. These percentages are not all that different from the 86 percent of white rape victims of African-American defendants that Wolfgang and Riedel documented. While we do not know the percentage of African-American victims in the Wolfgang and Riedel study, it is nonetheless stunning that still today there is not one white man on death row in any of the four states for the rape-murder of an African-American woman.

These statistics and cases suggest that a form of the racialized sexual mythology of rape Roberts observed exists in rape-murder death penalty cases. While the percentages have shifted in terms of who the defendants are on death row for murder cases involving rape, they have not changed materially in the percentage of white victims. The rape-murder of African-American women is virtually ignored and the notion of defending white womanhood persists.

Women's Historical Opposition

The confluence of racial and sexual bias that permeates crimes involving rape is not new. Even before the racist application of the death penalty to the crime of rape began in the 1940s, the charge of rape served as a vehicle to terrorize the African-American community.[105] After the Civil War, lynching of African-American men for the supposed rape of white women became a frequent occurrence.[106] In 1892, Ida B. Wells, an African-American journalist, asserted that "[to] palliate this record . . . and excuse some of the most heinous crimes that ever stained the history of a country, the South is shielding itself behind the plausible screen of defending the honor of its women."[107] Indeed, the South appealed to the North to suspend its judgment of southern lynchings on the ground of protecting "its women." Yet, as Wells was first to document, in 1894 only one-third of those lynched had been charged with rape, "to say nothing of those of that one-third who were innocent of the charge."[108] By the 1930s, studies had confirmed that the primary motivation for lynching African-American men was "greed not women's honor."[109]

Within the category of lynchings because of rape, the concern was protecting white women's honor. As Wells observed, when it was a white man who raped a African-American woman, "very scant notice is taken."[110] Thus the rape of a woman was treated differently depending on the race of both the victim and the offender: rape of a white woman became a justification for lynching an African-American man, and rape of an African-American woman by a white man became an act to ignore, or for which to blame the woman.[111]

After Wells instigated an anti-lynching campaign in the 1880s,[112] over the decades women have opposed the idea that the "destruction of men's lives served to protect and honor women."[113] In the early 1900s, African-American women's clubs made the anti-lynching campaign a priority, emphasizing "shaming white society into accepting moral responsibility for its continued devaluation of Black life through lynching and rape."[114] Finally, albeit late, in 1930, through the Association of Southern Women for the Prevention of Lynching, many white women joined the cause,[115] acknowledging that: "Public opinion has accepted too easily the claim of lynchers and mobsters that they were acting solely in the defense of womanhood.... Women dare no longer permit the claim to pass unchallenged nor allow themselves to be the cloak behind which those bent upon personal revenge and savagery commit acts of violence and lawlessness."[116]

In 1976, when the U.S. Supreme Court was considering whether to hold the death penalty an unconstitutional punishment for the crime of rape, several national women's organizations joined with the A.C.L.U. and the Center for Constitutional Rights, as amici, to argue that the punishment was cruel and unusual under the Eighth Amendment. The brief pointed to both racial and sexual bias. It argued, "the death penalty for rape is an outgrowth of both male patriarchal views of women no longer seriously maintained by society, and gross racial injustice created in part out of that patriarchal foundation."[117]

The concerns that animated women in the early 1900s to fight against lynching, and the women in the 1970s to object to the death penalty for the crime of rape, are equally valid today. The state still may seek to invoke racial bias against African-American men to bolster its case when white women are the victims. And, it is only white women's honor that is sought to be vindicated by the application of the death penalty in rape-murder cases, not all women's. Thus, rape-murder death penalty cases reflect a gendered racism that has persisted over time whenever rape has been part of the calculus. We should, as did the women in the early 1900s and in the 1970s, repudiate the state's misuse of rape-murder in furtherance of the death penalty.

The Predominance of the Facts of the Rape-Murder at Sentencing

In at least four states in this country rape-murders constitute a remarkably high percentage of the murders for which men are on death row. This is not an accident: prosecutors understand the power that the facts of an emotion-laden crime such as rape-murder have on sentencers. Constitutionally, sentencers are supposed to consider not only the aggravating circumstances of the murder but also the mitigating circumstances including the defendant's individual character and background in deciding whether to sentence him to life imprisonment or death.[118] This dual requirement is intended to ensure both consistency, by limiting the crimes that make a defendant eligible for the death penalty, and fairness, by requiring the jury to consider the defendant's human frailties.[119] Far too often, however, the latter does not occur. Studies document that many jurors make up their minds on the proper punishment for the defendant while hearing evidence about the defendant's guilt.[120] The crime of rape-murder is especially susceptible to this premature decision-making because it combines many of the factors that make the imposition of the death penalty more likely such as the rape itself, the fact that the victims are women or children, and the involvement of torture before death.

The facts of rape-murder may overwhelm proper consideration of mitigating circumstances that would support a life sentence. This is certainly problematic in an individual case because it means that the defendant's frailties, such as mental illness, long-term impairments from childhood abuse, or mental retardation, are not given due regard. The dominance of the crime also prevents us from acknowledging the connection between the individual defendant's circumstances and broader societal ills.

The tension between giving full consideration to the crime and to the defendant's human frailties is exemplified by an unusual published exchange between Justices Blackmun and Scalia, prompted by Justice Blackmun's announcement that he would no longer find the death penalty constitutional. In a written dissent to the denial of certiorari in *Callins v. Collins*, Justice Blackmun concluded that he "no longer shall tinker with the machinery of death" because it was "virtually self-evident to me now that no combination of procedural rules or substantive regulations ever can save the death penalty from its inherent constitutional deficiencies. The basic question—does the system accurately and consistently determine which defendants 'deserve' to die?—cannot be answered in the affirmative."[121] This was significant because Justice Blackmun was one of the justices who had upheld the constitutionality of the death penalty in 1976.[122] In *Callins*, almost twenty years later, he concluded, "It seems that the decision whether a human being should live or die is so inherently subjective— rife with all of life's understandings, experiences, prejudices, and passions—that it inevitably defies the rationality and consistency required by the Constitution."[123]

Justice Scalia, in response, criticized Justice Blackmun for, among other matters, choosing Callins as the case in which to announce his changed view.[124] Justice Scalia characterized Callins as "one of the less brutal of the murders that regularly come before us—the murder of a man ripped by a bullet suddenly and unexpectedly."[125] He suggested that it would have been more difficult to find the death penalty unconstitutional in a more brutal murder such as in *McCollum v. North Carolina*,[126] where an "11-year-old girl [was] raped by four men and then killed by stuffing her panties down her throat."[127]

McCollum, however, proved to demonstrate Justice Blackmun's conclusion that the death penalty cannot be fairly applied. True, the facts of the rape-murder were horrifying, but, as Blackmun noted, "there is more to the story."[128] McCollum was mentally retarded and only nineteen years old at the time of the crime.[129] Moreover, of the four individuals involved in the crime, McCollum was the only one convicted of murder and sentenced to death despite the fact that "[h]e was not the one who initiated the rape, the one who proposed the murder, or the one who actually committed the murder."[130] Thus the full facts of McCollum's case, those of his individual characteristics as well as the circumstances of the crime, showed that the system does not "accurately and consistently determine which defendants most 'deserve' to die."[131]

This tension between considering mitigating circumstances or only the facts of the crime is present in other rape-murder cases.[132] In one of the Florida cases, *Hall v. State*,[133] Chief Judge Barkett dissented from the Florida Supreme Court's decision upholding Hall's death sentence. Barkett maintained that while the crime was heinous, Hall was not among the most culpable of murderers:

> A young woman, seven months pregnant, was raped, beaten and shot to death. The horrible nature of the crime is uncontroverted, and it is certainly among the types of offenses for which the death penalty may be imposed. However, Freddie Lee Hall is not among the most culpable of

murderers. Hall's judgment, thought processes, and actions are unques-
tionably affected by his mental retardation. He cannot understand right
from wrong in the way that most members of our society do, and while he
should spend the rest of his life in prison, he should not be executed.[134]

The majority of the court found that the aggravators, including that the
crime was heinous, atrocious, or cruel, outweighed the mitigators for this
"cruel, cold-blooded murder."[135]

While the tension between considering mitigating circumstances and
the facts of the crime is not unique to rape-murder cases,[136] it is noteworthy that Justice Scalia chose a rape-murder as the type of case with which
to challenge Justice Blackmun's repudiation of the death penalty. It
speaks to the power of the crime of rape-murder itself to make jurors, and
us as a community, ignore individual frailties, be they mental retardation,
lasting impairments from childhood abuse, or mental illness.

Many of the men who are sentenced to death suffer from mental and
emotional impairments.[137] The few studies conducted of men on death
row found that they often have extensive neurological damage, psychological difficulties, and histories of extreme childhood abuse.[138] As with
Henry Lee McCollum and Freddie Lee Hall, these impairments may contribute to a person's lack of judgment, inability to consider alternative
courses of action, and often violent behavior.[139] This may be especially
true in tense and volatile situations such as those involving rape and
murder.[140] The import of these mental and emotional deficiencies in the
death penalty context is not that they excuse the defendant's commission of the crime, but that they explain his conduct in a way that enables
the sentencer (and us) to see that he should not be sentenced to death.

It is especially important in rape-murder cases for women to
acknowledge the import of an individual defendant's impairments.
Rape-murder is the kind of case in which we might readily be inclined to
blind ourselves to the character and background of the individual defendant and focus on the facts of the crime. These are horrible crimes:
Rape-murder is so closely related to rape[141] that, to the extent we have
been or fear being raped, we may identify, personally, with the victim.[142]
We may believe, therefore, that the severest punishment is the only
appropriate response.[143]

Yet even in the context of rape-murder, we must be willing to step
back from the horrifying nature of the crime and consider the individual
defendant and the culture in which he was raised and lived. Defendants
who are convicted of and sentenced to death row for rape-murder are
among those who were severely physically or sexually abused as children, or were mentally retarded or mentally ill.[144] The difficulties in judgment and behavior that they suffered due to these impairments per-

sisted, unabated,[145] into adulthood and undoubtedly affected them during the commission of the crime.

As each defendant lived with his own personal dysfunctions, he lived in a society where women are raped on a daily basis. I do not mean to suggest a direct connection between mental impairments and crimes of violence against women. Indeed, much progress has been made in establishing that men who rape women are not "crazy" but more normal than we might like to know.[146] The connection that exists among these forces is that they are all part of the mix that contribute to how the defendant thinks and behaves.

As a matter of deciding whether the defendant is guilty of committing the rape-murder, we may not want to let any of these factors alter our judgment about his degree of criminal responsibility. As a matter of determining punishment, however, we should be willing to consider as mitigating how the circumstances of rape and murder itself,[147] as well as circumstances of the defendant's background and current mental and emotional impairments, affected his behavior. On a broader scale, we need to acknowledge how aspects of our culture, be they a lack of respect for women or lack of concern for those who are mentally impaired, infiltrate the commission of rape-murder. When we ignore how the defendant became a man who raped and murdered a woman, and only focus on the bare facts of the crime, we fail to acknowledge the dire consequences of the uncaring nature of our society.

NOTES

1. This chapter is based on two prior articles, *Crossing the Line: Rape-Murder and the Death Penalty*, 26 Ohio N.,U. L. Rev. 689 (2000) and *Is the Death Penalty Good for Women*, 4 Buff. L. Rev. 917 (2001).
2. Coker v. Georgia, 433 U.S. 584, 597 (1977).
3. Godfrey v. Georgia, 446 U.S. 420, 428-29 (1980).
4. McCollum v. North Carolina, 512 U.S. 1254, 1254 (1994) (Blackmun, J., dissenting from denial of cert).
5. See *Crossing the Line*, supra at 694 n.27 (listing state statutes).
6. See, e.g., David C. Baldus et al., *Racial Discrimination and the Death Penalty in the Post-Furman Era: An Empirical and Legal Overview With Recent Findings from Philadelphia*, 83 Cornell L. Rev. 1638, 1643-44 (1998); Jeffrey J. Pokorak, *Probing the Capital Prosecutor's Perspective: Race of the Discretionary Actors*, 83 Cornell L. Rev. 1181 (1998).
7. The death penalty is supposed to be based on reason and not emotion. See Gardner v. Florida, 430 U.S. 349, 358 (1977) (plurality opinion). However, prosecutors recognize the important, even if unspoken, role that jurors' feelings play in deciding whether to sentence a defendant to life imprisonment or death. See, e.g., Joan Howarth, *Deciding to Kill: Revealing the Gender in the Task Handed to Capital Jurors*, 1994 Wis. L. Rev. 1345, 1396.
8. I use "gendered racism" to refer to two phenomena of racial and sexual exploitation. First, the devaluation of the crime of rape-murder by white men of African-American women and, second, the heightened valuation of the crime of rape-murder of white women particularly when committed by an African-American man. Other authors have used the term gendered racism when referring to lynching. See, e.g., Amii Larken

Barnard, *The Application of Critical Race Feminism to the Anti-Lynching Movement: Black Women's Fight Against Race and Gender Ideology, 1892–1920*, 3 UCLA Women's L.J. 1, 2-3 (1993) (describing how lynching was about more than seeking "retribution for the alleged rape of a white woman by a Black Man" and noting that "[t]he gendered racism of lynch ideology cast Black women as immoral and unworthy of respect which facilitated their sexual exploitation by white men."). Still others have identified the connection between sexual and racial bias as sexual racism. See, e.g., Charles Herbert Stember, *Sexual Racis*, ix (1976); Kimberle Crenshaw, *Mapping the Margins: Intersectionality, Identity Politics, and Violence Against Women of Color*, 43 Stan. L. Rev. 1241, 1272-75 (1991). As Darren Lenard Hutchinson observed: "Much of the oppression and discrimination blacks have endured has been sexual in nature. The sexualized oppression directed at blacks, given a patriarchal social structure, has produced gendered effects—creating different experiences for black men and women.... [B]lack men are constructed as promiscuous, threatening to white women.... [B]lack women are often considered promiscuous and sexually aggressive 'Jezebels.'" Darren Lenard Hutchinson, *Ignoring the Sexualization of Race: Heteronormativity, Critical Race Theory and Anti-Racist Politics*, 47 Buff. L. Rev. 1, 81-84 (1999); see also Dorothy Roberts, *Rape, Violence, and Women's Autonomy*, 69 Chi-Kent L. Rev. 359, 367 (1993). Both phrases (gendered racism and sexual racism) reflect what James Weldon Johnson saw: "At the core of the heart of the race problem is the sex problem." Stember, supra at xi (citation omitted).

9. Nationwide, 93 percent of rape-murder victims are women, compared to 24 percent of all murder victims. See James Alan Fox, NACJD-Supplementary Homicide Reports, 1976–1997 (visited September 5, 2000) http://www.icpsr.umich.edu/NACJD/SDA/shr7697.html. This internet site contains the data in the F.B.I. Supplemental Homicide Reports (SHR) 1976-1997. The date is a compilation of monthly reports made by local law enforcement agencies across the country that consist of information about homicides, where known at the time of reporting, including the identification of numerous variables, such as race of victim and offender, relationship between victim and offender, and factual circumstances of the murder. See Lawrence A. Greenfield, U.S. Dept. of Justice, Sexual Offenses and Offenders 27 (1997) [hereinafter 1997 Sexual Offenses and Offenders Study] (explaining the data collection process of the F.B.I. SHR). The website provides an online statistical data analysis program that allows visitors to access subsets of the data for individual states. My analysis of race and relationships for rape-murders comes from using this program.

10. See Coker, 433 U.S. at 592. The Court held that the rape of an adult woman could not be punished by death. Ibid. In recent years at least one prosecutor has sought the death penalty for the rape of a child. See State v. Wilson, 685 So.2d 1063 (La. 1996) (holding death penalty constitutional for the rape of a child under twelve).

11. See, e.g., Joan W. Howarth, *Review Essay: Feminism, Lawyering, and Death Row*, 2. S. Cal. Rev. L. & Women's Stud. 401, 412 (1992).

12. Martha Minow, *Between Vengeance and Forgiveness: Feminist Responses to Violent Injustice*, 32 N.E. L. Rev. 967, 972 (1998).

13. See Fox, supra. The percentage of rape-murders is a percentage of all reported murders with known circumstances. From 1976 to 1994, 77 percent of all murders were reported with known circumstances, 23 percent were unknown. One of the known circumstances is "forcible rape," defined as "the carnal knowledge of a female forcibly and against her will." Assaults or attempts to commit rape by force or threat of force are also included; statutory rape (without force) and other sex offenses are excluded. See 1997 Sexual Offenses and Offenders Study, supra at 31. The percentage of rape-murders may be somewhat higher than 1.1 percent because not all circumstances are known at the time of reporting. Furthermore, as one group of researchers pointed out, "[t]he number of sexual homicides occurring in a given year is difficult to assess for a number of reasons"; the sexual assault may not be reported as such, it may be undetected, or insufficient evidence may exist to substantiate whether a sexual assault took place. See Robert K. Ressler et al., *Sexual Homicide*, (Lexington, Mass.: Lexington Books, 1988), 1.

14. This is not different from felony-murder generally. Studies show that felony-murder represents a large percentage of those sentenced to death despite the relatively small percentage of homicides that are felony-murders. See, e.g., Samuel R. Gross and Robert Mauro, *Death and Discrimination*, (Boston: Northwestern University Press, 1989), 45-46 (reporting that in three of the states studied, the felony-murder rate among those on death row was much greater than the felony-murder rate among all homicides in those states: in Georgia 80 percent compared to 17.5 percent; in Florida, 80 percent compared

to 18.1 percent; and, in Illinois, 75 percent compared to 27.1 percent); David Baldus et al., *Arbitrariness and Discrimination in the Administration of the Death Penalty: A Challenge to State Supreme Courts*, 15 Stetson L. Rev. 133, 138 (1986) ("More than 80% of the defendants on death row today became death eligible because they killed in the course of a contemporaneous offense, usually an armed robbery or rape."); Daniel Givelber, *The New Law of Murder*, 69 Ind. L.J. 375, 413-14 (1994) (citing studies finding similar results).

15. For purposes of consistency I use "rape-murder" to refer to a murder that occurs concurrent to a sexual assault.

16. Crocker, *Crossing the Line*, supra.

17. At the time of my inquiry, the only information readily available was from the Greenfield study of sex offenders and offenses from 1976 to 1994. See 1997 Sexual Offenses and Offenders Study, supra. The study analyzed the F.B.I. SHR and reported on sexual assault murders, among other matters. Sexual assault included "rape and other sexual offenses . . . includ[ing] sexual assault such as statutory rape, sodomy, and incest and attempts to commit these crimes." Ibid. at 28. The 1997 Study reported that, nationwide, sexual assault murders were 1.5 percent of all murders with known circumstances. Ibid. at 27. Murders with known circumstances were 78.5 percent of all murders. Ibid. at 28. Rape-murder cases constituted 12 percent of those on Ohio's death row. Crocker, supra, at 699. Using the NACJD online statistical data analysis program., I ascertained that from 1976 to 1994 sexual assault murders were 1 percent of murders with known circumstances in Ohio (93 of 9029) and rape-murders were 0.8 percent (75 of 9029).

18. Crocker, *Crossing the Line*, supra, at 700-01. For sexual assault murders nationwide, where the race of offender and victim is known, the percentages are: 55 percent, white offender/white victim; 24 percent, African-American offender/African-American victim; 15 percent, African-American offender/white victim; and 2 percent, white offender/African-American victim (the remaining 4 percent are other racial combinations). 1997 Sexual Offenses and Offenders Study, supra, at 30. For Ohio sexual assault murders, 1976–1994, where the race of the offender and victim is known (68 of 93 cases), the breakdown is: 56 percent, white defendant/white victim; 30 percent, African-American defendant/African-American victim; 12 percent, African-American defendant/white victim; and 1.5 percent, white defendant/African-American victim. For Ohio's death row rape-murder cases: 45 percent, white, defendant/white victim; 23 percent, African-American defendant/African-American victim; 27 percent, African-American defendant/ white victim; 5 percent, latino defendant/white victim; and 0 percent, white defendant/African-American victim. Crocker, *Crossing the Line*, supra, at 700-01. The Ohio rape-murder death row cases are, therefore, equally disparate from both the nationwide and state percentages.

19. Crocker, *Crossing the Line*, supra, at 699. Nationwide sexual assault murders where the relationship of the offender and victim is known: 10.2 percent, family/intimate; 50.6 percent, acquaintance; and 39.2 percent, stranger. 1997 Sexual Offenses and Offenders Study, supra, at 38. Ohio's sexual assault murders where the relationship of the offender and victim is known (66 of 95 cases): 8 percent, family/intimate; 67 percent, acquaintance; and 26 percent, stranger. Ohio's death row rape-murders cases: 9 percent, family/intimate; 36 percent, acquaintance; and 55 percent, stranger. Crocker, *Crossing the Line*, supra, at 699. The acquaintance and stranger percentages are almost the reverse of the national and state figures.

20. I chose these states for different reasons. First, I thought it would be useful to contrast the northern state of Ohio to a southern state, especially because of the documented racial bias in the application of the death penalty in the south. Second, Colorado and Oregon both have small death rows, six and twenty-seven inmates respectively. See N.A.A.C.P. Legal Defense & Educational Fund, Inc., Death Row U.S.A., Winter 2000, at 34, 51 [hereinafter Death Row U.S.A.]. I thought it would be instructive to see how many, if any, were rape-murder cases. As my analysis shows, men on death row for rape-murder are relatively more prevalent in Colorado and Oregon than either Ohio or Florida

21. For each state my analysis is based on considering rape-murder death row cases and the F.B.I. SHR data on rape-murders available through the NACJD website. These are not perfectly comparable for a number of reasons. First, for consistency, I analyzed the national and state rape-murder cases from 1976 to 1994, but some of the men on death row in each state may have committed their crimes after 1994. (In addition, the F.B.I. SHR database for Florida does not include data for the years 1988–91.) Second, the definition of rape used in the F.B.I. SHR is not necessarily the same as the statutory defin-

ition of rape/sexual battery/sex offense used in each state. Third, whether a murder that involves rape is classified as such (even when the circumstances are known) is subject to a fair amount of discretion for both the police and prosecutor. See Michael L. Radelet and Glenn L. Pierce, *Prosecutorial Discretion in Homicide Cases*, 19 L. & Soc'y Rev. 587 (1995). Further, even if a murder is a rape-murder, the prosecutor has considerable discretion in whether to seek the death penalty. Finally, even if a prosecutor seeks the death penalty, the defendant may not be sentenced to death for a variety of reasons: he may plea bargain for a life sentence; he may be acquitted or convicted of a lesser included offense; or he may be sentenced to life. See Baldus, supra, at 234 fig. 30 (providing chart showing the disposition of death eligible cases in Colorado from 1980 to 1984, beginning with 171 indicted capital murder cases and ending with 4 death sentences). Despite the lack of comparability in many respects, it is nevertheless useful to look at this data to provide a context in which to evaluate the rape-murder populations on these states' death rows, and to consider how the state uses rape-murder as a death penalty case.

22. See, e.g., Sheri Lynn Johnson, *Unconscious Racism and the Criminal Law*, 73 Cornell L. Rev. 1016, 1028 (1988).

23. Death Row U.S.A., supra, at 24-25 (listing death row populations by state), 10 (listing executions by state).

24. My analysis is based on date from four sources: Death Row U.S.A., supra, published court decisions, newspaper articles, and information from the Florida Capital Cases database, maintained by Dr. Michael Radelet, Chair of the Sociology Department at the University of Florida.

25. Studies of Florida's death row consistently have found that race affects virtually every aspect of the death penalty system. See, e.g., Michael L. Radelet and Glenn L. Pierce, *Choosing Those Who Will Die: Race and the Death Penalty in Florida*, 43 Fla. L. Rev. 1 (1991) Hans Zeisel, *Race Bias in the Administration of the Death Penalty: The Florida Experience*, 95 Harv. L. Rev. 456 (1981).

26. The number is small—124 of 13,755. See Fox, supra. It may be artificially small because Florida numbers are not included for four of the nineteen years. Still, the percentage is close to the national percentage of 1.1.

27. The number of cases is 79 of 124. See Fox, supra. Because we are dealing with such a small number, the percentages represent very small numbers in some instances: forty-seven white offender/white victim, fourteen African-American offender/African-American victim, seventeen African-American offender/white victim, and one white offender/African-American victim. The F.B.I. SHR uses the categories white, black, American Indian, and Asian-Pacific Islander. It does not identify ethnicity apart from race. Thus, offenders and victims who are Hispanic will not appear in the state or national numbers. See Baldus, supra, at 1717 n.151 (considering problems with racial and ethnic categorizations). Because the numbers are missing for four of the nineteen years, it may be helpful to consider the national data. Nationwide the percentages for the race of defendant and victim in 1976–94 rape-murders are: 54 percent, white offender/white victim; 23 percent, African-American offender/African-American victim; 18 percent, African-American offender/white victim; and 2 percent, offender/African-American victim. See Fox, supra. The remaining 3 percent are other race combinations, each less than 1 percent.

28. The numbers are: forty-six white defendant/white victim; ten African-American defendant/African-American victim; sixteen African-American defendant/white victim; and, zero white defendant/African-American victim. The sum of the percentage is 91. The remainder are: one white defendant/Hispanic victim (1.25 percent), two African-American defendant/Hispanic victim (2.25 percent), three Hispanic defendant/white victim (3.75 percent), one Hispanic defendant/Hispanic victim (1.25 percent), one white defendant/"other" victim (1.25 percent). The Florida Capital Cases database uses the designations W/B/H/O.

29. This number reflects cases where the race of both the offender and victim are known (79 of 124 cases). See Fox, supra. The percentage of African-American victims among all cases where the race of the victim is known (123 of 124) is much higher—26 percent. Ibid.

30. Another way of looking at this difference is that about one in five Florida rape-murders, where the victim and offender race is known, involves an African-American victim, but only about one in eight rape-murder cases on Florida's death row involves an African-American victim.

31. These figures seem to comport with findings Radelet and Pierce reported in 1991. See Radelet and Pierce, supra. They found that "those suspected of killing white women are

over 5 times more likely to be [sentenced to death] than those suspected of killing black women." Ibid at 25 (9.7 percent and 1.8 percent respectively). Furthermore, a black man suspected of killing a white woman was fifteen times more likely to be condemned than a black man who is suspected of killing a black woman. Ibid. (24.4 percent and 1.6 percent respectively).

32. It is true that two white men are currently on death row for the rape-murder of two non-white women, one Hispanic (Mike Mansfield) and one designated "other" (Warfield Wike). Also, one white man who died on death row, George South, was convicted of raping and murdering a Hispanic woman. Ibid. So, I cannot say that the rape-murder by a white man of any nonwhite woman has been ignored completely by the state. Still, that number is so very small, especially in a state with a sizable hispanic population, that it should not bring comfort to anyone. See U.S. Census Bureau, Statistical Abstracts of the United States 34 (1999) [hereinafter U.S. Census Bureau] (listing population of those of hispanic origin in Florida, in 1998, at 2,243,000, fifteen percent of the total population of 4,916,000).

33. During the time of slavery in this country, it was not illegal to rape an African-American woman slave. See Thomas D. Morris, *Southern Slavery and the Law 1619–1860*, (Chapel Hill: University of North Carolina Press, 1996), 305. For example, in George (a slave) v. State, 37 Miss. 316, 320 (1859), the Mississippi Supreme Court held that the common law did not apply to slaves and statutory law did not "embrace[] either the attempted or actual commission of rape by a slave on a female slave." See Jennifer Wriggins, *Rape, Racism, and the Law*, 6 Harv. Women's L. J. 103, 118 (1983) (discussing case). See also Linda L. Ammons, *Mules, Madonnas, Babies, Bath Water, Racial Imagery and Stereotypes: The African-American Woman and the Battered Woman Syndrome*, 1995 Wis. L. Rev. 1003, 1025 n.104.

34. This is based on 72 of 124 cases. See Fox, supra. Nationally, rape-murders, where the relation is known are: 1 percent, family/intimate; 52 percent, acquaintance; and, 47 percent, stranger. Ibid.

35. The numbers are: 5 family/intimate; 23 acquaintance; 52 stranger.

36. See, e.g., Givelber, supra, at 412-14; Rapaport, supra at 380.

37. See, e.g., Susan Estrich, *Rape*, 95 Yale L.J. 1087, 1092 (1986) (identifying "real rape" as one where "[a] stranger puts a gun to the head of his victim, threatens to kill her or beats her, and then engages in intercourse" and as one that the law recognizes as a serious crime, even though "most cases deviate in one or many respects from this clear picture"). Fear of rape by strangers also may be tinged with racism. As Dorothy Roberts observed, "Women's fear of strangers on the street is complicated by the deeply embedded image of the dangerous Black man. In the South, a Black man's glance at a white woman signified a threat of rape." Roberts, supra, at 378. The most familiar example of the power of this fear is that of Emmitt Till, a fourteen-year-old African-American boy who was lynched because he whistled at and/or propositioned a white woman in Mississippi in 1954. See Stephen J. Whitfield, *A Death in the Delta: the Story of Emmet Till* (New York: Free Press; London: Collier Macmillan, 1988).

38. This number is based on analyzing the four sources referred to supra, in particular, the direct appeal decisions of the Florida Supreme Court. These eighty cases are ones in which the prosecution established that the defendant committed murder and sexual battery as part of the same criminal episode. Most often that means that a woman was both raped and murdered, but it also includes cases where one person was murdered and another sexually battered. See, e.g., Cole v. State, 701 So.2d 845, 848-49 (Fla. 1997) (stating that the defendants beat and stabbed a man to death and raped his sister).

39. This represents nine additional defendants. This includes two types of cases, one, where no one was raped in relation to the murder, and the other, where the state did not charge the defendant with rape, but some suggestion of it was made during the guilt phase.

40. See Ohio Rev. Code Ann. § 2929.04(A).

41. See Ohio Rev. Code Ann. § 2929.04(B).

42. See Ohio Rev. Code Ann. § 2903.01(A) (prior calculation and design); ibid. § 2903.01(B) (purposefully causing death while committing, attempting to commit or fleeing the commission or attempt to commit a felony). Three relatively new, additional forms of aggravated murder are: purposely causing the death of a person under thirteen years of age; purposefully causing the death of another while under detention for a felony conviction; and purposely causing the death of a law enforcement officer. Ibid. at § 2903.01(C)-(E) (2000 Supp).

43. See Ohio Rev. Code Ann. § 2929.04(A).
44. See Ohio Rev. Code Ann. § 2929.04(B).
45. Ibid. See State v. Wogenstahl, 662 N.E.2d 311, 321 (Ohio 1996) (reiterating that "'the nature and circumstances of the offence'" may only enter into the statutory weighing process on the side of mitigation) (quoting Ohio Rev. Code Ann. § 2929.01(B).
46. See Ohio Rev. Code Ann. § 2929.04(A).
47. See, e.g., State v. Benner, 533 N.E.2d 701, 703-05 (Ohio 1988) (stating that the indictment charged the defendant with twenty-two counts including aggravated murder of two victims and rape of two others).
48. See Ohio Evid. R. 404(B) (Banks-Baldwin 1995); see, e.g., State v. Durr, 568 N.E.2d 674, 677 (Ohio 1991) (stating that testimony at trial included reference to the defendant being arrested for two unrelated rapes).
49. See Fla. Stat. Ann. § 921.141 (setting forth criteria for sentencing a person to death); ibid. § 782.04 (defining murder that constitutes a capital felony). As in Ohio, the State may present evidence of other sexual batteries if they are sufficiently similar. See Duckett v. State, 568 So.2d 891, 895 (Fla. 1990) (affirming introduction of testimony by two women that the defendant, a police officer, picked them up in his patrol car while on duty and tried to make passes at them, but finding harmless error in the introduction of third woman's testimony because the sexual contact was consensual, in case where the defendant was charged with picking up a young girl, sexually assaulting, and killing her); Rivera v. State, 561 So.2d 536, 537-38 (Fla. 1990) (finding no error in state introducing, at guilt phase, testimony about the defendant sexually assaulting, choking, and trying to kill another young girl because sufficient similarities existed).
50. Fla. Stat. Ann. § 921.141(2)(b). The Florida Supreme Court has interpreted this provision to require that the State establish the existence of an aggravating circumstance by proof beyond a reasonable doubt. Swafford v. State, 533 So.2d 270, 277 (Fla. 1988) ("Aggravating circumstances must be proved beyond a reasonable doubt.").
51. Fla. Stat. Ann. § 921.141(3). In order for a judge to override a jury recommendation of a life sentence, "the facts suggesting a sentence of death should be so clear and convincing that virtually no reasonable person could differ." Tedder v. State, 322 So.2d 908, 910 (Fla. 1975). In several rape-murder cases the Florida Supreme Court reversed the trial court's refusal to follow the jury recommendation of a life imprisonment. See, e.g., McCrae v. State, 582 So.2d 613 (Fla. 1991) (finding a "reasonable basis" for jury life sentence recommendation based on evidence that the defendant suffered from temporal lobe epilepsy and probably experienced a seizure at the time of sexually battering and murdering an elderly woman, his condition improved with treatment in prison, and testimony about his good character); DuBoise v. State, 520 So.2d 260, 266 (Fla. 1988) (reversing trial court override of jury life sentence recommendation based on nonstatutory mitigating evidence such as the fact that the codefendants had not been apprehended, the defendant acted under the influence of his brother, a codefendant, the defendant was young (18), had a low I.Q., and a "deprived family background").
52. Fla. Stat. Ann. § 921.141(5)(b), (h). Many states include a comparably worded aggravating factor. James R. Ackers and C. S. Lanier, "Parsing This Lexicon of Death": *Aggravating Factors in Capital Sentencing Statutes*, 30 Crim. L. Bull. 107, 125 (1994) (reporting that seventeen of thirty-seven states have a heinous atrocious or cruel factor and that in some states, 60-80 percent of the death sentences were based on this as an aggravating factor). "Heinous, atrocious, or cruel" may be an avenue for the race of the victim to influence the jury's decision. See, e.g., Kristie R. Blevins, *Patterns of Aggravating and Mitigating Circumstances: An Examination of Tennessee's Death Row*, 79 and 102 tbl. 6 (2000) (unpublished master's thesis on file with the author) (showing that in Tennessee death penalty trials, 1977-1998, the jury found "heinous atrocious or cruel" more frequently when the victim was white than when the victim was African-American [59 percent versus 39 percent of the cases]).
53. Fla. Stat. Ann. § 921.141(5)(b) ("The defendant was previously convicted of another capital felony or of a felony involving the use or threat of violence to a person.").
54. See, e.g., Long v. State, 610 So.2d 1268, 1270-71 (Fla. 1992) (describing testimony about two prior sexual battery convictions introduced by the State); Tompkins v. State, 502 So.2d 415, 418 (Fla. 1987) (noting that the State presented testimony of three witnesses that the defendant had been convicted of sexual battery and kidnapping on two separate occasions after the victim here had disappeared); see also Kimbough v. State, 700 So.2d 634, 636 (Fla. 1997) (listing sexual battery as the basis for the trial court finding the aggravating circumstance of prior violent felony); Barwick v. State, 660 So.2d 685,

689 (Fla. 1995) (same); Schwab v. State, 636 So.2d 3, 7 (Fla. 1994) (same).

55. See, e.g., Whitfield v. State, 706 So.2d 1, 3 (Fla. 1997) (noting that the trial court found the contemporaneous sexual battery of another victim in case to constitute the prior violent felony aggravator); James v. State, 695 So.2d 1229, 1236 (Fla. 1997) (holding that in double homicide, the sexual assault and murder of one victim constituted proof of a prior violent felony that aggravated the murder of the other victim).

56. See, e.g., Coney v. State, 653 So.2d 1009, 1011-13 (Fla. 1995) (describing punishment phase testimony by victim of sexual battery by the defendant that occurred sixteen years earlier, incase where the defendant was convicted of first-degree murder for torching his homosexual lover in prison); Thompson v. State, 553 So.2d 153, 155 (Fla. 1989) (affirming death sentence where the defendant was convicted of kidnapping, beating, shooting, and throwing victim overboard at sea and punishment phase evidence including the defendant's 1950 rape conviction); Rose v. State, 461 So.2d 84, 87 (Fla. 1984) (permitting presentation, at punishment phase, of prior conviction for breaking and entering with intent to commit rape in case where the defendant was convicted of kidnapping and first-degree murder of an eight-year-old girl).

57. Chandler v. State, 702 So.2d 186, 191-92 (Fla. 1997) (allowing testimony about the defendant raping a woman on a boat in the Gulf of Mexico in a case where three women were strangled or drowned on a boat in the Gulf with the defendant; the women were found nude from the waist down but the state made no charge of sexual battery); Alvord v. State, 322 So.2d 533, 535-40 (Fla. 1975) (permitting punishment phase testimony about prior rape of a child in a case were the evidence showed the presence of semen in the vagina of one of the three women murdered, but the court described the murder as occurring in the course of a burglary).

58. Fla. Stat. Ann. § 921.141(5)(h).

59. Hall v. State, 614 So.2d 473, 478 (Fla. 1993) (holding that this instruction is not unconstitutionally vague because the terms are defined). Previously, the U.S. Supreme Court found a comparable aggravator of "wicked, evil, atrocious or cruel" unconstitutionally vague because none of the terms were defined. Espinosa v. Florida, 505 U.S. 1079, 1081 (1992).

60. At least 81 percent of the rape-murder cases (sixty-five of eighty) included a finding of "heinous, atrocious, or cruel." The percentage may be higher because in some cases I was not able to ascertain the particular aggravating circumstances found by the trial court due to the case pending on direct appeal and the most readily available information was from newspaper articles.

61. Forty-one percent of the eighty cases included strangulation as the manner of death. In comparison, 23 percent of the victims were shot to death, 15 percent were stabbed, and the remaining 20 percent were beaten, drowned, or the manner of death was unknown. This is consistent with studies of sexual homicide that note the prevalence of strangulation as a manner of death. See, e.g., Don Grubin, *Sexual Murder*, 165 Brit. J. of Psychiatry 624, 627 (1994) (reporting that in a study of twenty-one men who sexually attacked and murdered women, 67 percent [fourteen] of the victims were strangled).

62. Tompkins v. State, 502 So.2d 415, 421 (Fla. 1987).

63. Carroll v. State, 636 So.2d 1316, 1320 (Fla. 1994).

64. Ibid.

65. The number is twenty-three of eighty. See, e.g., Banks v. State, 700 So.2d 363, 366 (Fla. 1997) (finding the heinous, atrocious, or cruel aggravator supported by evidence that the defendant sexually assaulted a ten-year-old girl for twenty minutes before shooting her); Hoskins v. State, 702 So.2d 202, 206 (Fla. 1997) (citing evidence that the defendant attacked and raped an eighty-one-year-old woman with "sufficient force to tear her perineum" as supporting the finding of heinous, atrocious, or cruel); Mendyk v. State, 545 So.2d 846, 847-50 (Fla. 1989) (affirming heinous, atrocious, or cruel based on facts including that prior to killing the victim, the defendant "tied each of her legs to the legs of a saw horse, and sexually tortured her by several means, including inserting a broom handle in her vagina"); Quince v. State, 414 So.2d 185, 187 (Fla. 1982) (holding "severe beating, wounding, raping, and manual strangulation of an eighty-two-year-old, frail woman easily qualified as heinous").

66. See, e.g., Andrew Hacker, *Two Nations: Black and White, Separate, Hostile, Unequal* (New York: Scribners. 1992), 180; Roberts, supra, at 378.

67. See Johnson, supra, at 1028.

68. In both states experts have indicated that only the worst cases receive the death penalty. See Richard Perez-Pena, "The Death Penalty: When There's No Room for Error," *New York Times*, February 13, 2000, sec. 4 at 3. (noting that in Colorado, prosecu-

tors rarely seek the death penalty "in part, experts say, because they believe that the Colorado Office of the Public Defender will defeat all but the strongest cases"); Brad Cain, "Death Penalty Foes Optimistic They'll Make Oregon's Fall Ballot," AP Newswires, April 2, 2000 (quoting head of Oregon Crime Victims United stating, "[a]nd it's also a fact that it's very difficult to get a death penalty conviction in this state").

69. Death Row U.S.A., supra, at 31.

70. See People v. Harlan, 8 P.3d 448, 459 (Colo. 2000) (Robert Harlan); Julia C. Martinez, "Panel OKs Change in Death-Penalty System," *Denver Post*, February 4, 2000, A17 (Francisco Martinez); ibid. (William Neal); State v. Rodriguez, 794 P.2d 965 (Colo. 1990) (Frank Rodriguez).

71. The number is 46 rape-murders of 2,980 murders with known circumstances. See Fox, supra. There were 3,514 murders in total. Ibid.

72. See Martinez, supra, at A17. In four of the cases the rape was contemporaneous to the murder (Martinez [D.], Martinez [F.], Riggan, Salmon), in one the rape of one woman was in addition to the first-degree murder of three other women all in the same month (Neal), and in the remaining one, the rapes were prior to the first-degree murder of a woman, and the defendant was serving sentences of 216 years for these prior rape convictions (Richardson). Ibid.

73. Ibid. (Martinez [F.]) (gang rape and murder of fourteen-year-old young woman); Neal (rape of woman in the same month and in the same room as murder of three other women).

74. The mother of one of the victims was hispanic and her father white. Interviews with defense attorneys in Colorado (June and July 2000).

75. Ibid.; see also Death Row U.S.A., supra, at 31.

76. The relationship of victim and offender (where known) for 1976–94 Colorado rape-murder cases is: 11 percent, family/intimate; 48 percent, acquaintance; and 41 percent, stranger. See Fox, supra. Once again, the percentage of stranger rape-murder death row cases greatly outstrips the actual percentage in the state.

77. One might be tempted to discount the significance of these racial disparities in Colorado because the percentage of people of color is relatively small in that state. Indeed, in 1998, the most recent year for which information is available, approximately 92 percent of the population in Colorado was white. U.S. Census Bureau, supra, at 34. Nonetheless, African-Americans were both offenders and victims in Colorado rape-murder cases. From 1976 to 1994, for those rape-murders in which the race of offender and victim is known (28 of 46), the breakdown is: 68 percent, white offender/white victim, 11 percent, African-American offender/African-American victim; 14 percent, African-American offender/white victim; and 7 percent, white offender/African-American victim. Despite the small number, it is still worth recognizing that the small percentage of people of color in Colorado does not explain away the dearth of women-of-color victims in rape-murder cases on death row.

78. Death Row U.S.A., supra, at 51.

79. List on file with author.

80. This represents 50 of 2,026 murders with known circumstances, out of 2,428 total murders. See Fox, supra.

81. See Death Row U.S.A., supra, at 51. One of the defendants (Marco Montez) is of dual race, his father was hispanic and his mother Native- American. Interview with Montez's defense attorney (July 2000).

82. Interviews with defense attorneys in Oregon (June and August 2000).

83. The paucity of men of color among those convicted of rape-murder on Oregon's death row is not inconsistent with the rest of Oregon's death row. Only four of the twenty-seven men are nonwhite: one is Native-American, two are hispanic, and one is African American. Death Row U.S.A., supra, at 51. As with Colorado, the population of Oregon is overwhelmingly white: 93.5 percent in 1998. U.S. Census Bureau, supra, at 34. From 1976 to 1994 in rape-murder cases where the race of offender and victim is known (39 of 50), the breakdown is: 77 percent, white offender/white victim; 2.5 percent, African-American offender/African-American victim; 5 percent, African-American offender/ white victim; and 2.5 percent, white offender/African-American victim. See Fox, supra. Additional cases involve white offenders and victims of other races: 8 percent, white offender/American-Indian victim; 2.5 percent, white offender/Asian-Pacific Islander victim; 2.5 percent, white offender/"other" victim. Ibid.

84. In 1976–1994 Oregon rape-murders where the race of both the offender and victim are known, 18 percent were victims of color (7 of 39 cases). Ibid. Of these victims of color, 86 percent were female (6 of 7). Ibid. Even though this represents a small number, it

seems noteworthy that it is such a large percentage. As with Colorado, the absence of women of color as victims of men on death row for rape-murder should not be dismissed merely as a function of the relatively small percentage of people of color in the population.

85. These percentages are based on rape-murders where the relationship is known. Ibid.

86. See Coker v. Georgia, 433 U.S. 584 (1977).

87. By this I mean the spectacle lynchings that occurred from the late 1800s through the 1950s. See Grace Elizabeth Hale, *The Making of Whiteness: The Culture of Segregation in the South, 1890–1940*, (New York: Pantheon Books, 1998), 202-03; Martha Hodes, *White Women, Black Men: Illicit Sex in the Nineteenth-Century South*, (New Haven: Yale University Press, 1997), 176–77.

88. Roberts, supra, at 367. See also Katharine K. Baker, *Once A Rapist? Motivational Evidence and Relevancy in Rape Law*, 110 Harv. L. Rev. 563, 594-97 (1997).

89. Marvin E. Wolfgang and Marc Riedel, *Race, Judicial Discretion and the Death Penalty*, 407 Annals Am. Acad. Pol. & Soc. Sci. 119 (1973). This study was described as "'one of the most definitive pieces of research ever done on capital punishment." See Dennis D. Dorin, *"Two Different Worlds": Criminologists, Justices and Racial Discrimination in the Imposition of Capital Punishment in Rape Cases*, 72 J. Crim. L. & Criminology 1667, 1669 (1981) (quoting *Capital Punishment in the United States*, [New York: Published for the American Orthopsychiatric Association AMS Press, 1976], xvii [Hugo Bedau and Chester M. Pierce, eds.]).

90. Wolfgang and Riedel, supra, at 129 tbl. 2. The article focused on race discrimination against African-American defendants, so the races of the defendants and victims in the "other" category are not specified. However, in the Maxwell litigation, data specific to Arkansas showed that no white man was convicted of raping an African-American woman. See Maxwell, 398 F.2d at 144 (summarizing evidence presented to the federal district court). Apart from this one piece of information, I am unable to identify how many, if any, of the victims were African-American women. It is unlikely, however, that many, if any, of the victims were African-American women given that, for the most part, raping an African-American woman was not a crime in the South until after the Civil War. The unspoken rule, after the Civil War, was that, with the crime of rape, the death penalty was reserved for African-American men who raped white women. See Michael Meltsner, *Cruel and Unusual Punishment: The Supreme Court and Capital Punishment*, (New Tork: Random House, 1973), 321 n.2 (citing the experience in Georgia).

91. Ibid. at 132.

92. This is sixteen of the eighty men on death row for rape-murder.

93. Three of the four men on death row for rape-murder are men of color.

94. Only one of the thirteen men on death row for rape-murder is a man of color.

95. Robinson v. State, 520 So. 2d 1, 7 (Fla. 1988).

96. See ibid. at 6.

97. Ibid. On remand, Robinson was resentenced to death. See Robinson v. State, 574 So.2d 108 (Fla. 1991) (affirming new death sentence).

98. Robinson, 520 So. 2d at 7.

99. State v. Harlan, 8 P.3d 448, 499 (Colo. 2000).

100. Ibid. at 500.

101. Ibid.

102. Roberts, supra, at 365.

103. Mona Lynch and Craig Haney, *Discrimination and Instructional Comprehension: Guided Discretion, Racial Bias, and the Death Penalty*, 24 Law & Hum. Behav. 337, 353 (2000) (finding that in study on the relationship between racial bias and jury instruction comprehension, with mostly white participants, "those who sentenced a Black defendant were significantly more likely to undervalue, disregard, and even improperly use mitigating evidence as opposed to those who sentenced a white defendant," especially when the defendant and victim were of different races).

104. In two cases (Juan Chavez and Mark Schwab) the victims were white males, both young boys ages nine and eleven. See list on file with author. In one case, the defendant was white, in the other hispanic. Ibid. So the total number of cases involving white female victims is sixty-three out of eighty.

105. See, e.g., Robert L. Zangrando, *The NAACP Crusade Against Lynching, 1909–1950*, (Philadelphia: Temple University Press, 1980), 4–13 (1980) (reporting that 72.7 percent of recorded lynchings, from 1882 to 1968, were of African-Americans [3,446 out of 4,743]); ibid. at 8 (discussing how lynching and mob violence "reminded all black peo-

ple of white America's determination to impose its will and authority in a biracial society"); Jacquelyn Dowd Hall, "'The Mind That Burns in Each Body': Women, Rape, and Racial Violence," 328, 330 in *Powers of Desire: The Politics of Sexuality* (New York: Monthly Review Press, 1983) (Ann Snitow et al. eds., 1983) ("Like whipping under slavery, lynching was an instrument of coercion intended to impress not only the immediate victim but all who saw or heard about the event.").

106. Zangrando, supra, at 4 See also Paula Giddings, *When and Where I Enter: The Impact of Black Women on Race and Sex in America,* (New York: W. Morrow, 1984), 27–28 (1984) ("The charge [of raping a white woman] was leveled so consistently against Black men, and came from such impeccable sources, that the whole nation seemed to take it for granted. Not only Harper's but other scholarly and reputable magazines and newspapers wrote about the 'new crime.'")

107. Ida B. Wells-Barnett, "Southern Horrors," 14, in *On Lynchings* (New York: Arno Press and The New York Times, 1969) (1892); The governor of South Carolina once stated, during a gubernatorial campaign, "the one crime that warrants lynching, and Governor as I am, I would lead a mob to lynch the negro who ravishes a white woman." Whitfield, supra, at 3.

108. Ibid. at 14. What constituted "rape" was questionable: "With the Southern white man, any mesalliance existing between a white woman and a colored man is sufficient foundation for the charge of rape. The Southern white man says that it is impossible for a voluntary alliance to exist between a white woman and a colored man, and therefore, the fact of an alliance is proof of force." Ida B. Wells-Barnett, "A Red Record," 11, in *On Lynchings,* supra. See also Jacquelyn Dowd Hall, *Revolt Against Chivalry: Jessie Daniel Ames and the Women's Campaign Against Lynching,* (New York: Columbia University Press, 1979), 154 (noting that "popular opinion [and] very often in law [presumed] that any white woman having intercourse with a black man had been 'raped'' and that this was used to justify lynchings and legal executions). In addition, "[l]ynching could be triggered by offenses as trivial as failure to observe the racial courtesy of moving aside to let a white woman pass." Emma Coleman Jordan, *Crossing the River of Blood Between Us: Lynching, Violence, Beauty and the Paradox of Feminist History,* 3 J. Gender, Race & Just. 545, 558 (2000).

109. 2 Blanche Weisen Cook, *Eleanor Roosevelt, 1933–38* (New York: Viking, 1999), 178 (citing studies produced under the auspices of the Southern Commission of the Study of Lynching); see also Giddings, supra, at 26–27 (discussing the economic motive behind lynchings); Zangrando, supra, at 8 tbl. 3 (reporting causes of lynching from 1882–1968—rape was the third highest, after homicides and "all other causes"); ibid. at 8–11 (discussing economic, social, and political explanations of lynchings).

110. Ida B. Wells, *On Lynching,* 74, in *Words of Fire* (New York: New Press: Distributed by W. W. Norton, 1995) (Beverly Guy-Sheftall ed., 1995).

111. Barnard, supra, at 11–12; Wriggins, supra, at 119–21 (discussing how post–Civil War law continued to deny that African-American women were raped).

112. Barnard, supra, at 13–20; Hall, supra, at 149.

113. ACLU et al., Brief of Amici Curiae, Coker v. Georgia (1977), in 97 Landmark Briefs and Arguments of the Supreme Court of the Untied States: Constitutional Law 843,861 (Philip B. Kurland and Gerhard Casper eds., 1978) [hereinafter Amici Brief].

114. Barnard, supra, at 27; ibid. at 23–27 (discussing the Clubwomen's anti-lynching strategy). African-American clubwomen later joined forces with the NAACP which became the principal organization fighting lynching. Ibid. at 27-31 (discussing the creation of the NAACP and the role of African-American women). See generally Mary Jane Brown, *Eradicating This Evil: Women in the American Anti-Lynching Movement 1892–1940* (New York: Garland, 2000).

115. From 1932 to 1936, over 43,000 white women signed pledges against lynching. Hall, supra, at 180 tbl. 3. Hall observed that the many years of struggle against lynching that black women had engaged in made the creation of the Association possible. Ibid. at 165. Even then it was not easy: "For decades, black women had filled the front ranks of the fight against lynching. They had developed an analysis of the relationship between racial violence and sexual exploitation that the white ASWPL adopted only haltingly and with mixed feelings." Ibid. As Emma Coleman Jordan observed, "Perhaps a more balanced explanation of the role of white women in the anti-lynching campaign would confirm the contradiction of their willingness to accept all of the benefits of white supremacy, even as they battled lynching." Jordan, supra, at 556. Even though many white women eventually opposed lynching, other white women were complicit in African-American men being lynched. As Jordan reminds us: The history of rape would not be complete without an exploration of the abuse of rape accusations by white

women who used their power as whites to terrorize black men, women, and children. White women aided and abetted lynching actively by direct participation in the utilization of lynch mobs. They precipitated lynching passive-aggressively by falsely crying rape, staying home and letting their husbands go out to defend their honor with racial barbarity. Ibid. at 570–71 (citations omitted); Hodes, supra, at 178–97 (discussing the "agency of white women" in charging rape to cover up illicit relationships with African-American men); see also Hall, supra, at 340 (noting that "Ida B. Wells-Barnett was threatened with death and run out of town for proclaiming that behind many lynchings lay consensual interracial affairs").

116. Hall, supra, at 194 (quoting ASWPL, A New Public Opinion of Lynching).
117. Amici Brief, supra, at 871 (citing, among other sources, the Wolfgang and Riedel study).
118. Eddings v. Oklahoma, 455 U.S. 104, 110 (1982) (quoting Lockett v. Ohio, 438 U.S. 586, 604 (1978)); Gregg v. Georgia, 428 U.S. 153, 206 (1976) (plurality opinion of Stewart, Powell, and Stevens, JJ.).
119. See, e.g., Woodson v. North Carolina, 428 U.S. 280, 304 (1976). "A process that accords no significance to relevant facets of the character and record of the individual offender or the circumstances of the particular offense excludes from consideration in fixing the ultimate punishment of death the possibility of compassionate or mitigating factors stemming from the diverse frailties of humankind. It treats all persons convicted of a designated offense not as uniquely individual human beings, but as members a of a faceless, undifferentiated mass to be subjected to the blind infliction of the penalty of death." Ibid. Whether both fairness and consistency can be fulfilled constitutionally is a source of intense disagreement on the Court. See, e.g., Callins v. Collins, 510 U.S. 1141, 1151-52 (1994) (Blackmun J., dissenting from denial of cert.) (discussing other justices' recognition of a "'tension' between the need for fairness to the individual and the consistency promised in Furman"); Walton v. Arizona, 497 U.S. 639, 656, 673 (1990) (Scalia, J., concurring in part and concurring in the judgment). See generally David R. Dow, *The Third Dimension of Death Penalty Jurisprudence*, 22 Amer. J. Crim. L. 151 (1994).
120. Williams J. Bowers et al., *Foreclosed Impartiality in Capital Sentencing: Jurors' Predispositions, Guilt-Trial Experience, and Premature Decision Making*, 83 Cornell L. Rev. 1476, 1495 (1998) (reporting that in eleven states studied, almost one-half of jurors decided what punishment was appropriate before the penalty phase began).
121. Callins, 510 U.S. at 1145 (Blackmun, J., dissenting from denial of cert.).
122. Ibid. at 1147.
123. Ibid. at 1145-46.
124. Ibid. at 1142 (Scalia, J., concurring in cert. denial).
125. Ibid.
126. 512 U.S. 1254 (1994).
127. Callins, 510 U.S. at 1142.
128. McCollum, 512 U.S. at 1254.
129. Ibid. (noting that the jury that sentenced McCollum to death found seven mitigating factors including that he was mentally retarded, easily influenced by others, and under a mental and emotional disturbance at the time of the crime).
130. Ibid. See also Gretchen Engel, "Even Brutal Cases Show Death Penalty Is Unconstitutional," *New York Times*, February 27, 1994, 4: 14 (explaining sentences of the other participants: one was convicted only of rape, the other two were not tried because they were juveniles).
131. McCollum, 512 U.S. at 1254.
132. See e.g., State v. Cooey, 544 N.E.2d 895, 919 (Ohio 1989) (finding aggravating circumstances of rape and kidnapping outweighed mitigating evidence of mental disorder, severe childhood abuse, and other factors that "suggest[ed] that Cooey may have been less responsible for his acts than were most people"); State v. Benner, 533 N.E.2d 701, 720 (Ohio 1988) (Wright, J., dissenting) (dissenting on ground that the majority did not find error in three-judge sentencing panel considering the "brutal and depraved manner" in which the defendant killed the victims, when, by statute, the nature and circumstances of the offence may be only considered as mitigating).
133. 614 So. 2d 473 (Fla. 1993).
134. Ibid. at 481-82. Barkett recounted Hall's other difficulties in addition to his mental retardation. As the trial court found, "he suffers from organic brain damage, has been mentally retarded all of his life, suffers from mental illness, suffered tremendous emotional deprivation and disturbances throughout his life, suffered tremendous physical abuse and torture as a child, and has learning disabilities and a distinct speech imped-

iment that adversely affected his development." Ibid. at 479-80. The childhood abuse Hall suffered included: "[His] mother tied him in a 'croaker' sack, swung it over a fire, and beat him; buried him in the sand up to his neck to 'strengthen his legs'; tied his hands to a rope that was attached to a ceiling beam and beat him while he was naked; locked him in a smokehouse for long intervals; and held a gun on Hall and his siblings while she poked them with sticks. Ibid.

135. Ibid. at 479.

136. See, e.g., Gary Goodpaster, *The Trial for Life: Effective Assistance of Counsel in Death Penalty Cases*, 58 N.Y.U. L. Rev. 299, 334-35 (1983) (explaining that in all death penalty cases, the punishment phase inquiry is "whether the defendant, notwithstanding his crimes, is a person who should continue to live").

137. Based on twenty years of studying the lives and background of capital defendants, Professor Craig Haney concluded that a "nexus between poverty, childhood abuse and neglect, social and emotional dysfunction, alcohol and drug abuse, and crime is so tight in the lives of many capital defendants as to form a kind of social historical 'profile.'" Craig Haney, *The Social Context of Capital Murder: Social Histories and the Logic of Mitigation*, 35 Santa Clara L. Rev. 547, 580 (1995).

138. See Dorothy Otnow Lewis et al., *Psychiatric, Neurological, and Psychoeducational Characteristics of 15 Death Row Inmates in the United States*, 143 Am. J. Psychiatry 838 (1986) (reporting findings of study of 15 individuals on death row); Marilyn Feldman et al., *Filicidal Abuse in the Histories of 15 Condemned Murderers*, 14 Bull. Am. Acad. Psychiatry & L. 345 (1986) (reporting incidence of extreme childhood abuse among same 15 individuals); Dorothy Otnow Lewis et al., *Neuropsychiatric, Psychoeducational and Family Characteristics of 14 Juveniles Condemned to Death in the United States*, 145 Am. J. Psychiatry 584 (1988) (reporting findings on juveniles on death row). See also Pamela Y. Blake et al., *Neurologic Abnormalities in Murders*, 45 Neurology 1641 (1995) (finding extensive evidence of severe childhood abuse, brain damage, and mental illness among study of 31 murderers). See generally Haney, supra, at 600-01 (describing social histories of capital defendants and noting, "[m]any capital defendants have led lives that are the criminogenic equivalent of being born into hazardous waste dumps"). While the exact number of those on death row who are mentally retarded is not known, experts believe that about 10 percent of the 3,600 on death row are mentally retarded. Raymond Bonner and Sara Rimer, "Executing the Mentally Retarded Even as Laws Begin to Shift," *New York Times*, August 7, 2000, A1 (citing James Ellis, Professor of Law at the University of New Mexico and leading expert on mental retardation).

139. See, e.g., Dorothy Otnow Lewis, *From Abuse to Violence: Psychophysiological Consequences of Maltreatment*, 31 J. Am. Acad. Child & Adolescent Psychiatry 383, 388 (1992) (concluding that a history of childhood abuse, mental impairments and brain damage create a "matrix for violence" because the person's ability to make rational judgments, understand consequences and make appropriate choices is fundamentally altered); Phyllis L. Crocker, *Childhood Abuse and Adult Murder: Implications for the Death Penalty*, 77 N.C. L. Rev. 1143, 1156-76 (1999) (discussing long term effects of childhood abuse and how it may contribute to the commission of murder for which a person may be sentenced to death).

140. Dorothy Otnow Lewis et al., *Toward a Theory of the Genesis of Violence: A Follow-Up Study of Delinquents*, 28 J. Am. Acad. Child & Adolescent Psychiatry 431, 436 (1989).

141. Women often report that the rapist told them to be quiet or he would kill her. See, e.g., Nancy Venable Raine, *After Silence*, (New York: Crown Publishing Group, 1999), 20 (reporting rapist saying, "Shut up, you shut up, you bitch, or I'll kill you"); Estrich, supra, at 1087 (stating that rapist said, "Push over, shut up, or I'll kill you").

142. See Wriggins, supra, at 130 ("[T]he fear and threat of rape influences many women who are never actually raped.").

143. Indeed, the very availability of the death penalty as a punishment may foster this belief: One might argue that we show disrespect for the victim of rape-murder if we do not impose the most stringent sentence. But see Susan Bandes, *When Victims Seek Closure: Forgiveness, Vengeance and the Role of Government*, 27 Fordham Urb. L.J. 1599, 1599-1601 (2000) (discussing differing responses of victims' families to whether the defendant should be sentenced to death or life imprisonment). The problem with the argument is that it ignores flaws that exist with the death penalty, including those that directly relate to victims. For example, it ignores the racial and gender biases that permeate the application of the death penalty to rape-murder cases.

144. See, e.g., Cole v. State, 701 So.2d 845, 852-53, and n.5 (Fla. 1997) (referring to mitigating

evidence of mental incapacity, and physical and psychological childhood abuse, all discounted by the trial court); Bogle v. State, 655 So.2d 1103, 1105 (Fla. 1995) (reporting mitigating evidence including physical and mental childhood abuse, drug use encouraged by father, personality disorder, and mental disturbance at the time of the crime); Doyle v. State, 460 So.2d 353, 358 (Fla. 1985) (Overton, J., concurring in part and dissenting in part) (reciting mitigating evidence including low I.Q., borderline mental retardation, and organic brain deficits). The existence of these types of impairments is often a reason Florida Supreme Court vacates death sentences on appeal. See infra (discussing examples). The question is sometimes raised as to how I might feel about a defendant who committed rape-murder (or any other death-eligible murder) who did not have any impairments. Based on my experience representing men on death row for five years, and my continued work in the area, I find this possibility to be virtually nonexistent. See Welsh White, *Effective Assistance of Counsel in Capital Cases: The Evolving Standard of Care*, 2 U. Ill. L. Rev. 323, 342 (1993) (reporting a capital defense attorney as stating about mitigating evidence, "If the attorney did not find it, it was because he 'didn't look hard enough.' ").

145. See Haney, supra, at 574-78 (discussing the effects of the failure of juvenile institutions and adult prisons to address trauma and mental impairments); cf. Abby Stein and Dorothy Otnow Lewis, *Discovering Physical Abuse: Insights from a Follow-Up Study of Delinquents*, 16 Child Abuse & Neglect 523, 523 (1992) (discussing how adults deny or minimize their own childhood abuse).

146. See Baker, supra, at 582; Morrison Torrey, *When Will We Be Believed? Rape Myths and the Idea of a Fair Trial in Rape Prosecutions*, 24 U.C. Davis L. Rev. 1013, 1022-25 (1991) (discussing studies that show rapists are not mentally deviant but similar to "normal" men).

147. For example, in a rape-murder case, death by strangulation may suggest less premeditation or greater impulsiveness. As the Florida Supreme Court recognized, "[i]t is a tragic reality that the murder of a rape victim is all too frequently the culmination of the same hostile-aggressive impulses which triggered the initial attack and not a reasoned act motivated primarily by the desire to avoid detection." Doyle, 460 So.2d at 358. As a matter of punishment this could make the defendant less worthy of death. I thank Margery Malkin Koosed for suggesting this possibility.

13

AN EAGLE SOARS: THE LEGACY OF MR. SMILE

CECILE C. GUIN

Watching Feltus walk though the reception area to the lethal injection room at the Louisiana State Penitentiary at Angola was the most difficult experience I have ever had. I had previously sat with my father as he died of cancer and with my beloved friend as he died of AIDS. But this was different.

As the entourage of correctional personnel, witnesses, clergy, and victims passed through the waiting room, I, along with other friends of Feltus, waited for word that the execution was completed and that Feltus was dead. I discreetly dug my nails into my arms in that quiet room to avoid losing complete control of myself. As an emotionally healthy and strong professional, I was surprised at my psychological devastation, pain, and sorrow. I was also very worried that some technical aspect of the execution would go awry, and the results would be grisly for Feltus. He had approached his death with such dignity and grace and we all wanted him to die in the same manner.

As I waited for what seemed like an eternity, I reflected on the professional path that led me to be part of Feltus Taylor Jr.'s life. Feltus epitomized the many children and youth with whom I had worked since graduating from college in 1974. Like Feltus, many of these youth were propelled into the juvenile justice system through educational failure, developmental disabilities, child maltreatment, and a variety of other difficulties. The majority of the youth with whom I had been involved through direct practice or research were African American. Many were from very poor homes and suffered from various effects of malnourishment and maltreatment. The characteristics of these children who became delinquents—as well as the delinquents who progressed into adult criminality—have become all too familiar to me. Poverty, mental illness, mental retardation, learning disabilities, and child abuse are consistent factors in the life stories of these prison inmates. Feltus's story was no different.

I had been to death row at Angola several times before I met Feltus; the walkway to death row had become a major part of my existence. When I met Feltus in the fall of 1997, death row was managed in an unusually humane manner. Professionals and advisors were able to sit face-to-face with clients in a room that could be considered very pleasant for a prison. Inmates have produced a great deal of artwork, and some of it is seen in the building housing death row inmates. In the room where I first met Feltus, a large mural on the wall depicts an eagle flying above a lake in a rural, forest setting. Since I generally had to wait a few minutes for Feltus to be brought downstairs, I often studied that mural until I heard the characteristic flip-flop of slippers signaling the close proximity of an inmate and correctional officer.

Those previous meetings were vivid as I gave Feltus my final good-bye. As I hugged Feltus for the last time, I looked into his eyes and told him how proud I was of his accomplishments over the past ten years. As I waited for the death pronouncement, I felt my heart would break for the loss of him. What I saw in Feltus's eyes always reminded me of the plight of so many children and youth. Feltus and I had spent hundreds of hours talking about his path to death row. In the course of an armed robbery, he killed one person and gravely wounded another. He did not intend to hurt anyone and, in fact, had little memory of the incident. But he committed the crime and repented it to the end of his life.

Sister Helen Prejean was Feltus's first spiritual advisor. She had to give up this role when the success of the book *Dead Man Walking* provided her with the opportunity to take her work into the international arena. Sister Helen explained Feltus's pathway as it related to his intense need for human intimacy and connection. Most of the trouble Feltus experienced was somehow related to his financial support of women and their families, a responsibility that he believed was key to their love and acceptance of him. The stress of that type of daily urgency and burden proved to be overwhelming.

His story is like the stories of many other inmates, but unlike many other death row inmates, Feltus had developed a tremendous support group that included his attorneys, a magnificent spiritual advisor, social workers, and volunteers from both his grandmother's church and a local Episcopal church. His story captivated those in the research office that I direct at the Louisiana State University School of Social Work. Our students and a talented young writer who was employed with the office spent two years preparing Feltus's handwritten autobiography for publication. From his book and our life history investigation, some of the primary points of Feltus' life are depicted in the life history chart.

My office initially became involved with Feltus in 1997 through the faith and legal community that had become such a huge part of his life. All of these circumstances and relationships enabled Feltus to meet his death with the peace and certainty felt only by those with great faith.

MR. SMILE

Feltus had a habit of signing his letters "Mr. Smile," with a drawing of a happy face. Ever since I had known him on death row, the many notes he sent to people around the world were decorated with this smiling face. Mr. Smile was an accurate descriptor of Feltus, because he had a contagious sense of optimism and an undying hope of a better existence. Seeing his sunny attitude triggered thoughts of Haley Mills playing the eternal optimist in the movie *Pollyana*, which tells the story of a young girl who invented the "Glad Game" and used it to bring joy, optimism, and hope to the citizens of her small town. But Feltus was real, and his smile, his faith, and his hope for life were gifts he gave to his community: to his fellow inmates, to professionals who dealt with him, and to loved ones around the world.

Not only did I learn about hope from Feltus, but I also learned about life on death row. The row was a multifaceted community to Feltus. He emerged as a leader there, encouraging other men to be productive, to seek forgiveness, and to develop insight about their lives. To accomplish these ends, Feltus used his time on the row to write, paint, and read the Bible. He became a communications system: he communicated with God, with himself, and with other people both in and out of prison. He spent hundreds of hours communicating with people of all ages and all walks of life around the world. For instance, he advised and "mentored" a young man from the local Episcopal church. His daily activities, his participation in life both inside and outside the walls, and his role in his community all combined to make Feltus a vital part of his very real community. He made a positive impact.

I often told him how much he meant to people. Feltus was morally and spiritually rehabilitated in a way that most people imagine to be possible only in the next world. Through his remorse and faith, Feltus reclaimed more lost souls on death row and in the free world than anyone will ever know. The only burden that still weighed on him was his former friend, his living victim. Feltus desperately wanted to communicate his remorse to this victim, through letter, video, or any other form of

FELTUS TAYLOR TIMELINE

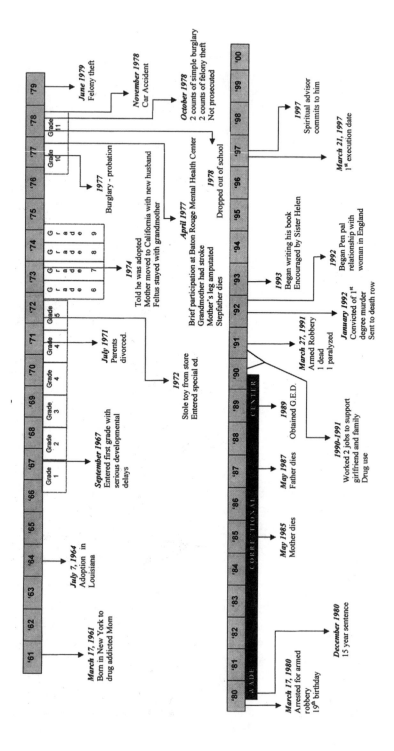

'61 | '62 | '63 | '64 | '65 | '66 | '67 | '68 | '69 | '70 | '71 | '72 | '73 | '74 | '75 | '76 | '77 | '78 | '79

March 17, 1961
Born in New York to drug addicted Mom

July 7, 1964
Adoption in Louisiana

September 1967
Entered first grade with serious developmental delays

Grade 1 | Grade 2 | Grade 3 | Grade 4 | Grade 4 | Grade 5

July 1971
Parents divorced.

1972
Stole toy from store
Entered special ed.

Grade 6 | Grade 7 | Grade 8 | Grade 9

1974
Told he was adopted
Mother moved to California with new husband
Feltus stayed with grandmother

April 1977
Brief participation at Baton Rouge Mental Health Center
Grandmother had stroke
Mother's leg amputated
Stepfather dies

1977
Burglary - probation

Grade 10 | Grade 11

1978
Dropped out of school

June 1979
Felony theft

November 1978
Car Accident

October 1978
2 counts of simple burglary
2 counts of felony theft
Not prosecuted

'80 | '81 | '82 | '83 | '84 | '85 | '86 | '87 | '88 | '89 | '90 | '91 | '92 | '93 | '94 | '95 | '96 | '97 | '98 | '99 | '00

ACADEMY CORRECTIONAL CENTER

March 17, 1980
Arrested for armed robbery
19th birthday

December 1980
15 year sentence

May 1985
Mother dies

May 1987
Father dies

1989
Obtained G.E.D.

1990-1991
Worked 2 jobs to support girlfriend and family
Drug use

March 27, 1991
Armed Robbery
1 dead
1 paralyzed

January 1992
Convicted of 1st degree murder
Sent to death row

1992
Began Pen pal relationship with woman in England

1993
Began writing his book
Encouraged by Sister Helen

1997
Spiritual advisor commits to him

March 21, 1997
1st execution date

communication, but the prison and legal systems never allowed this communication. The victim never was able to hear Feltus's remorse and to benefit from it. Feltus, however, had gained peace through his relationship with God, a faith that had grown in his nine years on death row. He felt God's forgiveness and kept believing that his victims and their families would feel the same sense of peace. Although he was sad at the prospect of his death and upset over the uncertainty of changing execution dates, Feltus faced his situation as if he knew exactly what was going to take place next. When the execution date finally arrived, I was overwhelmed by despair at the loss of someone who had become a productive and valuable part of our society—someone who had become a part of all of our lives.

It troubles me that Feltus's transformation took place on death row. If society had responded differently to him as a troubled youngster, would he have achieved his potential as a free man? Would he have avoided death row? Why did society wait until he was on death row to provide the supports he needed to grow into a self-aware, self-controlled, giving man? The sorrow of the situation is that, judging by the high-quality man he became on death row, he surely could have been a fine and responsible citizen had there been more effective intervention in his family life and early problems. My grief for Feltus is also grief for all the children who are on a collision course with prison and death row, and who are not getting the human supports they need to avoid that collision.

The fact is that something remarkable does happen to many people who live on death row; perhaps it is the solitude, the protection from society, or the psychological trauma of facing death. All these elements— as well as his internal strength—helped transform Feltus. As he developed, he reached out to others and developed reciprocal relationships. He blossomed through his relationship with his spiritual advisor. Another key ingredient was his elderly grandmother, who gave undying love and support. Feltus's deep sense of concern and compassionate love for his young "neighbor" on death row and a paternal communication with a legal aide and her young children demonstrated and expanded his sense of duty and ability to "give" to others. These people, as well as many others, created a community in which individuals believe that Feltus contributed to their own human development.

There is another community involved in this drama: the community of victims. This community includes direct victims of crime, and the "hidden" victims who are the family members and loved ones of both victim and offender. Feltus was keenly aware of his victims, and so is society. No discussion of death row is complete without examining the shadows of the victims who permeate death row.

JUVENILE TO ADULT CRIMINALITY

Feltus's face represented to me the 832 incarcerated youth I studied in my doctoral research,[1] and the 92 men and women who have been a part of our criminological life history research. He also represented the youth and young adult offenders who were identified as child abuse cases in another research study my office conducted on the effects of violence in early childhood.[2] It is true that the manner in which Feltus died was different from the end most of these people will experience, but the similarities are often stunning.

Since I have worked with this population for many years, several juveniles with whom I was involved in direct practice or in other research studies are now adults facing capital trials in a number of states. This is a horrifying statement of the failure of our juvenile justice system. Youth who have been in Louisiana's correctional institutions are entering the adult justice system at an alarming pace. My own doctoral research documented this ongoing adult criminality of 90 percent of individuals being tracked (of a total 832 males between the ages of thirteen and twenty-one). My interviews with youths who were a part of the Human Rights Watch Children's Rights Project[3] and U.S. Department of Justice investigation have often led me to be involved in such capital trials, describing the conditions of confinement for Louisiana children. I think one of the most compelling situations that I have faced took place in Oklahoma.

JACK

A Louisiana native named Jack[4] faced a high-profile capital trial, and I was asked to help develop his life story to present as mitigating evidence at sentencing in the event he was found guilty. He described in detail the circumstances that had led to his commitment to Bridge City Correctional Center for Youth (formerly Louisiana Training Institute at Bridge City). Since I have many clients who had been sent to this facility when they were very young, I asked Jack if he had known any of them there. Jack recognized several names and remembered one person named Robert very well. I had developed a life history on Robert for his capital trial and knew that Robert had been on death row in Louisiana for five or six years. When I told Jack of Robert's fate, Jack was very surprised and hurt.

Jack's trial ended in conviction and confinement on death row in Oklahoma. When I visited Robert on death row in Louisiana and told him of Jack's fate, Robert was distraught. He remembered Jack well, vividly recalling the extreme abuse and terror that Jack had suffered at Bridge City. Jack had gone to Bridge City as a small boy from a rural area; he could not protect himself from the correctional officers or the other boys. Robert, who had grown up in a very rough urban neighborhood, had, by necessity, learned to protect himself in order to survive. Both boys had entered the institution at very young ages (eleven and thirteen years old, respectively). Robert described some of the horrors of Jack's incarceration, and they were very consistent with the way Jack related those stories, right down to the nicknames of correctional officers. In fact, Jack's capital crime was linked to the abuses he suffered at Bridge City, even though the capital crime occurred some fifteen years later.

Jack maintained a productive and noncriminal lifestyle from the time he left Bridge City until his arrest for first-degree murder, in spite of his deteriorating mental condition. Although undiagnosed and untreated, Jack suffered from bipolar disorder, a mental illness that took him from the depths of depression to an extreme emotional high. He increasingly lived life as if he was on an uncontrollable roller coaster. Late one night, as he entered the downward swing of the disease after being awake for several days, Jack began to believe that demonic forces possessed the child in his care. These forces led the child to wake Jack up each time he had fallen asleep for a few moments. When Jack fell asleep, the child began crying. After several hours, in an emotional fit, Jack threw the child against the wall. The child became lethargic and non-responsive. Jack placed him in the closet and went to sleep. When the child's mother came home and found him in the closet, she physically attacked Jack. As they scuffled, the woman fell and hit her head on a brick that was supporting a sofa. The head injury killed her.

Jack panicked and reverted to a prior mental state that had helped him through his traumatic experiences as an incarcerated youth. His escalating bouts with mental illness, combined with the traumatic memories of his life as a child, led him to believe the child he harmed was actually being protected. In Bridge City, Jack had actually felt safer in "the hole," a dreary lockdown room with no lights, no furniture, and no clothing for the youth placed there. When Jack harmed the child in his care, he believed the child would be safe from harm in "the hole." The first "hole" was the closet in the apartment. Tragically, the second "hole" was underneath a house, where the child was placed in a basket in sub-zero degree temperatures with a severe head and neck injury. When Jack was arrested, he continually informed the police that the child was "safe in the hole." In fact, Jack loved the child and his mother and was despondent over his puzzling behavior that had killed one person and critically injured another.

Robert insisted on getting Jack's address so he could write him. With the press of work, I forgot to send Robert that address, and he was so intent on writing Jack that Robert, about two weeks later, sent a message all the way through death row to Feltus so Feltus could ask his attorney to ask me for Jack's address. Robert and Jack began corresponding.

ROBERT

Robert's story truly demonstrates the plight of poor, African-American males in Louisiana, where the actions of the juvenile justice system all but ensured that he would never have a chance at productive life. Robert was committed to the Louisiana Department of Public Safety and Corrections when he was thirteen for an aggravated battery. He was raised without love or tenderness in juvenile correctional facilities, having been sentenced for "juvenile life." His tumultuous seven years in that system meant that Robert, in order to protect himself, had to become aggressive and mean. He obtained additional charges while in the juvenile institution, generally related to fighting. The persons that Robert was convicted of hurting have a right to be extremely angry with a state system that bred callous cruelty and lack of impulse control. Robert's life could have been quite different with appropriate early childhood intervention.

But that was not to be the case. He moved from juvenile facilities to several adult prison facilities. Robert was finally released in 1994, at the age of twenty-five; he had no skills, minimal education, and no money. His impoverished mother was on dialysis three times weekly. His poor, violent, disorganized neighborhood offered no hope for him. His twelve years of incarceration had produced an embittered man, and set him on a twisted path. He had almost no way to become a productive member of society.

While awaiting his trial for shooting and killing a store clerk, Robert said to me, "Honestly, what does anyone expect? Did anyone really think I was going to leave the adult prison at this age and find a job with twelve years of imprisonment as my reference? I have no formal education, no skills, and no one to help me find a place to work. Really, does my situation surprise you?"

Indeed it did not. Robert's history matched the life scenarios of many incarcerated persons. The real surprise is that society continues to commit very young teens to juvenile prisons for "juvenile life," ensuring they have no hope of early release, no incentive to behave, and no opportunity to learn meaningful skills that could lead to employment after release. The system bears a heavy responsibility to the victims when these mistreated juveniles are released and, predictably, go on to commit crimes.

During the penalty phase of Robert's trial, it was alleged that an older woman whom Robert reportedly savagely beat during his brief crime spree was so badly injured that she could not leave her home and was completely unable to sleep. Robert has no real memory of the beating, a not uncommon response to rage-related crime. Not only was Robert a victim of the judicial system that incarcerated him at age thirteen—leaving him to raise and protect himself in a violent environment—but his victim was, too.

Robert has matured on death row and has developed unusual insight about the life trajectory that led him to the ranks of the condemned. When we prepared for Robert's trial, he admitted to being in the store (the crime scene), but denied being the shooter. Strong indicators uncovered during the past few years seem to support his contentions of being innocent. However, without another trial or a successful appeal, Robert will be executed for that murder, and the true guilty party will never be revealed.

If our system actually discovered who the real shooter was and released Robert, what would become of him? He still has no skills, no education, and no support system at home. Would a "juvenile life commitment" and death row experience prepare him to live effectively in society?

Whatever Robert's fate will be, his letters and requests show heartwarming signs of human development and potential. Feltus's relationship with Robert, I believe, is a factor in Robert's personal growth. Feltus and Robert were close to each other. Feltus's transformation must surely be credited to his own innate goodness and the devotion and dependability of his spiritual advisor. Robert and others on death row witnessed this transformation and observed Feltus's grace as he faced death. Robert was particularly inspired by Feltus's cheerful attitude, and I hope that their relationship will make Robert's future more meaningful and peaceful. Robert has requested a spiritual advisor, but the men on death row typically have difficulty securing one.

What about the many other children that have gone from pitiful childhoods to juvenile delinquency to adult criminality? The routes to death row vary. Robert's route wound through poverty, violence in the neighborhood, and a social system and judiciary which were inadequate to meet his needs. Feltus's path to criminality was childhood abandonment and developmental disabilities. Jack's trajectory moved through extreme poverty, unspeakable child abuse, and an untreated mental illness. From my professional vantage point, it appears that an increasingly large number of children with mental disabilities and retardation are being propelled into the criminal justice system.

JOHN

In 2000, before Feltus was executed, an attorney from another southern state called me. The attorney had recently been appointed to the case of a Louisiana native, John, who had been on death row in that other state for over fifteen years, and he was alarmed that time had simply run out for his client. John's story is quite compelling. He had been tried only once though the evidence in the case is quite questionable, and no evidence at all was submitted to demonstrate the fact that John had a lifelong history of mental illness and mental retardation. The documentation of child abuse in his early life would likely provide enough mitigation evidence to sway the most determined jury.

I agreed to examine John's case material and decide if we could assist in developing a criminological life history. When I referred to my 1976 dissertation records, I found that John had been a subject in that research. This prompted me to search my original files, stored in boxes in my attic. They verified that John had had a substantiated mental retardation diagnosis since the time he was very young. It amazed me that in the course of an entire death penalty trial, evidence of this diagnosis, substantiated by the Department of Corrections itself, using multiple methods, had not been entered.

I visited John, and found that his story was eerily familiar to the stories told by people like Robert and Jack. John was incarcerated at Louisiana Training Institute in Monroe, Louisiana, where the treatment he received was generally brutal. As bad as that was, John's treatment at home was worse: His parents hated and abused him terribly, and his siblings have not spoken to him in years. And, John reported, he was sexually abused numerous times in the institution for retarded children at which he lived for several years. It seems that John, at age forty, has finally found the one place where he cannot be easily violated or abused: death row. But his isolation is intense; he has no family communications, no pen pals, no money, and no real connection to the outside world. In the relative solitude of his life, John has been able to educate himself through reading the Bible and studying legal documents. Since his IQ is in the mid-50s, this accomplishment is rather remarkable. Unlike Feltus, John lacks any human support and spiritual connection to raise him to a higher level in life. John may be the only person I have ever met who has never had a soul who loved him or a person whom he could trust. It is possible, however, that he can trust the state to make good on its promise to execute him this spring, despite his continued protestations of innocence.

I am afraid for John. He is retarded and mentally ill, and cannot even understand what is happening to him. Without doubt, he does not understand the concept of lethal injection.

DALTON

John's situation bears some resemblance to Dalton's case. Dalton, another youth from my dissertation sample, came very close to being executed in 1989. Since he had been one of my subjects, the Department of Corrections allowed me to talk to him and use the research to help make his case for life imprisonment rather than death. I knew his case very well from my research, but I did not know him personally. The fact that he was soon to be executed unnerved me. I wanted to reconstruct, while I still could, all of the evidence that showed how he reached death row.

I had become so involved with ascertaining the tortured path by which Dalton progressed through the criminal world that I lost sight of him as a person. The criminological predictors and the circumstances that had led to his brain damage, retardation, and criminal activity were clear; his human needs and emotions were more difficult to uncover. The deep emotions that I felt about his execution—he was the first of those I had studied to be executed—set the stage for my fascination with discovering the life paths of children who become lifers or death row inmates.

What made Dalton's case so compelling was that much of his brain was apparently not operational. He had been battered and beaten so badly as a child that his brain was irrevocably damaged. His records, which were corroborated by correctional officials who had worked with him, demonstrated not only that he was unable to survive in the "free world," but that he did not have the mental capacity to live without structured supervision. A former institutional administrator described the prospect of releasing Dalton as similar to releasing a wild animal in a civilized society. Left alone, provided with food and shelter, and never threatened, that animal could perhaps safely coexist with others. But if the animal were threatened or hungry, it would naturally aggressively protect itself and fight for food and survival. Dalton's brain was so damaged it no longer governed his behavior when he felt threatened or hungry. His diagnosis was not sociopathic; he simply did not have a fully functioning brain. He needed to be in a structured living arrangement. That was not to be the case. Dalton was released, and he killed a state trooper several months later when the trooper behaved in a way that Dalton interpreted as aggressive. As his juvenile records had predicted, Dalton believed that the state trooper was behaving in an aggressive and threatening manner when he stopped Dalton and his brother on the interstate. In reality, the trooper probably did appear threatening to the two young African-American men as they were stopped on a dark, isolated portion of the highway. Dalton responded to the threat (real or perceived) by shooting the trooper. He never could understand why his actions were not considered to be in self-defense.

The months leading up to Dalton's execution were tumultuous. The Department of Corrections had graciously provided me space and assistance for the year or two that it took to collect all of the data for my doctoral dissertation. Each day, I witnessed the delivery of hundreds of letters to the Department of Corrections headquarters begging for clemency for Dalton. The execution had become a very high-profile case because of Dalton's brain damage. Dalton's story was featured on several documentary news shows, including *60 Minutes*, in which neighbors of Dalton described horrific episodes of abuse inflicted upon Dalton as a child.

The Department of Corrections was willing to let me interview Dalton. When I talked to him by phone, Dalton, quiet and polite, agreed to my interview but said, "it is just so hard to keep going through all of this." He was scared and emotional. I did not have the heart to interfere with his final days, and I never interviewed him. I did attempt, however, to get all of my records to the governor for consideration of clemency. It was to no avail; the governor reported that he felt duty-bound to execute Dalton because the crime involved killing a state trooper. Dalton met his end at 12:01 A.M. on May 18, 1990.

According to a friend who was also a confidant to the governor, the governor also had trouble sleeping that night. Apparently, he was quite torn about the execution because of Dalton's brain damage and the many pleas for clemency that had come to him. On hearing about the governor's sleepless night, it struck me that Dalton, as a child, must have had many nights of troubled sleep, anticipating the physical and sexual abuse that was his lot in life.

Dalton's story matters because his life path was so clearly beyond his control. As a defenseless child in a violent home, and suffering from brain damage resulting from abuse, Dalton never had a chance to control his life. Correctional officials clearly predicted that Dalton would be unable to live in the free world. The family of the dead trooper still, no doubt, wishes that someone in power had heeded those predictions.

In the early 1990s, when I was asked to testify before the legislature on the rights of unborn children, I thought of Dalton. Did Dalton feel that his tortured life was worth living? No one can know. Though the political question before the legislature revolved around abortion, I found myself testifying about Dalton. To begin life unwanted, emotionally abandoned, and physically maltreated, and to end life through legal execution, is a scenario that forces us to move beyond abortion and consider quality of life. This society must find a way to ensure the rights of the unborn, not to existence, but to a meaningful and bearable life.

Undoubtedly, the state trooper's family wonders about policy and practice with unwanted children, and Dalton's family does, too. During the course of conducting interviews for the Department of Justice investigation into juvenile correctional facilities from 1996 to 1998, I interviewed one of Dalton's second cousins. Though she did not know Dalton, she knew he had fathered a son. Dalton's plight, she said, had affected the family, but a number of his relatives were in the juvenile and adult justice systems—including the cousin I was interviewing.

Dalton's case is often cited in the literature about mentally retarded persons who have been executed. Though I try to think of the good points in Dalton's situation, it still remains unclear to me exactly what good came of his very sad time on earth.

A CIRCLE OF FRIENDS

Thinking of "the good" points was something that Feltus often talked about. True to his self-portrayal as "Mr. Smile," Feltus approached his death with hope for the next phase of his being. Ten to twelve of us (ranging from lifelong friends from his neighborhood to the devoted employer of Feltus's elderly grandmother) gathered to comfort Feltus and comfort ourselves on the day of his execution. Feltus, in his typical style, gathered everyone together and led us in prayer, and he thanked us for being part of his life. He then asked each of us to say a few words about our relationship with him and how we had developed through this experience. It was a very difficult and emotional time, as we all said goodbye to him and expressed our gratitude for his impact on us. We reminisced about first meetings and impressions, and we all laughed at Feltus's infectious sense of humor.

Quite frankly, I was so overcome by grief that I was unsure I could participate. But I was ultimately able to articulate the main thing Feltus brought into my life: hope.

Those who deal with persons in the criminal justice system on a daily basis often find the enormity of human wreckage overwhelming. Given the life circumstances of people like Feltus, John, and Robert, how can society create situations to allow these people to develop in more productive ways? When I conduct criminal history investigations into the lives of abused, neglected, and/or disabled children, I am often struck with how hard they have had to work just to survive, let alone to be productive. It is a struggle to glean the meanings of their lives, and to understand, not only their suffering, but also the suffering they inflict on their victims.

What Feltus's life did was to show me, in a most remarkable way, the value and sacredness of life. Feltus's existence exemplifies the miracle of redemption and transformation, providing hope that others in his circumstances can turn their lives around. Because of Feltus's remarkable impact on other people, I will never conduct another interview with a person facing capital charges without seeing his or her potential for accomplishment.

On the day of the execution, I haltingly explained these feelings to our "circle." Feltus inspired me to face any situation with an offender or victim with hope and faith, believing in the potential for recovery in their lives. This is a magnificent gift, and a vital one to professionals who work in the justice system, where hope is often hard to find.

When we completed our prayers, those who were leaving were allowed physical contact with Feltus as they said their good-byes. I was very grateful that I had been approved to remain with Feltus until it was time for him to enter the execution room. I was equally grateful that his spiritual advisor and attorney were witnesses to the execution and that I had been spared this experience.

WHAT ARE WE DOING?

Of the clients I knew well, Feltus was the first to be executed. But his life story is like that of many other inmates; in fact, the life histories are beginning to replicate themselves. Their stories seem to involve ever more horrifying examples of abuse, and violence, and callousness toward children. Increasingly, I find myself asking, What are we doing with entire generations of poor children, particularly poor children of color? How can we, as a society, continue to ignore the needs of children, particularly children with disabilities? Can we justify seeing so many of them enter into a life of crime?

The incarceration rates continue to increase in Louisiana, as does the death row population. More and more children with disabilities are entering the justice system and following a progression into adult criminality. The United States remains one of three countries in the world that executes retarded persons.

If the system is inhumane for inmates, it is equally inhumane for victims. Most victims tell me that they are greatly embittered by the arrogance of the state in assuming that the crime is against the state. Victims feel that the crime was against them. Communities bear the brunt of expenses, fiscal and humane, when crime is committed. There is some comfort in the idea of recognizing that the offenders, the victims, their families, and their communities all suffer when a crime is committed. Most of our criminals are just grown-up victims. Looking at all these elements creates a sense of urgency for society to promote community healing and individual peace and recovery.

Can we recover when we execute persons who are, in fact, rehabilitated? This question surfaced when Karla Faye Tucker faced execution in Texas. Retribution, an important principle to the legal system, does not necessarily contribute to community recovery. The contributions that Feltus could have made had he been allowed to live are countless—from mentoring others on death row, to advising youthful offenders to make better decisions, or to reconcile with his victims so they could finally achieve some internal peace and understanding.

THE END COMES

As I waited to hear the pronouncement of Feltus's death, I thought of all the Jacks, Roberts, Johns, and Daltons. Saying good-bye to Feltus meant saying good-bye to the hope of meaningful life for people in Feltus's situation. Seeing him walk toward the execution chamber meant also seeing the end of the pathway for many, many children who end up in crime.

But Feltus had overcome the world of crime and had found meaning in life. Moments before his execution, he told me he was ready to meet his end and that it would be all right. I had a fleeting thought about the craziness of the situation: The condemned man comforts the social worker. Looking into his big eyes and his smiling face, I told him he would always be in my heart. Kissing his bald head, I bade him good-bye.

The chaplains, attorneys, various friends, correctional officers, and I then watched the macabre processional into the execution room. Within five or ten minutes—the longest moments of my life—the entourage flowed back into the reception area: victims, correctional officers, Feltus's support group, and prosecutors all in the same room. The spiritual advisor comforted us by saying that the execution occurred without any flaws. Feltus was strong until his death, delivering a very eloquent message to his victims with courage and humility. His short statement was, "I want to tell you, Keith, and the Ponsano Family, that I have always regretted what I've done. . . . It was my own doing. After this is over, I hope you can find the peace to move on."

Later, we learned that Feltus's living victim had empowered the warden to relay the victim's forgiveness to Feltus. We were all very grateful to know that Feltus, shortly before he died, had obtained the forgiveness that he so much craved.

Feltus had a last wish granted: he was taken from Angola that night to the funeral home in charge of his arrangements. How we had laughed about that request when Feltus described it to us; he said, "As soon as I'm free, I want out."

Feltus's funeral was a tribute to his life and death. It was a joint service offered through his grandmother's Southern Baptist church and the upper-middle-class Episcopalian church that had "adopted" Feltus. It was a truly "integrated" natural setting, and the connective power was Feltus and the hope he conveyed. The service inspired the participants to develop a commitment to life. Feltus had helped arrange this funeral, explaining to me, "Now, you know my funeral isn't going to be one of your white-type funerals; it is going to be rocking and rolling." And he was right.

One of Feltus's attorneys spoke at his funeral about the artwork that was painted in the visiting area of death row, eloquently describing the mural of the eagle flying over a lake. Feltus had told the attorney that he often thought of his execution as freedom from his earthly life to a better life in heaven. That mural, which pictorially describes Feltus's longings, energizes those of us who develop relationships with other death row inmates. It symbolizes eternal hope for meaning in life and in the lives of our clients, their families, and their victims.

Before the funeral services began, I asked Feltus's friend Rodney to place in Feltus's hands a cross that my sister had brought from Jerusalem. This was more for me, I suppose, than Feltus. Though I had thought that Feltus might be able to carry the cross to his execution as a comfort, I think I needed the cross more than he did. When I tried to give it to Feltus on the day of the execution, he looked at me and said, "I won't be needing that. Can you give it to my attorney?" He was very concerned about his attorney having to witness the execution.

Feltus's imprint is with me during much of my life now. He has left me with wonderful informational tools and stories that help me deal with those who have followed him. I understand his path now, as well as his moral and spiritual rehabilitation. Now I never see the depths of despair without seeing the potential for development.

Thankfully, Feltus was able to face the unknown with the certainty of knowing his eternal fate. Whether through his ability to seek the freedom of a bird or the optimism of a happy face, he has left me and many others with the hope and the faith to continue with this difficult, compelling work on death row, while coping with societal attitudes which tell us we should not honor the life of a man like Feltus. But Feltus's life *is* a celebration, a celebration of the chance that we all have to reach our potential and make a meaningful contribution before we die—even if death comes through government-sponsored lethal injection.

NOTES

1. Cecile C. Guin, "Juvenile to Adult Criminality in Louisiana." Ph.D. dissertation, University of Texas-Arlington, 1991.
2. Cecile C. Guin and Ariana Elizabeth Wall, *An Examination of the Relationship between Child Abuse and Neglect and Violent Criminality: Summary of Findings* (Baton Rouge, La.: Children's Trust Fund, 1995).
3. Human Rights Watch, Children's Rights Project, *Children in Confinement in Louisiana* (New York: Human Rights Watch, 1995).
4. Some names used herein are pseudonymns.

14

IN MEMORY OF
ANDREW LEE JONES

SARAH OTTINGER

uly 1991 was an unusually oppressive, hot, and humid month, even for Louisiana. I was working as an attorney at the Loyola Death Penalty Resource Center. We were a small office: three attorneys, an investigator/paralegal, and an office administrator. We represented men on death row in Louisiana, generally in the final stages of their appeals before executions were to be carried out. I had worked in the office a little over a year, and throughout that period of time there was always the threat of an execution. We worked around the clock, through the weekends, in an almost desperate manner, seeking stays of executions. Our offices were housed in an old bank building in downtown New Orleans. It was not air conditioned on weekends but tended to retain at least some of the coolness of the previous work week. By Sunday night, however, it became unbearable. When I was overwhelmed by the heat, I would take a break from my computer and lie down on the cool marble floor in the hallway outside our offices.

I did not know Andrew Lee Jones very well until the last week of his life. In the final stages of Andrew's case, Nick Trenticosta, director and attorney at the Resource Center, drafted and filed most of the court pleadings. Neal Walker, the third attorney at the Resource Center, represented Andrew at the pardon board hearing along with Michelle Fournet, a private attorney who worked pro bono on the case. The Louisiana Pardon Board hearing would be Andrew's last chance for a reprieve in the likely event the courts failed him. I was much more involved in the cases of other men on death row, but of course was available to do whatever I could to help the attorneys representing Andrew. In the end, I drafted some court pleadings protesting the fact that the prosecution struck all black jurors from the jury that heard Andrew's case. I met with members of Andrew's family to assist in preparing for the pardon board hearing. And, most importantly, it became my job to prepare Andrew for the hearing. His testimony would be pivotal to the request that his death sentence be commuted to life imprisonment. This preparation involved discussing with Andrew in detail the crime he had been convicted of committing.

I still consider the content of those conversations to be confidential. But what I want to convey is that I spent several hours with Andrew several days in a row the week before he was executed and came to know him well. He shared significant details of his life with me because I asked him to, because it was necessary, and because it was the last week of his life. He did so despite the fact that it brought him great pain. Andrew literally believed that he would not survive the telling of some parts of his life. Like many of us, he feared that no one would love him who really knew him. Andrew's courage and honesty moved me a great deal, and I felt privileged to come to know him better.

Andrew had a remarkable smile. It was a quiet, childlike smile that lit up his face. Yet the sparkle of pleasure was mixed with a hint of immense pain. Andrew's life, like those of many of my clients on death row, was marked by pain and deprivation. He grew up in poverty and enslavement. Like his father before him, he was born and raised on a sugar cane plantation. Andrew was the seventh of fourteen children. The family worked the fields, picking cotton and harvesting cane, and Andrew's father doubled as a chauffeur. Despite the fact that parents and children worked, they were never paid enough to survive. Their lives were bound to the plantation by credit owed to the plantation store.

When Andrew was seventeen, his father became very ill. Initially, a country doctor diagnosed a pulled muscle in his back. Later, when Mr. Jones sought competent medical advice, he was diagnosed with cancer of the liver, which by that time had spread to his lungs. Of all the children, Andrew was most affected by his father's prolonged and painful death. The fabric of his life slowly unraveled. Shortly after his father's death, when Andrew was eighteen, the family was evicted from the plantation. Andrew found himself thrust from a rural life into the urban environment of Baton Rouge. Not long after moving, Andrew dropped out of school. Records show that he never progressed beyond the second grade in learning; from that time forward, he was socially promoted to the tenth grade. Testing conducted only after Andrew had been sentenced to death revealed the explanation. Andrew had an IQ of seventy-seven.

Not long after moving to Baton Rouge and dropping out of school, Andrew started drinking. He was soon arrested for burglarizing a convenience store and stealing beer. Despite the fact that he had never been arrested before, the judge denied probation and sentenced him to three years at Angola, where he spent the remainder of his teenage years. Not surprisingly, Andrew emerged from Angola, at that time one of the harshest prisons in this country, a different person. His youth had been marked by poverty and deprivation, but not by violence. This changed after Andrew's first stint at Angola. He spent the next eight years of his life in and out of Angola, living on the streets while he was out of prison and getting involved in a string of tumultuous and violent relationships with women. He became addicted to drugs and began experiencing psychotic episodes for which he did not receive treatment. Ultimately, he was arrested at age twenty-eight for the rape and murder of a thirteen-year-old girl, the daughter of his girlfriend at the time. Andrew was charged with first degree murder, punishable by death.

Because neither Andrew nor his family could afford to hire an attorney, the court appointed an attorney with the Office of the Public Defender in Baton Rouge. Andrew's lawyer had only practiced law for four years, so that did not qualify him under Louisiana law to represent Andrew at trial. However, another lawyer with more experience enrolled on the case as co-counsel. Even though the second lawyer did not participate actively in Andrew's representation, his enrollment satisfied the state law requirement that Andrew be represented by a lawyer who had practiced for at least five years. The trial lawyer's inexperience would prove fatal.

In Louisiana, a capital trial is divided into two parts. First, a jury of twelve must determine whether a defendant is guilty of first degree murder, guilty of a lesser crime, or not guilty. If and only if the jury determines that a defendant is guilty of first degree murder, the same jury proceeds to the sentencing phase, at which it determines whether a sentence of life imprisonment or death should be imposed. If the jury unanimously recommends that a sentence of death be imposed, the court imposes the sentence of death. If the jury is unable to reach agreement on the sentence to be imposed, or if the jury unanimously recommends a sentence of life, then the court imposes a sentence of life.

The jury must consider several factors in reaching a determination as to the sentence to be imposed. Among those factors that mitigate against imposing a sentence of death, and particularly relevant to Andrew's case were first, that the offense was committed while the offender was under the influence of extreme mental or emotional disturbance; and, second, that at the time of the offense, the capacity of the offender to appreciate the criminality of his conduct or to conform his conduct to the requirements of law was impaired as a result of mental disease or defect, or intoxication.

At Andrew's trial, there was a legally sufficient amount of evidence linking him to the rape and murder of the thirteen year-old girl, and the jury unanimously found him guilty of first degree murder.[1] At sentencing, Andrew's inexperienced lawyer argued that Andrew had consumed a great deal of alcohol on the night of the murder and was intoxicated. Andrew's lawyer did not seek funds to hire any experts to evaluate Andrew's level of intoxication and its effect on his actions, nor did he seek any funds for experts to conduct psychological testing and determine whether Andrew had a "mental disease or defect."[2]

Such evaluation would have produced a wealth of mitigating evidence for the jury to consider in recommending a sentence in the case. Years later, in the course of his appeals, Andrew was thoroughly evaluated by a neuropsychiatrist and a psychologist. They concluded that Andrew had experienced psychotic episodes throughout his adult life, that he suffered from organic brain damage, and that he was borderline mentally retarded. Intoxication likely augmented all three conditions at the time the crime was committed, although it was not clear whether Andrew was experiencing a psychotic episode at that time.

Crucial information regarding Andrew's state of mind at the time the crime was committed only came to our attention a few months prior to Andrew's execution, when we requested jail records that documented his pretrial incarceration. These records established that two weeks after Andrew's arrest, the jail asked a state psychiatrist to examine him. The doctor diagnosed psychosis and prescribed Thorazine, a powerful antipsychotic drug. Andrew was told he was taking sleeping pills. The prosecutor never informed Andrew's defense attorney of the psychiatrist's diagnosis, despite the fact that she was under a legal obligation to reveal all information in her possession critical to Andrew's defense in the penalty phase of trial. The state psychiatrist's diagnosis and course of treatment established conclusively that Andrew was psychotic during the period of time the crime was committed.

The end result was that the all-white jury that sentenced Andrew to death did so without the benefit of crucial evidence mitigating against a sentence of death. Andrew was executed because of his attorney's inexperience, the prosecutor's dereliction of duty, and the criminal justice system's failure at that time to provide a mechanism whereby indigent defendants could secure expert funding.

Andrew pursued his appeals through state and federal courts with various attorneys representing him on a pro bono basis. Suffice it to say that the courts never allowed Andrew to supplement the record in his case with the testimony of experts later hired to evaluate him. The courts refused to allow Andrew a hearing at which he could prove the wealth of mitigating evidence discovered after his trial. As a result, Andrew moved through his appeals at a fairly rapid pace. It was not until Andrew had exhausted his appeals and was pursuing a course of successor appeals, that the Louisiana Supreme Court finally sent his case back to the trial court for a hearing on the prosecutor's use of peremptory challenges to exclude all blacks from Andrew's jury.

Andrew alleged that the prosecutor had intentionally discriminated against blacks by excluding all potential black jurors from the jury. After a hearing on the issue, the trial court ruled that the prosecutor had enunciated race-neutral reasons for excluding the black jurors. The ruling ignored the obvious bias with which the prosecutor exercised its challenges to exclude all blacks. The appellate courts upheld the trial court's ruling, and the claim of discrimination was turned down for the final time by the United States Supreme Court shortly after 9:00 P.M. on July 21, 1991, the night Andrew was executed.

My own participation in Andrew's case, as I have said, was limited. Looking back, I think my most meaningful role was being present with Andrew in the final hours before his execution. It seems an impossible task to convey what it is like to spend the last hours of a man's life with him, in prison, watched by guards, waiting for the appointed hour of death. Nevertheless, it is a task worth undertaking since Andrew would never have a chance to describe what happened.

Several of us sat with Andrew throughout the evening in a large room directly outside the execution chamber. In addition to Andrew and me, Debra Voelker (our investigator), Neal Walker, and Michelle Fournet were there. We sat around a table talking. There were guards in the room as well, but they kept their distance. Andrew was handcuffed and shackled at the waist throughout the evening. His feet were also shackled. We would talk for a while, then Andrew would get up and shuffle away to go call his family, and the rest of us would pull ourselves together. We tried as much as possible to take our cues from Andrew. More than anything, he seemed to want distraction, and we took turns providing it. *Surreal* is the only word that comes to mind when I think about that evening. Yet it was real.

One of the most difficult times for Andrew in the long wait came at 9:30 P.M. when we received word that his last appeal had been denied by the Supreme Court. Andrew refused to talk to Nick, who had called from the office to give him the news, because Nick was crying. Andrew had forbidden any tears. He came back from the phone to the waiting room and sat down quietly. Then he looked straight into my eyes and asked, "Why can't they just do it now? How am I going to get through the next few hours?" I had no answer. I tried to imagine that in a few hours his life would be over while mine would be beginning a new day. I tried to imagine what it was like for him to look at me, knowing this. We stared at each other, and I shook my head. Someone suggested that Andrew purchase something else from the vending machine, and we all laughed thankfully. For Andrew, one of the great thrills of the last day of his life was his ability to put coins in a vending machine, punch a button, and receive food or drink. It had been over seven years since he had come in contact with coins or a vending machine.

Forty-five minutes before Andrew was executed, guards removed him from the visiting room, saying he would return soon. Fifteen minutes later, he walked back in with that smile of his, but awkward and blinking ferociously. In preparation for attaching the electrodes, the guards had shaved his head, one leg, and, as Andrew pointed out, "even my eyebrows." He was embarrassed. He wondered how he looked. Of course there were no mirrors. Andrew kept blinking. He explained that there were tiny bits of hair from his shaved eyebrows that were getting in his eyes. He was shackled at the waist and couldn't reach his eyes. Neal pulled a handkerchief from his pocket and asked if it would be okay to wipe Andrew's eyes for him.

One of the many silences crept over the table where we sat. Andrew laughed. "At least," he said, "they let me keep my Air Jordans. I thought they'd take those too, but they didn't. I've spent my whole life running and I want to hit the other side running." Michelle reminded Andrew that he'd always dreamed a plane would crash at Angola, setting him free. Andrew said it wasn't too late. We all laughed.

The worst moment came when Andrew was led into the execution chamber. It stays with me. Andrew had passed by us in the hall on the way to the door to the chamber. He gave a strained smile and flapped his shackled hands at us. I watched his back after he passed. At the door to the execution chamber, the guards stopped and made Andrew take off his Air Jordans. As he bent to do so, he looked back, directly into my eyes. I will never forget the raw fear in his eyes. There were tears in mine. All pretenses were gone.

I spent the next fifteen minutes doing deep breathing exercises, pacing the floor, looking at the drab prison surroundings, trying to comprehend but not be overwhelmed by the fact that Andrew was being electrocuted in the next room. We were separated by a wall. At some point, I decided that action, any action, would be better than waiting. I went into the guards' room and demanded Andrew's Air Jordans so I could take them to his mother. Earlier in the evening, I had promised Andrew I would let his mother know he wanted to be buried in them. The guard I spoke with calmly explained that Andrew's effects could only be released to his next-of-kin and that the prison would ship the running shoes to

Andrew's mother. I knew at that moment that Andrew's mother would not receive the shoes in time for Andrew's funeral.

Shortly after I returned to the main room, eight guards exited the execution chamber holding their hands away from their bodies. They had just removed Andrew's body from the electric chair. They formed a line at the men's rest room and, one by one, washed the touch of his skin off their hands.

NOTES

1. The fact that the evidence was legally sufficient does not mean that it really explained the crime. Notably missing from the evidence against Andrew was any explanation of how Andrew, who did not own a car, had traveled a great distance to the little girl's home and transported her to the scene where her body was found.
2. The year after Andrew's trial, the U.S. Supreme Court ruled that all indigent defendants are constitutionally entitled to such funding when they make a showing that it is necessary to their defense. When Andrew's case was tried, there was little funding available for experts, and his lawyer did not even request funding.

15

REPRESENTING ROBERT SAWYER

SARAH OTTINGER

ebra Voelker, our investigator, used to say that Robert Sawyer *looked* like a man destined to be executed. I would protest, but deep down I knew she was right. During the time I represented him, he came very close to execution four times in one year and each time I believed it was over. Robert actually came to believe that as long as I was representing him, he wouldn't be executed. When I quit my job representing men on death row in Louisiana and told Robert that other lawyers would continue working for him, he looked at me aghast. In his mind I had just pronounced the sentence of death.

Robert was the hardest client to say good-bye to when I quit working full-time on capital cases, because he was the most vulnerable. As it turned out, he is the only client of those I worked closely with who has been executed since I left the work. About Robert, Debra was right.

To this day I feel Robert's death and my life are intertwined. The days when Robert was fighting for a sentence of life imprisonment were the same days that I was struggling against a powerful, unrelenting pull toward death by suicide. Somehow the forces at work destroying Robert's life were present in my own psyche, destroying my own life. Pulling away from those forces, leaving them behind, was a life-affirming choice I made for myself. Our lives have value, all of them.

I have shunned blending these two life stories, Robert's and mine. I was ashamed of linking them together. Capital punishment is a political issue and I, with my privilege in this society, should not link it with depression and suicide attempts. But that is the voice of me *then*, not the voice of me now. The struggle to save Robert's life was the same struggle to save my own.

I first met Robert on death row at the Louisiana State Penitentiary in Angola in September 1990. At the time I had just finished spending two months investigating Louisiana's electric chair and the way in which it burned and mutilated those executed in it. The investigation had covered everything from scholarly writings on electrocution to descriptions of execution by electrocution across the United States, to botched executions in Louisiana, to understanding the mechanics of how the Louisiana electric chair functioned, to examining the autopsies of all those recently executed in Louisiana, to finding and interviewing embalmers who had direct contact with the bodies of men executed in Louisiana. It had been a morbid summer and the results of the investigation were appalling. Louisiana's electric chair was riddled with design defects that caused horrible burning to the skin of men who died in it. We were raising the claim in all the cases of men on death row in Louisiana, illustrating our argument that electrocution in Louisiana constituted cruel and unusual punishment with ghastly color photographs and grisly narratives of the condition of bodies postexecution.

I remember meeting Robert right before I was scheduled to take a much-needed weekend break from the pace of investigating electrocution. It was early September and Robert was scheduled to be executed on October 10, 1990. He had completed the full appellate process in a capital case: direct appeal to the Louisiana and U.S. Supreme Courts, a round of state postconviction appeals from the trial court through the Louisiana and U.S. Supreme Courts, and a round of federal postconviction appeals from the federal district court through the federal circuit court of appeals to the U.S. Supreme Court. He was entering a phase of appeals called *successor postconviction*—a phase in which there is little to no hope of preventing execution.

My initial impression of Robert was that he had been totally neglected for the ten years he had spent on death row by his lawyers and family alike. He was a desperately lonely man struggling very hard to understand what was happening around him. He had very little understanding of what had occurred in his appeals to date and even less understanding of what we would be doing next. I think our strategy appealed to him mainly because he was about to get a lot more attention than he was accustomed to. I was prying into every aspect of his life history.

During the ten years of neglect, Robert had narrowly missed having his sentence of death overturned all along the way. On direct appeal, the U.S. Supreme Court had remanded his case to the Louisiana Supreme Court for reconsideration of an issue involving the jury's consideration of an unfounded and unproven aggravating circumstance in reaching its sentence of death. The Louisiana Supreme Court reasoned that the error had not affected the outcome of the trial and upheld the sentence of death.

In state postconviction proceedings, the state supreme court twice sent Robert's case back to the trial court to fully consider the issue of whether Robert received ineffective assistance of counsel. The ineffective assistance of counsel claim revolved around the fact that Robert's chief trial attorney had less than two years' experience as a lawyer, and his second lawyer, who became involved in the case just days before it went to trial, had only been a lawyer for four years. State law in Louisiana requires that capital defendants be represented by at least one lawyer who has been a member of the bar for at least five years. There was no question that Robert, by law, should have been represented at trial by more experienced attorneys. The question the Louisiana Supreme Court wanted addressed was whether Robert's representation had suffered as a result.

It is common practice in postconviction appeals of capital cases to investigate not only what happened on the record at trial, but also all the evidence that could have been presented to the jury but wasn't. Robert's first postconviction lawyers never investigated Robert's life history. Instead, they relied on the record of the trial to prove that Robert's lawyers were ineffective. The record revealed that Robert's lawyers didn't make a closing argument to the jury in the culpability phase of the trial and only argued incredibly briefly against a sentence of death, labeling Robert a sociopath in the process. The lawyer made other mistakes as well. But all the mistakes were reviewed in terms of what was on the record at trial, not in terms of things that had been missed. The trial court upheld the sentence of death finding that even though inexperienced, counsel was not ineffective. The Louisiana Supreme Court upheld Robert's conviction and sentence of death by a narrow margin of 4 to 3. Three justices thought that Robert's trial lawyers had been ineffective and that he should have been given a new trial.

In federal postconviction proceedings, while ineffective assistance of counsel was reviewed and dismissed by the federal courts, a whole other issue became the focus of the appeals. The prosecutor had argued to Robert's jury that it was not solely responsible for sentencing him to death—that its sentence of death was a recommendation and that others would review the decision after the jury made it. A 1985 U.S. Supreme Court case held that such argument on the part of the prosecutor diminished the jury's sense of responsibility in returning a sentence of death in a capital case and that the argument was therefore improper, with the result that the case was sent back to the trial court for a new sentencing hearing. Without getting into what are somewhat incomprehensible arguments and theories even to experienced lawyers, suffice it to say that Robert was denied relief on this claim because it wasn't recognized as a claim until 1985 and Robert's case had gone to trial in 1980. The U.S. Supreme Court simply decided not to consider the claim because it didn't exist in 1980. It upheld his conviction and sentence of death by a 5 to 4 vote. Once again, one vote would have resulted in Robert's death sentence being overturned. The conclusion to Justice Thurgood Marshall's dissent was blistering. He wrote, "The jury that sentenced Sawyer to death was deliberately misled about the significance of its verdict. That Sawyer was thus denied a fundamentally fair trial was as apparent when Sawyer's conviction became final as it is today. This Court's refusal to allow a federal habeas court to correct this error is yet another indication that the Court is less concerned with safeguarding constitutional rights than with speeding defendants, deserving or not, to their execution. I dissent." Robert's October 10, 1990, execution date was scheduled after the U.S. Supreme Court narrowly denied him relief. He got a new set of lawyers, myself and Nick Trenticosta, and we set out to investigate his case anew and make sure nothing had been missed by previous lawyers.

Debra Voelker was fond of saying that all that was needed to uncover the horrific truths of Robert Sawyer's life was a phone, a few stamps, and a desire to find out why Robert behaved the way he did on the day of the murder in question. After Robert had been on death row for ten years, we developed the case against death based on mitigating factors in his life in less than one month, discovering some of the most compelling and easily verified mitigation I have seen. When Robert went before the Louisiana Board of Pardons on October 8, 1990, less than two days before his scheduled execution, we were able to present a wealth of information about him and his impairments by way of affidavits from family members, hospital and school records, and thorough evaluations conducted by a psychiatrist and a neurologist.

Robert was born in Memphis, Tennessee, on October 8, 1950, to a sick mother and a sadistic father. His mother gave birth to twins, Robert and a sister. She was constantly ill and bedridden during the nine months of her pregnancy, suffering from Asian flu and uremic poisoning. She was also abused, battered, and raped by her husband throughout the pregnancy.

The birth of twins was an unanticipated and unwelcome event to a mother engaged in her own day-to-day struggle to survive. Not long after Robert's birth, his mother became increasingly depressed. She twice tried to kill her newborn son, once with a fireplace poker and once by suffocation. Less than four months after Robert's birth, his mother climbed in the back seat of the family car, propped a shotgun against the front seat, aimed it at her heart, and pulled the trigger with her toe, killing herself.

His mother's suicide left Robert, his twin sister, and an older sister in his father's care. They lived in a crowded, dilapidated two-room shack in rural Tennessee. The house had no electricity, no running water, not even an outhouse. The family initially consisted of the three children, Robert's father, and his father's parents. However, not long after his mother's suicide, his grandmother had a nervous breakdown and could not care for both infants. An aunt took in Robert's twin sister, removing her forever from the devastating abuse Robert went on to suffer at his father's hands.

Robert's father was described by all who knew him (with the notable exception of Robert) as vicious and sadistic. Relative after relative, on both Robert's mother's and father's side of the family, recounted abuse upon abuse inflicted upon Robert as a child by his father who, according to one aunt, believed Robert "was the only thing in the world that was his and that he could do anything he wanted with." Robert's father beat Robert with anything he could get his hands on—whips, plow lines, fists. He verbally berated Robert constantly. He kept Robert working in the fields from the time he was very young, doing work all described as man's work. Robert grew up isolated, abused, and neglected while the whole neighborhood looked on, powerless to stem his father's rage.

Very early in his life, Robert began to exhibit the signs of a child who was not only abused but also mentally retarded and brain damaged. In school, he failed first grade twice and then was socially promoted to second grade. After failing second grade, he was placed in a special education class for the "educable mentally retarded." He was assessed with an IQ of 68. His scores on standardized tests were abysmal. In his eighth and last year in school, Robert was reading and spelling at a fourth-grade level and his arithmetic performance was consistent with a third-grade level. When he was fourteen and dropped out of school, his teacher reported that his social progress was "poor" and that he had "developed an attitude that the world is against him, however I believe this is due to his home environment." A school social worker commented at one point that Robert's father had so little concern for his son that he had no idea how poorly Robert was performing in school.

At the age of fourteen, Robert began his first in a series of mental health treatments. He became a patient at a mental health clinic in Memphis where he was diagnosed as moderately retarded with chronic brain syndrome. The clinic prescribed antipsychotic medication.

When Robert was fifteen, he was hospitalized in the psychiatric unit of a local hospital. There he was prescribed a powerful psychotropic medication for the treatment of schizophrenia and psychosis. At discharge he was diagnosed with "chronic brain syndrome with unknown cause manifested by mild mental retardation and abnormal EEG with behavioral disturbances." One month after his discharge, Robert was adjudicated incompetent and committed to a state psychiatric hospital. There he was diagnosed as schizophrenic. During his commitment he underwent shock treatments and was prescribed antipsychotic medication and tranquilizers. Robert turned sixteen while hospitalized. Despite the fact that Robert was found not competent to conduct his own affairs, he was discharged from the state psychiatric hospital five months after beginning treatment there. Upon discharge his psychiatrist noted the following: "stress: severe; predisposition: severe; impairment: severe, apparently this patient failed to identify himself with parents and siblings and lack of ego strength and ego ideal is the dynamic cause of patient's illness; prognosis: guarded." After his discharge, Robert left his home and made his way in the world on his own.

Having uncovered all this previously unknown information about Robert's early life, we decided to have Robert thoroughly evaluated by a psychiatrist and neurologist. Both doctors reviewed the records and affidavits from family members that we had amassed. Both conducted extensive clinical interviews and testing of Robert on death row. And in the end, both concluded that Robert's mental retardation, organic frontal lobe brain damage, previous abuse, and heavy use of alcohol on the night the crime was committed contributed to his very aggressive actions in killing a baby-sitter he thought had abused his girlfriend's children. The psychiatrist concluded that the diagnosis of organic personality syndrome (formerly organic brain syndrome) read "like a veritable summary of the life history of Robert Sawyer." Probably due to early abuse at the hands of his father, Robert's brain function was compromised in such a way that he lacked impulse control and responded to psychosocial stressors with impulsive or explosive behavior grossly out of proportion to the trigger that precipitated it. The neurologist detected, and later confirmed by magnetic resonance imaging, prefrontal brain injury. This type of neurological impairment "results in an inability to inhibit and control aggressive thoughts and actions. It affects the decision-making process: impulsive action precedes measured consideration. Intoxication exacerbates the impairment." Both doctors noted that those with Robert's impairments usually do very well in highly structured environments. In fact, Robert was well-liked on death row by inmates and guards alike because he was so mild-mannered, simple, and fair.

In what proved to be a fatal mistake, Robert's trial lawyers and initial appellate counsel never uncovered any information about Robert's childhood and never had him evaluated by qualified doctors. His documented mental retardation and profound neurological impairment were never presented to the jury to consider in deciding whether Robert should live or die. Neither was this information presented in Robert's first round of postconviction appeals in support of his claim of ineffective assistance of counsel. Instead, we raised all the information on the successor round of appeals, and courts uniformly replied that we were too late. I found myself on October 8, 1990, before the Louisiana Board of Pardons presenting evidence and arguing for a recommendation of clemency. October 8 was Robert's birthday. His scheduled execution date, October 10, was my own birthday. He would be forty; I would be twenty-eight. Robert thought this was a good sign. I didn't.

I remember well driving back from Angola, where I had visited extensively with Robert, to Baton Rouge, where I would spend the night in a hotel with Robert's family and other witnesses late the night of October 7, 1990. It was raining hard and I was running very late. I needed to meet with the psychiatrist at the hotel before either of us could go to bed, and we both needed to be up early to drive back to Angola for the pardon board hearing the next morning. I knew I was driving recklessly fast for the weather conditions and didn't care. At least an accident would likely stay the execution, as I was solely responsible for presenting Robert's case for clemency to the pardon board. Nick remained in New Orleans to keep filing appeals as courts turned them down. We were prepared to go through all the state and federal courts in the next two days.

What was particularly troubling to me was how inadequate I felt for the job before me. We had thrown together all the information we would present in a month of frenzied investigation. I was exhausted and had been working without much sleep for at least the last week. I'd never appeared before a pardon board and this one was rumored to be merciless. At least three members would turn down the request for clemency. Two might vote for it, but a majority was required. I would be arguing the electrocution claim—that Robert would suffer unspeakable torture if executed in Louisiana's electric chair. I would argue that Robert's trial lawyer with less than two years' experience had completely failed to adequately represent Robert at trial. I would argue that the lawyer's inexperience was responsible for Robert's failure to take the plea to the life sentence offered him before trial. His inexperience was responsible for the failure to uncover all we had found. His inexperience was responsible for his failure to raise Robert's incompetence to stand trial due to his very limited mental capacity. And it seemed some kind of sick, cruel joke on Robert that he would be depending on me, a lawyer with just two years' experience, to persuade the board in favor of clemency. I was literally the only person available for the job at that time. And I was conscious that Nick stayed in New Orleans to deal with the courts and had me do the pardon board hearing because the chances were so great, going in, that we would lose the bid for clemency. The only comfort to be had was that even a really good, experienced lawyer wouldn't make a difference. I was sure we were looking at an inevitable execution on my birthday and had promised Robert I'd be there to witness.

Robert, his older sister, her husband, the psychiatrist, Debra, and I went before the pardon board the next day with the passionate conviction that executing Robert would be wrong. The first setback came when we discovered only four board members would hear the case and the absent member was one of the two likely to vote in Robert's favor. I was terrified and spoke from my heart. Robert spoke from his heart. The psychiatrist spoke from his heart. Robert's sister and brother-in-law spoke from their hearts. The hearing went on most of the day. At the lunch break Wilbert Rideau, who was covering the hearing for *The Angolite*, told me that one pardon board member commented to him it was a shame that someone as young and seemingly innocent as me would lose my first pardon board hearing. We continued after lunch presenting the case for clemency. When it came time for my closing argument, I literally begged. I said Robert's case felt like a train running out of control. After ten years of neglect, we had just begun investigating the facts of the case. We needed more time: more time to investigate the crime; more time to obtain neurological testing that couldn't be scheduled before the execution date and was currently scheduled a week after execution. They were sitting as the conscience of the community and in good conscience, we couldn't execute Robert with so many unknowns. They should recommend clemency.

In the end, the board requested that the governor stay the execution for thirty days and the governor granted their request. A new date could not be set until the thirty days expired, which would give us approximately two more months in which to work before the next execution date. We were exultant. Robert held my hand like a little boy as the pardon board gave us its decision.

So it was back to the office in New Orleans. More testing. The magnetic resonance imaging revealed visible prefrontal lobe damage to Robert's brain. We exulted in this confirmation of Robert's severe impairment. More investigation, this time of the crime itself and why it was that Robert's codefendant had been sentenced to life by a jury while Robert, whom the state initially acknowledged was less culpable in its offer of a life sentence, was sentenced to death. We uncovered evidence that the state's chief witness against Robert at trial had testified in exchange for immunity, a deal that wasn't revealed to the defense. We discovered that the state lied about the statement of a child witness who had exonerated rather than implicated Robert in the crime. I thought I discovered that a critical piece of evidence had never made it to the evidence room and spent literally nights poring over crime scene photographs in an attempt to prove my theory. (I never did.) We wrote another impassioned plea to the pardon board with all the new facts we had uncovered again requesting clemency. As we approached Robert's next execution date, December 15, 1990, the pardon board voted 2 to 2 on clemency. A tie is a loss; a majority vote is required for the board to recommend clemency to the governor.

In the meantime, our new claims had made it through state postconviction and into federal district court. We were alleging ineffective assistance of counsel based on all the new information we had discovered, the state's withholding of exculpatory evidence, Robert's incompetence to stand trial, and the claim that electrocution in Louisiana's electric chair would constitute cruel and unusual punishment. We had little hope for any of the claims, thinking the substantive ones would be rejected because they were not raised in Robert's first round of appeals. Miraculously, though, the federal district court granted a stay of execution on December 12, 1990, two days before the scheduled execution. It wanted to hear evidence on our claim that Louisiana's electric chair was riddled with design defects.

The district court scheduled the hearing in January 1991. Once again we were thrown into a frenzy of preparation. Neal Walker, who had just joined the office and was the most experienced lawyer, particularly in the courtroom, took over coordinating the hearing in federal district court. We hired another expert to review the functioning of the electric chair. We spent several surreal days inspecting the electric chair with our expert and interviewing prison personnel present at previous executions, generally members of what was then known as the strap-down team. We conducted a macabre experiment with the electric chair, attaching the head electrode to a wooden skull covered with chamois soaked in saline. Our expert opined that the wooden head covered in chamois was the most accurate inanimate representation of the human head. A pig would be better, he said, but impossible to experiment on in light of laws protecting animals against cruelty. In the end our video of the wooden head was spectacular. It erupted in flames as soon as the electricity was switched on.

After all our preparation, we spent several days in federal district court in January 1991, presenting our evidence of the Louisiana electric chair design defects. Neal marshaled the evidence, primarily. I sat next to Robert, who was brought to New Orleans for the hearing. While Robert's understanding of the scientific concepts around electrocution was minimal, he understood too well the testimony about the grisly condition of bodies following execution. It was hard for him to hear and sit through, but he had decided to be there as a representative of all the men on death row and because he hoped the judge would see him and appreciate that he was a person, small in stature and very human. The state rebutted our evidence with evidence that electrocution at Angola was performed professionally and painlessly. The state introduced a video prepared specifically for the hearing that showed guards efficiently strapping a man short in stature, like Robert, into the electric chair. Robert was profoundly disturbed by the video. As far as I know, he is the only condemned man to view the electric chair and execution chamber prior to his execution, by way of video. Both nights Robert was held over in New Orleans for the hearing I visited him at the local jail. His direct witnessing of the manner in which his own execution would take place seemed to constitute an added dimension of cruel and unusual punishment. Yet Robert persevered in being present as something he needed to do for everyone on death row.

When the hearing was over, the court denied relief, saying it found Louisiana's electric chair to be compatible with evolving standards of decency in this society. We left the courtroom to await the final written decision of the court, which we knew would deny Robert relief on all his claims. The court did not issue its opinion until July 1991, giving us, for the first time since September, a bit of breathing room in Robert's case. (This is not at all to suggest that work on other cases relented. I worked up to the last minute on two other cases getting stays of execution that spring.)

When the federal district court released its opinion on July 16, we were a little more than a week away from the scheduled execution of another client on death row, Andrew Lee Jones. Robert's new execution date was scheduled for August 22, 1991, exactly one month after Andrew's. Those were very dark days in our office as we held out little hope for either man. I did not put any work into Robert's case until after Andrew's execution. Then I came back to work staggering under the reality of execution, steeling myself to deal with a second one in the next month. Neal had witnessed Andrew's execution at Andrew's request. I would witness Robert's at Robert's request.

Everyone had given up hope for Robert. We had narrowly escaped two execution dates in less than a year, and hoping for a third stay of execution seemed delusional. Only Robert had confidence that he'd get a stay. After all, he always did. Like much of Robert's thinking, his confidence was completely unfounded.

I was assigned the task of writing the appeal to the federal circuit court of appeals. Neal agreed to draft the electric chair claim. That summer, the Louisiana Legislature voted to do away with electrocution. Beginning September 15, 1991, execution in Louisiana would be by lethal injection. We thought our best shot might be to stay Robert's execution until that time. While some were frustrated by the meaninglessness of such a stay, I thought it would at least eliminate what had been one of the most difficult aspects of Andrew's execution—his fear of electrocution.

As I looked through all our pleadings and talked with Nick, I discovered an issue that Nick had alleged in our federal court pleadings but that the court had not addressed. I looked at the federal law on the issue more carefully, and saw that conflict had recently developed in federal appeals courts on the issue. Two courts had come to opposite conclusions. The conclusion of one court would arguably spare Robert's life. The conclusion of the other court would result in execution in Robert's case. Federal courts and the U.S. Supreme Court are most likely to address a conflict of law of this nature. The conflict of law gave meat to a claim that had sat unaddressed.

Before beginning work on the appeal to the federal circuit court, I met with the chair of the Louisiana Board of Pardons and requested another clemency hearing before the full board. She denied the request, citing a rule that allowed only one hearing per year before the pardon board. Robert would not be entitled to a new hearing until after October 8, 1991. No matter that his previous hearing had proceeded before only four of the five members of the board, and the fifth member could break the tie vote. There would be no exceptions.

I threw myself into the appeal. The petition was limited to fifty pages and by the time I'd finished pouring out the injustices in Robert's case, I was up to seventy pages and had to ruthlessly cut back on a good bit of what I wanted to say. The claim we raised was particularly conducive to putting forward all the mitigation that the jury never heard. We were arguing that Robert was "innocent" of his death sentence. Federal habeas law allowed successor appeals to be addressed when there was a claim of actual innocence of the crime. We wanted the court to address the issue of under what circumstances a condemned man could be innocent of the death sentence imposed. We argued that Robert was "innocent of death," given all the mitigation we had uncovered that the jury never considered. It was one of those nearly impossible-to-understand arguments that exist only in the realm of postconviction law. At the time I had difficulty explaining even to other lawyers the gist of what we alleged. But it allowed us to dwell on the substantial mitigation in Robert's case and presented the opportunity for the court to actually listen to what we were saying and address it rather than dismiss it because it had been raised too late.

Once again, miraculously, Robert got a stay of execution. The federal appeals court wanted us to fully brief and argue the innocence of death issue. It put us on an expedited briefing and argument schedule. If memory serves me correctly, we had two weeks to file a brief and argued the case to the court a week after the brief was filed, in September 1991. Because I had worked so closely on Robert's case for almost a year and was the only lawyer in the office who had actually read transcripts of every proceeding to date, I was the only lawyer enough up to speed to get the argument together in a couple weeks. As it turned out, my first appellate argument ever was before the federal circuit court of appeals. Once again, Robert would receive inexperienced representation at a critical juncture, on a life and death matter. I did not sleep well on any night between the time the stay was granted and the case was argued.

While the argument went smoothly, it was clear Robert would lose when the court released its opinion, and he did. The opinion was released on October 10, 1991. It was a year to the date after the first execution date I had been involved with in Robert's case. Robert had just celebrated another birthday on death row. I was out of town celebrating my own birthday with a friend the day the opinion was released, but came back immediately to begin working on the soon-to-be-set next execution date.

The next date was set for November 15, 1991. This time we would have the chance to go before the pardon board again requesting clemency. If we could keep the two votes we got the year before, and gain a third from the absent member who was rumored to be open to clemency, we would get a recommendation for clemency to take to the governor. And we still had the U.S. Supreme Court to petition, asking them to review the federal appeals court decision. Our worry about the Supreme Court was that it had already heard Robert's case argued in his first round of appeals. The chances of having a case argued before the Supreme Court are slim. The chances of having a case argued before the Supreme Court *twice* seemed nonexistent. But the issue of what constituted actual innocence of a death sentence was ripe for the Court to address, so we hoped against hope.

This time Neal and I worked together on the pardon board hearing. I did not have the sense that I was on my own, as before. That was a relief. We decided to present everything we had presented the year before, but to concentrate on mental retardation. We worked with experts to describe mental retardation in depth to the pardon board and explain why several states had outlawed the execution of mentally retarded persons as inhumane. Robert literally had the comprehension of an eleven- or twelve-year-old. It would be like executing a child. We pulled together more evidence on Robert's thinking from those who knew him—his family members, other men on death row, even me. I had spent innumerable hours over the last year trying to explain the goings-on in Robert's case to him. As the man in the cell next to Robert put it, watching Robert try to grasp legal concepts was like watching a man circling a pool trying to get in. You'd explain how, he'd seem to understand, then go right back to circling with no better idea of how to get in. Robert truly only understood a fraction of the complexities of his case.

The pardon board hearing went well. The board was receptive and Robert was characteristically perplexed, but sincere throughout. At one point a board member asked him to define murder. After much thought he said, "it's when the breath leaves the body." "Well, that's almost it but not quite," replied the board member. "There's just one thing you're missing. Can you think of what it is?" Again Robert thought hard. "Somebody *makes* the breath leave the body?" "Very good," replied that board member and proceeded at the end of the hearing to vote against clemency. Our expert on mental retardation described the incident as a classic example of a mentally retarded person's desire to please others and mask the disability. Robert did not understand that we were arguing his lack of understanding of legal proceedings. He wanted to appear as smart as he could to the pardon board.

At the end of a very long day, by a vote of 3 to 2, the pardon board recommended clemency. In Louisiana, only the governor can grant clemency, and only upon a recommendation of the pardon board. We were one huge step closer to a life sentence for Robert. The governor scheduled a meeting the following day for us to make our clemency case directly to him. Nick, Neal, and our expert on mental retardation attended the meeting. I returned to the office to work on the petition to the United States Supreme Court.

That day in the office I took one of the most amazing calls I think I've had in a capital case. A man called asking to talk to one of Robert Sawyer's attorneys. He had read in the morning paper's coverage of the pardon board hearing that Robert was mentally retarded. He was one of the jurors in Robert's case and had voted for the sentence of death. He said he never would have voted for death if he had known Robert was retarded. In fact, he said, he told the lawyers when they were picking the jurors for the case that he couldn't impose a death sentence on a retarded man. He wanted to know if there was anything he could do to prevent Robert's execution. He said it didn't seem right since he would have voted for life if he'd had all the facts.

While a juror's change of heart based on newly learned information may sound like one of the most relevant factors we could uncover, in fact it was legally irrelevant, and there would be no way to structure a claim of a constitutional violation around it. Instead, I had the juror come into the office and write an affidavit attesting to what he told me on the phone. We forwarded the affidavit to the pardon board and the governor hoping it would weigh into the governor's clemency decision.

Nick and Neal returned from the Baton Rouge meeting with the governor feeling fairly dejected. Things did not look good. We all threw ourselves into completing our last appeal to the Supreme Court and filing it. By the time we filed, Robert's execution was a little over twenty-four hours away.

Nothing looked good the next morning. The governor announced his denial of Robert's request for clemency. Neal had initiated another new claim in state court that I had missed but he discovered upon reading the full transcript of Robert's trial. The jurors in Robert's case had been instructed that a reasonable doubt was a grave doubt, and the instruction was found to be unconstitutional and required reversal of a conviction in another Supreme Court case. On that day before Robert's scheduled midnight execution, we got news that the Louisiana Supreme Court had denied a stay of execution by a vote of 5 to 2. Our last hope would be the United States Supreme Court.

Robert was at Angola, moved the week before from death row to a cell near the execution chamber. He was enjoying his last time with his family, and Debra and I began our preparations for the two and a half hour drive out to Angola to spend the late afternoon and evening with Robert. Then a call came from the Supreme Court clerk's office. They wanted us to fax affidavits and hospital records that we had alluded to but not included in our appeal. That was a good sign. Debra and I decided to wait a bit longer before leaving the office. I think the call came around 4:00 that afternoon that the U.S. Supreme Court had granted a stay of execution and would hear Robert's case one more time. For the moment we were very relieved. I called Robert, who was still visiting with his family, and gave him the news. From the sound of it, the whole room erupted in tears. Robert said in a voice I knew meant he was grinning ear to ear that he knew we would pull it out. He said thanks.

I spent the weekend celebrating. Once again, I had been certain that Robert would be executed. This stay would last until the following summer because it would take the Supreme Court that long to hear Robert's case and write an opinion. We had to brief the case and argue it quickly, but there wouldn't be another execution date for a while. The following Monday I came to work and cleared off my desk. Neal and Nick were going to begin writing the brief for the Supreme Court, and Neal would argue the case. In the midafternoon that Monday, I hitched a ride with someone else in our office to a psychiatric hospital, where I checked myself in as a patient. I was alone with one suitcase of belongings.

I became a patient on a unit called the Center for Emotional Recovery. It was an understatement of what I needed at that time. I'd made the arrangements to go there a couple weeks before Robert's November execution date. Since early summer, before Andrew was executed, I had felt desperately suicidal. I wanted to live, I wanted to leave the pull to kill myself behind, but I simply didn't know how. On some very deep level I was tired of struggling with myself to validate my existence. My desire to simply not exist had overwhelmed me.

I found myself in an environment that cared very little about the woes of my clients on death row, about their tragic lives, the tragic crimes

they committed, and the deaf ear that courts were turning to basic violations of their constitutional rights. The social workers, psychologists, and
psychiatrists questioned my need to fight to the end for the lives of others while caring so little for my own. I was to learn to love myself, to take
care of myself first. At the outset I deemed their philosophy the vapid
expression of people without a political conscience. Nothing was wrong
with me. If the world weren't such a bad place, I wouldn't be as
depressed as I was. Like fourteen-year-old Robert, I had come to believe
that the whole world was against me. In addition, I was beginning to
think I was the only sane person in it. Any sane person would feel as I
did. Any sane person would want to die.

I had little choice, though, but to go with the program. I was barely
functioning at the time and knew I didn't have any alternatives. And in
truth, I didn't much like myself. There were issues that had been part of
my existence since childhood that I had to explore. I'd been pretty
severely depressed since I was a teenager. My personal life at the time
was a mess, and very painful. I had very little in the way of a support system. All those problems needed addressing.

But something more than just the psychological turmoil was going
on. I was also in the midst of a profound spiritual crisis. I worked most of
my waking life against a justice system that had lost its heart and soul. I
was in despair, running on less than empty, and had nothing more to
offer than all I had already brought to the struggle.

Robert's case to me was simple from the time I had my first conversations with him. Robert was a man deserving, as we all are, of compassion and love. He had been completely neglected for years when I first
met him. I had watched his life grow in the short time we represented
him, just in response to our commitment to him. His connection to some
members of his family grew much stronger, he found a spiritual advisor
he liked and trusted and began talking with her, he communicated regularly with me as well and called in times of despair. A lot was happening
in response to what Robert experienced as kindness and caring.

None of this was acknowledged, none of it was relevant in the system in which I functioned as a lawyer. Each step of the way, Robert's case
showed how very far we had come from the individualized sentencing
determinations that supposedly distinguish a sentence of death from
lightning striking. Would Robert have been sentenced to death if an
unsupported aggravating circumstance had not been introduced at sentencing? Would Robert have been sentenced to death if he were represented by an experienced attorney, even absent the attorney's total failure to investigate his case? Would Robert have been sentenced to death
if the jury hadn't been instructed that their verdict was only a recommendation and that others would review it to make sure it was correct?

And the really devastating question to me: Would Robert have been sentenced to death if jurors had known about his mental retardation, his organic brain damage, his childhood of horrific abuse? I knew the answer to that question from the mouth of one of the jurors. No. He would not have been sentenced to death.

The legal system's response to those last two issues—an erroneous sentencing instruction and the fact that jurors received no information regarding Robert's debilitating impairments—was that while such errors would be considered in the cases of other men on death row, Robert's timing was bad. His trial occurred too early in time for him to benefit from the clearly erroneous jury instruction. He raised the significant mitigation in his case too late for courts even to consider the impact such information would have had on the jury's verdict. The timing was bad—struck by lightning. But with Robert it wasn't a natural phenomenon. It was the product of intellectual acrobatics. It was the higher functioning of our human intellect at its most inhumane.

I spent about a month in the hospital making a start on reclaiming my own life. I left the hospital and returned to work representing the men on death row with the idea that I would be able to do the work in a more balanced way, taking time away for myself and for more enriching, not debilitating, pursuits. When I returned to work, Neal was in the last stages of writing Robert's Supreme Court brief. He had been working night and day while I was away and had mastered the voluminous record in Robert's case as well as the vast body of Supreme Court case law from the time it found capital punishment constitutional under current state statutes. It was strange to have so little involvement in Robert's case, but my connection to him and his family was still very strong and I spoke with them frequently.

Neal argued Robert's case before the Supreme Court in February 1992. I was sworn in as a member of the Supreme Court Bar the morning of the argument, and Nick and I sat with Neal as cocounsel. There's no question that it was a momentous event—arguing a case in the highest court in the country. But it was my own undoing. I turned a corner that day and in the ensuing months and will never go back. I'll never again participate in that kind of cynicism. I choose not to. I choose to live my life and do my work in environments that care about people.

Neal has a majestic presence and is a truly gifted orator. He held his own against a skeptical court, responding well to question after question. As we had anticipated, the questions focused on the huge burden to courts of reviewing every case that came along like Robert's. Neal repeated, over and over, that the court was addressing a very small number of cases in which a jury sentenced a man to death based upon misinformation, lies, about the character of the defendant.

MR. WALKER: ... The picture of Robert Sawyer that the jury considered was a picture of a person portrayed by psychiatrists, and even his own lawyer, as a sociopath, a person who has the ability to control his behavior but freely chooses to engage in conduct harmful to others; a person who beat up and ultimately set Fran Arwood on fire because he likes to do those things; a person who had been in a mental hospital one time, quote, for no reason.

A very different picture of Robert Sawyer emerges from the evidence presented in support of the successive habeas claim. That picture of Robert Sawyer is a picture of a person who has been committed twice in his life to mental hospitals and in fact had been declared on one occasion incapable of competing for employment in the outside world.

For that Robert Sawyer the world is a very confusing place, and when that Robert Sawyer arrived back at his residence the day the homicide was committed, he was confronted with a terribly confusing situation, because after entrusting the care of his adopted children to Fran Arwood, the babysitter, he thought one of them had been drugged.

Now, Robert Sawyer's world is a very menacing world, one where people are constantly out to get him. A normal person may not have thought that the child was drugged, but Robert Sawyer thought that child was drugged, because Robert Sawyer sometimes sees problems where they don't exist because of his disabilities.

Robert Sawyer couldn't think this problem through. His mind doesn't work this way. His mind won't work that way. His mind became clouded with rage and he exploded, his rage feeding on itself, and he beat and brutalized Fran Arwood.

The crux of the issue before the Supreme Court was whether in capital sentencing, when a jury is deciding whether to sentence a defendant to life imprisonment or death, a miscarriage of justice could arise equivalent to the miscarriage of justice that arises when an innocent man is wrongly convicted. Justice Antonin Scalia scorned the very idea. Neal responded eloquently, but it was like screaming underwater. The man on the side of the pool was oblivious:

JUSTICE SCALIA: Why should [the innocence exception to convictions] be translated into the penalty phase at all? I mean why—I had thought that we're making an exception for compelling circumstances to our normal rules that you've had a fair trial and that's the end of the matter, and we've said, you know, why isn't it reasonable to say well, if in fact you weren't guilty of the crime, that's an extraordinary circumstance, but you're saying even if you are guilty of the crime you might have gotten a lesser sentence. I don't find that as extraordinary a circumstance at all.

MR. WALKER: Well, Justice Scalia, just as we have a right to have a fair trial under this Court's jurisprudence, there was an equally strong right to a fair sentencing hearing.

JUSTICE SCALIA: Well, that's certainly not our jurisprudence in most areas. You wouldn't be making the argument if he got 50 years instead of 10 years, would you?

MR. WALKER: No, we wouldn't, because we're talking now about a fundamentally different sort of proceeding, and we're talking about a proceeding where the stakes are not whether he goes to prison or not, or the degree or length of a period of incarceration, we're talking about whether or not a person will live or die, and this Court has noted in its jurisprudence since *Gregg* itself that death is a qualitatively different kind of punishment than any other punishment that can be doled out by a sentencing judge in the United States of America.

And again I think that if we reference the facts of this case, all reasonable people would agree that it's fundamentally unfair that Robert Sawyer has not at least had a chance to put before some tribunal his severe and crippling mental disabilities and have a tribunal at least evaluate whether or not if that evidence had been presented the jury may have voted for a life sentence.

But the court's bottom line was that it would simply take too much time to weed out the bad claims of this nature from the good claims of this nature. Justice Anthony Kennedy summed it up in one of his questions to Neal: "[L]istening to your argument today, and your very moving description of Sawyer's condition, I would have to read the sentence—the transcript of the trial itself, of the sentencing hearing and all of the affidavits and all of the submissions before I could pass on the validity and strength of your argument." At that moment I felt the huge gulf between me and the Supreme Court justice, sitting up there brushing Robert's life and the trial that determined his fate aside like too many words on paper. It was hopeless. Neal responded that it wouldn't take too much time to review the written claims because appeals courts remain assigned to the same capital cases throughout the appeals process. I hung my head in defeat. Wasn't getting it right worth the time it would take? Wasn't fairness? Weren't time and thought essential to the constitutional prohibition against arbitrary and capricious sentences of death?

I quit my job a month later. I phoned in my resignation from the hospital, back in the Center for Emotional Recovery. After my release from the hospital, I traveled to death row and told my clients I was leaving. I no longer worked in the office when the Supreme Court issued its opinion refusing to consider the mitigation we discovered in Robert's case. The vote was 9 to 0, a resounding defeat.

Robert Sawyer was killed by lethal injection on March 5, 1993. I had promised him I would be there with him and was, up until the time he was led from his cell to the execution chamber. One of the last things he told me was that he would be with me in spirit whenever I worked into the wee hours of the morning as I had so many times for him. I have felt his gentle, childlike presence with me while writing about the two of us. I owe him my life as I live it today, with compassion for all, including myself.

PART VI

TOWARD ABOLITION

16

KILLING THE DEATH PENALTY WITH KINDNESS

CLIVE STAFFORD-SMITH

ack in 1996, I was trying to stop the state of Georgia from electrocuting Larry Lonchar. The prison employees who conduct an execution have to be volunteers, which tends to distill the class of guard that gets involved. Shortly before Larry was to be strapped into Ol' Sparky, the polished oak electric chair, one of the sadists handed him a description of what was about to happen:

> When the executioner throws the switch that sends the electric current through the body, the prisoner cringes from torture, his flesh swells, and his skin stretches to the point of breaking. He defecates, he urinates, his tongue swells and his eyes pop out. In some cases I have been told the eyeballs rest on the cheeks of the condemned. His flesh is burned and smells of cooked meat. When the autopsy is performed the liver is so hot it cannot be touched by human hand.

That time, we stopped Larry's execution well into the eleventh hour—actually just thirty-two minutes before the seven o'clock deadline. At night, sometimes, I still see a black-and-white negative of his wild eyes when he handed the crumpled paper to me.

Later, the stays were lifted and they went ahead and killed Larry. As his lawyer, I had to be there. You don't see all the horrors, of course, because they covered his face with an appalling leather mask, and strapped his mouth so tightly that he could not scream. But I knew what he was going through.

On June 11, 2001, Timothy McVeigh was strapped onto a gurney, and poison was injected into his arm. Lethal injection is meant to be a kinder, gentler form of death. Within minutes, he was dead, and his passing was celebrated by some, and observed in studied silence by the anti–death penalty movement. Tim McVeigh was not our poster child.

We all have our bigotries, and I hate capital punishment. I've spent the past seventeen years representing people facing execution. Our charity has an amorphous name—the Louisiana Crisis Assistance Center—because then nobody knows what we do, and that stops the bomb threats from frustrated advocates of the death penalty.

Before McVeigh, the last time the federal government executed a prisoner was before a human being had trod on the moon. Although McVeigh was convicted of blowing up 168 people in the Oklahoma City federal building on October 19, 1995, his death is yet another small step for humankind—backwards. The filip it gives to death penalty supporters cannot obscure the writing on the wall. Today there are 108 countries that don't execute, and only 87 that do. The death penalty is dying, suffocated in the effort to make it kinder.

Perhaps it is unwise simply to count countries. That's like asking whether we should still be driving on the lefthand side: most countries don't do it, but more people still live in countries that do. The "Big Eight" countries that retain the death penalty on the books (China, India, Indonesia, Japan, Nigeria, Pakistan, Russia, and the USA) account for 3.4 billion of the world's 6 billion people, yet few countries remain serious about executions. While a century ago capital punishment was routine everywhere, by the year 2000 almost 90 percent of all executions took place in China, Iran, Saudi Arabia, and the United States. Japan had just three; Russia, none.

No matter what the numbers, the real story is a human one. I always ask jurors the ultimate question of capital punishment when they must decide whether my client should die: "Why did we *need* to kill Tim McVeigh?" If a killing is unnecessary, we should not do it.

There are, of course, execution exponents who believe that the noose, or at least the needle, will reign again. When Louisiana introduced the death penalty for statutory rape in 1996, the state court suggested that the new law was "the beginning of a trend" that other states might follow, an evolution in the "standards of decency" of our society. But from where I stand, the decline in the death penalty seems inexorable, and I find it difficult to believe that future history books will describe a twenty-first-century renaissance where public executions made a comeback.

So why do particular countries maintain the death penalty, as it dies out elsewhere? Among the serious advocates of capital punishment, the United States finds itself in unfamiliar company, divorced from its habitual Western European allies. On closer inspection, the United States is already three-fourths of the way along the road to abolition.

The two primary justifications for the death penalty are deterrence and retribution. Of the two, retribution carries ancient credentials, but we swallow hard when we read that the Iranians actually sentenced Gholamhossein Aryabakhshahye to have an eye removed last year for blinding Mohammad Ali Qorbani in an argument. As Old Testament scholars will tell anyone prepared to listen, Mosaic law *limited* private acts of vengeance by allowing the government to exact *only* an eye for an eye. Given that this three-thousand-year-old law's purpose was to restrain revenge rather than foster it, the *lex talonis* argument has a questionable pedigree for a modern justice system.

It would be a strange society that spent money to make the relatives of murder victims feel better with rituals of revenge, rather than trying to prevent the crime in the first place. England's National Health Service does not spend its limited resources on helping the families of an ill person feel better about their loved one's untimely death; it spends money on a cure.

Thus, governments generally fall back on the deterrence argument—that capital punishment really is a "cure" for crime. The Chinese and Saudis carry out their executions in public for a reason—deterrence is not served by discreet executions, conducted in the dead of night. On an intuitive level, for deterrence to work, the punishment has to shock the spectator, and even the British solution, hanging, failed in this respect, since watching someone dangle at a distance failed to evoke sufficient horror. British officials were disconcerted by the picnic atmosphere that often prevailed at a public execution, and by the large number of pickpockets working the crowd at the hanging of a colleague.

In the West, we are now repelled by close-up pictures of a Chinese woman being shot in the back of the head; still more by the image of a scimitar being swung in a Saudi square. These punishments have moved beyond our pale. Our own subjective revulsion is the first stage of squeamishness that spells death for the death penalty. In America, it has already prompted a series of reforms that, ironically, deprive capital punishment of any justification.

The second stage of squeamishness is to bar the public from the executions. Executions are not pleasant. Therefore, the state carefully censors what the witnesses see. The black curtain did not rise on Tim McVeigh until the needle had already been inserted (in case they had to probe for an hour to find a vein, as had occurred not long before in South Carolina). The viewer could not even see Tim writhing on the gurney as he died, because a sedative and a paralyzing agent were injected prior to the poison.

Because the execution protocol is designed *not* to shock the audience, why should executions not be broadcast? It is partly because politicians have lost the will to kill, even kindly; partly, they fear that televising a modern execution would only highlight its diminished deterrent effect. The government, which now blames societal violence on vivid Hollywood films, cannot turn around and sponsor *Execution Television*. With 3,726 people on death row, and media *mo-ghouls* keen to screen every one, ETV would have no shortage of footage: an execution a day for ten years. But because the ritual has been neutered, the ratings would soon slip—Hollywood does it so much better.

So as the second stage of squeamishness sets in, the execution is carried out in the dead of the night, without fanfare. In recent years, Americans have routinely opted for midnight. The Japanese go a step further. Three people were executed in Japan last year, all on November 30. Each had been on death row for more than ten years, and their appeals had been turned down more than five years earlier. Without warning, the condemned men were simply taken from their cells and executed in secrecy. Such furtive punishment destroys even the pretense of deterrence: future killers can't be expected to fear something they are not permitted to know.

The third stage of squeamishness comes when we start placing limits on the number of executions. China executed over a thousand people last year. America, with a far higher crime rate, had eighteen thousand murders. To kill every killer would require fifty executions a day, which is too much blood for society to stomach. So the Americans purported to select only the worst crimes, and executed just eighty-seven. However, the kinder the numbers, the weaker the pretext of deterrence. One cannot expect a crack addict to pause mid-robbery to ponder whether he may have a one-in-two-hundred chance of spending a decade on death row. On a school trip, Adam Pinkton went to the Mississippi State Penitentiary to see the gas chamber. Three years later, high on drugs, Adam shot Louis Coats. Adam could not spell *deterrence*, let alone contemplate its consequences. He was sentenced to death.

The fourth stage of squeamishness comes when we start worrying about the danger of executing the innocent. If we hook 'em, book 'em, and cook 'em, we might instill fear, but we will make mistakes. A kinder, gentler society insists that we get the right guy. Here, due process ultimately sounds the death knell of deterrence. Three years ago, I was suing the state of Mississippi over whether Willie Russell should have to represent himself in his appeals—a lonely task for a developmentally handicapped man locked in his cell all day, not even allowed a pencil. Willie won. Now he has a lawyer, and a lengthy appeal detailing why he should have been found not guilty was due to be filed on the day that Tim McVeigh was originally set to die.

Due process means that we have to take care when we punish people. In part, that means slowing the rush to judgment. In 1987, I tried to delay Edward Earl Johnson's death and I failed; an innocent man was executed. In Japan, the average time between arrest and execution is now ten years; in the United States, it is eight. Delay does not decrease the number of venal police, incompetent defense lawyers, and overzealous prosecutors. However, delay, combined with resources, does allow the condemned to expose erroneous convictions. It is no coincidence that people are now being exonerated from death row in increasing numbers; ninety-five since 1976—so far.

In the future, the focus will shift from how to get the innocent out of prison to the more significant question of how they got in prison in the first place. Due process poses some harsh questions for advocates of executions.

Ultimately, as capital punishment seeks to become kinder, politicians are left with a punishment in search of a justification. For a while, it will persist, fueled by the desire among politicians to find someone for us to despise. Those on death row are handy scapegoats for many of society's ills. Yet the ills persist. A recent poll of American police chiefs found that only one in a hundred felt that the death penalty had a serious impact on crime.

There is no doubt that, in the United States, the tide of public opinion in favor of the death penalty is running out. Support for capital punishment climbed to 80 percent in 1994 (over 90 percent in some southern states), and we are now back to 66 percent. No tide in the affairs of humankind could sweep away the death penalty in time for Tim McVeigh, but Bud Welch was one person who did not watch Tim's execution. Bud's only child, Julie, died in the explosion in Oklahoma City. There was once a time in the wake of the bombing when he wanted to watch Tim die—he calls it his "insanity period." He changed his mind when he remembered riding cross country with his daughter, listening to a newscast about yet another execution. Julie's response was, "Dad, all they're doing is teaching hate to their children."

Bud is an inspirational figure. When he is not filling up cars at his service station, he finds his eloquence in the power of his message. He says this message persuaded a fifth of the families of McVeigh's victims to oppose McVeigh's execution. Bud and the organization he now represents, Murder Victims' Families for Reconciliation, reflect the reality of a kinder process: mercy. Their mercy will deal the death penalty its final blow. When the history books record June 11, 2001, Timothy McVeigh will probably be a footnote; the hero will be Bud Welch.

17

SPEAKING OUT AGAINST THE EXECUTION OF TIMOTHY McVEIGH

BUD WELCH

I am the third oldest of eight children, raised on a dairy farm in central Oklahoma. I have run a gasoline service station for thirty-four years. I lived a quiet, unassuming life until April 19, 1995, when my daughter, Julie Marie, was killed in the Oklahoma City bombing. Julie was my only daughter. She was my pal, my sidekick, and my best friend. My wife understands that, that Julie was my best friend. We hung together, we fought together, we did everything together. Julie attended the public school system in Oklahoma City, K through 8. In the eighth grade, she met a young Mexican girl who was a foreign exchange student. The school was mostly white. Some of the children had been picking on the little Mexican girl because she couldn't speak English quite the same as the rest of them. Julie befriended this little girl, and in March or April, it suddenly dawned on Julie that this little girl was speaking English, and she was speaking it fluently. Being a thirteen-year-old kid, Julie was intrigued by that. The following year, when she started at Bishop McGuinness High School, a Catholic school, she enrolled in German, Latin, and Spanish. She did the same thing in her sophomore year.

She had decided by about January to apply for a foreign exchange to a Spanish-speaking country. She was accepted by a program called Youth For Understanding and went to live with a family in Pontevedre, Spain, on the Atlantic Ocean, about thirty miles north of the Portuguese border. Her host family could barely speak English, and Julie couldn't speak Spanish, even though she had had two years of it in high school. But she got a crash course because when she sat down at the dinner table and wanted a food item passed, she had to learn how to request it. Her host father was an attorney for a bank in Pontevedre, and they had many friends down in Portugal. Often on weekends they would travel there, and through this travel, Julie was paying close attention, and so in addition to Spanish, she learned to speak Portuguese.

She returned to Oklahoma City for her junior and senior years in high school. She enrolled in more foreign language courses, including French and Italian. Her senior year, after being accepted at a number of universities, she received a letter from Marquette University saying they were having a foreign language competition, and inviting her to attend. She had never been to Milwaukee, and neither had I. So I bought us a couple of tickets, thinking that even if she didn't do well in the contest at least she would get to see the campus. She competed with ninety-one other kids, got lucky, and finished first. That provided about $6,000 per year in grants and scholarships, so it enabled a service station owner to send his daughter to what I consider a high profile—and expensive—private university.

When I took Julie to Milwaukee in August of 1990 for freshman orientation, I did not have any shirt that would fit my swollen chest because I was so proud of her. I never attended college myself, and I think parents are certainly guilty of reliving their childhood through their children. That's what I was doing with Julie.

In January of Julie's freshman year, the university got a request from the Society of St. Vincent de Paul in Milwaukee for a Spanish major to accompany them to the Dominican Republic. Out of twenty-one people, Julie went down to help out down there. In her sophomore year in college, she went back to Madrid, where Marquette has a campus. She graduated in March of 1994, with a degree in Spanish and a minor in French and Italian. I brought her back to Oklahoma City over the Fourth of July weekend in 1994. The next month, she got a job as a Spanish translator for the Social Security Administration in the Federal Building.

Julie had met a young lieutenant at the Tinker Air Force Base, a recent graduate from the University of Arizona. She had heard about a prayer group that met at Tinker, a Catholic Chapter, and they said the rosary, I think, every Friday night, along with a few other prayers. I always jokingly accused them of praying for twenty minutes and drinking and dancing the rest of the night. She and Eric fell in love, and they dated until her death. I found out after Julie's death that they had planned to announce their engagement, and that still tears at my heart.

I have opposed the death penalty all my life. So has my entire family, even going back to my grandparents. I'd often been told over a cup of coffee with friends who supported the death penalty—or thought they supported the death penalty—that if something violent ever happened to one of my family members, I would change my mind. When Julie got to be a teenager, they would always use her as an example, because they knew how close we were. They would make such statements to me as, "What if you get a call tonight that Julie had been raped and murdered in Milwaukee?" That's something a father just cannot contemplate. They would say, "If that happens, you'll change your mind about the death penalty."

After Tim McVeigh bombed the Oklahoma City Federal Building, I was filled with rage, hate, the urge for revenge. I cannot describe how I felt. And I did change my mind about the death penalty. After McVeigh and [Terry] Nichols were charged, I thought, Fry the bastards. We don't need a trial, that's just a delay. People speak of temporary insanity—and lawyers try to use it in court. I know that temporary insanity is real. I can assure you that it exists, because I lived about five weeks of it. Perhaps you recall TV images of McVeigh or Nichols being rushed from an automobile to a building with bulletproof vests on. The reason that the police did that is because people like me would have killed them. The police presence around Tim McVeigh and Terry Nichols was the deterrent that keeps me from being on death row in Oklahoma today. Because had I thought that there was any opportunity to kill them, I would have done so. I did not come up with a plan because I knew there was no way to succeed. If there had been, I would not have cared if they had killed me in the process. That is how I thought during that insanity period.

For about the next eight months, I struggled with the thought, What is going to happen to these people? How am I going to get some peace? The bombing took place on a Wednesday morning at nine o'clock. On Thursday afternoon, I think, while Julie's body was still missing—her body was not recovered until Saturday—I heard President Bill Clinton and Attorney General Janet Reno say that they were going to seek and obtain the death penalty for the perpetrators. That sounded so wonderful to me at the time, because here I had been crushed, I had been hurt, and that was the big fix. We were going to find these guys and we were going to kill them. I thought about that over the next eight months.

I also remembered the statement that Julie had made to me driving across Iowa one time, during her junior year, on our way from Milwaukee to Oklahoma City. We heard a newscast on the radio about an execution in Texas the night before. Julie's response to that was, "Dad, all they're doing is teaching hate to their children in Texas. It has no socially redeeming value." I didn't think a hell of a lot of it at the time, but I remembered her saying that. Then after she was killed, and after I got past this initial five-week period, what she said kept echoing in my mind.

Across the street from the bomb site, there's an old American elm tree, the only living thing left there. All the survivors had been relocated, all the dead had been buried, and just one thing survived the bombing, and it's that old American elm. It's said to have come up from a seedling about the turn of the century, which would make that tree older than the state of Oklahoma, which became a state in 1907. I went down and stood under that tree one cold, January day. There were no leaves on it. I was watching the people walk the chain-link fence that surrounds the "footprint" of the building. People hang wooden crosses, wheel covers, rosaries, and everything imaginable on that fence. People will be traveling from Boston across the country, and they will suddenly want to leave something.

I see them open the trunks of their cars and pull out an old license plate they've had there for two or three years, find a piece of wire and hang it on the fence. Thousands of people who walk past every day. I kept looking at those people, just watching them, and I was in deep pain. It was nine months after the bombing. I was drinking too much, I was smoking three packs of cigarettes a day, twice as much as I had been smoking when Julie was killed.

I was in anguish about what was going to happen. The trials had not even begun, yet I was already asking myself, Once they're tried and executed, what then? How is that going to help me? It isn't going to bring Julie back. I had asked that question for a period of about two weeks, and I came to realize that it's all about hate and revenge. And hate and revenge are the reasons why Julie and 167 others are dead today. It was McVeigh and Nichols's hate for the federal government, their revenge for Waco, for Ruby Ridge, for whatever other cause they felt justified in what they did. After I was able to get that revenge and hate out of my system, I made a statement to an Associated Press reporter one day, saying that I did not believe in the death penalty. This came after a long conversation of bragging on my child, of saying what a wonderful daughter she was and how close we were. And yet, I told the reporter, I didn't want her killer killed.

The reporter's mouth didn't exactly drop open, but she simply could not imagine how I could be so close to this child and not want her killers killed. Anyway, she wrote a wire story on it. Soon I heard from people such as Renny Cushing of the organization Murder Victims' Families for Reconciliation. It had never occurred to me that it was unusual in this country to be a victim's family member and not want the killers executed.

I saw Bill McVeigh, Tim's father, on television a few weeks after the bombing. He's a very quiet kind of person who does not grant many television interviews. There was a crew out at his house in rural New York, just outside of Buffalo. He was working in his flower bed. The reporter asked him a question. I don't know what the question was, or the answer. But I saw him look into the television camera for a short two or three seconds, and I saw a deep pain in a father's eye that probably few people could even recognize. I recognized it because I was living that pain. And I knew that some day I would have to go tell that man that I truly cared about how he felt, that I did not blame him or his family for what his son had done.

I had made a number of speeches across the country, and in June of 1998, a nun by the name of Sister Rosalyn called me from Attica prison. She has been a minister in Attica for about ten years, and she wanted me to come to the Buffalo area to speak at colleges and universities, civic groups meetings, and churches, about the death penalty. Through our hour or hour-and-a-half conversation of getting to know one another, I told her what I had seen in Bill McVeigh's eyes. I asked if the McVeigh family was from someplace around Attica. She described to me exactly where they were and asked, "Well, would you want me maybe to pursue that?" And I told her that I would. I wanted the message to go to him that I did not want any media involved, that I wanted a very private thing between the two of us.

Sister Rosalyn contacted a parish priest where Bill goes to mass. The priest's biological sister, Liz McDermott, is a former nun, now married, and a bit older than I am. And she had been a neighbor of the McVeighs while her children and theirs were growing up. She has a daughter, twenty-four, and a son, nineteen; Jennifer McVeigh is twenty-four, and Tim is now thirty. Bill and Nikki McVeigh divorced about fifteen years ago; Nikki now lives in Florida. Bill moved a few miles away from the McDermotts, got himself a couple acres of land, and built a small house. That was where the television crew was when I saw him working in his flower bed.

McDermott contacted Sister Rosalyn in early August with the news that she had made the arrangements for us to meet on September 5, a Saturday, at ten A.M. I'll never forget that date or time. I went to Buffalo six days earlier, to make a series of speeches in the area. I had heard that Bill McVeigh had quite a large garden in his backyard. I was desperately trying to find out other things about him, and I finally met Liz McDermott, and she and I were able to sit down and she told me a lot of things about him.

Sister Roslyn is a careless, careless driver. On that Saturday, she takes me out to Bill McVeigh's house, pulling into his gravel driveway at probably fifty miles per hour and screeching to a halt. Then she says, "There's the door. Go knock on it." I didn't know how I was going to be able to do this at all. I didn't know what I was going to be able to say. Bill came to the door, and I introduced myself. I said, "I understand that you have a large garden in your backyard." He said, "Oh, yeah, would you like to see it?" I said, "I'd love to." That just put relief all over me. I knew what big gardens were all about. There were ten of us in the family in Central

Oklahoma, and we always had a big garden. I hoed gardens every year when I was a child. So, Bill and I spent the first half-hour in that garden getting to know one another. Then we went into the house, where we spent about an hour-and-a-half visiting at the kitchen table. His twenty-three-year-old daughter Jennifer was there.

As I walked into the kitchen I had noticed a particular photograph among the family photos on the wall above the table. It was a photo of Tim. I kept looking at it as we were sitting at the table, with Bill sitting off to my left. I knew that I had to comment on it at some point, so finally I looked at it and I said, "God, what a good looking kid." And Bill says to me, "That's Tim's high school graduation picture." By Bill's own admission, he has always had a difficult time showing emotion. He told me that when we were in the garden. But then I saw a tear roll out of his right eye. He's a big guy, about 6'2", and I saw love in a father's eyes, at that moment, for his son. And I know without a doubt that Bill McVeigh loves his son more today that he did four years ago. Because we, as parents, have a way of loving our children more the more they need us.

We talked about Jennifer's starting to teach school. She's twenty-four now, a year older than Julie when Julie was killed. And, unknown to us at the time, Julie had had a job teaching Spanish at a Catholic elementary school in Oklahoma City at the time of her death. (We know that because in July, three months after the bombing was in April, the principal of that school called to tell Julie when the first day of school was, not knowing that she had been killed in the bombing.) So Jennifer and I talked about Julie wanting to teach school as well. She told me about how several family members have threatened to withdraw their children from that school because a McVeigh was going to be teaching there. As it turned out, there was one family that did withdraw their children. And I assured her that she was better off, the school was better off, and that that family was better off.

Tim's guilt or innocence never came up. That was not my purpose in going there. I didn't need Bill McVeigh to look me in the eye and say, "I'm sorry my son killed your daughter." I didn't have to hear that. But I was able to tell him that I truly understood the pain that he was going through, and that he—as I—was a victim of what happened in Oklahoma City. We talked about how many generations of McVeighs had been in western New York. They were Irish Catholic, I'm Irish Catholic, and I told him that I was from a third generation of the Welches in central Oklahoma. So that was more common ground for us. But after our hour-and-a-half-long visit, I got up from the kitchen table and Jennifer came from the other end of the table, and gave me a hug, and we sobbed, and I was able to hold her face in my hands—I'll never forget it—I was able to hold her face in my hands and tell her, "Honey, the three of us are in this for the rest of our lives. And we can make the most of it if we choose. I don't want your brother to die. And I will do everything in my power to prevent it." And she hugged me again, and I left.

They had left a rental car for me outside of the house so I could drive the twenty miles back into Buffalo. I wanted to get back to Hope House, a halfway house for released prisoners, which I had spent a few days visiting. I was getting to know Sister Karen, who runs Hope House, and I knew Sister Rosalyn would be there as well. As I was driving back to Buffalo, I couldn't see through my glasses because I was still crying. When I got back to Hope House I sat in the living room and sobbed for another hour. I have never felt closer to God in my life than I did at that moment. Once I was through sobbing, I felt as though a load had been taken completely off my shoulders. I wish I could explain it to you; I wish I could make you understand the way it felt to me.

I left the next day to go back to Oklahoma City. On Monday morning, Liz McDermott (the next-door neighbor) called. She said, "Bud, I haven't heard a spirit in Bill McVeigh's voice for three and a half years like I've heard now." She said, "I want you to understand that this is the greatest thing you ever could have done for him."

And I wasn't doing it for Bill McVeigh, I was doing it for myself. It was a selfish thing on my part. But, as it turned out, it worked for all three of us.

The death penalty is about revenge and hate. Many people profess to be Christians, but if we are truly going to follow Christ, as I feel that I try to do, then I think we must ask ourselves this one question about the death penalty: "Would Jesus pull the switch?" I don't think that he would, because Jesus stopped an execution when he said, "Let those who are without sin cast the first stone." I think Gandhi put it very well when he said about the Old Testament, "An eye for an eye leaves the whole world blind."

18

AMAZING GRACE: REFLECTIONS ON JUSTICE, SURVIVAL, AND HEALING

RENNY CUSHING

In the fall of 1998 I traveled to Cambridge, Massachusetts, to watch Nelson Mandela honor Harvard University by accepting an honorary degree. In the presence of Nelson Mandela, I couldn't help but think what an amazing story he represented, because this a person who at one time faced the death penalty; who was found guilty in court and sentenced to life in jail; who spent twenty-seven years in prison; and, at the end of that, walked out without much bitterness. He didn't look back, because he had things to do; he had to free a nation from the burden of apartheid. He eventually took his place as the leader of a new South Africa, as the president of a free South Africa, a country that as part of its rebirth abolished the death penalty. The Harvard ceremony included a song in Mandela's honor. The song was "Amazing Grace." My youngest daughter's name is Grace, and it happened that my wife Kristie Conrad and I had brought her there to see Mandela as a first birthday present.

"Amazing Grace" was written by a man named John Newton, who was a slaveholder in the early part of his life. He was someone who trafficked in human beings, who extracted people in bondage from Africa and transported them to bondage here in the New World. John Newton was a man who, by his own admission, was responsible for the deaths of scores of innocent men, women, and children. In another time and in another jurisdiction, John Newton would have been subject to the death penalty. But as fate would have it, he was not subject to death, and eventually went on to reevaluate his life. He went about a transformation from slaveholder to ardent abolitionist, and he also gave us the gift of that song. He once was lost but now he's found, was blind but now he sees.

Hearing "Amazing Grace" while thinking of Nelson Mandela made me
pause and contemplate the possibilities that exist in the aftermath of
murder and in the aftermath of crime.

On June 1, 1988, Robert and Marie Cushing planted a garden in the backyard of their home in New Hampshire. It was a ritual of the seasons: the
same twelve-hundred-square-foot plot of land in which they had
planted a garden, the backyard of the same home they had bought in
1951 on the GI bill, and where they had raised their seven children.
Robert had retired as an elementary school teacher, and Marie was sev
enteen days away from retiring after twenty-three years as a readin
teacher. They were celebrating the birth of a new granddaughter, also
named Marie, who was the first child of their oldest son—me. Life for
them was very good. They were happy.

At about ten o'clock at night, there was a knock on the front door. My
mother was lying on the couch watching the Celtics in a playoff game. My
father was at the kitchen table reading the newspaper, and he got up to
answer the door. As he did so, a couple of shotgun blasts rang out, ripped
his chest apart, and he died in front of my mother. From that day, from
that moment, I became the survivor of a homicide victim. And in the
aftermath of that I had reason to contemplate—on numerous occasions
and in some depth—how we deal as a society and individually in the
aftermath of murder.

I can just tell you that murder is awful. I would not wish any of you
to have the experience. Because after the killing begins a whole series of
events makes you feel like a victim again and again. Revictimization is
constant. Funerals and caskets; cemetery plots and headstones; empty
chairs at holidays; police investigations; hearings, trials, sentencing,
appeals...I refer to this all as the "dead zone." Those things were hard,
but there was something harder. In the aftermath of the murder, the
most difficult thing I had to do was to ask someone for help to get my
father's blood cleaned off the walls of the house.

Prior to my father's murder, I opposed the death penalty. Although
I'm from the Irish-Catholic tradition, whose teachings include "Thou
shalt not kill," being against the death penalty was for me more akin to a
set of principles upon which I had consciously decided I want to lead my
life, a vision I had of the world in which I wanted to live. It was simply a
matter of wanting to live in a society where life is respected. In the aftermath of my father's murder, I never really wavered from that position.
But I found that there was a presumption on the part of many people,
maybe even most people, that my position would waver. A few days after
the individuals who murdered my father were taken into police custody,
a friend came up to me in the grocery store. He was someone I have

known my whole life, and he said to me, "I hope they fry the bastards so you and your mother and your family can get some peace."

He meant well. He meant to offer me some comfort, I think. But at that time, there was probably nothing that he could have said that would have caused me more angst. His comment implied that my father's murder should cause me to change my position about executions. I was threatened with losing my values. I thought that not only had the murderer taken my father's life, and taken him from me and from his family; but that now the murderer was reaching out from his cell to take my values as well. People who knew me presumed that the murder of my father would make me change, would make me become or want that which I had abhorred. They presumed that I would want somehow to balance my father's life being taken by extinguishing the life of someone else.

I think that people who are the survivors of homicide victims want three basic things. First, we want to know the truth. By "the truth," I mean a precise, almost literal, understanding of what took place: the chronology, the details, how it happened that somebody we loved could be taken from us. I think we need to know these things because homicide is unlike other deaths. We are accustomed to death coming by natural causes, we can accept disease, we can accept an automobile accident, we can accept some force that's outside all of us. But what is very difficult for us to contemplate, I think, with homicide, is how another human being who seemingly has all the same faculties that you and I have could take it upon himself to make a conscious decision to be the deity. We believe in our own selves that that is not something we would do, and so it is hard for us to understand how somebody else could do it. We need to know the truth just to help us gain some kind of control over our lives; we want to understand how it is that such control could have been removed.

The second thing that survivors of a homicide want is justice. Justice is one of those concepts that is real but is a difficult thing to grasp and even harder to explain. Particularly in the case of murder, there is a sense in which the only way to achieve justice is for the murderer and the victim to trade places: for the murderer to be in a grave and for the victim to be walking the earth. But of course we cannot make that happen, much as we might want to. So we have to fashion something as best we can to secure justice. An objective of justice is to make whole those who most deeply feel the loss. One of the ways we feel whole and repaired is to restore that sense of security that has been lost. And that means people need to be separated from society. The objective of incarceration fulfills this need; it removes the offender from our midst.

The third thing we want is healing. To a certain extent, an understanding of the truth and an attempt to fashion justice are necessary preconditions for healing. The healing to which I refer is a process; it cannot be reduced to an event. One of the things that the proponents of the death penalty incorrectly assume is that an execution can serve as the singular event that results in healing. Healing does not come in so sudden a fashion. And indeed, death penalty proponents falsely raise the expectations of survivors of murder victims when they suggest that the execution will bring healing, when they suggest that extinguishing the life of someone who took a life can serve as a healing event, when they say that if you just kill the bastard it will all of a sudden be better, and you will feel better, and then you can just go on.

The reality is that healing is a process that goes on all the time. It is part of the burden, the reality that the survivors of homicide victims come to grips with: healing is a process that will go on for the rest of your own life.

Not only does an execution not contribute to healing, but there are actually a couple of reasons why the death penalty might present some impediments to healing. One is that the existence of the death penalty itself, and the whole carnival-like atmosphere that exists in our society around executions, is incredibly demeaning. It is demeaning to life, to our own lives and to the life of the victim. The death penalty makes us offender-oriented; we take our focus off the life of the individual we have lost, and off that person's good works. The death penalty makes icons out of demons. So we all know the names of John Wayne Gacy, or Gary Gilmore, or Ted Bundy, or Timothy McVeigh. There are very few of us who know the name of a single one of their victims. And at the same time, there are very few of us who know the name of a murderer who was sentenced to life in prison rather than death. Death penalty proponents complain, justifiably, that the criminal justice system too often forgets the victims, but the death penalty itself is one feature of the system that causes that.

In addition, the criminal justice system is supposed to help heal victims, but the death penalty creates new victims. I remember coming out of the courthouse after a pretrial hearing and running into a man named Robert McLaughlin Jr. He is the son of the man who murdered my father. We had never met before. As we stood next to each other for a moment in that parking lot, I had the sensation of a black hole being laid between the two of us, with both of us trying desperately not to get sucked down into it. I said to him, "We both lost our fathers on June 1, 1988. My father is dead in the grave, and your father is in jail." Then I realized that in a way I was the lucky one, because I had my father's life to celebrate. Of course I don't wish that my father had been murdered, but I honor his life; I am the son of a murder victim. But for Robert McLaughlin Jr. it's a different legacy. He lives his life as the son of a murderer. And I would not want the pain that I felt in losing my father to be placed on Robert

McLaughlin Jr. The idea that I would be healed, that any murder victim would be healed, by inflicting pain upon the child of the family of a murderer is nonsense. Life is not a zero-sum game. My pain does not get eased by inflicting pain on another.

The final reason for my opposition to the death penalty is the most difficult to articulate. It involves the way in which I relate to the murderers. I cannot ignore that I am linked to two people who are serving life sentences, without the possibility of parole, because they killed my father in June of 1998. I cannot ignore the fact that I am linked to those people, and I have felt an urge to figure out how to relate to two human beings who have caused me such pain. So, at one point, I decided to go to the New Hampshire State Prison to meet with one of the people responsible for my father's murder. It was something I wanted to do but that I was also wary of doing. I knew that some people would think I was betraying my father by conceding that his murderer was a human being who had any value at all. Yet I did it. I went to the state prison and I had an exchange with her. I do not know what exactly I was expecting, and although I was glad that I did it, it was not very fulfilling.

A few weeks later, I went for a walk on the beach with an old friend of mine. We talked a little bit about life, about how our paths had meandered. At some point I told her about my visit to the women's prison, and I said out loud, for the first time, "You know, on some level, I'm going to end up spending the rest of my life trying to figure out a way to help the McLaughlins get me to forgive them." That's a convoluted way of putting it, and yet I cannot put it any simpler. I do not want to be consumed by hate. I do not want to create any more victims. I do not know whether I can interact with any of these individuals who have hurt me, but I do know I will not feel better by causing more hurt.

The death penalty is final. When we kill people who kill our loved ones, we forever preclude the opportunity for those of us who want to figure out how to have an interactive forgiveness. The existence of the death penalty in and of itself becomes a barrier to healing. I do not want to live in a society where, in the aftermath of murder, the criminal justice system, which should help victims heal, instead prevents them from doing so.

BIOGRAPHIES

Stacy Abramson is Executive Producer at Large with WNYC radio in New York. She was previously with Sound Portraits Productions, where her production credits included *Witness to an Execution* and *The Jewish Giant*. She is co-author of *Flophouse* (2000).

Shawn Armbrust was the case coordinator for the Northwestern University Law School's Center on Wrongful Convictions. She currently attends Georgetown University Law Center.

Stephen B. Bright, one of the best-known death penalty attorneys in the country, is director of the Southern Center for Human Rights (SCHR) in Atlanta. SCHR is a public-interest legal project that provides representation to persons facing the death penalty and to prisoners in challenges to cruel and unusual conditions of confinement. A visiting lecturer at Harvard and Yale Law Schools, Bright is the author of dozens of articles published in law journals and popular periodicals.

Richard Burr is one of the preeminent death penalty attorneys in the United States and former director of the Capital Punishment Project at the Legal Defense Fund in New York; he represented Shaka Sankofa (nee Gary Graham), who was executed in Texas in 2000.

Bob Burtman is an investigative reporter with the *Houston Press* who has written about the death penalty and other criminal justice issues in Texas. His story about convicted rapist Roy Criner, later featured on the PBS *Frontline* documentary *A Case For Innocence*, ultimately led to Criner's exoneration.

Phyllis L. Crocker is Associate Professor of Law, Cleveland-Marshall College of Law, Cleveland State University. She was a staff attorney from 1989-94 at the Texas Resource Center.

Renny Cushing is the Executive Director of the National Board of Directors of Murder Victims' Families for Reconciliation, based in Cambridge, Massachusetts.

David R. Dow is the George Butler Research Professor of Law at the University of Houston, where he teaches and writes in the areas of constitutional law and theory, death penalty law, contract law, and law-and-literature. Since 1988 he has represented more than 25 death row inmates in their habeas corpus appeals. In addition to scholarly works in legal periodicals, he is also a frequent contributor of essays and opinion pieces to popular publications, including *The Christian Science Monitor*, *The Texas Observer*, *The Houston Chronicle*, and *The Dallas Morning News*.

Mark Dow is a freelance writer and poet whose work has appeared in the *Boston Review*, *Threepenny Review*, *Conjunctions*, *Index on Censorship*, *Prison Legal News*, *The Miami Herald*, *The Texas Observer*, *New Politics*, *The Progressive*, and many other publications. He won a 1996 Project Censored Award for his reporting on immigration detention centers.

Cecile C. Guin is the Director of the Office of Social Service Research and Development at the Louisiana State University School of Social Work in Baton Rouge. She regularly testifies in the sentencing phase of capital trials and is currently working with individuals whom she met some fifteen years ago when they were juvenile offenders and who are now adults on death row in Texas, Louisiana, and Oklahoma.

Andrew Hammel was a staff attorney at the Texas Defender Service in Houston, Texas, from 1996 to 2000. The opinions expressed in "Jousting with the Juggernaut" essay are solely those of the author.

Christopher Hitchens, a columnist for Vanity Fair and The Nation, is author of numerous books, including *Letters to a Young Contrarian* (2001), *The Trial of Henry Kissinger* (2001), *Unacknowledged Legislators: Writers in the Public Sphere* (2000), and *No One Left to Lie To: The Values of the Worst Family* (2000).

David Isay is the founder of Sound Portraits Productions in New York. His numerous broadcasting honors include the Peabody Award (three times) and the Robert F. Kennedy Award (twice). He has also received the Prix Italia, and was a 2000 MacArthur Fellow. He is author or co-author of *Holding On* (1995), *Our America: Life and Death on the South Side of Chicago* (1997), and *Flophouse* (2000).

Sarah Ottinger, an attorney with the Juvenile Justice Project of Louisiana, has represented death row inmates at the Louisiana State Penitentiary at Angola for almost ten years.

Ken Silverstein is a writer based in Washington, DC. He is contributing editor to *Harper's* and *Mother Jones*, as well as a regular contributor to *The Nation* and *Salon*. Silverstein previously worked with the Associated Press in Latin America. His fourth and most recent book is *Private Warriors*.

Clive Stafford-Smith, Director of the Louisiana Crisis Assistance Center in New Orleans, is an attorney who has represented death row inmates in the south for twenty years. Born in England, he is also the founder of Reprieve, an organization dedicated to training civil rights attorneys in Britian.

Bud Welch in on the National Board of Directors of Murder Victims' Families for Reconciliation, is based in Cambridge, Massachusetts.

Mandy Welch, cocounsel with Richard Burr for Timothy McVeigh in the sentencing phase of the Oklahoma City bombing trial, is former director of the Texas Resource Center, which provided representation to capital defendants until it was defunded by Congress in 1994.

INDEX

healing, 284–87
Heath, Larry, case of, 23
Herrera v. Collins, 18
Hilliard, Jerry (Porter case victim), 159,
    162, 163
Hitler, Adolf, 190
Holmes, Johnny (district attorney),
    111–12
Hubbard, Ronald (Graham case witness),
    131, 133–34, 136, 142n4
Human Rights Watch Children's RIghts
    Project, 230
Humphrey, Johnny Ray (Barnes case wit-
    ness), 148–49, 153
Hunt, Jim, 146

I
IASG. *See* independent and adequate
    state ground (IASG) doctrine
Illinois
    black judicial officials in, number of,
        71n28
    executions in, 2
    felony-murder in, 213n14
    moratorium on executions in, *vi,* 1–2,
        155
    releases from death row in, 157
    reversals of death sentences in, 114
    Witherspoon v. Illinois, 31–32
independent and adequate state ground
    (IASG) doctrine, 30–31, 35n37,
    35n42
India, 270
Indiana
    black judicial officials in, number of,
        71n28
    judicial override of jury decisions in, 83
Indonesia, 270
Ingram, Kenneth (judge), 84–85
innocence
    in appeals, role of, 33, 140–41
    in death penalty debate, 4–6
    definition of, 4, 5
    of Graham, 128, 147, 155
    and habeas corpus appeals, 18, 259
    impossibility of proving, 4
    of Edward Johnson, 155
    to the public, 142
    when evidence of is found, importance
        of, 141–42
Iran, 270, 271
Iraq, 11

J
Jack (pseudonym), case of, 230–32, 233
Jackson, Inez (Porter case witness), 160,
    162–64

Jackson, Walter, 162, 164
James, Fob, 86
James, Frank, 180
Japan, 270, 272, 273
Jefferson, Albert, case of, 49
Jimerson, Verneal, case of, 165
John Paul II, Pope, *vii,* 27
John (pseudonym), case of, 234
Johnson, Edward Earl, case of
    attempted delays in, 273
    Cabana and, 175, 181, 182, 191
    innocence of, *xi*
    Samuel Johnson and, 93, 101, 103
Johnson, Libby (Barnes case investiga-
    tor), 151
Johnson, Samuel Rice, case of, 91–103
Johnson, Wayne (Lee case judge), 87
Johnston, Joseph (judge), 81
Jones, Andrew Lee, case of, 241–47, 258
Jones, Ken, 102
Jones, Lloyd (sheriff), 93–94, 95
Jordan, Leamon, case of, 158
Jospin, Lionel, 145
judges
    appointment of death penalty lawyers
        by, 24
    political pressures on, 16, 84–85
    power to override jury decisions, 79,
        83–84
    prosecutors writing opinions for,
        114–15
    racial prejudice among, 48–49, 80
    relationship with district attorneys,
        54–55
    state *vs.* federal, 15–16
    weariness with appeals process, 27, 33
    See also named judges
juries
    change of heart about a sentencing,
        261
    death qualification of, 53, 85
    decision-making prior to sentencing
        hearings, 126n16, 212n7
    diversity and, 55
    exclusion of blacks from, 49–50, 53–55,
        59–63, 65–67, 206, 242, 245
    instructions to, 72n43, 202
    intimidation of jurors, 95
    law-and-order jurors, 110–11
    overrides of jury decisions, 79–80,
        83–84, 217n51
    pretty women required on, 88
    psychological tendencies of whites on,
        55, 75n112
    selection of, 112–13, 126n15
    in Texas, 112–13
jury strikes

McVeigh, Timothy, case of
  AEDPA and, *v*
  as exceptional case, 11
  execution of, *viii–ix, x,* 181, 269–70,
    271, 273, 275–81
  FBI in, *viii*
  reason for not executing, 190
  survivors of victims and, *vii–viii*
Mears, Michael, 37
Mease, Darrel J., case of, 27
Menendez brothers, case of, 21
Michigan, black judicial officials in, number of, 71n28
Miller, Charles, 88
Milstein, Lisa (Barnes case investigator),
  149, 150, 153
Minow, Martha, 198
Miranda v. Arizona, 67
Mississippi
  capital sentencing scheme in, 100
  caps on fees paid death penalty
    lawyers in, 21, 109
  conviction rate in death penalty cases,
    4–5
  death row inmates in, 100
  executioners in, fees paid to, 96
  Parchman Farm prison (*See* Parchman
    Farm prison)
  racial discrimination in bringing death
    penalty cases in, 58
Missouri
  correctional institutions in, 179
  racial slurs during death penalty trials
    in, 63
Missouri State Penitentiary, Cabana at,
  175
mitigating factors
  in Alabama, 83
  in backgrounds, life histories of death
    row inmates, 14, 223n144, 225–26
  definition of, 13–14
  failure to present, 16, 48, 86–87,
    133–34, 136, 138–40, 234
  in John case (pseudonym), 234
  in Jones case, 243–44
  in Ohio, 201
  in *Penry v. Lynaugh,* 115–16
  racial discrimination in attention paid
    to, 220n103
  in rape-murder cases, 209–12
  in Sawyer case, 252
  in sentencing, 47
  in Texas, 13, 112, 116
Mock, Ron (Graham case lawyer), 130–31
Murder Victims' Families for
  Reconciliation, 273, 278

murderers, "frying them until their eyeballs pop," 87
murders
  felony-murder, 213n14
  in Georgia, 25, 57
  with known circumstances, 214n17
  Lake Waco murders, 21
  of loved ones, dealing with, 284–85
  per year in U.S., 12
  rape-murder, 195–212, 213n9, 213n13,
    214nn18–19, 219n84, 243
  sexual assault murders, 214n17,
    214n18, 214n19

N
Neelley, Judy, case of, 85–86
Neilson, Claud (Alabama Supreme Court
  candidate), 84
New Jersey, racial discrimination in
  bringing death penalty cases in,
  58
Newton, John, 283–84
Nichols, Terry, case of, 277, 278
Nigeria, 270
North Carolina
  automatic death sentences in, 13
  executions in, 146
  McCollum v. North Carolina, 210
  racial discrimination in bringing death
    penalty cases in, 58

O
O'Connor, Sandra Day, 31
Odom, Mike (lawyer), 88
Ohio
  aggravating circumstances in, 201, 203,
    216n42
  mitigating factors in, 201
  rape-murder in, 198–99, 200, 201–2,
    203, 204, 206, 207, 214nn18–19
  sentencing in, 201
  sexual assault murders in, 214n18,
    214n19
Oklahoma
  black judicial officials in, number of,
    71n28
  living conditions of death row inmates,
    12
"Old Sparky" (Texas electric chair), 46, 269
Oregon
  death row inmates in, 203–4, 214n20,
    219n83
  rape-murder in, 199, 203–4, 206, 207,
    219n84
  sentencing scheme in, 116
Oshinsky, David M, 92